Lecture Notes in Computer Science 8309

Commenced Publication in 1973
Founding and Former Series Editors:
Gerhard Goos, Juris Hartmanis, and Jan va

Editorial Board

Juan Carlos Augusto   Reiner Wichert
Rem Collier   David Keyson
Albert Ali Salah   Ah-Hwee Tan (Eds.)

Ambient Intelligence

4th International Joint Conference, AmI 2013
Dublin, Ireland, December 3-5, 2013
Proceedings

 Springer

Volume Editors

Juan Carlos Augusto
Middlesex University, London, UK
E-mail: j.augusto@mdx.ac.uk

Reiner Wichert
Fraunhofer IGD, Darmstadt, Germany
E-mail: reiner.wichert@igd.fraunhofer.de

Rem Collier
University College Dublin, Ireland
E-mail: rem.collier@ucd.ie

David Keyson
Delft University of Technology, The Netherlands
E-mail: d.v.keyson@tudelft.nl

Albert Ali Salah
Boğaziçi University, Istanbul, Turkey
E-mail: salah@boun.edu.tr

Ah-Hwee Tan
Nanyang Technological University, Singapore
E-mail: asahtan@ntu.edu.sg

ISSN 0302-9743   e-ISSN 1611-3349
ISBN 978-3-319-03646-5   e-ISBN 978-3-319-03647-2
DOI 10.1007/978-3-319-03647-2
Springer Cham Heidelberg New York Dordrecht London

Library of Congress Control Number: 2013953905

CR Subject Classification (1998): I.2, H.4, H.3, C.2.4, H.5, I.2.11, K.4

LNCS Sublibrary: SL 3 – Information Systems and Application,
incl. Internet/Web and HCI

Typesetting: Camera-ready by author, data conversion by Scientific Publishing Services, Chennai, India

Printed on acid-free paper

Springer is part of Springer Science+Business Media (www.springer.com)

Preface

We are living through exciting times. Technology is becoming available for a substantial portion of the population and humans have in their hands a number of tools that were not available in such a high number and degree of versatility to our species before. The previous time our species shared the same number of tools all around the globe, the ubiquitous tools were of a different nature, they were for farming. Now many of us carry small computers around, some of them disguised as a phone.

Technology is everywhere and becoming more common, more powerful, more accessible; it is being immersed in our daily lives and starting to influence our decisions and to some extent our lives. This scientific community has embraced the wealth of options opening in front of our society and is mining the possible richness; we have the privilege of being the first to explore this new world. At the same time we also have the responsibility to offer to the world nothing else but the true richness of this area and to clearly understand the risks and limitations of the options we offer to society.

This fourth edition of the International Joint Conference on Ambient Intelligence - the most prestigious event in the field - summarizes the effort of colleagues from 33 different countries, and the papers are the result of a review process that selected 38% of the submissions. The material included in this edition gives us the opportunity to get to know the latest advances in the area, to examine the different products being built by some of the most renowned experts in this area worldwide, to understand the current challenges of the state of the art, and to suggest innovative ways to develop this blending of humans and technology one step further.

This preface is an opportunity for us to acknowledge all the effort of the people who helped to make this meeting of minds a reality, some of their names are listed at the end of this document; it also gives us the opportunity to invite all you who are active in this field to join us in our effort of changing the world for good.

October 2013

Juan Carlos Augusto
Reiner Wichert
Rem Collier
David Keyson
Albert Ali Salah
Ah-HweeTan

Organization

Honorary Chair

Emile Aarts   Eindhoven University of Technology, The Netherlands

General Chair

Gregory O'Hare   University College Dublin, Ireland

Program Chairs

Juan Carlos Augusto   Middlesex University, UK
Reiner Wichert   Fraunhofer IGD, Germany

Workshop Chair

Michael O'Grady   University College Dublin, Ireland

Posters Chair

Ah-Hwee Tan   Nanyang Technological University, Singapore

Demos Chair

Rem Collier   University College Dublin, Ireland

Landscape Chair

David Keyson   Delft University of Technology, The Netherlands

Doctorial Colloquium Chair

Ali Salah   Bogazici University, Turkey

Publicity Chair

Hedda Schmidtke   CMU

Tutorial Chair

Davy Preuveneers   Katholieke Universiteit Leuven, Belgium

Program Committee

Adrian D. Cheok   National University of Singapore
Asier Aztiria   University of Mondragon, Spain
Alessandro Vinciarelli   University of Glasgow, UK
Babak Farshchian   Sintef, Norway
Ben Krose   University of Amsterdam, The Netherlands
Brian Lim   Carnegie Mellon University, USA
Bjorn Schuller   Technical University of Munich, Germany
Boon-Chong Seet   Auckland University of Technology,
                                  New Zealand
Boris de Ruyter   Philips Research
Carmen Santoro   CNR-ISTI, HIIS Laboratory, Italy
Cem Ersoy   Bogazici University, Turkey
Cem Keskin   Microsoft Research Cambridge, UK
Christine Julien   University of Texas at Austin, USA
David Lillis   University College Dublin, Ireland
Eric Pauwels   CWI, The Netherlands
Emilio Serrano   Polytechnic University of Madrid, Spain
Fabio Paternò   CNR-ISTI, HIIS Laboratory, Italy
Fahim Kawsar   Alcatel-Lucent
Hirozumi Yamaguchi   Osaka University, Japan
Hans Guesgen   Massey University, New Zealand
Irene Kotsia   Middlesex University, UK
Joseph Paradiso   MIT
Javier Caminero   Telefónica ID, Spain
Juan Ye   Saint Andrews University, UK
Jilei Tian   Nokia Research Center, China
Jin-Hyuk Hong   Carnegie Mellon University, USA
Juan Wachs   Purdue University, USA
Karin Coninx   University of Hasselt, Belgium
Kostas Stathis   Royal Holloway University of London, UK
Kaori Yoshida   Kyushu Institute of Technology, Japan
Kyriakos Kritikos   FORTH-ICS, Greece
Kin Choong Yow   GIST College, Republic of Korea
Kaori Fujinami   Tokyo University of Agriculture and
                                  Technology, Japan
Lei Xie   Nanjing University, China
Lars Braubach   University of Hamburg, Germany
Laurence Nigay   LIG-IIHM, Grenoble, France
Luis Carriço   Universidade de Lisboa, Portugal

Table of Contents

Part I: Full Papers Track

Part II: Landscape Track

Part III: Doctoral Colloquium

Part IV: Demos and Posters Track

Part V: Workshops Descriptions

Part I

Full Papers Track

An Implementation, Execution and Simulation Platform for Processes in Heterogeneous Smart Environments

Serge Autexier, Dieter Hutter, and Christoph Stahl

German Research Center for Artificial Intelligence (DFKI), Bremen, Germany
{serge.autexier,dieter.hutter,christoph.stahl}@dfki.de

Abstract. Developing ambient intelligence for a smart home is a complex task. We present how to define intelligent system behavior through processes on an adequate level of abstraction with the SHIP-tool. Based on the representation of the environment in a formal logical description, communication with the environment is realized via updates of the logical description. Processes are built from basic actions to update the current logical descriptions and include means to monitor the evolution of the environment in a temporal logic formalism. The SHIP-tool implements the process language and serves both for simulation and execution. The paper describes two examples of assisting services in a real smart home living lab, one for light and door control in emergency situations, and one for the scheduling of two parallel wheelchair transports.

1 Introduction

Smart homes typically comprise a variety of different systems that range from rather primitive ones, like motion sensors or remotely controllable lights, to more sophisticated ones, like gesture recognition systems or autonomously driving robotic vehicles. Realizing intelligent behavior in such environments is a major task as it has to go all the way up from protocols to communicate on a low signal level to sophisticated services recognizing, mediating, and planing high level activities. Explicit representation of the environment in a logic [13] allows for the assessment of complex situations and an adaptive behavior. However, smart homes comprise various individual components acting almost autonomously. They have to cope with humans changing spontaneously the environment and thus the basis for their activities. Furthermore, the system as a whole has to follow mandatory rules regulating, for instance, its safety and security. Enforcing such rules requires the orchestration of the different activities.

This paper illustrates the technology and the corresponding tool to orchestrate and monitor such heterogeneous processes. The SHIP-tool provides an implementation, simulation, and execution environment for ambient intelligent processes. It uses Description Logic (DL) to represent the states of the environment as it is a formalism well suited to represent data and its logical dependencies. Any state change of the real environment gives rise to a change of the logical representation. Vice-versa every change on the logical representation triggers changes in the

J.C. Augusto et al. (Eds.): AmI 2013, LNCS 8309, pp. 3–18, 2013.
© Springer International Publishing Switzerland 2013

real environment. DL provides sound and complete means to detect and remove invalid data as well as derive implied data. This is described in (see Sec. 2). Processes based on basic actions to change the logical representation are defined in a dynamic description logic language (DDL, [7]). As a means to describe behaviors over the evolution of the environment, the SHIP-tool uses a linear temporal logic formalism over Description Logic properties (Sec. 3). The monitoring consists of observing a specific behavior over environment updates. Integrating success and failure of the observation into the process semantics allows one to monitor the evolution of the environment and to react to non-conformant behavior. The SHIP-tool has been connected to the Bremen Ambient Assisted Living Lab (BAALL, `www.baall.de`) shown in Fig. 1 and used both for simulation of the processes in a 3D model of the lab and as a runtime environment to control the lab (Sec. 4).

Running Example. To illustrate the SHIP-tool, we realized a showcase for the BAALL. The BAALL allows to control doors and lights remotely through speech and mobile devices and it is equipped with electric wheelchairs that can autonomously navigate and drive handicapped persons to certain destinations, e.g. the bed or fridge. Given an existing system in which only a single person uses her/his autonomous wheelchair in the flat, the showcase utilizes the SHIP-tool to realize a system in which multiple persons share various wheelchairs available in the flat. Now, persons can request transportation to various places in the flat and the designated service assigns an available wheelchair, which picks up the person and transports her/him to the desired destination. Though the wheelchairs do sense and avoid obstacles, they are not aware of each other's planned route. This can result in a deadlock situation if they block each other in a narrow corridor. Hence, the designated service must also schedule the rides of the wheelchairs accordingly. This is presented in Sec. 5 along with other applications.

We deliberately present all the examples in the SHIP-programming language syntax to emphasize the integrated scripting language style and to highlight that this really is the programming language one has to use. Nothing else is required once the corresponding protocol adapters to the real environment are available.

2   Modeling the Data Using Description Logic

Description logic is a formalism well suited to represent data and its logical dependencies. The SHIP-tool provides a simple description logic syntax SHIP-DL to represent the environment. The language supports modularization and renaming. As usual in description logic [2], an application domain is modeled in an *ontology* consisting of three parts: *concepts*, representing a class of objects sharing some common characteristics, and *roles*, representing binary relationships between two objects, and *individuals*, which are concrete objects in the domain and can belong to several concepts. A SHIP-ontology consists of a terminological part defining the concepts and roles and an assertional part (ABox) describing a specific state by defining individuals along with their relations.

(a) Living room with kitchen, doors open   (b) Bedroom with Desk, doors closed

Fig. 1. Smart home living lab BAALL serving as test environment

We use the standard Description Logic SROIQ, in which concepts are formed from the top and bottom concepts T and F, concept names and nominal concepts $\{i_1, \ldots i_n\}$ built from individuals i_j by union +, intersection &, complement not, existential, universal and number role restriction (ex R.C, all R.C, = n R.C, > n R.C, < n R.C). Roles R are either role names or inverses of roles inv(R).

The terminological part of an ontology consists of declarations and definitions of concept and role names. Concept names C can be declared as sub-concepts of concepts D (C < D) or defined by concept equality C = D. An example are WheelChairs, which are supposed to always have a route indicated by the relation wheelchair_route. Subconcepts are wheelchairs WCNonEmptyroute having a non-empty route and those having an empty route WCEmptyroute:

```
WCEmptyroute = WheelChair & ex wheelchair_route . EmptyRoute
WCNonEmptyroute = WheelChair
                  & ex wheelchair_route . NonEmptyRoute
```

Roles are declared together with a signature that indicates domain and range of the property. Role composition is supported using the symbol '.'. Similar to concepts, subroles can be declared as super-roles of role composition using the symbol < or defined as being equal to a composition of roles using the symbol =. The usual role properties can also be defined by respective keywords: Sym for symmetric roles, Asym for asymmetric roles, Trans for transitive roles, Ref for reflexive roles, Irref for irreflexive roles, Func for functional roles, and FuncInv stating that $inv(R)$ is functional. An example is the functional role associating wheelchairs to their current route through the living lab, and the composed roles associating a wheelchair to its next position and next area:

```
wheelchair_route : WheelChair * Route
Func(wheelchair_route)
wcnextposition : WheelChair * Position
wcnextposition = wheelchair_route . route_next
wcnextarea : WheelChair * Area
wcnextarea = wcnextposition . isinarea
```

We provide the notation $r = r_0*$ to define a role r which is *exactly* the reflexive, transitive closure of role r_0. This is not expressible in DL where it is only translated to $r_0< r$, `Trans(r)`, `Ref(r)` but used to compute updates in the SHIP-tool.

In addition we use the following syntactic sugar to ease the definition of ontologies in a style inspired by abstract datatypes:

$$C ::= C_1(r_{11} : D_{11}, \ldots, r_{1n_i} : D_{1n_i}) | \ldots | C_m(r_{m1} : D_{m1}, \ldots, r_{mn_m} : D_{mn_m})$$

defines the concept C to be equal to the disjoint union of the concepts C_i and each individual $c : C_i$ has exactly one r_{ij} relation to some individual in D_{ij}. As an example consider the DL declaration defining `Lists` over elements `Elem`.

```
List ::= EmptyList  | NonEmptyList(hd:Elem,tl:List)
```

which is expanded to

```
List = EmptyList + NonEmptyList
F = EmptyList & NonEmptyList
tl:NonEmptyList * List
Fun(tl)
hd:NonEmptyList * Elem
Fun(hd)
NonEmptyList < (ex hd . Elem) & (ex tl . List)
```

Another example is the definition of the concept `WheelChair` as having a route and carrying either a `Person` or `Nobody`:

```
IDObject ::= WheelChair(wheelchair_route:Route,
                   wheelchair_carries:OptPerson) | OptPerson
OptPerson = Person | Nobody
```

The ABox part consists of a list of concept assertions `a:C`, declaring `a` to be a member of the concept `C`, and role assertions `(a,b):R`, stating that relation `R` holds between the individuals `a` and `b`. For every SHIP-DL-ontology we assume the unique name assumption. Complex ontologies can be composed by importing and renaming existing ontologies. Given, for instance, the `List`-ontology above, we build an ontology for `Routes` specifying routes along `Positions` by

```
import basic.Lists with
  concepts Elem as Position, List as Route, EmptyList as
     EmptyRoute, NonEmptyList as NonEmptyRoute
  roles hd as route_next, tl as route_rest
  individuals nil as emptyroute
```

where `nil:EmptyList` is declared in the `List`-ontology as an empty list.

This allows one to model the application domain of the smart home. Concepts are defined for the doors and different kinds of lights and their respective possible states along with the specific doors and lights in assertions about the corresponding individuals and the concepts encoding their current state (cf. Fig. 2).

SHIP-DL-ontologies can be converted to OWL-ontologies and vice versa a subset[1] of OWL-ontologies can be imported into SHIP-DL-ontologies. This could

---

[1] Currently, we do not import OWL datatypes, but this is currently added.

```
Door   ::= Closed | Open              bathroomLight : Off
Light  ::= On | Off                   bathroomMirrorLight : Off
DimLight  ::= DimOn | DimOff |         bedroomLight1 : Off
    DimBright | DimDark | DimHalf      bedroomLight2 : Off
AbstractLight = Light | DimLight       bathroomdoor : Open
On < AbstractOn                       lowerLeftDoor : Closed
DimOn < AbstractOn                    lowerRightDoor : Open
Off < AbstractOff                     lowerLeftDoor : Closed
DimOff < AbstractOff
```

Fig. 2. Ontological Description for Doors and Lights

be used to reuse smart environment related ontologies such as the OpenAAL ontology http://openaal.org. For example, importing the well-known wine ontology is done by import http://www.w3.org/TR/owl-guide/wine.rdf.

Updates. A major advantage of using Description Logic ontologies to model data and its dependencies is that upon changing data it provides sound and complete means to detect invalid data as well as to derive implied data.

The states of the environment are represented by ABoxes with respect to a fixed terminology and the transition of states correspond to ABox-updates. Thus ABox-updates are not meant to change the underlying terminological semantics characterizing the environment states, so the approach to ABox-updates from [10] is unsuitable in our setting and we are in the spirit of the updates in [6].

Following this line of reasoning we interpret the construction of complex concepts as a kind of specification for abstract datatypes. The use of an existential restriction in IDObject < ex at . AbstPosition corresponds to the definition of a mandatory attribute "at" indicating a position in the abstract datatype denoted by IDObject. Conjunction of concepts combine the attributes of the corresponding datatypes while disjunction of concepts resembles the notion of variants.

From this we have worked out in [1] the notion of a constructive ontology, which depending on the given terminology, categorizes concepts and roles into primitive and non-primitive. The ontology is constructive, if all ABox assertions are exclusively primitive concept and role assertions and all existential role assertions have a witness among the declared individuals. As an example consider the ontology of Lists from Sec. 2 (p. 6). The only primitive concept is EmptyList and the primitive roles are hd and tl. An ABox containing only the primitive assertions nil:EmptyList, (a,nil):tl is not constructive. Adding the primitive assertion (a,e):hd makes it constructive.

The main benefit from sticking to constructive ontologies and only admitting ontology updates that are constructive in that sense is that computation of the updated ontology is efficient. This is important in our setting, since ontology updating is the basic computation step in the SHIP-tool.

Ramification: Indirect Effect Rules. Sometimes actions do also have indirect or implicit consequences that are not necessarily known to the process that performs

```
indirect effect CarriedPersonMovesAsWell = {
  init = (wc,p):at
  causes = (x,p):at
  cond = (wc,x):wheelchair_carries , x:Person, wc:WheelChair}
```

Fig. 3. Indirect Effects

the update. In such a situation, it might be necessary to integrate the indirect consequences immediately into the ontology in order to prevent some monitors to fail, as sending another update would introduce a new point in time on our time axis. The problem of how to describe the indirect effects of an action – or more generally, an arbitrary update – in a concise way is known as the *ramification problem*. In SHIP we use causal relationships as introduced in [4] called *indirect effect rules* to describe indirect effects that are caused by *arbitrary* updates.

An example of an indirect effect rule is shown in Fig. 3. It works as follows: Given an ontology update from O to O', the init-assertions are checked on O'. If additionally cond is satisfied by O, then the indirect effects described by causes are an additional update on O'.

3   Monitors, Actions and Processes

Monitors. To monitor behaviors in the environment, SHIP uses a linear temporal logic formalism (LTL) [11] to specify temporal properties about ontology updates that result from processes and their environment. Typically LTL is used to specify a system behavior over time in a symbolic and declarative style. Moreover, there exist techniques to monitor such specifications over time and detect, when a behavior has been completely observed, if it is still possible to observe it or if something happened that definitely violates the specified behavior. We integrate it into the SHIP-language to allow to specify and monitor behavior of the environment in order to initiate processes once a behavior has been successfully observed or to detect unreliable or uncooperative environments and react by taking appropriate actions. We call programs that monitor such properties simply *monitors*. In SHIP, monitors can be started at any time and are evaluated w.r.t. a finite set of ontology updates that occurred between the start of the monitor up to the current time or its termination. Thereby, it does not matter whether the update was performed by a SHIP-process or the environment.

When monitoring a property, different situations can arise: (i) the property is satisfied after a finite number of steps – in this case, the monitor evaluates to true and terminates successfully; (ii) the property evaluates to false independently of any continuation – in this case, the monitor terminates with failure; (iii) the behavior that was observed so far allows for different continuations that might lead to a failure as well as success – in this case, the monitor is still running.

The language is a first-order temporal logic over description logic ABox-assertions and similar to that used in [3]. First-order quantification is over individuals and interpreted over the current world. Fig. 4 shows the grammar for

⟨*monitor*⟩ ::= 'monitor' ⟨*string*⟩ ⟨*params*⟩ '=' ('"'⟨*formatstring*⟩'"')? ⟨*foltl*⟩

⟨*formatstring*⟩ ::= Any string without ¨ . Formal Parameters to be substituted should be surrounded by %, e.g. %p% for the formal parameter p.

⟨*foltl*⟩ ::= ⟨*aboxass*⟩ | 'not' ⟨*aboxass*⟩ | ⟨*string*⟩ ⟨*params*⟩ | ⟨*foltl*⟩ 'and' ⟨*foltl*⟩
  | ⟨*foltl*⟩ 'or' ⟨*foltl*⟩ | ⟨*foltl*⟩ '=>' ⟨*foltl*⟩ | ('all' | 'ex') ⟨*aboxass*⟩ '.' ⟨*foltl*⟩
  | '(' ⟨*foltl*⟩ ')' | ('X'|'F'|'G') ⟨*foltl*⟩ | ⟨*foltl*⟩ 'U' ⟨*foltl*⟩

Fig. 4. SHIP-TL language to describe SHIP-tool-monitors

monitors. The temporal operators are: X indicating the next world, F indicating some point in the future, G stating that a property must hold globally, and U stating that a property must hold until another property becomes true.

As an example for a monitor formula we consider our running example: the BAALL includes two wheelchairs that are actually autonomous vehicles operating in the lab, where they can drive around along routes consisting of positions. The SHIP-tool has been used to add a control layer on top of the wheelchairs to avoid conflicting situations by scheduling the routes of the wheelchairs. One simple behavior one wants to monitor is when a new schedule must be computed. In Sec. 2 (p. 5) we introduced the part of the ontology specifying wheelchairs with empty and non-empty routes (WCEmptyroute, WCNonEmptyroute). To know if a new schedule must be computed, we must have observed the following behavior:

```
(ex wc:WCEmptyroute . F(wc:WCNonEmptyroute))
or
(ex wc:WCNonEmptyroute . F(wc:WCEmptyroute and F (wc:
    WCNonEmptyroute)))
```

This expresses that either in the current situation we have a wheelchair with an empty route and that wheelchair eventually gets a non-empty route. Or there is a wheelchair which currently has a non-empty route, eventually gets an empty route and then again eventually a non-empty route. If one of these behaviors is observed, then we must compute a new schedule. The actual monitoring is performed by formula progression (see, e.g., [5]) after each update.

Actions represent parametrized atomic interactions of the service with the environment and consist of a finite set of A-Box assertions pre, the preconditions, and a set of A-Box assertions effect, the effects. The syntax to declare actions is illustrated in Fig. 5. Effects can be unconditional (Fig. 5.(a)) or conditional (Fig. 5.(b)). Sometimes effects cannot be described statically, but are the result of a purely functional computation based on information contained in the ontology. An example from our wheelchair scenario is the computation of the route for a wheelchair to go to a target position (Fig. 5.(c)). This is based on the route graph, which is encoded in the ontology, the current position src of the wheelchair and the specified target position trg. This is achieved by allowing the call of a function defined in Scala[2], the programming language of the

---

[2] www.scala-lang.org

```
action switchOff (l) = {          action switchLight (l) = {
  pre = l:LightOn                   pre = l:Light
  effect = l:lightOff               if (l:LightOn) l:LightOff
}                                   if (l:LightOff) l:LightOn }
```

      (a) Simple Action   (b) Action with conditional effects

```
action computePlan = {
 pre = r:PlanRequest , (r,wc):planrequest_wheelchair ,
       (r,src):planrequest_source , (r,trg):planrequest_target
       (wc,oldroute):wheelchair_route
   exec = RouteComputation.computeRoute(src,trg,r,oldroute,wc)}
```

(c) Action with computed effects

Fig. 5. SHIP-tool Sample Action Descriptions

SHIP-tool, to perform that computation. Technically these are static Java methods with a specific signature in a compiled library available at runtime and invoked via Java's reflection mechanism. The result of these methods must imperatively be an ABox-update. This serves to perform purely functional computations but also, for instance, to access external data contained in databases, and which is then serialized into the ontology using specific concepts and roles.

An action is applicable on an ontology O if all its preconditions are satisfied in O. In this case, O is updated to a new ontology O' by applying the effects of the action, including conditional effects which conditions hold in O. If O' is inconsistent, then the action fails and we keep O as the current ontology. Otherwise the action succeeds and O' is the new current ontology. If the preconditions are not satisfied, the action stutters, i.e., waits until it gets applicable. skip is the action which is always applicable and does not modify the ontology.

Using free variables in the effects, new individuals can be added to O, where a fresh name is created at run-time. By annotating a variable with the keyword delete, individuals can be removed from the ontology.

Processes. SHIP provides a language to define complex processes that interact with the environment. They are dynamic description logic processes based on actions and similar to those in the literature (e.g, [7]), but augmented by monitors to easily integrate processes and behavior observation.

Starting from *actions*, complex processes are defined using the combinators shown in Table 1. To allow for recursive processes, named processes parameterized over individuals can be declared and used in process descriptions similarly to actions. As an example consider the declaration of a process used in the wheelchair coordination scenario to detect situations using the monitoring formula from the previous section:

```
process watchfornewroutes(schedulecontroller) = {
  switch case x:WheelChair => {
   init ((ex wc:WCEmptyroute . F(wc:WCNonEmptyroute))
```

Table 1. Process combinators

Name	Syntax	Semantics
simple condition	`if a then b else c`	branches according to a or waits until a can be decided
complex condition	`switch case c_1 => p ... case c_k => p`	branches according to the specified cases which are checked in order. _ can be used as default case, then, the condition never stutters.
iteration	`p*`	applies p until it fails, always succeeds
sequence	`p ; q`	applies p then q
monitor start	`init m`	starts the monitor, continues when the monitor succeeds or fails when the monitor fails
guarded execution	`p +> q`	executes p; if p fails, q is executed, but the modifications of p are kept
parallel	`p ∥ q`	executes p and q in parallel (interleaved), terminates when both p and q terminate, fails when one of them fails
bounded parallel	`forall c => p`	executes p for all instances matching c in parallel, terminates when all terminate, fails when one of them fails

```
    or (ex wc:WCNonEmptyroute .
        F(wc:WCEmptyroute and F (wc:WCNonEmptyroute))));
  stopScheduling(schedulecontroller);
  watchfornewroutes(schedulecontroller) }}
```

The monitor is only initialized if there is at least one wheelchair, and once a new schedule must be computed, via the shared controller individual stops the processing of the current schedule (which is a parallel process) and then recurses.

4   Simulation, Visualization and Execution

The actual components of the SHIP-tool are depicted in Fig. 6.(c). The setting comprises the smart home BAALL (see Fig. 1) and an interactive simulator, which has been implemented in two different instances that share the same code base: a desktop VR environment (Fig. 6.(a)) and a physical small-scale model (Fig. 6.(b)). The BAALL represents an apartment suitable for the elderly and people with disabilities. On $60m^2$ it includes all standard living areas, i.e. kitchen, bathroom, bedroom, and living room. All devices within the lab are controlled by a KNX bus system. Besides the usual control of light, shades and heating, the lab features five electric sliding doors to let the wheelchair pass through. The lab also includes height-adaptable furnishing (bed, kitchenette and shelves, washing basin, WC) to suit the needs of wheelchair users. The KNX bus can be accessed through an IP-gateway, and we use the LinKNX[3] interface on top of it (based on XML/HTTP protocol) to get and set the status of the KNX actuators in order to symbolically represent the environment in a SHIP ontology.

---

[3] http://sourceforge.net/apps/mediawiki/linknx/

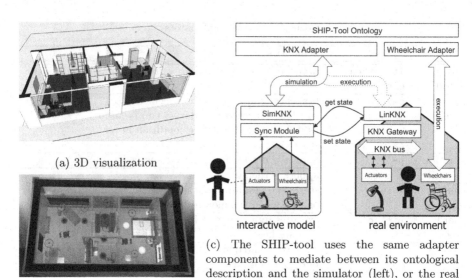

(a) 3D visualization

(b) scale model (1:35)

(c) The SHIP-tool uses the same adapter components to mediate between its ontological description and the simulator (left), or the real environment (right) for execution

Fig. 6. 3D visualization (a) and physical scale model (b) serve as interactive simulation environments for the SHIP-tool, and the architecture (c) shows the synchronization between them and the real BAALL environment

During the design and implementation phase of the SHIP-tool, a simulator has been required because the testing with real wheelchairs has not been practical. They are not always available due to maintenance, and running the scenario in real-time is quite limiting. Furthermore, the control of real devices always poses the risk of costly hardware damage in case of software errors. Hence we have implemented a virtual simulation environment (see also Fig. 6.(a)) based on [9]. The modeling toolkit provides the necessary objects for lights, doors, and height-adaptable furniture, which are not only visualized in 3D, but also implement the same properties as their real KNX-connected counterparts. Lamps are visualized as cones that appear either black (off) or bright yellow (on) and the sliding doors appear either open or closed. The toolkit also implements a simplified motion model to animate the virtual wheelchairs. The simulator implements the same interface as the living lab (accordingly named SimKNX) so that the SHIP-tool can switch between the real and virtual world at any time. The configuration is transparent to the SHIP-tool, i.e. processes are not aware of the simulation.

Recently, [8] went even further and realized the SmartCase, a physical scale (1:20) model of a real apartment. They argue that scale models help architects to elaborate, explain and communicate complex design decisions. The SmartCases walls and interior are made of polyurethane foam components, whereas transparent surfaces, such as table lamps, windows, stove and oven, are refined with acrylic glass. However, the interaction with the model is limited to the windows and doors. Our model (see Fig. 6.(b)) has been made completely from acrylic glass (interactive objects are red, others white) and it has been designed at a smaller scale (1:35). We wanted it to be fully interactive, so it uses a 18" TFT display as base (below the walls and acrylic furniture items) and a touch sensor pane as top. We project the interactive components of the virtual 3D model onto the floor to indicate the status of the lights, doors, and wheelchairs. All of the devices can be controlled through touch gestures from the top: tapping the lights toggles their state, and a slide gesture moves the doors or height-adaptable furniture. In our experience, the scale model simulator is more natural and engaging than 3D graphics, even though the displayed digital content is very similar.

As described in [14], the perfect match between the real environment and the simulator realizes dual (or synchronized) realities that mutually reflect each other. Besides simulation, the model can be used to visualize and control the living lab in real time. In our setting, this is achieved by the synchronization module. The model can be configured to poll the real world state and mirror it, so that changes are immediately visualized. Vice versa, as the user interacts with the model, i.e. to toggle the status of a virtual lamp, a corresponding request is send to the real environment's LinKNX interface. Hence the simulator model can be used as intuitive, tangible user interface that is cognitively more appropriate than symbolic representations. It avoids the mapping problem between labels and devices, since all devices support direct manipulation.

5   Applications

The SHIP-tool has been used to realize two ambient services in the BAALL from Fig. 1 (p. 5).

Night Surveillance Service. The first service is a night surveillance service, where at night time, doors are automatically closed. If persons move around in the flat and open doors, the doors are automatically closed again after a short delay. In case of an emergency such as a fire alarm, doors are automatically opened and the whole flat is illuminated. For this we extended our ontology to model day time and emergency situations:

```
Time ::= Day | Night          Situation ::= Normal | Emergency
```

The concept assertions about lights and doors (see Sec. 2, p. 7) indicate the current states of the doors and lights. The interface component to the living lab (resp. the visualization tool) maintains the mapping between these individuals and their counterpart in the flat (resp. in the model). If for instance the concept assertion of light `bedroomLight1` in the ontology changes to `bedroomLight1:On`, the corresponding lamp is switched on in the flat (resp. in the model). Vice versa, if the real lamp is switched on, this results in a respective ontology update sent from the interface component to the SHIP-tool-kernel system. The current situation and the daytime are modeled as individuals `situation:Normal` and `time:Day`. The whole surveillance process is implemented by the recursive process

```
process NightSurveillance (sit,time) = {
 Control(time); (Emergency(sit,time)||DoorControl(sit,time));
 NightSurveillance(sit,time) }
```

The first process Control waits until night comes and then, if there is no emergency, closes all doors and turns off the lights. Then the processes Emergency and DoorControl are started in parallel. Emergency waits until there is an emergency or it is day time again and in case of an emergency opens all doors and illuminates the flat:

```
process Control(time) = {
  switch
  case time:Day => init NightComes(time) ; Control(time)
  case situation:Emergency => skip
  case time:Night and adefault:Authority =>
    ((forall d:Open => CloseDoor(d)) ||
      forall l:AbstractOn => LightOff(l,adefault)) }
```

DoorControl is the process responsible for closing doors again if they are opened:

```
process DoorControl(situation,time) = {
 switch
 case situation:Emergency => skip
 case time:Night => {
    (init MonitorDoors(situation,time)) +> {
 switch
 case sit:Emergency => skip
 case _ => {CloseAllDoors ;
            DoorControl(situation,time)}}}
 case _ => skip }
```

The process stops if there is an emergency or if it is day time again. At night it monitors that the doors are closed until either there is an emergency or it is day time again:

```
monitor MonitorDoors(sit,time) =
 all d:Door . (d:Closed U (sit:Emergency or time:Day))
```

That monitor fails in case a door is opened manually. If so, the alternative process on the right-hand side of +> is started, which in case of an emergency does nothing, and otherwise before recursively calling DoorControl again, closes all doors using

```
process CloseAllDoors =  { forall d:Open => CloseDoor(d) }
```

Transportation Assistance Service. The second service is the running example used in the paper and comprised the equipment of the living lab with a transportation assistance for the occupants. In addition to managing the transportation requests and wheelchair rides, the service should also open closed doors if a wheelchair has to drive through it. For the comfort of the residents, the service also takes care that when wheelchairs drive autonomously at night time in rooms where persons are present, the lights should be on.

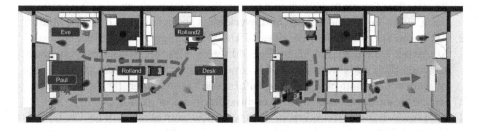

Fig. 7. Conflict Situations resolved by Scheduling

The ontology used in this setting extends the ontology used for the night surveillance service by having a finite number of positions in the flat, where persons and wheelchairs can be. These are connected in a route graph the wheelchairs used already for navigating in the flat. We modeled these in the ontology and added the definitions of route graphs and routes:

```
import basic.Graph with
 concepts Node as Position
 roles edge as neighbour, reachable as connected
import basic.Lists with
 concepts Elem as Position, List as Route, EmptyList as
    EmptyRoute, NonEmptyList as NonEmptyRoute,
        SubList as SubRoute, CompleteList as CompleteRoute
 roles hd as route_next, tl as route_rest
 individuals nil as emptyroute
at: IDObject * AbstPosition
Func(at)
```

The space of the whole flat is geometrically segmented into spatial areas, so that wheelchair positions and lights can be related to them.

```
import basic.Set with
 concepts Elem as Position, EmptySet as EmptyArea,
    NonEmptySet as NonEmptyArea, Set as Area
 roles iselem as isinarea
 individuals emptyset as emptyarea
(Table,kitchenliving):isinarea
(BedRight,bedroom):isinarea
(bedroomLight1,bedroom):associated_light
(livingLight1,kitchenliving):associated_light        ...etc...
```

Finally, the relationships between doors and positions is modeled. Some doors are located adjacently to a position and others are on a position:

```
(173123804,lowerLeftDoor):adjacent_door
(11480149,lowerLeftDoor):adjacent_door
(lowerRightDoor,296758459):door_position        ...etc...
```

The whole service consists of seven main processes running in parallel

(1) `RequestHandler` manages incoming requests, possibly aborts running requests, assigns available wheelchairs and overlooks the pickup and delivery phases;

(2) `AutoReserver` schedules the rides of the wheelchairs to avoid conflict situations as shown in Fig. 7 by forbidding or allowing wheelchairs to drive towards their next position, and computes a new schedule in case the route of some wheelchair changes; this information is delivered by the process

(3) `watchfornewroutes`, which we presented in Sec. 3 on p. 10;

(4) `WCPlanner` handles requests to compute new routes for a wheelchair; this is the iterated execution of the action `computePlan` from Fig. 5 on p. 10 exploiting the connection to Scala to perform route computations;

(5) `WheelChairProcessAssist` updates the routes of the wheelchairs when they moved from their current position to the next position on their route;

(6) `controldoors` opens closed doors if a wheelchair has to drive through and closes them again afterwards;

(7) `illuminationTransportAssistance` controls the lights during the rides of the wheelchairs, turning them on at night in the areas the wheelchair are or are about to drive into and there are persons in these areas or the wheelchair carries a person.

The transport requests are modeled as `Goals` in the ontology and whether a goal is open or already assigned to some wheelchair are derived concepts. Similarly, the different modes of a wheelchair are modeled and the derivable subconcepts of wheelchairs are defined:

```
Goal ::= Goal(goal_subject:Person,goal_target:Position,
    goal_wheelchair:OptWheelChair)
OpenGoal = Goal & ex goal_wheelchair . Unassigned
AssignedGoal = Goal & all goal_wheelchair . WheelChair
WCMode = WCIdle | WCPickup | WCDelivery
WCAvailable = WheelChair & ex wheelchair_mode . WCIdle
```

The derivable concepts are available to the processes via the underlying deductive machinery of an OWL reasoner, in our case the Pellet reasoner [12]. This allows for succinct formulation of behaviors, such as when a new schedule must be computed (the LTL formula on p. 3), or when some light `l` should be on depending on the current day time `time`:

```
monitor LightShouldBeOn (time,l) =
 time:Night and l:AbstractOff and
 ex area:(Area & (ex inv(associated_light) . { l })) .
 (/* 1. Either there is a wheelchair with a non-empty route,
     which ... */
  (ex wc:WCNonEmptyroute .    (
   /* carries a person or there is a person in the area... */
   (wc:WCCarriesPerson or ex person:(Person & (ex
       elementIsInArea . { area })) . true)
   and
   /* the wheelchair is already in or about to enter */
   ((wc,area):elementIsInArea or (wc,area):wcnextarea)))
```

```
or /* the wheelchair is assigned to a person on the same
   area*/
(ex person:(Person & (ex elementIsInArea . { area })) .
 ex wc:(WheelChair & (ex wcAssignedToPerson . { person })) .
    (wc,area):elementIsInArea))
```

The assignment of the nearest wheelchair available to a person also exploits derived information on the status of the wheelchairs and exploits the connection to Scala for computations. Similarly, a new schedule is computed in Scala and then serialized in the ontology using specific concepts and roles.

The communication with the wheelchairs (see also Fig. 6.(c)) is realized using an interface component which sends new target positions to the wheelchair when these are cleared in the current ontology, tracks the movement of the wheelchair and possibly updates the position information of the wheelchair in the ontology and informs when the wheelchair has reached its destination.

The night surveillance and the transportation assistance services are fully functional in the living lab with two autonomous wheelchairs. The services can also be executed in simulation mode and visualized in both the VR and physical scale model of the flat (see Fig. 6 (a) and (b)). Realization of further assistance processes is currently under development, such as a dressing assistant and cooking assistant. Also the combination of independently designed assistance processes, such as integrating night surveillance with transportation assistance, is currently investigated.

6   Related Work and Conclusion

We presented the SHIP-tool to implement services for smart environments on a definable high-level of abstraction. The SHIP-tool programming language is an attempt to bring together formalisms well-suited to deal with data dependencies, data change and behavior monitoring in an integrated script-language style. It enables the programmer to select the adequate formalism for each aspect and to easily combine them to build an ambient intelligent service and not having to deal with the complexity of the underlying formal logic deductive machinery. The actual connection to a real environment or a simulation environment is realized via interfaces encapsulating the protocol of the specific devices in the environment and mediating between the states of the devices and their ontological representation. This provides a clear principle how to hide the technological protocol layer to communicate with the integrated systems from the design of the assistance services that make use of the capabilities of the systems. Two services realized for the smart home living lab BAALL have been presented to demonstrate the suitability of the approach to develop and experiment with ambient intelligent services both in simulation and reality. As related work we consider existing solutions built in different smart homes. They provide solutions for very specific tasks, but to our knowledge there is no system that provides a programming layer to develop new services based on existing or new systems. In order to make them easier to integrate and interoperable beyond the pure protocol level in different environments, an ideal extension of such systems would be to equip these (or only individuals sensors and devices) with an ontological description.

References

1. Autexier, S., Hutter, D.: Constructive dl update and reasoning for modeling and executing the orchestration of heterogeneous processes. In: Krötzsch, M., Eiter, T. (eds.) Proceedings 2013 Intl. Workshop on Description Logics (DL 2013), Ulm, Germany, July 23-26. CEUR-WS.org (2013)
2. Baader, F., Calvanese, D., McGuinness, D.L., Nardi, D., Patel-Schneider, P.F. (eds.): The description logic handbook: theory, implementation, and applications. Cambridge University Press, New York (2003)
3. Baader, F., Ghilardi, S., Lutz, C.: LTL over description logic axioms. ACM Transactions on Computational Logic (2012)
4. Baader, F., Lippmann, M., Liu, H.: Using causal relationships to deal with the ramification problem in action formalisms based on description logics. In: Fermüller, C.G., Voronkov, A. (eds.) LPAR-17. LNCS, vol. 6397, pp. 82–96. Springer, Heidelberg (2010)
5. Bauer, A., Falcone, Y.: Decentralised LTL monitoring. In: Giannakopoulou, D., Méry, D. (eds.) FM 2012. LNCS, vol. 7436, pp. 85–100. Springer, Heidelberg (2012)
6. Chang, L., Lin, F., Shi, Z.: A Dynamic Description Logic for Representation and Reasoning About Actions. In: Zhang, Z., Siekmann, J.H. (eds.) KSEM 2007. LNCS (LNAI), vol. 4798, pp. 115–127. Springer, Heidelberg (2007)
7. Chang, L., Shi, Z., Gu, T., Zhao, L.: A family of dynamic description logics for representing and reasoning about actions. J. Autom. Reasoning 49(1), 1–52 (2012)
8. Frey, J., Bergweiler, S., Alexandersson, J., Gholamsaghaee, E., Reithinger, N., Stahl, C.: Smartcase: A smart home environment in a suitcase. In: Intelligent Environments, pp. 378–381. IEEE (2011)
9. Laue, T., Stahl, C.: Modeling and simulating ambient assisted living environments – A case study. In: Augusto, J.C., Corchado, J.M., Novais, P., Analide, C. (eds.) ISAmI 2010. AISC, vol. 72, pp. 217–220. Springer, Heidelberg (2010)
10. Liu, H., Lutz, C., Milicic, M., Wolter, F.: Updating description logic aboxes. In: Doherty, P., Mylopoulos, J., Welty, C.A. (eds.) Proceedings of the 10th Int. Conference on Principles of Knowledge Representation and Reasoning, Lake District of the United Kingdom, June 2-5, pp. 46–56. AAAI Press (2006)
11. Pnueli, A.: The temporal logic of programs. In: FOCS, pp. 46–57. IEEE Computer Society (1977)
12. Sirin, E., Parsia, B., Grau, B.C., Kalyanpur, A., Katz, Y.: Pellet: A practical owl-dl reasoner. J. Web Sem. 5(2), 51–53 (2007)
13. Springer, T., Turhan, A.-Y.: Employing description logics in ambient intelligence for modeling and reasoning about complex situations. Journal of Ambient Intelligence and Smart Environments 1(3), 235–259 (2009)
14. Stahl, C., Frey, J., Alexandersson, J., Brandherm, B.: Synchronized realities. JAISE 3(1), 13–25 (2011)

Generating Explanations for Pro-active Assistance from Formal Action Descriptions

Sebastian Bader

MMIS, Computer Science, University of Rostock
sebastian.bader@uni-rostock.de
mmis.informatik.uni-rostock.de

Abstract. In this paper we show how to generate explanations for an automatic assistance system for smart environments. In particular, we address dynamically changing environments in which devices and services can enter and leave at any time. All components employ the same simple action definitions. They are used to analyse the underlying intention, to synthesise a supporting strategy and to generate explanations that provide insights into the internals of the system. As tool of communication, we employ automatically generated question and corresponding answers. We furthermore detect sub-optimal behaviour and provide explanations that help to improve the usage of the system. All explanations are generated in natural language by utilising an intermediate representation as discourse representation structure and the SimpleNLG natural language generation framework.

Keywords: Explanation generation, pro-active assistance, smart environments.

1 Introduction

Controlling complex hard- and software systems is becoming more and more demanding due to the increasing complexity and the number of options and choices offered to the user. This is particularly true for intelligent environments in which the composition of devices and corresponding services is subject to frequent and usually unforeseen changes. The compound reaction that emerges from the interplay of the different components is hard to predict, which prevents the construction of a useful mental model of the overall system. The objective of this work is three-fold. We show how to: (a) analyse user intentions and to support assistance, (b) construct explanations (in form of question answer pairs) which help building a correct mental model of the system, and (c) detect sub-optimal usage and to construct a correcting explanation.

The construction of intelligent environments is an ongoing research topic for the last decades. It gained momentum by the availability of small embedded and wirelessly connected devices which form our todays working and living environments. Those devices (or to be more precise: the resulting compound meta-device) are supposed to support their users by helping them fulfilling their goals. Unfortunately, most of the constructed environments appear to the user as black box, and are not able to explain their internal reasoning, or provide explanations for the automatically chosen actions. The lack of the system's ability to explain its behaviour might lead to a loss of trust as pointed out

J.C. Augusto et al. (Eds.): AmI 2013, LNCS 8309, pp. 19–31, 2013.

in [8] within the area of context-aware web applications. Therefore it is crucial to build explanation aware systems for supporting the user.

In this paper we try to answer the question whether an assistance system for smart environments can be enhanced by explanation capabilities. For this we rely on previous work from the area of activity recognition, intention analysis and strategy synthesis as described in Section 2. First attempts have been made to add explanation capabilities to different algorithms as investigated for example within the Exact workshops [25] over the last years. But to the best of our knowledge there are almost no real systems able to provide assistance in some physical environment and able to explain what happens. Exception are [27] in which a small museum like installation has been constructed and [20] in which alerts within an AMI environment are validated.

Below we show how to construct different types of explanations based on a simple description of actions within a situation calculus like formalisation. This formalisation is used to analyse the underlying intentions, to synthesise supporting strategies and to answer different types of questions. This shows that generating explanations is possible, even within heterogeneous and dynamic environments, as already constituting our daily living and working environments. Even though this research originates from smart meeting rooms the approaches developed below are not limited to that, but are applicable in other settings involving users interacting with complex device infrastructures.

After introducing some related work and basic notions next, we show how to enable pro-active assistance based on a formal description of available actions in Sec. 3. In Sec. 4 we show how to generate explanations and how to correct sub-optimal usage. A first evaluation is reported in Sec. 5 and some conclusions are drawn thereafter.

2   Basic Notions and Related Work

Because our system utilises ideas from different areas, we introduce some related work and the necessary notions first. Recognising the current *activities* of a user is important to predict the underlying goals of his behaviour. Several approaches have been proposed in the literature and recent overviews can be found in [1] and [4]. Most of the system rely on probabilistic models like Hidden Markov Models, Dynamic Bayesian networks, particle filters, or Kalman filters. Depending on the sensor and type of background knowledge very high accuracies are obtained by the system (up to 100% accuracy in certain domains). Here, we only assume that the system provides a sequence of probabilities over user actions, but we are not restricted to any particular one.

In the area of *intention analysis*, researchers try to infer the intentions underlying the currently executed sequence of actions. This allows to predict the goals of the user and thus to provide pro-active support. The notion of intention as used below is strongly related to the *Belief-Desire-Intention (BDI)* model and the *Theory of Rational Interaction*. Based on sensory information the long term user plans are recognised. This can be used to predict the ultimate goal, namely the final state of the world. As above, most systems rely on probabilistic models initialised by background information depending on the application domain [17,23].

Once the underlying intentions of the user are analysed, *pro-active assistance systems* try to support the user by executing useful actions automatically. Different systems and approaches have been introduced before. Prominent examples of larger installations, namely complete smart houses are the *MavHome* [7], the *Gator Tech Smart House* [14], the *Georgia Tech Aware Home* [16], and the *Adaptive House* [19]. But also other application scenarios have been addressed, as for example intelligent classrooms [9], team meeting rooms [3,13], command and control rooms and living environments [5]. Good introductions and overviews can be found in [6,21] and [22].

Unfortunately most assistance systems are black boxes to their users. Researchers in the area of *explanation aware computing* try to tackle this problem by making the systems more intelligible and able to provide explanations. This idea has recently gained momentum as indicated, for example, by the series of *Explanation-aware computing (ExaCt)* workshops [25] and the *Workshops on Intelligibility and Control in Pervasive Computing* [26]. It has been shown that the automatic generation of questions (in particular *"Why ...?"* and *"Why not ...?"* questions) and corresponding answers helps users to predict the reactions of context aware applications [18]. A proactive dynamic system able to answer why and why-not questions has been proposed in [27]. In this paper, we show how to derive different kinds of explanations from the same formal description that is used to analyse the human activities and to infer a supporting strategy.

Discourse representation theory provides an abstract and formal representation of meaning in natural language and allows to handle references within and across sentences [15]. *Discourse representation structures (DRS)* are used to represent the meaning of sentences. Without going into details, we present a slightly adapted example taken from [15]: The meaning of the sentences *"Jones owns Ulysses. It fascinates him."* is represented within the following DRS: [X,Y] : [jones(X), ulysses(Y), owns(X,Y), fascinates(Y,X)]. A DRS consists of two parts, a list of referents and a list of conditions. Those data structures can be used in natural language understanding and interpretation as well as for the generation of natural language. For example the *Attempto Controlled English (ACE)* project[1] uses similar structures to interpret and construct natural language sentences [10]. Below we use DRSs as intermediate representation of explanations and as input for our language generation module.

Natural language generation (NLG) is concerned with the construction of natural language from a formal representation. Several approaches have been proposed in the past. A fairly up-to-date overview can be found on the website[2] of the Special Interest Group on Natural Language Generation (SIGGEN). NLG systems are usually constructed in layers [24]: *Layer 1 (Document planner)* determines the content and the structure of the document to convey the communicative goal. *Layer 2 (Micro-planner)* performs the lexicalisation, referencing and aggregation of paragraphs and sentences. *Layer 3 (Surface realiser)* applies grammar rules to convert an abstract representation into text. In our system described below, the document- and part of the micro-planning is done by the explanation generation process. As surface realiser, we use the SimpleNLG[3] framework [11], which is also able to perform some micro-planning (in particular the aggregation), provides a lexicon with a fair coverage of English words and performs the morphological realisation.

---

[1] http://attempto.ifi.uzh.ch

[2] http://www.siggen.org/

[3] http://code.google.com/p/simplenlg/

3 Enabling Pro-active Assistance in Smart Environments

To illustrate the ideas we discuss a simple example often occurring in academic settings, involving projectors, projection screens and laptops with presentations. In most meeting and lecture rooms, all devices have to be controlled directly, that is, the projector needs to be switched on, the screen lowered for projection and the video output be directed to the correct projector. In a smarter meeting room however, it suffices to connect the laptop to the room. Sensing this event triggers the assistance, which should result in a situation showing the video output on an appropriate screen. There are several cases to consider here, that require explanations:

A) the user is aware of the assistance, but does not know how to trigger it exactly,
B) the user (by accident) connects the laptop first, which results in some (probably unexpected) automatic assistance,
C) the user performs the full action sequence manually.

In the first case, the user might like to ask the system how to bring about a certain state of the environment, e.g., how to start a presentation. As shown below, the set of likely questions can be limited based on the current situation and the available options. In case B, the user might be surprised by the assistance and will require some explanation showing why the automatic actions have been taken. In the last case, the system might inform the user about the possible assistance by showing how to achieve the goal more efficiently. All three cases are discussed in detail in the following section. We show how to detect the different situations, how to construct appropriate explanations and how to present them to the user. The approach presented below is based on the following steps:

1. *Intention analysis*. Based on current and past activities, and a formalisation of actions and intentions, the intention recognition infers likely user goals.
2. *Strategy synthesis*. Supporting strategies are synthesised wrt. to the current state of the world, available actions and potential goals.
3. *Explanation generation*. The user actions, the goals and the synthesised strategy are integrated into an explanation that helps to explain the overall system.

We use the setting from above as a running example to illustrate all concepts.

3.1 Formalising Actions and Intentions

As customary within the automatic planning domain [12], all actions are described using preconditions and effects. Before diving into the formalisation, we discuss a simple example (all examples show actually used Prolog code of the system):

Example 1 (Action turnOn(P)). *The action to switch on a given projector P is formalised as follows:*

```
action(turnOn(P) by user,   % name, arguments and agent
  [P=projector],            % types
  [-isOn(P)],               % preconditions
  [isOn(P)]).               % effects
```

Every action consists of a name including arguments (turnOn(P)), the agent able to perform the action (user), a set of static types and precondition, and the effects.

Definition 2 (Action). *An action* A *is a 7-tuple:* $A := (N, Ag, T, P^+, P^-, E^+, E^-)$, *with* N *being an action name, possibly containing variables,* Ag *being an agent capable of performing* A, *and* T *being a mapping from variables occurring in* N *to types. The sets* P^+, P^-, E^+ *and* E^- *contain predicates and represent the positive and negative preconditions as well as the positive and negative effects of* A. *All variables occurring in* Ag, T, P^+, P^-, E^+, *and* E^- *must also occur in* N.

The associated semantics underlying our action descriptions, has been adapted from the situation calculus. A situation S is described as a set of predicates assumed to hold in S. An action A can be applied in a given situation S whenever all preconditions are satisfied, i.e., if $P^+ \subseteq S$ and $\forall_{p \in P^-} p \notin S$ hold. The resulting situation S' is computed by removing negative effects and adding the positives, i.e., $S' := (S \setminus E^-) \cup E^+$. In our code (see Example 1), we use one list `preconditions` containing the union of E^+ and E^- with items from E^- prefixed by "-". The typing information added to the action description can be seen as additional preconditions, but as types are assumed to be static, they are handled separately for reasons of efficiency. We call a sequence of actions $[a_1, \ldots, a_n]$ applicable in S_0 if we find for all a_i that a_i is applicable in S_{i-1} and leads to state S_i. Intentions are specified as shown in Example 3.

Example 3 (Intention `presentation(P)`). *The possible intention of giving a presentation is formalised as follows:*

```
intention(presentation(P),    % name and arguments
  [P=projector, L=laptop],    % types
  [isOn(P), conn(L,P)]).      % conditions
```

Definition 4 (Intention). *An intention* I *is a 4-tuple* (N, T, C^+, C^-), *with* N *and* T *as introduced in Definition 2. The sets* C^+ *and* C^- *contain predicates representing the positive and negative conditions of* I.

The conditions attached to intentions constrain the valid states of the world in which this intention is achieved. Together, actions and intentions constitute the basic building blocks of our overall system descriptions. They enable to infer possible intentions given a situation and a sequence of user actions, and to compute optimal supporting action sequences leading from a given situation to a desired one as described below. For the remaining part of this paper, we assume that there are only finitely many ground instances of actions and intentions.

3.2 Analysing User Intentions

As mentioned above, we assume that the activity recognition module repeatedly outputs (a probability distribution over possible) user actions. In addition, we assume that the state of the world is (partially) observable, at least such that preconditions of intentions can be tested. Under this conditions, we are able to analyse the user's intentions. Please note, that we are not concerned with identifying the one-and-only intention underlying the user's actions, but to keep track of all those intentions which are plausible in the current situation. This allows to present the explanations in a meaningful order, namely with decreasing likelihood with respect to the underlying intention.

While running the system, we track the current state of the environment and the probability distribution over user actions as computed by the activity recognition. For every state, we identify all intentions which are plausible. An intention is called plausible, if the specified goal can actually be achieved from the current situation, that is, if a plan exist that leads from the current to a desired state of the world. For every plausible intention, we compute the number of necessary actions to be executed. Then we compute the "gradient" of this number over the last x steps, with x being a natural number (e.g., $x \leq 10$, depending on the granularity of actions). The underlying idea is the following: if a rational user tries to reach a goal, he will behave goal-directed, that is, he will try to take steps towards reaching the goal and thus the gradient will be negative. Comparing the gradient of the individual intentions is better than comparing the pure number of necessary actions, because the number of necessary actions depends largely on the complexity of the intention.

Example 5 (Intention tracking). *Assume a smart meeting room with two projectors and corresponding projection screens which have to be moved down for projection. In this setting, there are three intentions possible: I_1: Give a presentation using projector 1 (present(scr. 1)), I_2: Give a presentation using projector 2 (present(scr. 2)), and I_3: Shutdown the system and leave the room (leave room). Starting from an initial state (in which all projectors are switched off and the screens are in top-position), Figure 1 shows the evolution of the system while performing the following sequence of actions: A_1: connect the laptop to projector 2 (connect(lap1,proj2)), A_2: switch on projector 2 (proj2:switchOn), A_3: lower projection screen 2 (scr.2:down), A_4: switch off projector 2 (proj2:switchOff), and finally A_5: move up screen 2 (scr.2:moveUp) The first three actions are performed to give a presentation via projector 2, and the latter two to leave the room. The dashed lines show the gradients of the three intentions. Already after performing the first action, towards the first goal, this intention can be recognised by its negative gradient. Likewise for leaving the room after performing proj2:switchOff.*

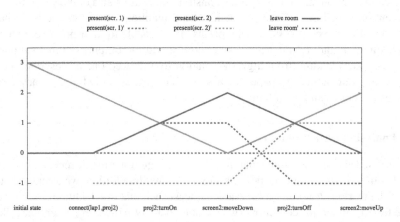

Fig. 1. The evolution of the number of necessary actions to achieve the intentions discussed in Example 5 and of the corresponding "gradients"

3.3   Synthesising Supporting Strategies

Once the most likely intentions have been identified, a supporting strategy can be generated based on the action definition and the goal conditions attached to the intentions. This can be done using basically every automatic planner. In our setting, we use a self-developed system which is able to generate all valid minimal plans (action sequences). A plan is called valid in a given situation, if it is applicable as defined above. A plan is called minimal, if the resulting state sequence does not contain cycles. Our planner works by simple forward chaining, which is possible due to the finite nature of the sample domains. Among all these plans, we select one with minimal number of user actions involved. For this, every action is annotated with the agent as shown in Example 1. In more complex domains, other planners can be used as long as they are able to compute an optimal plan in our sense.

Example 6. *Assume again the meeting room with two projectors and a video switcher able to connect any input source to any of the projectors. All devices can be handled either manually by the user, or remotely by the assistance system. There is only one action that has to be performed by the user, namely to connect the laptop to the system. In a situation in which all devices are switched off and the user connects the laptop, the analysis yield a maximum probability (minimal gradient) for the intention of giving a presentation. This triggers the planning process which: switches the projector on, move the screen down for projection and directs the laptop's output to the projector.*

4   Generating Explanations for Pro-active Assistance

Before actually showing how to derive explanations within our system, we briefly discuss the natural language generation and its input format based on discourse representation structures (DRS).

4.1   Explanation Generation from DRS

The natural language generation module is an important part of the explanation generation. We use a syntactically slightly modified form of DRSs used in the ACE system [10]: Instead of listing all referents occurring, we keep only those which refer to the syntactic structure to be realised, which is for example the question referent Q in the examples above. In addition, we explicitly distinguish between definition and condition statements. All constructs of the form Id=... are called definitions. This syntactical distinction simplifies the conceptual construction of explanations and the construction of the SimpleNLG statements. As described below, the explanation generation components output fairly high-level descriptions of explanations. E.g., the following high-level description specifies a why-question:

```
[Q]:[P=isOn(projector), holds(P,S), S=state, Q=why-holds(P,S)]
```

That is, the question is defined as a DRS with four statements in it and only one referent (Q). Using simple transformation rules this DRS is further refined, by replacing high-level constructs into more low-level conditions. The resulting low-level DRS corresponding to the example above is:

```
[Q]:[P=nounPhrase(the, projector), Q=clause(P, is, switched on),
     interrogative-type(Q, why)]
```

In our system, the transformation rules are specified in Prolog and are basically syntactical conversions, which map sets of high-level components like why-holds to sets of low level constructs like nounPhrase.

To actually generate explanations in natural language, we rely on the SimpleNLG toolkit developed at the University of Aberdeen [11]. The toolkit is a realiser which allows to generate correct English sentences based on an abstract representation. Based on the DRSs, SimpleNLG code is constructed automatically. For this we adapted the syntax of the DRSs slightly. Instead of writing nounPhrase(P, the, projector) we use P=nounPhrase(the, projector) to indicate that this should be transformed into an object creation statement within the SimpleNLG framework. This notation allows to sort all conditions specified within a DRS such that in the right hand side only initialised objects occur. That is the condition Q=clause(P, is, switched on) should be evaluated only after evaluating the condition defining P, as it refers to it. After sorting the conditions, they are transformed into SimpleNLG statements. For the example above, the following Java-code is generated:

```
NPPhraseSpec p = nlg.createNounPhrase("the", "projector");
SPhraseSpec q = nlg.createClause(p, "is", "switched on");
q.setFeature("interrogative_type", InterrogativeType.WHY);
String question = realiser.realiseSentence(q);
```

After executing the statements, the variable question contains the following sentence: "Why is the projector switched on?".

4.2 Answering How-to Questions

As mentioned in Section 3 there are three different cases to consider while generating explanations. Here we concentrate on case A), in which the user is aware of the fact that automatic assistance can be provided, but is not aware of how to actually invoke it. Depending on the current state of the environment, different user goals are possible. As before we compute the set of possible intentions by synthesising plans from the current state to a state satisfying the condition attached to the intention. For all those intendables an optimal action sequence is computed as described above. Let I be an intention and let $[a_1, \ldots, a_n]$ be a corresponding optimal action sequence leading to a state that satisfies I's condition. Let furthermore $[a'_1, \ldots, a'_m]$ be the sub-sequence of user actions. We define the corresponding pair of question and answer as follows:

Definition 7 (How-to-question). *Let I be an intention with name n, and let $[a'_1, \ldots, a'_m]$ be the achieving sequence of user actions as defined above. We define the corresponding How-to-question Q_H and answer A_H as follows:*

$$Q_H := [Q]:[intention(I), state(S), Q=how-achieve(I,S)]$$
$$A_H := [E]:[intention(I), state(S), A=seq, item(A,a'_1), \ldots$$
$$item(A,a'_m), E=achieve(I,S,A)]$$

Those DRSs are later translated into question and answer like *"How to 'n'?"* and *"To achieve 'n' you have to perform the following sequence of actions: $a'_1, \ldots, a'_m$."*

4.3 Answering Why-Questions

The second case discussed in Section 3 describes a situation in which a user by accident triggers some automatic assistance. In this case, the user needs explanations why a certain action has been triggered or why a certain state of the environment has been achieved. A similar system – for a different control system – has been proposed in [2]. Those questions can be answered similar. For this the system reactions need to be stored, that is, the sequence of recognised activities, the assumed intentions and the resulting action sequences to support the intention. Based on this information, pairs of why-questions and answers are generated as follows:

Definition 8 (Why-question 1). *Let S be a situation, in which some automatic assistance is triggered. Let I be the assumed and supported intention and let* $[a_1, \ldots, a_n]$ *be the supporting sequence of actions executed automatically. Let furthermore S' be the resulting situation after executing the plan. For every* $P \in S'$ *and* $P \notin S$ *we define the following Why-question and answer, with* a_P *being the action that caused P to hold:*

$$Q_W := [Q] : [P = isOn(proj.), \ holds(P,S), \ Q = why\text{-}holds(P,S)]$$
$$A_W := [E,F] : [holds(P,S), \ state(S), \ intention(I),$$
$$A = seq, \ item(A,a_1), \ \ldots, \ item(A,a_m),$$
$$E = support(I,S,A), \ F = caused(P,a_P)]$$

Those DRSs are later translated into *"Why does 's' hold?"* and *"'s' holds because the system assumed you are planning to 'I' which has been supported by executing the following sequence of actions:* $[a_1, \ldots, a_m]$. *'s' has been caused by 'a_s'."* Please note, the explanation consists of two parts as indicated by the two referents within the DRS A_W. In addition to answering why a certain predicate holds, the system has to explain why the underlying intention has been assumed:

Definition 9 (Why-question 2). *Let S be a situation in which some automatic assistance supporting the intention I has been triggered. Let* $o_S, o_{S-1} \ldots, o_0$ *be the reverse sequence of observed activities which eventually lead to situation S. The resulting Why-question* Q_W *and answer* A_W *explaining why I has been assumed is defined as follows:*

$$Q_W := [Q] : [intention(I), \ state(S), \ Q = why\text{-}assumed(I,S)]$$
$$A_W := [E] : [intention(I), \ state(S), \ assumed(I,S), \ observed(O),$$
$$O = seq, \ item(O,o_{S-1}), \ldots, \ item(O,o_0), \ E = support(I,S,O)]$$

Those DRSs translate to *"Why has 'I' been assumed by the system?"* and *"'I' has been assumed because you performed* o_S *(and before:* $[o_{S-1}, \ldots, o_0]$). *This sequence of action made the system believe you are aiming at 'I'."* Of course more fine grained explanations can also be generated based on the exact algorithm used to analyse the intentions. Analogously the activity recognition engine could provide insights into its internals by linking activities and corresponding sensor information to explain why a given activity has been recognised.

4.4 Correcting Sub-optimal Behaviour

Finally, we discuss the third case mentioned in Section 3 in which the user performs actions which are actually not necessary because they can be performed automatically by the assistance system if triggered by some event. In this case the user actually behaves non-optimal in our sense, that is he performs some unnecessary actions to achieve a goal. Nonetheless, we assume the user to behave goal-directed within his mental model, that is, according to his internal ideas of how the system works he performs the correct actions. To point users to such sub-optimal behaviour, we track all actions triggered by the user and analyse the likely underlying intention as described above. At the same time, the state of the system is logged. If the system is sufficiently sure about the underlying assumption it identifies unnecessary actions and generates a hint as follows:

Definition 10 (Hint). *Let* $[(S_1, a_1), (S_2, a_2), \ldots, (S_n, a_n)]$ *be a sequence of pairs containing a situation and the executed action. And let I be some assumed intention. Let finally $l > 0$ be some natural number. If for every situations $S \in \{S_{n-l}, \ldots, S_n\}$ there exists an action sequence $a_S = [a_1, \ldots, a_i]$ leading to a state satisfying I, such that the corresponding sub-sequence of user actions $[a'_1, \ldots, a'_u]$ coincides for all S, then we generate the following message explaining this fact:*

```
H := [E]:[intention(I), state(S), assumed(I,S),
          A=seq, item(A,a'₁),..., item(A,a'ᵤ),
          E=hint-sufficient-actions(A, S, I)]
```

The parameter l controls how many unnecessary actions have to be executed before the system generates a hint. The resulting DRS is translated into *"To achieve 'I' it is sufficient to perform the following actions:* $[a'_1, \ldots, a'_u]$.*"*

5 Preliminary Evaluation

The system described above has been realised in a first prototype. As mentioned above, the text generation itself is done by the SimpleNLG toolkit available in Java. The remaining parts of the system are implemented in Prolog. Because a full evaluation of the approach has not yet been performed, the following should rather be understood as an anecdotal evaluation which is meant to show the system in action and to show that (at least for this case) the system works as intended.

The simple example used here describes a fairly frequent situation within an academic setting, but it should not be misunderstood as being the sole application domain. All ideas and algorithms can directly be transferred into different domains involving users that interact with (smart) devices, like for example assisted living scenarios and smart working places.

As mentioned above, our system currently performs the three steps from intention analysis up to explanation generation. To recognise user activities, we currently rely on external inputs. Given a sequence of user activities the system analyses the possible underlying intentions, provides automatic assistance and is able to generate explanations to describe the internals of its decision making as well as to guide the user to a more efficient use of the system.

Assume a setting similar to the one introduced in Section 3, that is a room with two projectors, associated screens, and a video switcher. In addition, there are dimmable lamps next to the projection screens and there is a whiteboard able to recognise that a pen is taken up by the user to use it. The system generates e.g. the following *How-to* questions:

- **How to start a presentation on screen 1?** *By connecting the laptop to video input 1. The system will execute all further necessary actions (e.g. switch on the projector, lower screen and dim the light).*
- **How to use the whiteboard?** *By taking up a pen. The system will execute all further necessary actions (e.g., switch on the light).*
- **How to switch off the room?** *By dis-connecting the laptop from video input 1, putting back the pen and leaving the room. The system will execute all further necessary actions (e.g., switch off the light and projectors).*

In addition to the necessary user action, the explanations contain details wrt. automatically executed actions that will be performed by the system. The question-answer pairs are shown sorted with respect to the probability associated with the underlying intention. After performing the optimal action by accident first, the system generates e.g. the following explanation for the changes made to the environment:

- **Why has the projector been switched on?** *The projector has been switched on to enable giving a presentation. This is assumed because you connected a laptop.*
- **Why has the projection screen been moved down?** *The projection screen has been moved down to enable giving a presentation. This is assumed because you connected a laptop.*

If the user manually performs part of the full action sequence by switching on the projector and lowering the screen, the system generates the following hint:

- **Hint:** *To give a presentation, it suffices to connect a laptop to the system. The system will execute all necessary actions (e.g. switch on the projector, lower screen and dim the light).*

In this example the parameter l in Definition 10 has been set to 2, i.e., whenever the user executes two actions that could have been executed automatically the hint is shown to the user.

A first user study [2] performed on a similar system shows that the generated answers are understandable and contain a sufficient amount of detail to explain the system's internals.

6   Conclusions and Future Work

In this paper we describe a system able to provide assistance for users within smart environments and at the same time able to explain its reactions. It is furthermore able to construct explanations describing how to utilise the system in a more efficient way. This research has been conducted to show the general feasibility, because there are only few explanation aware assistance systems available for intelligent environments.

All components are based on a formalisation of actions as known from the situation calculus and used within the automatic planning domain. Based on this formalisation, intentions underlying a recognised sequence of user actions can be analysed and supporting strategies are generated by planning algorithms. At the same time necessary information is logged which allows to explain the actions automatically taken by the system. Those information is transformed into human readable explanations in English.

This research shows that the automatic generation of supporting explanations is possible. The generated explanations help the user to construct and correct his internal mental model of the whole system and thus to utilise it more efficiently. A rigorous evaluation of the system and the confirmation of its usefulness in settings beyond simple meeting room scenarios will be subject to future work.

Surprisingly, the generation of explanations has been possible without any further information as the one contained within the action and intention descriptions. Nonetheless, there are many open issues raised by this work. Even though we believe our system to help improving the users trust, this claim needs to be evaluated by a larger user study. Explanations provided to one user need to be collected and to be investigated with respect to occurring patterns. If one user always requests a certain kind of explanation, this may indicate a certain misconception. This explanation tracking will be investigated next in combination with user-customisation of the explanations, depending on the background knowledge of the user. As already mentioned above, the activity recognition and intention analysis modules could be replaced by more powerful approaches. This will very likely be necessary while applying the overall system within more complex domains.

Acknowledgments. This work is supported by the german research foundation (DFG) within research training group 1424 MuSAMA.

References

1. Aggarwal, J., Ryoo, M.: Human activity analysis: A review. ACM Comput. Surv. 43(3), 16:1–16:43 (2011)
2. Bader, S.: Explaining the reactions of a smart environment. In: Proc. of Exact 2012, Montpellier, France (August 2012)
3. Bader, S., Dyrba, M.: Goalaviour-based control of heterogeneous and distributed smart environments. In: Proc. of the 7th International Conference on Intelligent Environments, pp. 142–148. IEEE (2011)
4. Chen, L., Nugent, C., Biswas, J., Hoey, J. (eds.): Activity Recognition in Pervasive Intelligent Environments, Atlantis. Ambient and Pervasive Intelligence, vol. 4 (2011)
5. Chin, J., Callaghan, V., Clarke, G.: An end user tool for customising personal spaces in ubiquitous computing environments. In: Ma, J., Jin, H., Yang, L.T., Tsai, J.J.-P. (eds.) UIC 2006. LNCS, vol. 4159, pp. 1080–1089. Springer, Heidelberg (2006)
6. Cook, D., Das, S.: Smart Environments. Wiley (2005)
7. Cook, D., Huber, M., Gopalratnam, K., Youngblood, M.: Learning to control a smart home environment. In: Innovative Applications of Artificial Intelligence (2003)
8. Dey, A.: Modeling and intelligibility in ambient environments. J. Ambient Intell. Smart Environ. 1, 57–62 (2009)
9. Dooley, J., Callaghan, H.H.V., Gardner, M., Ghanbaria, M., AlGhazzawi, D.: The intelligent classroom: Beyond four walls. In: Proc. of the Intelligent Campus Workshop (IC 2011) held at the 7th IEEE Intelligent Environments Conference (IE 2011) (2011)

10. Fuchs, N.E., Schwertel, U., Schwitter, R.: Attempto controlled english – not just another logic specification language. In: Flener, P. (ed.) LOPSTR 1998. LNCS, vol. 1559, pp. 1–20. Springer, Heidelberg (1999)

11. Gatt, A., Reiter, E.: Simplenlg: A realisation engine for practical applications. In: Proc. of ENLG 2009 (2009)

12. Gerevini, A., Haslum, P., Long, D., Saetti, A., Dimopoulos, Y.: Deterministic planning in the fifth international planning competition: PDDL3 and experimental evaluation of the planners. Artificial Intelligence 173(5-6), 619–668 (2009)

13. Heider, T., Kirste, T.: Supporting goal-based interaction with dynamic intelligent environments. In: Proc. of ECAI 2002, pp. 596–600 (2002)

14. Helal, S., Mann, W., El-Zabadani, H., King, J., Kaddoura, Y., Jansen, E.: The gator tech smart house: a programmable pervasive space. Computer 38(3), 50–60 (2005)

15. Kamp, H., Reyle, U.: From Discourse to Logic. Kluwer (1993)

16. Kientz, J.A., Patel, S.N., Jones, B., Price, E., Mynatt, E.D., Abowd, G.D.: The Georgia Tech Aware Home. In: CHI 2008 Extended Abstracts on Human Factors in Computing Systems, pp. 3675–3680. ACM, New York (2008)

17. Krüger, F., Yordanova, K., Hein, A., Kirste, T.: Plan synthesis for probabilistic activity recognition. In: Proc. of the 5th International Conference on Agents and Artificial Intelligence (ICAART 2013), Barcelona, Spain, pp. 283–288 (February 2013)

18. Lim, B., Dey, A., Avrahami, D.: Why and why not explanations improve the intelligibility of context-aware intelligent systems. In: Proc. of the 27th International Conference on Human Factors in Computing Systems, pp. 2119–2128. ACM (2009)

19. Mozer, M.C.: Lessons from an adaptive house. In: Cook, D., Das, R. (eds.) Smart Environments: Technologies, Protocols, and Applications, pp. 273–294. Wiley (2005)

20. Muñoz, A., Serrano, E., Villa, A., Valdés, M., Botía, J.A.: An approach for representing sensor data to validate alerts in ambient assisted living. Sensors 12(5), 6282–6306 (2012)

21. Nakashima, H., Aghajan, H., Augusto, J. (eds.): Handbook of Ambient Intelligence and Smart Environments. Springer (2010)

22. Poslad, S.: Ubiquitous Computing: Smart Devices, Environments and Interactions. Wiley (2009)

23. Ramírez, M., Geffner, H.: Goal recognition over pomdps: inferring the intention of a pomdp agent. In: Proc. of IJCAI 2011, pp. 2009–2014. AAAI Press (2011)

24. Reiter, E., Dale, R.: Building Natural Language Generation Systems. Studies in natural language processing. Cambridge University Press (2000)

25. Roth-Berghofer, T., Leake, D., Cassens, J. (eds.): Proc. of the Workshop on Explanation-aware Computing (2012)

26. Vermeulen, J., Lim, B., Kawsar, F.: Pervasive intelligibility - 2nd workshop on intelligibility and control in pervasive computing (2012)

27. Vermeulen, J., Vanderhulst, G., Luyten, K., Coninx, K.: Pervasive crystal: Asking and answering why and why not questions about pervasive computing applications. In: 6th International Conference on Intelligent Environments, pp. 271–276 (2010)

The Screen Is Yours—Comparing Handheld Pairing Techniques for Public Displays

Matthias Baldauf[1], Markus Salo[2], Stefan Suette[1], and Peter Fröhlich[1]

[1] FTW Telecommunications Research Center Vienna, Austria
[2] University of Jyväskylä, Finland

Abstract. Whereas mobile devices have been heavily investigated as remote controls for distant displays, research on the fundamental first step, the pairing with the display, is scarce. In a comparative user study with 31 participants we evaluated five potential pairing techniques concerning their performance and acceptance for connecting to a public display and gained insights into the general requirements for pairing techniques in this special usage context. Besides four established mobile interaction techniques (touching an NFC tag, capturing a QR code, scanning, and manual input), our study considered a recent appropriate pairing technique called display pointing, which allows passers-by to connect to available displays just by pointing their smartphone at the installation, for the first time. Our results show that display pointing is superior to traditional alternatives to a large extent. Yet, its quick response times can result in a perceived lack of control if not handled appropriately. Further, we learnt that long distance techniques are generally preferred while the type of device gesture as well as security concerns are of less relevance.

Keywords: mobile interaction, pairing, pointing, visual recognition.

1 Introduction

While digital signage technologies have been increasingly deployed in urban environments over the last few years, we currently observe a shift toward interactive content on public displays. Such emerging installations allow passers-by to fetch coupons, play games, or take part in contests and polls. Besides gestural and touch-based interactions which require special hardware to be deployed, smartphones are promising ubiquitous and versatile remote controls for such interactive applications. Respective previous research focused on the investigation of various mobile interaction styles [1], only little attention has been attached to the crucial first step in the interplay of mobile devices and public displays, the pairing process. Related work has mainly studied post-pairing interaction and innovative application concept for smartphones and public displays assuming an already established wireless connection and neglecting this obstacle for usage. However, creating a low threshold of use and thus allowing for highly serendipitous interactions might be one of the critical success factors for upcoming interactive applications [1].

J.C. Augusto et al. (Eds.): AmI 2013, LNCS 8309, pp. 32–47, 2013.

In this paper, we present a user study comparing potential pairing techniques. The most recent one, in this paper called "display pointing", allows for connecting the mobile device with a public display through a simple pointing gesture. Interested passers-by can just briefly target the distant display through the mobile camera viewfinder to immediately establish a connection to it (Figure 1). We compare display pointing with the following more established physical mobile interaction techniques [2,3] for the very specific use case of pairing a mobile device with a public display, deliberately independent of the subsequent actual interaction style:

- *Touching.* Bringing a mobile device very close (5cm or less) to a smart label near the public display to read the pairing information without contact (Figure 1b).
- *Short-range pointing.* Identifying an object by capturing a corresponding unique visual marker attached to the public display through the camera (Figure 1c).
- *Scanning.* Selecting the desired display from a list by scanning the environment for available public displays based on proximity (Figure 1d).
- *User-mediated pairing.* Manually entering a code on the mobile device to specify the public display to be paired (Figure 1e).

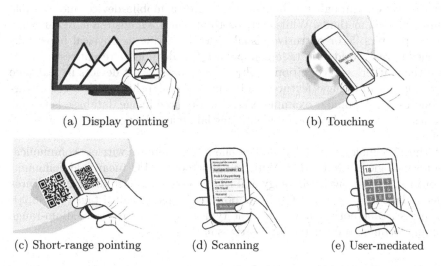

(a) Display pointing

(b) Touching

(c) Short-range pointing   (d) Scanning   (e) User-mediated

Fig. 1. We compared the recent display pointing approach (a) and four more established pairing techniques (b-e)

Our comparative study aims at investigating the characteristics of display pointing and evaluating the overall applicability of these pairing techniques in the context of public display interaction. Further, we are interested in the general requirements of such mobile pairing techniques for the given scenario. Do any of these arouse special security concerns? What role does the distance to the public screen play? And have explicit smartphone gestures such as pointing become socially accepted in public spaces?

2   Related Work

In the following, we summarize previous related research in the field of mobile interaction with real-world objects, so-called physical mobile interactions, and respective results from user studies in different contexts.

2.1   Mobile Real-World Interaction

Today's feature-rich smartphones provide several technological means to act as mediators to real-world surroundings and nearby smart objects and thus realize abovementioned interaction styles [4]. One popular approach are geospatial calculations based on built-in positioning technologies such as GPS. While the plain device location can be used to realize simple scanning features for typical location-based services, it can be combined with orientation information gathered from a compass to realize long-range pointing styles [4].

Another way to realize both short- and long-range pointing gestures is the visual detection through the built-in camera of a mobile device and suitable computer vision methods. While early prototypes utilized custom hardware such as laser pointers [5] or obtrusive visual codes [6] acting as physical hyperlinks attached to real-world objects (e.g. popular QR codes), more recent research enabled the markerless recognition of objects on mass-market devices in real-time exploiting natural image features and comparing snapshots with a set of target photos [7]. A popular example based on a remote image database is Google Goggles, a mobile application for identifying landmarks by pointing with a smartphone.

A third technological enabler for mobile interaction are wireless communication technologies such as NFC, Wifi, and Bluetooth. NFC (near field communication) is a short-range technology and can be used to realize touching gestures to fetch data from or write data to unpowered chips, so-called tags (e.g. [8,9]). In contrast, Bluetooth and Wifi are the typical cornerstones for medium-range scanning techniques for detecting nearby smart objects.

2.2   Evaluating Physical Mobile Interaction

Rukzio et al. [2,3] were amongst the first researchers who compared different interaction techniques to derive guidelines on what technique to apply for what scenario. According to their studies, scanning and user-mediated object interaction are the preferred techniques for tourist guide applications while in a museum context where visitors are close to objects touching is favorable. For smart (home) environments which are probably most related to the public display scenario explored in this paper, the distance is pivotal: again, for close objects touching is preferred, for object further away yet visible it is pointing (implemented by laser pointer attached to mobile device), for not visible object (in other room) scanning. Similar results are reported by Välkkynen et al. [10]. At that time, camera-based pointing with visual codes suffered from high execution times requiring up to a few seconds for decoding and informing the user about the success of the action. A more recent study comparing product identification techniques [11] shows that NFC is still preferable in terms of speed, however, very close to capturing visual codes. Yet, both techniques outperform manual code entry. Other studies proved advantages of NFC touches and visual codes over Bluetooth scanning approaches for dedicated use cases [12,13]. Comparing NFC and 2D codes directly in the context of smart posters unveiled the easier learnability of 2D code capturing, whereas trained participants preferred NFC [14]. However, related studies unveiled security concerns regarding touching gestures in public places [9].

In contrast to such previous studies, we investigate these techniques as pairing modes for public displays and thus as enablers for subsequent interaction. Further we are interested in the specific requirements in the context of public displays and the impact of contemporary technology such as improved QR code readers and NFC sensors.

2.3 Screen Pairing Techniques

Previous research on mobile interactions with public screens focused on innovative interaction styles to use smartphones as remote controls. However, work dedicated to the required pairing step is scarce. When applying visual markers (e.g. [15,16]) or custom displays equipped with a grid of NFC tags (e.g. [17]), these smart labels can be utilized for both determining the screen area a mobile device was targeted at and encoding the address of the hosting computer to establish a data connection it. For markerless setups, Bluetooth scanning approaches have been proposed to determine available public displays and select the desired one based on descriptive names. Whereas this approach probably takes more time, it is also feasible for environments with multiple displays deployed.

Purely location-based approaches which automatically connect to a nearby screen [18] might be suitable for home environments, however, fail for urban surroundings densely equipped with public displays. Pointing-like techniques for visual markerless screen recognition are considered in recent work on smart lens-based interaction with displays [19], however, only as part of the actual interaction, not as dedicated pairing techniques.

So far, no studies have been conducted to compare pairing techniques for enabling mobile interactions with public displays in depth. The experiment presented in this paper tries to shed light on this neglected aspect and studies pairing techniques independent from any task-related interaction with the remote display.

2.4 Research Hypotheses

Based on the abovementioned literature research and own experiences from a preliminary qualitative study [20], we formulated our expectations in the following research hypotheses.

H1. Due to its intuitive nature and common "photographing" gesture, display pointing is easier to learn than alternative techniques.
H2. Display pointing outperforms the alternative in terms of several key factors in physical mobile interactions: ease, mental and physical load, speed, innovativeness, fun and accuracy.
H3. Display pointing arouses less security concerns than for example NFC due to its long-distance contactless pairing approach.
H4. According to previous research in smart home environments, long-distance techniques for pairing with remote display will be preferred in the context of public screens.
H5. Due to the public context, participants prefer pairing techniques based on typical smartphone interactions such as manual input over explicit device gestures.

3 Method

To address our research questions and answer the hypotheses, we implemented a functional research prototype featuring five pairing techniques and conducted a comparative lab study.

3.1 Participants

32 participants (13 females, 19 males) were recruited from our institute's user database and through social media announcements took part in our experiment. The data of one male participant had to be excluded due to insufficiently provided data in the final interview phase. The participants' age ranged between 23 and 66 years (mean=36.8, median=31.5). We carefully selected the participating users to resemble the structure of the entire local smartphone users and thus gain representative results: the test group consisted of 15 participants (5 females, 10 males) younger than 29 years, 10 participants (5, 5) aged between 30 and 49, and 6 persons (2, 4) over 50 years. As remuneration for taking part in our study we offered vouchers for supermarkets and online shops.

Each participant owned on average 1.3 mobile devices. On five point Likert scales between strongly agree (1) and strongly disagree (5), the test persons stated a mean of 1.6 for the statement I like to experiment with new information technologies and of 2.1 for I often seek out information about new technology products. Further, they answered both I regularly use many kinds of mobile applications and I think I am skillful at using technology and mobile applications with 2.1 on average. All participants had seen visual codes before (20 had used one in practice), 23 participants had heard about NFC (3 had used it), and 27 participants knew Bluetooth scanning (25 had used it).

Fig. 2. The test setup contained two large screens with exemplary interactive applications (left). One of them was a public poll showing a topical question and three possible answers after the successful pairing (right).

3.2   Setup

In our test room, we arranged two flat screen TVs with screen diagonals of 47 and 55 inches, placed on bar tables at a typical height of public displays. The two screens were facing the same direction to resemble the scenario of adjacent windows in a shopping street (Figure 2, left). These two screens were no separate systems but were hosted by one desktop computer through a multi-monitor graphics card in order to facilitate data logging. Another smaller screen was attached for the test manager to change the system configuration via a simple console, e.g. remotely specifying the connection technique for the current user. For the two large screens we chose two typical applications: one was designed as an official information terminal of the city showing a poll for citizen participation after connecting to it (Figure 2, right), the other one acted as an advertisement screen of a travel agency offering a quiz to win a journey. In front of the screens, we attached custom boxes containing an NFC tag and a QR code to the tables. Labels with the screens' names and three-digit numeric identifiers were placed at the bottom right corner of the display as suggested by Rashid et al. [21].

As mobile device, we used a Samsung Nexus S smartphone running Android 4.0.3. This device meets all the required hardware requirements including a suitable camera and an NFC sensor.

3.3   Mobile Prototype

Our mobile application communicated with the remote system over Wifi and featured all five pairing modes as depicted in Figure 1:

- *Display Pointing.* We realized the display pointing technique utilizing *Qualcomm's Vuforia*, an advanced augmented reality toolkit for mobile devices. Our mobile user interface showed the camera viewfinder in full-screen. Instead of typical graphical overlays, we only used the toolkit's image recognition capabilities to visually identify the background images shown on the two screens. The toolkit provides an efficient markerless image recognition based on natural image features (i.e. no obtrusive visual markers such as black/white patterns are required) and works highly robust also from varying distances and angles. In the mobile application, we associated each background image used in the study with a screen identifier (i.e. a fictive IP address). While this simplified approach with predefined images is feasible for a lab study, a more sophisticated back-end system is required to enable display pointing on a large scale. We presented a respective framework continuously informing nearby mobile devices about the currently visible display content in previous work [22].

- *Touching an NFC tag.* The NFC approach was implemented using the standard Android framework and appropriate method calls. Our mobile user interface just showed the message "Please touch the NFC tag". As soon as the smartphone was brought into close proximity of about three centimeters or less to one of the tags, the screen identifier was read.
- *Capturing a QR code.* To efficiently decode the QR codes, we made use of the popular ZXing software library. On top of the full-screen camera viewfinder we placed a rectangular border as target area like in typical barcode scanner applications. Our solution worked in continuous camera mode and was very responsive, i.e. explicitly pushing a button to photograph the marker was not required.
- *Scanning.* For study purposes, we created a view resembling the well-known Bluetooth scanning process (Figure 1d). The scan could be started and stopped with a push of a button. Then, a scrollable list of 12 faked display names (including the two available in the test room) was built up in random order with random delays between 0.5 and 1.5 seconds for each list item resulting in a typical Bluetooth scanning experience. As soon as a display name was visible, it could be selected by touching it.
- *Manual input.* Finally, we implemented a traditional numerical on-screen keyboard featuring a backspace and a confirm button for entering numeric identifiers.

When a screen identifier was correctly recognized by the smartphone (whether visually from the display content, read from an NFC tag, decoded from a QR code, selected from the scanning list or entered manually), it was sent to the desktop computer over Wifi and the successful connection to the screen was indicated by a short vibration. Further, the corresponding screen changed its content and showed a quiz question or a poll, respectively, with multiple answer buttons (Figure 2, right). The questions were selected from a set of prepared questions to avoid routine and keep the participants interested. To select an asnwer, the mobile application featured two interaction modes:

- *Touchpad.* In analogy to publicly available mobile applications like *Logitech's Touch Mouse*, the participants could relatively move the remote enlarged mouse cursor by strokes on the mobile display and simulate mouse clicks by pressing a button.
- *Mini video.* This interaction technique showed a cloned scaled-down version of the distant display's content on the mobile device for direct touch interaction similar to available remote control software such as *Teamviewer*.

3.4   Procedure

During the study, each participant used each pairing technique in a training and a test phase to connect to the prepared screens. However, each participant was only confronted with one randomly assigned interaction technique. To collect the participants' experiences and final resumes, we prepared a questionnaire enquiring demographic data and including questions to estimate the participant's technology affinity and experience. We decided to follow an established method for comparing technologically heterogeneous interaction techniques (cf. [2,3]) by engaging participants in interactions and afterwards asking them for the subjectively perceived performance. As an example for the heterogeneity of the compared techniques and the arising difficulties for objective assessment, the time for scanning can be easily measured as the time between starting the scanning and selecting an item from the result list, whereas the precise start time of capturing a QR code cannot be determined.

For evaluating each pairing technique in practice, each participant started with a training phase and subsequently went through the test phase. The order of the pairing techniques was systematically varied to avoid any learning effects. When the connection to a screen was successfully established, the participant answered the question related to the given interaction technique. Then the screen showed a short "Thank you" message and both the display and the mobile device were set back to the original pairing mode.

Training phase. During the training phase, we asked the participants to use only one screen and connect to it using the given technique for several times until they felt comfortable with it. Afterwards, we wanted them to answer how easy it was to learn this technique on a five-point Likert scale, ranging from "very easy" to "very hard" and to give reasons for their decision.

Test phase. Familiar with the pairing technique, the participants were asked to use the technique again, but now to move over to the other screen after each screen interaction, imagining that they would be using it within an everyday situation on a shopping street. As a constraint for the test phase, we asked the participants to switch between four and eight times between the screens. Having completed the test phase, the participants were asked to state on five point Likert scales how easy they considered the pairing process through the given technique and rate it in terms of mental and physical effort, speed, innovativeness, fun and accuracy and give short explanations for their rating. These aspects have been previously identified as key factors in physical mobile interactions [2,3]. A further rating scale was related to whether subjects would have any security concerns when using their personal mobile device for this technique at the aforementioned public place.

Final Interview. Having tested all five pairing techniques, we asked the participants to rate the techniques according their overall preference. Finally, we wanted to know whether the participants in general preferred short-distance (NFC, QR code) or long-distance (display pointing, manual input, scanning) techniques and explicit gestures (display pointing, NFC, QR code) or traditional on-screen interaction (manual input, scanning) at a public place.

4   Results

Overall, our participants conducted 1,478 successful pairing operations: 569 in training mode and 909 in test mode. In the following, we report on results from the user inquiry directly after usage, as well as comparative preference rankings and comments from the final interview. Error bars in the figures indicate 95% confidence intervals. For inferential statistical analysis, we ran GLM repeated measures tests with SPSS to identify main effects of the registration techniques. In case of violated sphericity assumptions, the values reported are using the Greenhouse-Geisser degrees of freedom adjustment. When main effects were significant, post hoc pair wise comparisons with Bonferroni corrections were performed. To test potential biases by the sample composition or test design, we also investigated interaction effects of registration technique vs. several independent factors such as age groups, gender, technology affinity or the used interaction technique after registration, again using SPSS GLM analyses. For none of these independent factors, we identified a significant interaction effect with registration technique.

We found significant main effects for learnability ($F_{4,65.58}=8.38$, $p<0.001$), ease of connecting ($F_{4,59.43}=6.88$, $p<0.01$), speed ($F_{4,79.59}=10.52$, $p<0.001$), mental ($F_{4,116}=8.90$, $p<0.001$) and physical demand ($F_{4,87.69}=5.64$, $p<0.01$), fun ($F_{4,83.33}=32.06$, $p<0.001$), innovativeness ($F_{4,79.17}=17.45$, $p<0.001$), accuracy ($F_{4,116}=11.87$, $p<0.001$), overall preference ($F_{4,116}=6.96$, $p<0.001$), and preparedness to use in public ($F_{4,116}=4.57$, $p<0.01$). However, we did not find significant main effects for mean rating scores on security concerns (rating scores were around 2.9, the average SD was 1.35).

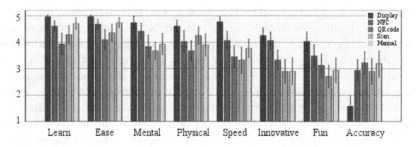

Fig. 3. Rating results for the five pairing techniques

Learnability. In general, participants' ratings after the training phase for each technique were rather positive (Figure 3), with mean scores of 4 and higher. When analyzing pairwise differences for learnability, we found that display pointing received an almost maximum mean rating of 4.97 (SD=0.18), followed by manual input (M=4.71, SD=0.59), NFC (M=4.61, SD=5.58), scanning (M=4.29, SD=0.94) and QR code (M=3.94, SD=1.12). We found significant pairwise differences between display pointing and NFC (p=0.28), display pointing and scanning (p<0.001), display pointing and QR code (p=0.004), as well as manual and QR code (p=0.015).

Ease of pairing. Also the ratings on how easy it was in overall to connect to the screen were quite positive for all techniques. A nearly perfect mean score was received for display pointing (M=4.97, SD=0.18). This was again followed by manual input (M=4.74, SD=0.51), NFC (M=4.68, SD=0.54), scanning (M=4.35, SD=0.92) and QR code (M=4.10, SD=1.04). Significant differences were found between display pointing and scanning (p=0.012), display pointing and QR code (p=0.001), as well as between manual input and QR code (p=0.023).

Mental demand. The rating scores for mental demand (1=high demand, 5=low demand) were best for display pointing (M=4.74, SD=0.68), second best for NFC (M=4.42, SD=0.81), followed by QR code (M=3.84, SD=1.19), manual input (M=3.94, SD=1.09), and scanning (M=3.68, SD=0.91). Significant pairwise differences were found between display pointing and QR code (p=0.002), display pointing and manual input (p=0.004), display pointing and scanning (p<0.001), as well as NFC and scanning (p=0.015).

Physical demand. Display pointing was rated best (M=4.61, SD=0.62) and QR code was rated worst (M=3.68, SD=1.05); only this pairwise difference was significant (p=0.001).

Speed. Display pointing (M=4.77, SD=0.48) was qualified significantly faster than the other techniques NFC (M=4.06, SD=0.96, p=0.009), manual input (M=3.77, SD=0.95, p<0.001), QR code (M=3.45, SD=1.15, p<0.001), and scanning (3.32, SD=1.35, p<0.001). No other pairwise differences were found.

Innovativeness. Figure 4 indicates that display pointing (M=4.26, SD=0.77) and NFC (M=4.06, SD=0.89) were perceived more innovative than the other techniques. We did not find a significant pairwise difference between them, but each of them had significant pairwise differences to the other techniques, namely to QR code (M=3.32, SD=1.05, both p<0.01), scanning (M=2.90, SD=1.19, both p<0.01), and manual input (M=2.90, SD=1.38, both p<0.01).

Fun. Display pointing provided most fun (M=4.65, SD=0.84), significantly more than the other techniques NFC (M=3.33, SD=1.16), QR code (M=2.87, SD=1.26), manual input (M=2.00, SD=0.86), and scanning (M=2.10, SD=1.04), all differences were highly significant (p<0.001). Further significant differences were NFC vs scanning (p=0.006) and NFC vs manual input (p<0.001).

Accuracy. Overall, the participants' accuracy ratings were comparatively low, with scores of 3.20. Display pointing was qualified as least accurate (M=1.58, SD=1.15), significantly less accurate than scanning (M=2.90, SD=1.33), NFC (M=2.94, SD=1.12), QR code (M=3.00, SD=1.15), and manual input (M=3.19, SD=1.33), all differences highly significant (p<0.001). There were no further significant pairwise differences.

Overall preference. Figure 4 shows that display pointing received the highest mean ranking score, i.e. it was significantly more often preferred than the other techniques (M=4.06, SD=1.34), NFC (M=3.00, SD=1.32), manual input (M=2.84 SD=1.10), QR code (M=2.81, SD=1.38), and scanning (M=2.29, SD=1.40), all pairwise comparisons significant (p<0.01). Figure 5 (left) shows that when participants were explicitly asked about the distance to a public screen while registering to it, 87.1% preferred long distance methods (such as display pointing, manual input or scanning) to short distance methods (such as NFC or QR code, 9.7%), only 3.2% were undecided. Confronted with the question whether they would like to apply a gesture (such as with display pointing or touching an NFC tag) vs a typical smartphone interaction (by manual input or scanning), the distribution of answers was balanced between these two alternatives (45.2% vs. 38.7%), and 16.1% participants were undecided (Figure 5, right).

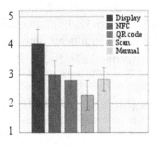
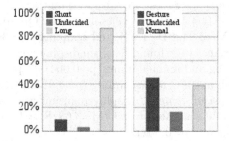

Fig. 4. Mean ranking scores for 'Overall Preference'

Fig. 5. Percentage of preference for distance (left) and gesture (right)

4.1 Observations and Statements

While most of the participants did not have any remarkable problems with NFC, scanning and manual input, some test persons struggled with capturing the QR codes. Even though the QR code scanner worked very well and responsive, targeting the code was difficult for them. In contrast, several people were obviously surprised by the speed of display pointing while some of them, especially elderly, described display pointing even as "too fast" and "too sensitive".

However, we observed that the subjective speed of a mobile connection technique in the context of public displays is perceived differently. While most of the participants experienced NFC, QR code and display pointing as fast techniques due to their short response times, others surprisingly considered scanning and manual input as faster alternatives. These techniques allow passers-by to start establishing the connection even while approaching the screen (given the screen identifier is known or well readable also from distance, respectively) and not to walk to a smart label, thus shorten the distance to be travelled and resulting in an earlier completed connection attempt.

During observation, we especially directed our attention to the moment after a successful connection attempt when the participants moved from the connection phase to the interaction phase and tried to identify issues in the combination of different connection and interaction techniques. As potential obstacle several participants mentioned that switching device orientation is impractical, e.g. when combining manual input in portrait mode (Figure 1e) with interaction in landscape mode such as mini video. Surprisingly, many of these participants used display pointing and the QR code reader in portrait mode, even though both also worked in landscape mode.

Further, some combinations resulted in a complete departure from the large display by some participants. In the previous example combining manual input with mini video, those were entirely focused on the mobile device throughout both pairing and interaction. Some even did not notice changes on the large screen at all and considered the action happening only in the mobile application. Typical statements in such cases included that the public screen actually would not be needed.

5   Discussion and Conclusions

In this section, we refer back to our research hypotheses and discuss the results of our study in view of our previous assumptions.

5.1   H1. Learnability

The hypothesis on the learnability of display pointing is confirmed. Display pointing received outstanding learnability scores and was considered significantly better than NFC, QR code and scanning and also better, yet not significantly, than the very trivial manual input method in terms of learnability. Whereas scanning consists of several interaction steps, QR code needs accurate pointing and NFC requires a special hand posture to position the NFC sensor of the device over the tag. Display pointing, by contrast, consists of one intuitive gesture and is very robust to varying distances and angles when based on state-of-the-art recognition algorithms. Since the recognition of parts of the remote display is already sufficient for establishing the connection, no precise pointing and targeting is required making this technique also tolerant against hand or arm trembling and thus suitable for both young and elderly users with varying experiences in smartphone usage and different physical conditions.

5.2   H2. Perceived Performance

The study results support this hypothesis in major parts, however, not entirely. Concerning the occurring mental load, NFC and display pointing are perceived best. Scanning and manual input require reading, mistakes in capturing a QR code easily leads to frustration. This is also true for the physical load, where display pointing is rated best with a significantly lower load than the QR code alternative. Furthermore, display pointing significantly outperforms all alternatives in terms of speed and fun. This finding is also supported by observations within the training and test phases, where participants positively noted the game-like targeting of display pointing. However, in contrast to capturing QR codes, display pointing was always successful and led to a sense of achievement for the participants. In our context of enabling mobile interactions with public displays, we especially regard the criteria ease of connecting, speed and fun as key factors and thus consider display pointing as very suitable: pairing techniques should be fast to allow users to quickly start doing the actual task, should be comfortable and easy to use to lower the threshold of starting an interaction and should be fun to animate passers-by to participate.

However, the major drawback of display pointing turned out to be the perceived accuracy: Participants were not satisfied with the technique's accuracy, they rated display pointing significantly worse than all other techniques. The participants' statements and our observations explain this drawback: for several (especially elderly) participants, the tested implementation of display pointing worked too fast and sensitively what resulted in a perceived lack of control and the fear of selecting a nearby screen by mistake. As appropriate countermeasures we suggest the integration of optional confirmation features to avoid such wrong selections. As soon as the remote display is detected, the mobile application should communicate the successful recognition and provide a simple approval mechanism. This might either be a short dwell time indicated by a progress bar or an additional button for explicit pairing. We consider the second approach as more promising since the mobile device can be brought down into a normal position after the pointing gesture.

5.3   H3. Security Concerns

The results of the study do not confirm our hypothesis on security. Surprisingly, we could not find any significant differences with regard to security: the participants considered remote connection techniques as secure as the alternatives in the evaluated context. With regard to the results of related previous studies, we interpret this as a consequence of the emerging ubiquity of mobile services based on QR codes and NFC tags and thus a familiarization and growing trust in these techniques. Further, we consider the type of interactive screen application to be crucial: With the quiz game and the poll we chose two very typical examples for our study, namely none security-critical applications. In contrast to mobile payment processes or similar, connecting to a public display to play a game or take part in an informal survey seems not to give rise to any security concerns.

5.4   H4. Distance

Our hypothesis on the preference of techniques allowing for connections from distance is fully confirmed. Whereas short-range techniques such as NFC were proven to work well for security-relevant interactions in the public, e.g. for purchasing tickets [8], more than 80% of our participants clearly stated that they appreciate long-distance techniques for connecting to a public display over pairing methods requiring immediate vicinity to the screen. As reasons for their decision, the test persons mentioned not to be forced to walk to the display as well as the applicability for multi-user applications at busy locations where interested passers-by could simply connect from distance instead of breaking through the crowd or queuing up in front of a corresponding smart label. Another major reason was the opportunity to literally operate from a position in the background and not to be immediately recognizable as the one responsible for the actions on the public display.

This clear preference for long-distance techniques in the context of mobile interactions with public displays is a strong point for scanning, manual input (if the screen identifier is known) as well as display pointing. Due to high-quality cameras and zoom features and dependent on the size of the remote display, this technique can also be applied from larger distance.

5.5   H5. Gesture

Our hypothesis on the preference of "normal" smartphone interactions over explicit device gestures is not confirmed. Slightly more participants preferred an explicit gesture for setting up the connection than a normal smartphone interaction such as on-screen typing. We ascribe this outcome to the positive experiences with the tested gestural techniques (especially touching the NFC tag and display pointing) and primarily their quick response times with regard to scanning and manual input. This result indicates that directional device gestures like touching and pointing are accepted when they are perceived useful. Further, this result may be a sign of changes in technology usage and acceptance over time: While in related early studies participants tended to avoid explicit smartphone gestures in public space or mentioned feeling awkward or embarrassed (cf. [5,14]), such gestures have become more mainstream in the meanwhile and thus socially acceptable. This is further confirmed by the technique ranking concerning the overall preference: the gestural display pointing method is significantly preferred to the alternatives.

6   Limitations

To gain systematic and comparable results for this first comparative study on screen pairing, we decided to conduct our study under controlled lab settings, accompanied by a test assistant to maximize data richness. We took several measures to alleviate the potential limitation of contextual validity by arranging a setup with two screens according to a typical scenario of a shopping street. Further, the test assistant emphasized the public context of the study several times when going through the questionnaire and also used photos showing public displays at busy locations. We assume that these points help to make clear the public context and were confirmed by several participants who mentioned the realistic setup and atmosphere of their own accord. In the light of the promising findings obtained, a field study to verify and contextualize these is definitely justified. This should especially be beneficial for the exploration of further benefits and functional restrictions of display pointing, e.g. depending on the impact of crowded places, varying distances and different light conditions.

7   Outlook

We presented a user study evaluating different pairing techniques for enabling serendipitous mobile interactions with public displays. Surprisingly, capturing

QR codes turned out to be difficult for a considerable number of users and lowers the learnability. NFC, by contrast, received good ratings in general, however, suffered from the general preference for distant techniques in the context of public displays. The distant techniques scanning and manual input are easy to learn and to use, but are perceived as less innovative and fun. Display pointing was proved to be good combination of a directional technique supporting distant pairing while being efficient and fun. Yet, mentioned improvements must be considered to address the perceived lack of control and avoid wrong selections.

Besides a replication study in the field, further work should investigate how to communicate available interactive features in the case of sophisticated markerless setups, i.e. how to optimally inform passers-by about the pairing opportunity. Further interesting research questions include the impact of multi-user applications on the preferred pairing technique. While we consider display pointing a suitable technique due to its support for pairing from distance and several participants of our study implicitly considered this aspect in their ratings, a dedicated study with groups of participants might clarify respective issues.

Acknowledgments. This work has been carried out within the projects b-Part and PRIAMUS financed by FFG and A1. Further funding was received from Nokia Foundation, the Research and Training Foundation of TeliaSonera Finland Oyj, and HPY Research Foundation. FTW Forschungszentrum Telekommunikation Wien GmbH is funded within the program COMET by BMVIT, BMWA, and the City of Vienna. The COMET program is managed by the FFG.

References

1. Ballagas, R., Borchers, J., Rohs, M., Sheridan, J.G.: The smart phone: A ubiquitous input device. IEEE Pervasive Computing 5(1), 70–77 (2006)
2. Rukzio, E., Leichtenstern, K., Callaghan, V., Holleis, P., Schmidt, A., Chin, J.: An experimental comparison of physical mobile interaction techniques: Touching, pointing and scanning. In: Dourish, P., Friday, A. (eds.) UbiComp 2006. LNCS, vol. 4206, pp. 87–104. Springer, Heidelberg (2006)
3. Rukzio, E., Broll, G., Leichtenstern, K., Schmidt, A.: Mobile interaction with the real world: An evaluation and comparison of physical mobile interaction techniques. In: Schiele, B., Dey, A.K., Gellersen, H., de Ruyter, B., Tscheligi, M., Wichert, R., Aarts, E., Buchmann, A.P. (eds.) AmI 2007. LNCS, vol. 4794, pp. 1–18. Springer, Heidelberg (2007)
4. Fröhlich, P., Oulasvirta, A., Baldauf, M., Nurminen, A.: On the move, wirelessly connected to the world. Commun. ACM 54(1), 132–138 (2011)
5. Mäkelä, K., Belt, S., Greenblatt, D., Häkkilä, J.: Mobile interaction with visual and rfid tags: a field study on user perceptions. In: Proc. of the SIGCHI Conf. on Human Factors in Computing Systems, pp. 991–994. ACM (2007)
6. Rohs, M.: Real-world interaction with camera phones. In: Murakami, H., Nakashima, H., Tokuda, H., Yasumura, M. (eds.) UCS 2004. LNCS, vol. 3598, pp. 74–89. Springer, Heidelberg (2005)
7. Wagner, D., Reitmayr, G., Mulloni, A., Drummond, T., Schmalstieg, D.: Real-time detection and tracking for augmented reality on mobile phones. IEEE Transactions on Visualization and Computer Graphics 16(3), 355–368 (2010)

8. Broll, G., Rukzio, E., Paolucci, M., Wagner, M., Schmidt, A., Hussmann, H.: Perci: Pervasive service interaction with the internet of things. IEEE Internet Computing 13(6), 74–81 (2009)
9. Riekki, J., Salminen, T., Alakarppa, I.: Requesting pervasive services by touching rfid tags. IEEE Pervasive Computing 5(1), 40–46 (2006)
10. Välkkynen, P., Niemelä, M., Tuomisto, T.: Evaluating touching and pointing with a mobile terminal for physical browsing. In: Proc. of the 4th Nordic Conf. on Human-Computer Interaction: Changing Roles, pp. 28–37. ACM (2006)
11. von Reischach, F., Michahelles, F., Guinard, D., Adelmann, R., Fleisch, E., Schmidt, A.: An evaluation of product identification techniques for mobile phones. In: Gross, T., Gulliksen, J., Kotzé, P., Oestreicher, L., Palanque, P., Prates, R.O., Winckler, M. (eds.) INTERACT 2009. LNCS, vol. 5726, pp. 804–816. Springer, Heidelberg (2009)
12. Scott, D., Sharp, R., Madhavapeddy, A., Upton, E.: Using visual tags to bypass bluetooth device discovery. SIGMOBILE Mob. Comput. Commun. Rev. 9(1), 41–53 (2005)
13. Seewoonauth, K., Rukzio, E., Hardy, R., Holleis, P.: Touch & connect and touch & select: interacting with a computer by touching it with a mobile phone. In: Proc. of the 11th Int. Conf. on Human-Computer Interaction with Mobile Devices and Services, pp. 36:1–36:9. ACM (2009)
14. O'Neill, E., Thompson, P., Garzonis, S., Warr, A.: Reach out and touch: Using NFC and 2D barcodes for service discovery and interaction with mobile devices. In: LaMarca, A., Langheinrich, M., Truong, K.N. (eds.) Pervasive 2007. LNCS, vol. 4480, pp. 19–36. Springer, Heidelberg (2007)
15. Ballagas, R., Rohs, M., Sheridan, J.G.: Sweep and point and shoot: phonecam-based interactions for large public displays. In: Ext. Abstracts on Human Factors in Computing Systems, pp. 1200–1203 (2005)
16. Madhavapeddy, A., Scott, D., Sharp, R., Upton, E.: Using camera-phones to enhance human-computer interaction. In: Sixth Int. Conf. on Ubiquitous Computing (Adj. Proc.: Demos) (2004)
17. Broll, G., Reithmeier, W., Holleis, P., Wagner, M.: Design and evaluation of techniques for mobile interaction with dynamic NFC-displays. In: Proc. of the Fifth Int. Conf. on Tangible, Embedded, and Embodied Interaction, pp. 205–212. ACM (2011)
18. Dachselt, R., Buchholz, R.: Natural throw and tilt interaction between mobile phones and distant displays. In: Ext. Abstracts on Human Factors in Computing Systems, pp. 3253–3258. ACM (2009)
19. Boring, S., Baur, D., Butz, A., Gustafson, S., Baudisch, P.: Touch projector: mobile interaction through video. In: Proc. of the SIGCHI Conf. on Human Factors in Computing Systems, pp. 2287–2296. ACM (2010)
20. Baldauf, M., Salo, M., Suette, S., Fröhlich, P.: Display pointing - a qualitative study on a recent screen pairing technique for smartphones. In: Proc. of the 27th Int. BCS Human Computer Interaction Conference. ACM (2013)
21. Rashid, U., Terrenghi, L., Quigley, A.: Labeling large displays for interaction with mobile devices: recognition of symbols for pairing techniques. In: Proc. of the Int. Conf. on Advanced Visual Interfaces, p. 417. ACM (2010)
22. Baldauf, M., Fröhlich, P., Lasinger, K.: A scalable framework for markerless camera-based smartphone interaction with large public displays. In: Proc. of the Int. Symposium on Pervasive Displays, pp. 4:1–4:5. ACM (2012)

Customized Situation Verification in Ambient Assisted Living Environments

Mario Buchmayr[1], Werner Kurschl[2], and Josef Küng[3]

[1] University of Applied Sciences Upper Austria, Research Center Hagenberg
`mario.buchmayr@fh-hagenberg.at`
[2] University of Applied Sciences Upper Austria,
School of Informatics, Communications and Media
`werner.kurschl@fh-hagenberg.at`
[3] Johannes Kepler University Austria,
Institute for Application Oriented Knowledge Processing
`jkueng@faw.jku.at`

Abstract. The demographic change in the European society leads to an increased demand for assistance and support systems for elderly people. To cope with the upcoming superannuation of the population a variety of projects for developing *Ambient Assisted Living (AAL)* solutions were funded. The usage of multiple sensor sources can increase the accuracy and fault tolerance of an ambient system, but increases the effort and complexity for decision making as well. In ambient assisted environments, where the decision making process has to consider different user specific behavior, complexity becomes an issue. Therefore, we propose the usage of a semantic layer, which encapsulates user specific information and enriches sensed user interactions with semantics. Within this paper we present an approach, which *(i)* allows to verify sensor events in a user specific context during decision making and *(ii)* ensures that actions are triggered corresponding to the user's needs. To demonstrate the feasibility of our approach we implemented the use case of detecting and handling a critical household event by using a simulation environment to evaluate different scenario set ups.

Keywords: Ontology-based data management, Semantic data, Ambient Assisted Living.

1 Introduction

Improved living standards, socio-economic prosperity and advanced medical treatment have lead to a higher life expectancy within the past decades [15]. Empowered by the demographic change in our society, various scientific research was initiated to tackle the problems of an upcoming superannuation of the population. *Ambient Assisted Living (AAL)* systems are going to become more and more popular in research and industry [25]. The purpose of AAL systems is to facilitate the daily living of elderly people by extending the time elderly can live independently in their own home [20]. By enabling elderly people to live a longer self-determined life a decrease in nursing and health care costs is

J.C. Augusto et al. (Eds.): AmI 2013, LNCS 8309, pp. 48–61, 2013.

anticipated. To get accepted by the user, such systems have to provide a reliable detection of life-threatening situations (household accidents, fires) and features for autonomy enhancement [4]. For situation detection it is necessary to monitor the resident's behavior and interpret the perceived data on higher levels of information processing to reliably provide proper assistance.

Many AAL systems deliver feasible results in laboratory environments, but their success rate drops when installed in real world facilities. Besides sensing and infrastructure issues, a lack of adaptability and customization to the individual user behavior causes several problems. The anticipated/trained user behavior often does not correlate with the behavior in the real world which leads to bad classification results. Nevertheless, it should be possible to define the basic system behavior suitable for all users, but to consider the individual characteristics of each user. Our idea is to create an AAL add-on system for verifying detected situations which overcomes this drawbacks. It should be possible to define the basic behavior of the system in a generic model and to refine the system behavior for each individual. Or to put it into a nutshell: *Provide customized situation verification by interpreting the default behavior in a user specific context.* Within this paper we will use the example of *handling an alarm from a smoke detector* to explain and evaluate our approach.

2   Related Work

A broad range of AAL systems, most of them tailor made for specific use cases, like supporting persons with dementia, providing fall detection or vital sign monitoring, have been developed over the years [18]. All these systems have to cope with two problems: *(i)* processing sensor input from multiple sensors, and *(ii)* triggering corresponding actions. Processing data from different sources is a typical data fusion problem which can be solved by applying a model for multi sensor data fusion, like the *JDL data fusion model* [14], if applicable. Such models typically describe a modus operandi from the perception of sensor data to the detection of specific situations and optionally the evaluation of possible situation evolution. Situation verification is an inherent part of the situation assessment step in most models. The adaptation of this step to the application domain is difficult. Especially in AAL environments, where individual user behavior influences the interpretation of sensed data and the actions to be triggered. Moreover, data fusion models only define a generic model for processing data which must be individually refined to the application domain.

In terms of sensor data processing Moraru et al. have proposed a framework, which is capable of *'processing sensor measurements for extracting more meaningful values for the properties observed'* [16]. They use additional information sources from the Internet to enrich the interpretation of sensed values or for creation of additional features [16]. This is done by getting sensor descriptions and measurements from Internet sources and enriching them by using a collection of ontologies for describing sensor characteristics. In contrast to Moraru et al. our approach does not focus on the extraction of observed properties, we observe properties and combine them to user activities.

For the description of sensor networks the W3C SSN Incubator Group [9] has created an *'ontology that can describe sensors in terms of capabilities, measurement processes, observations and deployments'* [8]. The SSN ontology does not focus on a specific application domain. Semantic is strongly related to the sensing infrastructure. No relations which allow the composition of sensor interactions to activities are provided. Sensors and temporal properties are not part of the SSN ontology, these *'are areas where other ontologies are required to fill in the details'* [8].

PERSONA uses an integration layer as part of their *'SAIL'* architecture [1] for acquiring context by transforming sensor output to ontological states. The transformation is done by context information providers, which know how to interpret sensor signals and generate context events [1]. This conceptual processing model is called *'SODAPOP (Self-Organizing Data-flow Architectures suPporting Onotology-based problem decomPosition)'* and was integrated into the universAAL platform [10]. A further project whose related concepts were integrated into universAAL is SOPRANO [10]. SOPRANO [22] names the enrichment of sensor data *'Semantic Uplifting'* [22]. Sensor devices have to fulfill defined contracts which *'contain semantically rich descriptions of the context data'* [28] and can be interpreted by SOPRANO's *Context Manager* [28] to get *semantically uplifted*.

The goal of UniversAAL is to provide an open platform for developing technically feasible AAL solutions, whereas our goal is to provide a tailor-made add-on system for situation verification for in-home monitoring systems. UniversAAL uses the ontologies from PERSONA and SOPRNAO which are implemented via proprietary Java classes [24]. In contrast to UniversAAL, our SENIOR ontology is defined in standard OWL2 [26] and decoupled from the data and processing logic. In UniversAAL the context and the processing logic for semantic uplifting are defined in Java code. Our approach uses decoupled rules written in standard JENA rule notation. Our ontology and rules are dynamically loaded which allows to adapt behavior interpretation during system runtime. Extensions for our lightweight SENIOR ontology can be added during runtime as well, with no need of rebuilding Java bundles, as this would be necessary in UniversAAL.

3   Problem Description

One issue of AAL systems is their customization. Concerning the detection of critical or life endangering situations, every system needs to be individually adapted for the inhabitant. The main factors hereby are: *(i)* the available sensing infrastructure for perceiving the environment, *(ii)* the available infrastructure for interacting with the inhabitant, and *(iii)* the actions that should be triggered when critical situations are detected.

Concerning AAL systems, a reliable handling of critical situations is an essential requirement for acceptance [17]. It must be guaranteed that *(i)* critical situations are detected reliably and *(ii)* appropriate actions are triggered correspondingly [25]. A high amount of misclassified situations (situations incorrectly classified as critical) or missing possibilities for customizing the user interaction lead to a low user acceptance [17]. The semantic of a critical situation is not always the same. For example, if a smoke detector triggers an alarm, it necessarily need not be a critical situation. Maybe a resident has just let his meal scorch. Depending on the semantics of the situation, it is not always required to inform professional help providers, like a fire brigade or an ambulance. In certain cases it is more effective to inform a neighbor or, in case of assisted living homes, a residential caregiver.

Consider the use case of a fire alert reported by a smoke detector installed in the kitchen. In *version 1* of the use case we can gain additional knowledge (via sensing devices) that the inhabitant has used the stove a short time before the smoke detector alert was triggered and that the stove is now switched off. By using a light barrier attached to the kitchen door or a motion sensor we know that the person is now (a short period after the alert) in the kitchen. Considering that the time the alert was triggered is a usual time the person cooks his/her meals, we can conclude that the situation is under control. So no need to call the fire brigade. Probably a better (and cost saving) action would be to inform one of the neighbors to check if the inhabitant is all right and to display a warning in the resident's home. Listing 1.1 shows how such constraints could be defined using an informal notation.

```
FireAlert uncritical :=
    (Person locatedNow Kitchen) AND
    (Stove wasUsedBefore FireAlertTime) AND
    (Stove switched Off) AND
    (FireAlertTime isUsualCookingTime Yes)

Handle uncritical :=
    (NeighbourNotificationAction triggeredBy FireAlert) AND
    (MessageNotificationAction triggeredBy FireAlert)
```

Listing 1.1. Version 1: verifying a fire alert as uncritical

In *version 2* of the fire alert use case the situation could be slightly different. By using a light barrier in the kitchen door or a motion sensor we know that the person is actually not in the kitchen. From the power switch sensor attached to the stove we know that the stove was used before the smoke detector alert was triggered, and is now still switched on. Additionally, the alert happened during a time which is usual for this person to prepare his/her meal. Therefore, we can conclude that something critical has happened and informing the fire brigade will be an accurate action. In addition a message could be triggered to warn the resident. Listing 1.2 shows how such constraints could be defined using an informal notation.

```
FireAlert critical :=
    NOT(Person locatedNow Kitchen) AND
    (Stove wasUsedBefore FireAlertTime) AND
    (Stove switched On) AND
    NOT(FireAlertTime isUsualCookingTime Yes)

Handle critical :=
    (CallFireBrigadeAlarmAction triggeredBy FireAlert) AND
    (MessageNotificationAction triggeredBy FireAlert)
```

Listing 1.2. Version 2: verifying a fire alert as critical

To verify a situation based on additional information interpreted in the context of user specific behavior we identified three problems: *(i)* the issue how to specify user behavior (like the usual cooking time), *(ii)* the issue how to verify a critical situation by using additional sensor information (like defining constraints to check if required prerequisites are met), and *(iii)* the issue how to choose a proper situation handling (like deciding whether to call help or display a notification). Within this paper we will develop a conceptual system which is capable of overcoming these three problems.

4   Approach

To solve the mentioned problems we decided to use a knowledge-driven approach based on an ontological model. The ontology serves as formal model, which we use to explicitly define the system behavior related to user interactions. Furthermore, various research suggests ontological models for specifying situations [12], [13], [3]. During the evaluation it turned out, that our ontological model is feasible for defining constraints and can be used for verifying situations as well. Beyond the integration and re-usability aspect, ontologies offer the benefit to support evolutionary requirements specification [11], which will be convenient when new sensing components should be added for improving the system accuracy.

We reused the SENIOR core ontology *(sen_core)* [6] together with the SENIOR sense ontology *(sen_sense)* [6] and introduced a new ontological layer for encapsulating user related concepts. *Sen_core* serves as base ontology for *sen_sense* which covers the available sensing infrastructure installed in an AAL home. Alternatively to *(sen_sense)* existing ontologies, like OntoSensor [21] could be reused. OntoSensor can be integrated by deriving the *OntoSensor:Sensor* class from the SENIOR core ontology class *sen_core:Sensor* and by introducing additional time relations between sensor and data objects. Queries and rules will get very complex due to the amount of objects and relations defined in OntoSensor (high amount of indirections). Therefore, we decided to stay with our simple and manageable ontology *sen_sense*, providing the objects and relations needed for preparing the data for the next step: semantic enrichment.

In this paper we introduce a new layer called SENIOR Semantic Ontology *(sen_sem)*. The purpose of *sen_sem* is: *(i)* to encapsulate the semantic information specific to the user behavior (behavior rules, like the typical stove usage time), and *(ii)* to encapsulate the user specific notification actions (like displaying a visual message or speaking an audio message). Figure 1 gives a simplified overview of *sen_core*, *sen_sem* and *sen_sense* related to the fire alarm use case we described in section 2. This paper only focuses on the *sen_sem* ontology and explains concepts from *sen_core* and *sen_sense* where they are necessary for understanding. A more detailed explanation can be found at [6].

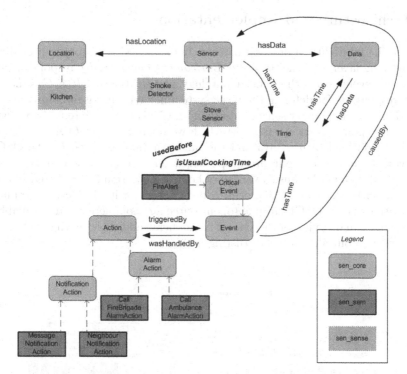

Fig. 1. SENIOR Core Ontology (sen_core)

The original core ontology defined the basic objects *Sensor*, *Data*, *Time* and *Location* which were extended by the objects *Action* and *Event*. On *sen_core* level basic relations are defined. Sensors are located in a room (*hasLocation*) perceive data (*hasData*) at a certain time (*hasTime*) and can cause *Events* (*causedBy*) which are handled by (*wasHandledBy*) *Actions*. Property chains are used to connect Data, Time and Sensors to draw conclusions if a sensor had some data during a given time period and vice versa. *Actions* can trigger notifications (*NotificationAction*) or alerts (*AlarmAction*). Additionally, the *sen_core* ontology can be used to verify, if an ontological model is valid (avoid data store corruption). Besides, it is possible to adapt the underlying ontologies (*sen_sense, sen_sem*) without changing the core behavior. On *sen_sense* level basic sensing objects (*SmokeDetector, StoveSensor*) and the building/sensor infrastructure (*Kitchen*) are modeled.

The sen_sem ontology was introduced to fill the gap between *sen_core* and *sen_sense*. Within *sen_sem (i)* additional information concerning user behavior (*isUsualCookingTime*) is specified, *(ii)* critical situations are verified by using additional information (StoveSensor, the person's location), and *(iii)* proper situation handling depending on infrastructure and severity is provided. *Sen_sem* serves as model and defines basic objects and relations, like the meaning of the *usedNow* and *usedBefore* relation. The user behavior and the specific actions triggered in case of an alarm are defined in rules based on *sen_sem*.

5   Architecture and Implementation

To prove the feasibility of our approach we implemented a prototype providing two reasoning layers: *(i)* the *Semantic Enrichment Layer (SEL)*, responsible for interpreting events using the sen_sem ontology, and *(ii)* the *SENIOR Core Layer (SCL)*, responsible for defining the basic system behavior using the sen_core ontology. For mapping binary sensor data to ontological objects we reused an existing data mapping framework (see [6]) which we reference as *Data Access Layer (DAL)*. We decided to use Java and the infrastructure provided by the OSGi framework to implement our prototype based on a service oriented architecture. We chose OSGi, because a variety of home automation projects and sensor devices are either based on OSGi or provide adapters for it. Besides, several implementations of the OSGi runtime (open source and commercial) are available. Figure 2 gives an overview of the system components and their runtime behavior with respect to our alert use case (listing 1.1).

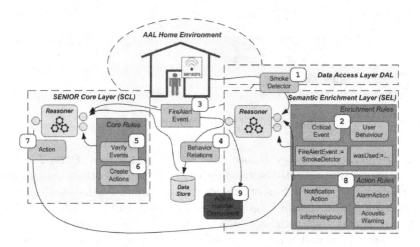

Fig. 2. SemanticEnrichmentApproachEnhanced

Sensor data from an *AAL Home Environment* is processed by the *Data Access Layer (DAL)* (1). The DAL is responsible for mapping sensor data to *sen_sense* data objects. For a detailed description of the data mapping mechanism we refer to [6]. The generated data objects are passed to the *Semantic Enrichment Layer (SEL)*. The SEL uses two different sets of rules for processing incoming data:

1. *Enrichment Rules* for enriching data objects coming from the DAL and defining *Critical Events* for a resident.
2. *Action Rules* for handling incoming objects from the (SCL) which are responsible for proper action handling.

In our example the SEL contains a set of rules which trigger on the incoming *SmokeDetector* (2) object. Therefore, the SEL reasoner creates a *FireAlertEvent*

(3) as well as *Behavior Relations* (4) depending on the user's behavior specified via rules. The derived *Behavior Relations* (like isRegularStoveUsageTime or is-UsualCookingTime) are stored in a global *Data Store*. Listing 1.3 shows how a relation is created using Jena rule syntax.

```
[ rule00_isRegularStoveUsageTime:
    (?fireEvt rdf:type sen_sem:FireAlertEvent)
    (?fireEvt sen_core:hasTime ?time)
    (?time sen_core:hasTimeValue ?timeValue)
    greaterThan(?timeValue, "06:00:00"^^xs:time)
    lessThan(?timeValue, "09:00:00"^^xs:time)
    ->
    (?fireEvt sen_sem:isRegularStoveUsageTime ?time)
]
```

Listing 1.3. Rule sample for creating behavior relations

The *FireEvent* is passed to the *SENIOR Core Layer*. In the *SENIOR Core Layer* rules are used to verify how critical a situation is and decide how it should be handled (5). Semantic information from the data store (consider the created *isRegularStoveUsageTime* relation) can be used for verification. In our case the *FireEvent* is verified (5) via rules similar to the informal rules from listing 1.1 and listing 1.2. A generic rule in the *SENIOR Core Layer* (6) (see listing 1.4) ensures that an *Action* object (7) is created and passed to the *Semantic Enrichment Layer (SEL)*. The SEL uses *Action Rules* (8) to decide for a proper handling of the occurred situation and triggers the *ActionHandlerComponent* (9) responsible for executing actions. In our demonstration prototype action handling simply means logging into a file to verify if correct reasoning decisions were made. In a real world installation the *ActionHandlerComponent* would trigger devices, like displays, speakers, email or SMS services.

```
[ rule01_handle_critical:
    (?evt rdf:type sen_core:CriticalEvent)
    noValue(?evt sen_core:wasHandled sen_core:True)
    makeSkolem(?newAction, ?evt)
    ->
    (?newAction rdf:type sen_core:AlarmAction)
    (?newAction sen_core:triggeredBy ?evt)
]
```

Listing 1.4. Generic core rule sample for handling critical events

The layers DAL, SEL and SCL are implemented as OSGi services [19] and installed on our SENIOR target platform. During development the usage of OSGi turned out to be an advantage, because it reduced the effort for integrating existing services for data mapping to a minimum and facilitated the reuse of existing infrastructure (data store, rule file storage and parsing components). *Sen_core* and *sen_sense* were defined using the widespread *Web Ontology Language (OWL)* [26], therefore we used OWL for *sen_sem* as well.

In contrast to the DAL, where the data mapping is done via a simple RDFS reasoner [27] provided by the JENA framework [2], we had to use an OWL 2 reasoner in the semantic and core layer. Besides other OWL 2 reasoning features, this allows the usage of property chain axioms when deriving our user specific relations. We decided to use Pellet [7] as OWL 2 reasoner because of the provided Java API and its compatibility with the Jena API. Therefore we could use the same rule notation (and infrastructure) which we already used for processing the rules used in the DAL.

6 Evaluation

To evaluate our approach we assumed a household of an elderly single person. The household is equipped with standard home automation technology, such as switch sensors, contact sensors, a motion sensor and a smoke detector. We used a simulation environment (see [5]) and equipped a simulated flat with the mentioned sensor devices. One switch sensor was used to indicate the usage of the stove, a contact sensor was used to indicate the usage (open/close) of the fridge, a motion sensor was used to detect movements in the kitchen / dining area and a smoke detector was placed in the kitchen. Figure 3 shows a screen shot of the sensors placed on the flat blueprint in more detail. The relevant sensors are marked with a red circle.

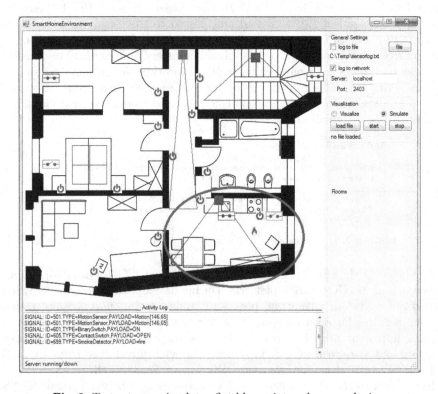

Fig. 3. Test set up - simulator flat blue print and sensor devices

6.1   Use Case Set Up

For testing we created two different rule set ups. *Person A* is supposed to have a light visual impairment, gets home delivered meals and sometimes cooks a warm supper. The evening time between 17:00 and 19:00 was defined as regular usage time of the stove. Due to the visual impairment a speaker device is supposed to be available for acoustic warning messages. In case of critical events an emergency call for an ambulance should be triggered.

Person B is supposed to have no visual impairment, but to suffer from a light form of dementia. The cooking is done by the person itself, therefore we defined morning (7:00 to 9:00), noon (10:30 to 13:30) and evening (17:00 to 19:00) as regular usage time spans for the stove. Warning messages should be displayed on the TV and in case of critical events nursing personnel and the neighbor should be informed.

6.2   Customized Situation Verification and Action Triggering

Both rule sets (Person A and Person B) were defined in the *Semantic Enrichment Layer*. In the *SENIOR Core Layer* the generic rules for verifying critical situations were defined (*if* (unhandled event) *then* action)). Listing 1.5 shows a snippet of the SCL rule file responsible for verifying critical/uncritical alarms using Jena rules syntax [23]. The rule *handle_critical_fe* can be interpreted as follows: When an unhandled *FireAlertEvent* occurs and the stove was used before the event and the person is actually not in the kitchen and the time the event occurred is not the usual usage time of the stove, then the event is critical and an *AlarmAction* object is generated (*makeSkolem(?newAction, ?evt)*). The rule *handle_uncritical_fe* can be interpreted similar with the difference that the person is in the kitchen and the time the event occurs is the usual cooking time. In this case only a *NotificationAction* should be generated, because the situation is not critical.

```
[handle_critical_fe:
  (?evt rdf:type sen_sem:FireAlertEvent)
  noValue(?evt sen_core:wasHandled sen_core:True)
  (?evtTime sen_core:hasTime ?evt)
  (sen_sense:Stove sen_sem:wasUsedBefore ?evtTime)
  noValue(sen_sem:Person sen_core:hasLocation Kitchen)
  noValue(?evtTime isUsualCookingTime Yes)
  makeSkolem(?newAction, ?evt)
  ->
  (?newAction rdf:type sen_core:AlarmAction)
  (?newAction sen_core:triggeredBy ?evt)
]

[handle_uncritical_fe:
  (?evt rdf:type sen_sem:FireAlertEvent)
  noValue(?evt sen_core:wasHandled sen_core:True)
  (?evtTime sen_core:hasTime ?evt)
  (sen_sense:Stove sen_sem:wasUsedBefore ?evtTime)
  (sen_sem:Person sen_core:hasLocation Kitchen)
  (FireAlertTime isUsualCookingTime Yes)
  makeSkolem(?newAction, ?evt)
  ->
  (?newAction rdf:type sen_core:NotificationAction)
  (?newAction sen_core:triggeredBy ?evt)
]
```

Listing 1.5. Core rule for verifying critical/uncritical events

6.3   Evaluation Results

In the first version of our prototype we had problems to avoid handling events twice. This happened when events occurred within a very short time span (the same event triggered redundant actions). Introducing a check in the core rules to only consider unhandled events for action triggering solved this problem. A further problem was, that semantic enrichment was done in one step by applying all the enrichment rules defined in the SCL to the data coming from the DAL and the data store. During evaluation it turned out to be more effective to separate the rules and apply them in two steps. The SCL distinguishes now between enrichment rules that need information from the data store (like the rule for creating *usedBefore* relations) and rules that don't (like the rule for creating *isUsualCookingTime* relations). Rules that don't need additional information are evaluated first by an in-memory Pellet instance which only knows the SENIOR ontologies. The inferred data model is passed to the second Pellet instance which does reasoning on the data model from the data store the and second set of rules. The split-up in two different rule sets and usage of two reasoner instances decreased the processing time of the SEL and lead to faster responses to sensor interactions.

Our simulation environment allows to generate, record and replay user interactions from different sensors. For verification we simulated the fire alert use case as defined in sections 2 and 6 and created for each person two use cases: (*UC1*) fire alert is critical, (*UC2*) fire alert is not critical. The use cases were simulated for the two persons using the same sensor set up, but different user configurations (rule sets). Via the simulation interface we generated and stored a set of user-sensor-interactions (entering/leaving the kitchen, interacting with the stove, triggering the smoke detector). These user interactions represent daily routines of *Person A* and *Person B* with special focus on the activities in the kitchen. Based on UC1 and UC2 we simulated fire alarms (by triggering the smoke detector in the simulator). For each use case set up we started with an empty data store and filled it with a predefined set of user-sensor interactions. To evaluate our approach we had to verify (*i*) if proper semantic relations were created, (*ii*) situations were verified correctly as critical and uncritical, and (*iii*) if proper actions were created. We were able to successfully query the expected relations from the data store after simulating UC1 and UC2 for each person. Concerning situation verification we analyzed the log file from the SCL if a detected situation was considered critical or not. For validating proper actions we used the log files created by the *ActionHandler Component* and successfully compared the result with the defined actions for *UC1* and *UC2* for *Person A* and *Person B*. To test the generic system behavior we run *UC1* and *UC2* without *Action Rules* defined for *Person A* and *Person B* and successfully verified that for all unhandled *Actions* an alarm was raised.

7 Conclusion and Further Work

With our prototype implementation and the use case based evaluation we were able to demonstrate the feasibility of our approach. We described our system which decouples the generic system behavior (SCL) from user specific behavior (SEL). This allows to *(i)* properly interpret user interactions considering individual user behavior and *(ii)* trigger suitable actions depending on the detected situation, available infrastructure and the user's needs.

In contrast to Moraru et al. who aim at creating additional sensor features [16], our solution is intended to interpret sensed data considering different user behavior. Our approach can be compared with UniversAAL (i. e. SOPRANO's semantic uplifting). In contrast to UniversAAL, which defines the processing logic for semantic uplifting in Java code and uses one layer for interpreting sensed data, we use three consecutively based layers: *(i)* sen_core to encapsulate the generic behavior, *(ii)* sen_sem for semantic interpretation, and *(iii)* sen_sense for sensor infrastructure abstraction. Furthermore, we decouple the user behavior definition from the generic system behavior, which allows to change the system behavior during runtime. UniversAAL does not provide such functionality, which is restricted due to their component design (context and contracts must be implemented in Java classes, no external rules used, no runtime-changes possible).

However, our work is still in progress and further experiments needs to be performed to evaluate the usability of OWL 2 reasoning features (property chains, inverse properties) as well as the system performance with complex decision rules. One open issue is how the system will cope with an increased amount of data. We expect three factors to be relevant for the growth of triples: *(i)* the sampling interval and number of installed sensors producing input, *(ii)* the number of use cases intended to be verified by the system, and *(iii)* the granularity of the semantic enrichment (amount of triples produced by the rules). Our preliminarily experiments showed, that the triples in our data store grew up to approximatively 50.000 triples within 5 hours of simulating regular behavior in an AAL environment. Due to our primary goal, which is situation verification, we just require data on a daily time span. Further tests need to be performed to figure out the limit of triples for providing feasible in-memory reasoning response times. For performing long term analysis on the data, other strategies (e. g. data mining) have to be considered.

Acknowledgements. This research was funded by the European Regional Development Fund (ERDF) in cooperation with the Upper Austrian state government (REGIO 13).

References

1. Amoretti, M., Wientapper, F., Furfari, F., Lenzi, S., Chessa, S.: Sensor data fusion for activity monitoring in ambient assisted living environments. In: Proc. 1st Int. Conference on Sensor Systems and Software (S-Cube 2009), pp. 206–221 (2009)
2. Apache. Jena Framework (2013)

3. Baumgartner, N., Retschitzegger, W.: A survey of upper ontologies for situation awareness. In: Proc. of the 4th IASTED International Conference on Knowledge Sharing and Collaborative Engineering, St. Thomas, USA, pp. 1–9 (2006)
4. Becker, M.: Software architecture trends and promising technology for ambient assisted living systems. In: Proc. of Assisted Living Systems - Models, Architectures and Engineering Approaches. Schloss Dagstuhl - Leibniz-Zentrum fuer Informatik, Germany (2008)
5. Buchmayr, M., Kurschl, W., Kueng, J.: A Simulator for Generating and Visualizing Sensor Data for Ambient Intelligence Environments. In: Proc. of the 2nd Int. Conference on Ambient Systems, Networks and Technologies (ANT 2011), Niagara Falls, Canada, pp. 90–97 (September 2011)
6. Buchmayr, M., Kurschl, W., Küng, J.: A rule based approach for mapping sensor data to ontological models in AAL environments. In: Castano, S., Vassiliadis, P., Lakshmanan, L.V.S., Lee, M.L. (eds.) ER Workshops 2012. LNCS, vol. 7518, pp. 3–12. Springer, Heidelberg (2012)
7. Clark and P. LLC. Pellet: OWL 2 Reasoner for Java (2013)
8. Compton, M., Barnaghi, P., Bermudez, L., Garcia-Castro, R., Corcho, O., Cox, S., Graybeal, J., Hauswirth, M., Henson, C., Herzog, A., Huang, V., Janowicz, K., Kelsey, W.D., Phuoc, D.L., Lefort, L., Leggieri, M., Neuhaus, H., Nikolov, A., Page, K., Passant, A., Sheth, A., Taylor, K.: The ssn ontology of the w3c semantic sensor network incubator group. Web Semantics: Science, Services and Agents on the World Wide Web 17 (2012)
9. W. I. Group. Semantic Sensor Network XG Final Report (2011)
10. Guillen, S.: Universaal Open Architecture and Platform for Ambient Assisted Living (2012)
11. Happel, H.J., Seedorf, S.S.: Applications of ontologies in software engineering. In: Proc. of the Int. Workshop on Semantic Web Enabled Software Engineering (SWESE 2006), Athens, USA, pp. 1–14 (2006)
12. Klein, M., Schmidt, A., Lauer, R.: Ontology-centred design of an ambient middleware for assisted living: The case of soprano. In: Proc. of the 30th Annual German Conference on Artificial Intelligence (2007)
13. Kokar, M.M., Matheus, C.J., Baclawski, K.: Ontology-based situation awareness. Inf. Fusion 10(1), 83–98 (2009)
14. Llinas, J., Bowman, C., Rogova, G., Steinberg, A.: Revisiting the JDL data fusion model II. In: Proc. of the 7th Intern. Conference on Information Fusion, Stockholm, Sweden, pp. 1218–1230 (2004)
15. Mackenbach, J.P.: Health inequalities: Europe in profile. Technical report, Department of Public Health, University Medical Center Rotterdam (2006), Expert report commissioned by the UK presidency of the EU
16. Moraru, A., Mladenic, D.: A framework for semantic enrichment of sensor data. In: Proc. of the 34th Conference on Information Technology Interfaces (ITI), pp. 155–160 (June 2012)
17. Nehmer, J., Becker, M., Karshmer, A., Lamm, R.: Living assistance systems: an ambient intelligence approach. In: Proc. of the 28th Int. Conference on Software Engineering, ICSE, New York, USA, pp. 43–50 (2006)
18. Nick, M., Becker, M.: A hybrid approach to intelligent living assistance. In: In Proc. of the 7th International Conference on Hybrid Intelligent Systems (HIS), pp. 283–289 (2007)
19. OSGi Alliance. OSGi Framework (2013)

20. Rennemark, M., Holst, G., Fagerstrom, C., Halling, A.: Factors related to frequent usage of the primary healthcare services in old age: findings from the swedish national study on aging and care. Health & Social Care in the Community 17(3), 304–311 (2009)
21. Russomanno, D.J., Kothari, C.R., Thomas, O.A.: Building a sensor ontology: A practical approach leveraging iso and ogc models. In: Proc. of the Int. Conference on Artificial Intelligence (ICAI), Las Vegas, US, pp. 637–643 (2005)
22. Schmidt, A., Wolf, P., Klein, M., Balfanz, D.: 2. Deutscher Kongress Ambient Assisted Living, Berlin, Germany
23. W. Technologies. Jena Rules Syntax (2013)
24. universAAL. universAAL White Book Advanced (2013)
25. van den Broek, G., Cavallo, F., Wehrmann, C.: AALIANCE Ambient Assisted Living Roadmap, vol. 6. IOS Press (2010)
26. W3C. OWL 2 Web Ontology Language (2009)
27. W3C. Resource Description Framework, RDF (2013)
28. Wolf, P., Schmidt, A., Klein, M.: SOPRANO - An extensible, open AAL platform for elderly people based on semantical contracts. In: Proc. of the 18th European Conference on AI, 3rd Workshop on AI Techniques for Ambient Intelligence, Greece, (2008)

Inferring Model Structures from Inertial Sensor Data in Distributed Activity Recognition

Pierluigi Casale and Oliver Amft

ACTLab, Signal Processing Systems, TU Eindhoven
Eindhoven, The Netherlands
{p.casale,o.amft}@tue.nl
http://www.actlab.ele.tue.nl

Abstract. Activity-Event-Detector (AED) digraphs can describe relations between human activities, activity-representing pattern events from sensors, and distributed detector nodes. AED graphs have been successfully used to perform network adaptations, including reconfiguring networks to reduce recognition complexity and network energy needs. In this paper, we present an approach to infer AED graph configurations from distributed sensor data. We utilise a non-parametric clustering procedure and derive all relevant information about the AED graph structure, including the detector-specific activity grouping and activity-detector relations from measured data. We analysed our approach using a previously published dataset and compared our inferred AED graph with those designed by an expert. The system based on the inferred AED graph yielded a performance boost of 15% in the final classification accuracy and reduced computational complexity of detectors. These results indicate that our approach is viable to automate the configuration of distributed activity recognition sensor-detector networks.

Keywords: context recognition, wireless sensor networks, clustering, inertial sensors.

1 Introduction

The recognition of human activities from raw sensor data finds one of its mayor application in Ambient Intelligence scenarios. Automatic activity monitoring enables the development of personalized ubiquitous services in health-care and assisted living domains [1] providing, at the same time, more natural interactions in smart homes and smart environments [2]. Although different types of sensor modalities are effective for classifying different activities, a sensors network gathering data from different objects and locations is potentially able to identify a large set of heterogeneous activities. This setting naturally envisions a recognition architecture where the set of non-divisible pieces of information that each node can sense, constitutes the alphabet of elements of complex activities.

Activity-Events-Detectors (AED) [3] digraphs describe these concepts in a formal way, showing the relationships between activities and sensor nodes under

J.C. Augusto et al. (Eds.): AmI 2013, LNCS 8309, pp. 62–77, 2013.

a distributed perspective. The graphs describe the dependencies between the activities that can be observed by each node, the detection performed at sensor level and the physical nodes, providing a conceptual abstraction where the set of activities is decoupled from the sensors network. The decoupling is achieved by introducing events that are groups of atomic activities with similar signal patterns for each detector. Events should be recognised by individual distributed detectors using their sensor measurements. Detectors actually report events that represent their perspective of an occurred activity. Task of a detector is the extraction of activities from the continuous data stream and the disambiguation of the events discriminable by the detector. This grouping reflects the local position and the sensing capabilities of the node. The paradigm provides clear advantages in terms of transmission bandwidth since, instead of sending raw or compressed data, only the detected events are transmitted over the network. Moreover, dynamic reconfiguration of the network can be allowed with significant benefits in the power consumption of the whole network.

Previous works show that by using domain knowledge, detectors can be manually configured by grouping atomic activities into events providing an enhancement in the recognition performance of the architecture ([4],[3]). In this paper, a data-driven methodology that infers the model structure of detectors is presented and evaluated. Given a set of atomic activities, the proposed approach automatically learns groups of patterns that look similar from the local perspective of the node and are relevant for the final recognition of composite activities. The methodology is defined on a non parametric clustering procedure that uses classification margin as patterns similarity measure, inferring all the relevant information from sensors data, using no a-priori assumptions on the relations between sensor nodes and activities.

The approach has been compared with manual detector configurations provided by experts and with configurations generated using the K-Means clustering methodology. Results obtained show that the methodology is able to retrieve relevant activities for all the detectors and grouping them consistently to the manual configuration provided by experts. In particular, for the majority of the detectors, the proposed methodology is able to retrieve relevant activities for sensor nodes as annotated by experts. Moreover, groups of activities not annotated in the manual configuration are also generated by the methodology. Recognition performance shows that the use of the AED digraphs improves the classification performance in the activity recognition process. In particular, detectors performance are considerably increased and the final performance of the recognition architecture has a boost of 15% in terms of classification accuracy. Furthermore, the detector configuration provides a reduction of the computational resources needed by the detector nodes of more than 90% for all the sensor nodes of the network.

The rest of the paper is organized as follows. In Section 2 an overview of related works in hierarchical and distributed activity recognition is provided. In Section 3, a formal description of the Activity-Events-Detectors paradigm is reported and in Section 4, the proposed configuration methodology is presented and described in details. Section 5 presents the validation protocol alongside the description of the dataset used. Experimental results are presented in Section 6. Finally, Section 7 concludes the paper.

2   Related Works

Many works address the necessity of using hierarchical abstractions for modeling human activities. Aggarwal et al. [5] provide a detailed overview of activity recognition research works with particular focus on hierarchical methodologies. Approaches are differentiated between statistical and syntactic approaches. Statistical approaches construct state-based models hierarchically concatenated, like layered hidden Markov models, to represent and recognize high-level human activities. Similarly, syntactic approaches, as in [6], use grammar syntaxes to model high-level activity as a string of atomic-level activities that sequentially compose complex human activities, allowing the generation of information fusion methodologies. Zappi et al. [7] investigate distributed information fusion using multiple classifiers strategies from sensors distributed on the body. Using classifiers fusion, recognition accuracy can be boosted using clusters of sensors. This distributed scheme, that shares with the AED approach the idea of aggregating the detection results, does not consider the simplification of the detector by aggregating atomic activities at detector level. Sarkar et al. [8] consider the possibility to identify key sensors in the network that are related to different activities. Clusters of sensors are defined based on the activation that sensors have during similar activities. Key sensors are identified based on the number of activation per sensor. The proposed methodology provides a clear improvement in terms of activity classification accuracy. Nevertheless, although the work share with the AED approach the idea of grouping similar activities, it still does not consider the grouping of those activities at sensors level. Storf et al. [9] describe an activity recognition architecture, where complex activities are recognized using a low-level activities decomposition. Atomic and complex activities are detected by a specialized detection agents that communicate by exchanging typed facts represented in a common data structure. The approach brings several practical advantages especially in terms of execution performance since only those parts of the overall functionality are invoked that are actually affected. Van Kasteren et al. [10] propose a two-layer hierarchical model with activities consisting of a sequence of actions where sensor data are automatically clustered during the training phase. Results obtained outperforms the non-hierarchical model providing the advantages of making easier the activity annotation process. The approach, that share with the AED approach the underlying idea of grouping similar activities at sensor level, does not provide any information about which activities were grouped and, in particular, the clusters found do not have any meaningful correspondence to actual actions.

3   The Activity-Events-Detectors Framework

Human activities are often considered under a hierarchical perspective in order to manage their inherent complexity. The suitable recognition architecture can be usually modeled in a layered organization were a set of non-dividable unities, the *atomic activities* processed and identified from raw sensor data, is considered at the lowest level. At higher levels, the atomic activities are agglomerated into more complex sequences of activities. Accordingly, Activity-Events-Detectors (AED) digraphs consider a set of distributed sensing and detection nodes that sense the contextual sensors data, identifies pattern events in the acquired sensor data and communicates the results of the detection for further processing. Often, the patterns of two or more atomic activities observed by detectors may look similar. In this case, several atomic activities can be mapped into one event to be recognised by the detector that represent the final detection result of the nodes. Detected events are communicated among the distributed detector nodes such that they can be further processed. In a formal description, the composite activities, represented by the set C, describes the activities that the system is able to recognize. The set of atomic activities A describes the detection alphabet and each composite activity C_n is a subset of unique atomic activities from A.

$$C = \{C_1, ..., C_n\}, \ A = \{a_1, ..., a_m\}, \ C_k \subseteq A \tag{1}$$

Each detector node D_i contains at least one detector event E_i, as described in Eq. 2. The number of detector nodes $|D|$ and the total number of detector events $\sum_{i=1}^{|D|} |D_i|$ are complexity metrics for the implemented architecture.

$$D_i = \{E_1^i, ..., E_t^i\} \tag{2}$$

When atomic activities cannot be discriminated from each other, but are detectable as sensor data patterns by a detector, the affected activities are grouped into one event of the detector: for each detector D_i, atomic activities a_j conflicting with each other are grouped to a single event E_j^i.

$$E_j^i \subseteq A, \ where \ \forall i : E_j^i \cap E_k^i = \emptyset, \ for \ j \neq k \tag{3}$$

The combination of multiple, distributed event detectors is used to recognize composite activities. The event-based composite activity C_n consists of a subset of events reported by different detectors D_i, where the set is empty, if the detector does not contribute to the recognition.

$$C^n = \bigcup_i D_n^i, \forall i : D_n^i \subseteq D^i \tag{4}$$

These relationships can be represented in the form of directed bipartite graphs, as shown in Fig. 1. Two directed graphs are presents. The AE graph maps atomic activities into events, the ED associates events with their detector nodes.

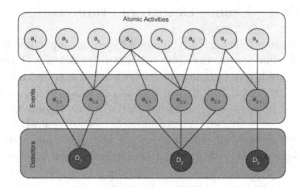

Fig. 1. Example AED digraph. Elements a_k correspond to atomic activities, e_j to events recognized, and d_i to detectors. Detectors represent sensors embedded in objects or infrastructure provided with computational power. High level activities are composed by groups of atomic activities.

Graph nodes of A are connected to graph nodes in E. No directed edges from E to A are present. Similarly, nodes in E are connected to nodes in D and no reverse edges are allowed. Graphs AE and ED may not have cycles or loops. The AED digraph helps in visualizing the main concepts of the AED paradigm showing which are the atomic activities that constitute events in each detector. In the following section, a data-driven methodology that automatically generates the detector configuration is presented. The methodology is decomposed in three steps: (i) identifying patterns of atomic activities that look similar from the local perspective of the detector, (ii) grouping them into events, and (iii) reject groups of activity patterns irrelevant for the detector.

4 Inference Methodology for Detectors Configuration

This work aims to automatically derive the AED graph configuration. In particular, the relevant atomic activities for each detector need to be found and grouped, such that the resulting events can be recognised. Grouping similar patterns is the task performed by clustering algorithms. The aggregation is computed on the base of a predefined similarity measure between data points. The classical K-means algorithm performs this procedure using a two steps iterative process which maximizes both the similarity between points belonging to the same cluster and the dissimilarity between clusters. The groups found are shaped in a predefined number of convex clusters [11]. For many clustering methodologies, the number of clusters is a parameter for the algorithm. When no a-priori knowledge about the number of clusters is available, different grouping methodologies should be considered.

The main steps of the proposed configuration methodology are shown in Fig.2. In the first step, a proximity measure between activities is computed. Since activities are generally described by multiple features, this problem can be identified

Fig. 2. Inference Methodology: Steps in the Detectors Configuration

as a geometric proximity problem. The resolution of this problem implies the identification of a boundary region of the data-points in the features space and the search of the closest points between all the neighbor activities. When low-dimensional spaces are considered, efficient solutions can be applied. However, the running time and memory requirements of these algorithms grow exponentially with the dimension of the features space.

For the purposes of this work, an estimation of the proximity between activities is computed using the classification margin between activity classes. The advantage of using this approach is twofold: (i) the classification margin represents a noise-tolerant proximity measure since it does not depends by specific data-points and (ii) its computational burden is limited when compared to a high-dimensional geometrical proximity problems. Using the proximity measure provided by the classification margin, groups of activities are found using a clustering procedure based on Minimum Spanning Tree. This step generates a linkage between activities that minimizes the overall classification margin through the graph. The final grouping is obtained by cutting the edges in the graph with highest margin. In this way, groups of activities that correspond to the *events* are discovered. However, not all the discovered events are relevant for the specific detector. As final step, the relevance of the events generated is quantified using a ranking procedure based on features selection. Based on the ranking, events were removed that were irrelevant for the detector. The overall procedure, resembling a single linkage agglomerative clustering algorithm, has a peculiar advantage. While the single linkage clustering works on actual data-points, the proposed methodology provides a high-level grouping of the activities that does not depend directly on activity data-points. In addition, the result of the procedure provides groups of activities that make no assumptions regarding the underlying activities distribution. In the following subsections, each step is described and explained in detail.

4.1   Compute Activity Proximity

Method: The classification margin is a measure of confidence in the classification process between two sets of patterns. In the simplest case of pairs of atomic activity patterns $\{a_i, a_j\}$ that are linearly separable, the classification margin is provided by the shortest distance of the closest examples from the separating hyperplane. This basic geometrical consideration can be extended for handling the case when maximum margin hyperplanes are difficult to find due to noisy data [12], and the classification problem is not linearly separable [13]. Nevertheless, the quantity is still able to provide an approximate measure of proximity between patterns. Given a classification function f able to compute the margin, a general algorithm for computing the pairwise classification margins between atomic activity patterns is defined in Algorithm 1. For each pair of activity patterns, the classification function f is trained on the dataset constituted by the considered patterns and the margin is computed on a separated testing set.

Implementation: When a limited number of examples is present in the dataset,

---

Input: A dataset T with labels in $A \in \{a_1, .., a_m\}$
       A classification function f
Output: An Activity Proximity Matrix $M \in \mathbf{R}^{m \times m}$
Split T in training set T_{train} and testing set T_{test}
foreach $i=1,..,m$ **do**
   foreach $j=1,..,m$ **do**
      Train f on $T^{i,j}{}_{train}$, with $T^{i,j}_{train} \subseteq T_{train}$ s.t. $T^{i,j}{}_{train}$ has only training points in $\{a_i, a_j\}$
      Compute the classification margin $M(i,j)$ for class a_i and class a_j on $T^{i,j}{}_{test}$
   end
end

Algorithm 1. Compute Activity Proximity

---

the resulting testing set may be not representative of the activity distribution. The Random Forest classification function [14] is based on a supervised ensemble methodology that aggregates decisions trees trained on randomly chosen bootstrap samples of the training set. Hence, the set of examples not used for training can be used to obtain an estimate of the classification margin without the need of using an explicit testing set. For binary classification problems, the margin provided by Random Forest is equivalent to the geometrical classification margin as previously described [15].

4.2   Grouping Activities into Events

Method: Given the proximity measure provided by the margin, the aggregation of atomic activities is generated using the clustering capabilities of the Minimum Spanning Tree (MST) [16]. The spanning tree provides an acyclic graph containing as vertices the atomic activities in the set A. The graph is built in order to minimize the sum of the weighted edges, i.e., the classification margins, along its path. In the graph, the edges with lower weights connect the previously classified atomic activities that exhibit small classification margin. Cutting the edges relative to the highest margins provides a partition of the graph in groups. The resulting connected components represent the events generated. Algorithm 2 describes the steps used in the grouping procedure.

> **Input:** A proximity matrix $M \in \mathbf{R}^{m \times m}$
>   A threshold θ_w
> **Output:** A set of events E
> Compute MST(N,E) Minimum Spanning Tree on M
> Cut the edges with weight $w > \theta_w$
> Set E as the connected components in the resulting graph

Algorithm 2. Clustering Activity using Minimum Spanning Tree

Implementation: In the algorithm, the optimal value of the cutting threshold θ_w can be easily found considering the discrete distribution of all the values of the margin. The threshold value is given by the value of the margin that provides the highest discontinuity in the distribution.

4.3   Select Relevant Events

Method: Depending on their local position and sensing modalities, different sensors cannot sense all the atomic activities in the set A in the same way. In particular, patterns related to activities or events not directly sensed by the local node can be interpreted as noise from the detector: they will not contribute in the final recognition of the composite activities in C. Therefore, a ranking procedure measuring the importance of the discovered events is useful to establish which events are important for each detector. Stacked generalization [17] is a pattern recognition scheme that uses a multi-level architecture. The architecture feeds the detected events, that represent the output of base or *level-0* classifiers, to the subsequent *level-1* classifier that provides the final recognition of the ongoing activity. Following this classification scheme, events relevance can be measured as a features selection process at the level-1 classifier.

Algorithm 3 describes the steps needed for this task using a general classification function f. Once the level-0 classifier is fit on the training set with labels E, the level-1 classifier is trained on the events predictions generated by the level-0 classifier. During the training of the level-1 classifier, the features selection process (i.e. the events ranking) is computed. Once events have been ranked based on their discriminant power for the final classification of the composite activity, events are chosen as the ones that provide at least 90% of the total importance in the ranking.

> **Input:** A dataset T with labels in $D \in \{E_1, .., E_t\}$ and $C \in \{c_1, .., c_n\}$
>   A classification function f
> **Output:** A set of events E_s
> Split T in training set T_{train} and testing set T_{test}
> Train f^0 on T_{train} with labels E
> Evaluate f^0 on T_{test} providing predictions E^{pred}
> Train f^1 on E^{pred} with labels C and rank the best features in E^{pred}
> Return E_s as the ordered set of events that provides the 90% of the total ranking importance

Algorithm 3. Compute Events Importance

Implementation: As in the case of Algorithm 2, when a limited number of examples is considered, the Random Forest classification function can be used for computing feature importance on the samples not used in training. The Random Forest features importance measure is computed considering the mean increment in the classification error when a randomly selected features is changed in the tree. If the random permutation of the considered feature over all the trees results in an increment of the classification error, the feature represents an important variable in the classification process. The mean value of the incremental error, averaged over all the trees, provides the final measure of the importance. This measure is in agreement with importance measures computed using linear regressors [18]. Nevertheless, Random Forest importance measure can be also computed for ill-posed problems where the number of data-points is much lower that the dimensionality of the features space.

5   Evaluation Methodology

The proposed methodology has been evaluated on a dataset collected in a car assembly scenario [19]. The dataset used and the data collection process are briefly described in Sec. 5.1. The validation protocol and the performance measures adopted are described in Sec. 5.2

5.1   Dataset Description

We evaluate our method using a dataset that has been previously analysed for an AED system design [19]. Here we briefly summarise the dataset and recording procedure. Using a car body installed in a laboratory environment has been used to gather data related to car assembling tasks. A total of 42 atomic activities have been collected using 12 distributed sensors worn by the workers and attached to different tools and parts of the car. Nine wireless sensor nodes have been used to record motion of different car parts. Two cordless automatic screwdrivers and a socket wrench have been used as tools for the assembly. Three wired sensors have been attached to a jacket at the wrist position of both right and left lower arms and the upper back. Two workers performed 10 repetitions of all the tasks. Experts manually annotated a total of 49 different detector events derived from the atomic activities for all sensor-detector nodes. Simple time-domain features are computed from raw 3-D accelerometer sensor data. The features includes sums and absolute sums, first and second deviations, minimum, average, and maximum amplitudes. The complete list of sensor nodes with their acronyms alongside the list of composite activities present in the dataset are shown in Table 1.

5.2   Validation Protocol and Performance Measure

Recall has been used to quantify the performance of the process and to evaluate the number of relevant atomic activities that the proposed configuration

Table 1. Sensor nodes and composite activities in the car assembly scenario

Sensor Nodes	Right Lower Arm (RLA),Left Lower Arm (LLA),Central Upper Back (CUB),Front Light (FLIGHT),Brake Light (BLIGHT),Driver 1,Driver 2,Front Door (FDOOR),Back Door (BDOOR),Rattle
Composite Activities	Hood Rod,Mount Back Door,Mount Bar,Mount Brake Light,Mount Front Door,Mount Light,Mount Water tank,Test Back Door,Test Front Door,Test Hood,Test Trunk

methodology is able to retrieve. The manual annotations and detectors configurations provided by experts have been considered as *ground-truth*. Recall is then expressed as the ratio between the number of annotated relevant activities that have been retrieved and the total number of annotated activities. A percentage of 100% of recall means that all the annotated activities relevant for the specific detector have been successfully retrieved.

In order to evaluate the coherence between manual and inferred configurations, the *events edit distance* has been used as performance measure. The events edit distance is defined as the minimum number of insertions, deletions and substitutions required to convert one event present in the automatically generated configuration into the correspondent manually configured event. A zero value of events distance means that the events considered are constituted by the same atomic activities.

A 3-folds cross-validation approach has been used for evaluating the methodology. At each step of the cross-validation approach, one fold has been used for inferring the detectors structure, one fold has been used for training the classification architecture and one fold for testing purpose. A total of 3 runs of cross-validation has been performed, for a total of 9 experiments. Final performance measures are obtained by averaging all results. Classification accuracy has been adopted as recognition performance measure. In all the experiments, the Random Forest classifier has been trained on 151 classification and regression trees.

The K-Means clustering algorithm has been used for comparison purposes. Being the number of events not previously know, the procedure described in [20] has been used for automatically evaluate the number of clusters.

6   Experimental Results

Experimental results and discussions on aspects of interest are reported in the following subsections. In particular, results of the configuration process are reported in 6.1 for both k-Means and the proposed methodology, denoted as *MST*. Recognition performances for both detectors and overall classification architecture are reported in 6.2. Finally, 6.3 presents quantitative results in terms of reduction of computational resources that the inferred configuration provides for each detector.

6.1   Detectors Configuration and Comparison with Experts Annotations

Recall is reported in Fig. 3 for all sensor nodes. For the wide majority of nodes, the MST methodology is able to retrieve all relevant activities per detector as annotated by experts. RLA and LLA exhibit the lowest recall. In particular, LLA exhibits a recall of less than 50%. On the other hand, k-Means is able to retrieve all the annotated activities only for the Trunk, Blight and Rattle sensor nodes. The mean value of the events distance computed over all the events in-

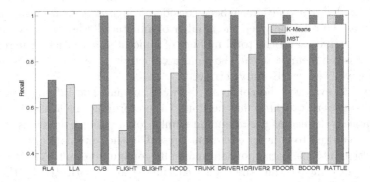

Fig. 3. Recall obtained for k-Means and MST: the value measures the percentage of relevant activities retrieved with respect to the events manually annotated for each detector node.

ferred in the detectors configuration is shown in Fig. 4. The MST methodology infers configurations that are very similar to the configurations manually set by experts. In most of the cases, the events discovered coincide with the manually annotated events. Nevertheless, the configuration generated with the k-Means grouping shows very high values of distance indicating events that deviate from the annotations. This is principally due to the fact that the algorithm collects data-points of contiguous activities in the same cluster generating events with elements derived from many different atomic activities. Both configurations generated by k-Means and MST contains events that experts did not annotate. This fact is exemplified in Fig. 5 where the configurations inferred for Trunk and Brake Light are reported. Both configurations identify one event that experts did not annotate. Nevertheless, the mutual presence of the events reflects the possibility that the activities of the nodes are related. Nevertheless, these hidden patterns cannot completely discriminable for the detector. This case and other similar ones obtained for different nodes, motivate the low recall measure obtained in the RLA, LLA and CUB detectors: in those nodes, the amount of activity patterns present makes extremely difficult an accurate manual grouping. Moreover, this fact represents the motivation why no null events distance is obtained. Finally, it is worth to be noted that, being the presence of these

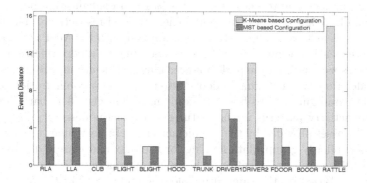

Fig. 4. Events distance obtained by k-Means and MST configurations: small values of events distance show that the configuration generated is consistent with the manually configured detectors

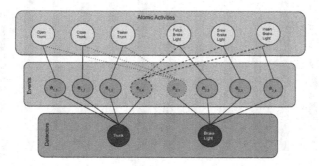

Fig. 5. Example of Detector Configuration for Trunk and Brake Light sensor nodes: dotted lines identify events not annotated by experts

non-annotated events a general case for all the detectors, measures like precision would exhibit very low performance value.

6.2   Classification Results

Events detection accuracy is reported in Fig. 6. Results derived by the manual and MST-based configuration indicate detection performances that are always higher than 99%. Although lower, detection accuracy derived by k-Means-based configuration still maintains a satisfactory level of performance. Detector performance without grouping are generally lower than 75% of accuracy and have been not reported. These results shows the capability of the AED approach to boost the detection performance in the sensor node. This enhancement is also reflected in the final classification step where composite activities are considered. Mean value and standard deviation computed over all the composite activities are reported in Fig. 7. Starting from a classification accuracy of 73% obtained without configuration, accuracy reaches 78% and 84% when configuration based on the manual and k-Means grouping methodologies are used respectively. The highest performance is achieved using detectors configured with the MST configuration with a classification accuracy of 88%, corresponding to a performance boost of 15% with respect the baseline performance. This significant improvement can be easily understand when looking in depth into the detector configuration process. The AED paradigm aims to find a maximum margin classifier that easily separates the activity patterns in the features space of the detector, disregarding the actual classes provided by the atomic activities. In particular, the MST configuration explicitly groups data looking for the maximal margin distance. Due to this behavior, the classification is boosted towards high level of recognition performance. Based on the same principle, the complexity of the detector will be also reduced thanks to the possibility of learn simple separation boundaries, as shown in the following subsection.

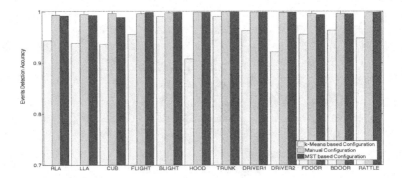

Fig. 6. Events detection accuracy for k-Means,manual and MST configurations: for the manual and MST grouping, detection accuracy reaches 99% for all the the sensors. Baseline accuracy obtained without configuration is 75%.

6.3   Reduction in Detectors Computational Resources

Detectors have been modeled by means of classification and regression trees (CART) composing the Random Forest classifier. Hence, a simple measure of complexity for detectors is provided by the number of nodes each CART is composed. This complexity measure gives an idea of the complexity of the dataset that the tree is modeling. Events that are simple to model are described by very simple CARTs: in these trees the splits, implemented by if-then rules, represent the detection boundaries that the learning algorithm use to model the events. The mean number of nodes computed over all the CARTs classifier is reported in Fig. 8, for each detector and all the grouping methodologies. For comparison purposes, the mean number of nodes when no configuration is applied, is also reported. For all the inferred configurations, the mean number of nodes is lowered. In particular, for the CUB detector, while approximately 470 nodes are needed for modeling the detector without events, a mean number of 100 and

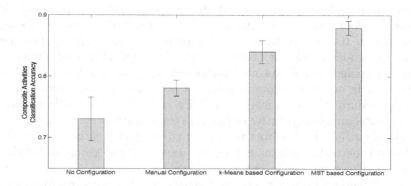

Fig. 7. Composite activities classification accuracy: mean value and standard deviation are reported for the the three grouping methodologies in comparison with the classification accuracy of the recognition process without grouping. The MST grouping provides a performance boost of 15%.

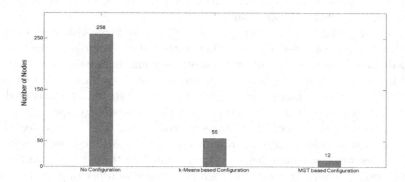

Fig. 8. Mean number of nodes in CARTs for each detectors: the number of nodes of the configured detectors is lower than in the baseline classifier

29 nodes are needed for the k-Means and MST configurations. Using the MST grouping methodology, detectors modeling events in Fligth, Blight, Trunk and Rattle sensor nodes use CARTs with less than 10 nodes. As previously stated, this behavior is symptomatic of the construction of maximum margin classifiers: few decision boundaries are enough for obtaining a consistent and powerful discrimination between events.

7   Conclusions and Future Works

In this paper, a data-driven methodology for inferring the configuration of distributed activity detectors has been presented and evaluated. The methodology, based on Activity-Events-Detector (AED) digraphs, learns groups of activity patterns that look similar from the local perspective of the sensor nodes and are relevant for the final recognition of composite activities. The methodology provides an high-level grouping of the activities that does not depend directly by activity data-points and makes no assumptions regarding the underlying data distributions. In addition, relevant groups of activities are discovered using a ranking procedure based on a features selection strategy in a hierarchical classification architecture. Comparative results with configurations manually designed by experts show that the detectors are configured coherently to the configuration provided by experts. In addition, the methodology generates groups of activities that, although not present in the manual configuration, help in the recognition tasks. Experimental results obtained using a multiple-runs cross-validation approach, show that the configuration provided by the proposed methodology boosts the recognition performance at both detector and architectural level. In particular, all the events are detected with accuracy generally higher than 99% and the classification performance of composite activities is enhanced. Furthermore, results obtained show that simple decision boundaries are needed when the AED configuration is applied and the correspondent detectors are simplified in terms of computational constraints.

Future works aim to further generalize the methodology. Although a cross-validation scheme was used for providing statistical correctness to the results obtained, an exhaustive series of experiments over multiple datasets will be required in order to study the behavior of the methodology under different scenarios. In particular, a more complex set of activities should be considered in order to gain insights about the limitations of the methodology, specially when datasets with a large number of activities are considered. The methodology has been developed in order to provide robustness to noise. Although not explicitly tested in this work, a comprehensive study related to testing the behavior of the methodology under different noise levels is needed in order to provide a further generalization step. Last but not least, a thorough investigation should be considered specially in relation to the theoretical aspects provided by the AED approach and the methodology proposed.

Acknowledgments. This work was supported by the EU FP7 Marie Curie Network iCareNet under grant number 264738.

References

1. Rashidi, P., Mihailidis, A.: A survey on ambient assisted living tools for older adults. IEEE Journal of Biomedical and Health Informatics 17(3), 579–590 (2013)
2. Schmidt, A.: Context-Aware Computing: Context-Awareness, Context-Aware User Interfaces, and Implicit Interaction (2013), http://www.interaction-design.org/encyclopedia/context-aware_computing.html
3. Amft, O., Lombriser, C.: Modelling of distributed activity recognition in the home environment. In: EMBC 2011: Proceedings of the 33th Annual International Conference of the IEEE Engineering in Medicine and Biology Society, pp. 1781–1784. IEEE (2011)

4. Lombriser, C., Amft, O., Zappi, P., Benini, L., Tröster, G.: Benefits of Dynamically Reconfigurable Activity Recognition in Distributed Sensing Environments. Atlantis Ambient and Pervasive Intelligence, vol. 4, pp. 261–286. World Scientific Publishing Co. (2010)
5. Aggarwal, J., Ryoo, M.: Human activity analysis: A review. ACM Comput. Surv. 43(3), 16:1–16:43 (2011)
6. Aloimonos, Y.: Sensory grammars for sensor networks. Journal of Ambient Intelligence and Smart Environments 1(1), 15–21 (2009)
7. Zappi, P., Stiefmeier, T., Farella, E., Roggen, D., Benini, L., Troster, G.: Activity recognition from on-body sensors by classifier fusion: sensor scalability and robustness. In: 3rd International Conference on Intelligent Sensors, Sensor Networks and Information Processing (ISSNIP), pp. 281–286 (2007)
8. Sarkar, A.M.J., Hasan, K., Lee, Y.-K., Lee, S., Zabir, S.: Distributed activity recognition using key sensors. In: 11th International Conference on Advanced Communication Technology, ICACT 2009, vol. 03, pp. 2245–2250 (2009)
9. Storf, H., Kleinberger, T., Becker, M., Schmitt, M., Bomarius, F., Prueckner, S.: An event-driven approach to activity recognition in ambient assisted living. In: Tscheligi, M., de Ruyter, B., Markopoulus, P., Wichert, R., Mirlacher, T., Meschterjakov, A., Reitberger, W. (eds.) AmI 2009. LNCS, vol. 5859, pp. 123–132. Springer, Heidelberg (2009)
10. van Kasteren, T.L.M., Englebienne, G., Kröse, B.J.A.: Hierarchical activity recognition using automatically clustered actions. In: Keyson, D.V., et al. (eds.) AmI 2011. LNCS, vol. 7040, pp. 82–91. Springer, Heidelberg (2011)
11. Jain, A.K.: Data clustering: 50 years beyond k-means. Pattern Recogn. Lett. 31(8), 651–666 (2010)
12. Cortes, C., Vapnik, V.: Support-vector networks. Mach. Learn. 20(3), 273–297 (1995)
13. Scholkopf, B., Smola, A.J.: Learning with Kernels: Support Vector Machines, Regularization, Optimization, and Beyond. MIT Press, Cambridge (2001)
14. Breiman, L.: Random forests. Mach. Learn. 45(1), 5–32 (2001)
15. Breiman, L.: Some infinity theory for predictor ensembles. Tech. rep. (2001)
16. Zahn, C.: Graph-theoretical methods for detecting and describing gestalt clusters. IEEE Transactions on Computers C-20(1), 68–86 (1971)
17. Wolpert, D.H.: Stacked generalization. Neural Networks 5, 241–259 (1992)
18. Ulrike, G.: Variable importance assessment in regression: Linear regression versus random forest. The American Statistician 63(4), 308–319 (2009)
19. Amft, O., Lombriser, C., Stiefmeier, T., Tröster, G.: Recognition of user activity sequences using distributed event detection. In: European Conference on Smart Sensing and Context (EuroSSC), pp. 126–141 (2007)
20. von Luxburg, U.: Clustering stability: An overview. Foundations and Trends in Machine Learning 2(3), 235–274 (2009)

Making Context Aware Decision from Uncertain Information in a Smart Home: A Markov Logic Network Approach

Pedro Chahuara, François Portet, and Michel Vacher*

Laboratoire d'Informatique de Grenoble
Grenoble 1/Grenoble INP/CNRS UMR 5217, F-38041 Grenoble, France
{pedro.chahuara,francois.portet,michel.vacher}@imag.fr

Abstract. This research addresses the issue of building home automation systems reactive to voice for improved comfort and autonomy at home. The focus of this paper is on the context-aware decision process which uses a dedicated Markov Logic Network approach to benefit from the formal logical representation of domain knowledge as well as the ability to handle uncertain facts inferred from real sensor data. The approach has been experiemented in a real smart home with naive and users with special needs.

Keywords: Sensing and Reasoning Technology, Knowledge-Based Systems, Decision making, Reasoning under uncertainty.

1 Introduction

As the development of Smart Homes (SH) has gained a growing interest among many communities — such as medicine, architecture, computer sciences, etc. — two major challenges have emerged in the area of Ambient Intelligence. Firstly, the need for knowledge representation models featuring high readability, modularity and expressibility. Secondly, the requirement to develop decision making methods that can leverage knowledge models to take context — the particular situation under which a decision is taken — and its uncertainty into account. Indeed, in most real cases context is inferred from sources affected by uncertainty.

In the literature, logical models, mostly ontologies and logic rules, seem to have reach a consensus due to the high readability and expressibility they offer. For instance, the Open AAL platform [25] uses an ontology that describes in-home entities belonging to low and high abstraction levels. The framework designed around this ontology is appropriate to facilitate the integration of devices from different providers, as they share a common taxonomy, and the implementation of computational methods to make context inference. The independence between knowledge representation and inference methods guarantees modularity, however it does not take advantage of the reasoning capacities supported by logical reasoners, as the

* This work is part of the Sweet-Home project founded by the French National Research Agency (Agence Nationale de la Recherche / ANR-09—VERS-011).

J.C. Augusto et al. (Eds.): AmI 2013, LNCS 8309, pp. 78–93, 2013.

only purpose of the ontology is to be an artefact of integration. Chen et al. [4] have proposed a method to perform activity recognition in home, an important element of context awareness, by using subsumption checking in an ontology, but uncertainty is not supported in this work. A more general approach was designed by Liao [15], in which some context elements, such as level of risk, are defined through logic rules using RDF-based events to perform activity recognition. However, uncertainty of the information sources is not considered even if a prior probability of risk is estimated. Answer Set Programming (ASP) is another logic approach for representation and reasoning that has been applied by Mileo et al. [17] to estimate the evolution of the inhabitant's health state. They present a framework that can properly deal with reasoning under incompleteness and uncertainty. Furthermore, the knowledge encoded in the ASP rules could be integrated into an ontology as well. Although their approach is very relevant for context recognition, they have not developed formal decision models containing essential elements such as utilities, risks and actions. On the side of decision methods for SH dealing with uncertainty, several Bayesian approaches have been suggested, as in the SOCAM project [7]. Influence diagrams [10], which are based on Bayesian networks, have been also applied to model the causal relation among decision actions, uncertain variables, risk, and utilities [20,5]. However in these works, the decision process is not supported by a formal knowledge representation that can be exploited in other tasks besides decision.

It seems that there exists a gap between the development of formal models to represent knowledge in pervasive environments and the methods for decision making that must act under uncertain information. In this paper, we propose an approach involving the representation of concepts by means of ontologies and a set of logical rules. In the decision stage, a part of the logical rules is employed to construct an influence diagram based on Markov Logic Networks (MLN), a statistical method that makes probabilistic inference from a model consisting of weighted logic rules. The rest of this paper describes the SH context in Section 2 and the framework in Section 3. Section 4 details the decision making model and Section 5 summarises experiments conduced in a real smart home. Finally, a brief discussion is given Section 6.

2   The Smart Home Context

The typical smart homes considered in the study are the one that permit voice based interaction. There is a rising number of such smart homes [11,2,8,6,14] that are particularly adapted to people in loss of autonomy [21]. Typically, such smart homes are multi-rooms and equipped with sensors and actuators such as infra-red presence detectors, contact sensors... This kind of smart home can support daily life by taking context sensitive decisions based on the current situation of the user. More specifically, the smart home can be *reactive* to vocal or other commands to make the most adequate action based on context, and can act *pro-actively* by recognising a specific situation in which an action must be made (e.g., for security issue). To illustrate this support, let's consider the following two scenarios:

Scenario 1. *The inhabitant wakes up at night and utters the vocal order "Turn on the light". This simple command requires context information (location and activity) to realize which light to turn on and what the appropriate intensity is. In this case, the system decides to turn on the bedside lamp with a middle intensity since the ceiling light could affect her eyes sensitivity at that moment.*

Scenario 2. *The inhabitant returns to her apartment after shopping, forgets to lock the door, and does her usual activities until night. She prepares to sleep and turns all the lights off but the bedside lamp as she usually reads before sleeping. After some minutes, she turns off the lamp and, from the sequence of her interactions with the environment, the system recognizes that she is about to sleep. The unlocked main door represents a relatively dangerous situation. The system could send a message through a speech synthesizer – considering the risk of interrupting her rest– to remind her to close the door.*

From these scenarios it can be noticed that contextual information, such as location and activity, play a major role in delivering the appropriate support to the user. In this paper, Location and Activity are defined as follows:

Definition 1 (Location). $l(t) \in L$, *where L is the set of predefined locations in the SH and $t \in \mathbb{N}$ is the time, specifies where the inhabitant is located.*

In this work, a specific area corresponds to a room and we assume a single inhabitant in the environment.

Definition 2 (Activity). *Routine activities performed during daily life; such as, sleeping, cooking, or cleaning. In an instant t the activity might be undetermined; so an activity occurrence, a is defined in an interval of time, $A(t_{begin}, t_{end})$. Thus $A : t_b, t_e \to a, t_b, t_e \in \mathbb{N}$ and $t_b < t_e$*

Moreover, much more information can be inferred from the raw data such as agitation, communication, etc. They are defined as sources of information:

Definition 3 (Source of Information). *The system contains a set of variables V that describes the environment. A source of information is a variable $V_i \in V$ with domain $Dom(V_i)$ representing the information provided by a sensor or an inference process i.*

Definition 4 (System state). *If Υ is the set of possible values of V, a system state is an assignment $v \in \Upsilon$ making $V = \{V_1 = v_1, V_2 = v_2, ..., V_n = v_n\}$*

The Situation is then defined by:

Definition 5 (Situation). *A situation $S \subset \Upsilon$ is defined by a set of constraints $C = \{C_1^{k_1}, C_2^{k_2}, ..., C_m^{k_m}\}$, where each constraint $C_i^{k_i}$ establish a set $D_i \subset DOM(V_{k_i})$ to constrain the value of a source of information V_{k_i}. Thus $S = \{v/\forall C_i^{k_i} \in C, v_{k_i} \in D_i\}$*

For example, in Scenario 2 we have : V_1, V_2 and $V_{3,...,n}$, which are the states of the main door, the user's location and the states of the blinds and lights. A situation can be defined by constraints, $C_1^1, C_2^2, ..., C_n^n$, holding the following sets: $D_1 = \{open\}$, $D_2 = \{\neg kitchen\}$, $D_{3,...,n} = \{off\}$. A situation is recognized when all the lights are off, the blinds are closed, the front door is open and the person is not in the kitchen (assuming the front door is in the kitchen).

Definition 6 (Temporal Situation). *A temporal situation R, is defined by a set of constraints $T = \{T_1, T_2, ..., T_m\}$, where each T_k is a tuple composed of a pair of situations (S_k^1, S_k^2) and a temporal constraint r between S_k^1 and S_k^2.*

Consider $T_1 = < S^1, S^2, r >$ with $r = [t_i, t_j]$, a temporal situation is recognized when $t_i \leqslant t_S^2 - t_S^1 \leqslant t_j$ where t_S^i is the occurrence time of S^i. r can also be a qualitative constraint such as $after(S_1, S_2)$ or $order(S_1, S_2, S_3)$. For more details about temporal representation and reasoning the reader is referred to [1]. In the rest of the paper we refer to temporal situations simply as situations.

The elements defined above compose the context that we define as follows:

Definition 7 (Context). *Set of informations characterizing the circumstance under which an inference is made.*

The main usage of context is disambiguation. When a situation is recognized, several decisions can be made with different effects. The context provides the complementary information to evaluate the circumstance in terms of risk (safety) and utility (safety, efficiency, comfort...). These two notions are defined below:

Definition 8 (Risk). *The risk is the probabilistic measure that a given action would have a negative outcome in the situation under consideration.*

Though risk definition varies according to the domains, in decision making, risk is often a consequence of uncertainty which is evaluated by enumerating all the possible outcomes with their probability and their consequences.

Definition 9 (Utility). *The utility $U \in [0, 1]$ is the degree of preferences of a system state caused by applying an action decided by the decision making system.*

Under uncertainty, an action can have numerous effects. If the effect leads to a negative outcome, U takes a negative value. There is thus a relationship between U and the risk: to compute risk for a given action, the probability of all the unwanted states (i.e., those with a negative value) must be computed.

For instance, in Scenario 1 the situation which triggers the decision making is the recognition of the voice order *"turn on the light"*. The context is the location (bedroom), the time (middle of the night) and the activity (sleeping). The action to make could be to light on the ceiling light or the bedside lamp or both. The effects could be do decrease or increase comfort. Thus the risk of each action is given by its probability of having an unwanted effect (here, decrease comfort). The utility is the numerical value associated to each effect.

It must be emphasized that the choice depends on the context. Indeed, in the case of Scenario 1, as the person has just awoken in the dark, the bedside lamp would be the best choice to avoid dazzling, but in a different context (e.g., when tidying up) the ceiling could be the best choice.

3   The Voice Controlled Smart Home System

The smart home system we are considering in the study has been developed in the SWEET-HOME project[24]. The reasoning capabilities of the system are implemented in the intelligent controller depicted in Figure 1. The bottom of the figure shows external systems that are connected to the controller to gather streams of data and send orders to the home automation system. All these streams of information are captured and interpreted to recognize situations and makes decisions.

The estimation of the current situation is carried out through the collaboration of several processors, each one being specialized in a specific source of information. All processors share the knowledge specified in both ontologies and use the same repository of facts. Furthermore, the access to the knowledge base is executed under a service oriented approach that allows any processor being registered to be notified only about particular events and to make inferred information available to other processors. This data and knowledge centred approach ensures that all the processors are using the same data structure and that the meaning of each piece of information is clearly defined among all of them.

We have considered that the main aspects for situation recognition are the location of the inhabitant and the current activity. These informations are useful to reduce ambiguity in the decision making process. Other works have also reckoned location and activity as fundamental for context-aware inference [17,23].

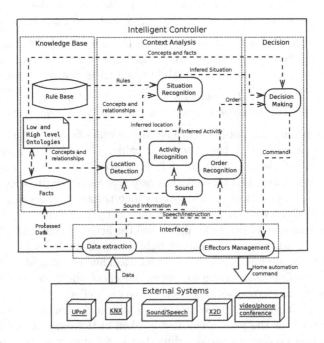

Fig. 1. The Intelligent Controller Diagram

In order to perform location and activity inference, two independent modules were developed and integrated in the framework. The former applies a method based on the modelling of the links between sensor events and location assumptions by a two-level dynamic network. Data fusion is achieved by spread activation on the dynamic network. The second module uses a classifier, based on Markov logic networks, to carry out activity recognition. Due to space limitation the reader is referred to [3] for further details.

The intelligent controller performs inference in several stages, from raw input data until the evaluation of situations. Each event is produced by the arrival of a sensor information. These events are considered of low level as they do not require inference. Once they are stored in the facts base, processing modules are executed sequentially (e.g., location then activity then situation). Thus, each inference corresponding to a high level event is stored in the database and used subsequently by the next modules. Within the controller architecture, other inference modules can be added without compromising the processing of the other components.

The knowledge of the controller is defined using two semantic layers: the *low-level* and the *high-level* ontologies. The two ontologies were implemented in OWL2, not only for domain knowledge representation, but also for storing the events resulting from the processing modules. Furthermore, situations are defined within the ontologies allowing description logic reasoners to evaluate if a situation is happening. Consequently, the importance of the ontology goes beyond the mere description of the environment.

The *low-level* ontology is devoted to the representation of raw data and network information description. State, location, value and URI of switches and actuators are examples of element to be managed at this level. The *high-level* ontology represents concepts being used at the reasoning level. These concepts are organized in 3 main branches: the Abstract Entity, the Physical Entity, and the Event concept that represents the transient observations of one abstract entity involving zero or several physical entities (e.g., at 12:03 the dweller is sleeping). Instances in the *high-level* ontology are produced by the inference modules (e.g. activity, location, and situations) after treating information coming from sensors. This separation between low and high levels makes possible a higher re-usability of the reasoning layer when the sensor network and the home must be adapted [13].

As situation are defined as temporal patterns of the system state, ontologies provide an appropriate foundation for situation recognition since they store all the facts (i.e., the system state) and a complete semantic description of the environment as well. Furthermore, temporal representation can be achieved by means of role properties among event concepts defining temporal relations such as *previous* and *next* which, through chaining property of OWL2, can generate the *after* and *before* relations. Under some restrictions, Datalogs describing situations as logic rules can be transformed in description logic and written on ontologies [9]. These rules are built using the Semantic Web Rule Language (SWRL). However, the scope of this approach is very limited as it does not allow to specify complex definitions. But, even when it is limited to safe rules, it overcomes several restrictions of description logics while having the definitions still as part of the ontology. In addition, SWRL built-in functions further extend the semantics of context definitions.

For instance, the situation in which a person is leaving her house without having closed her windows can be described by the SWRL rule 1 while the situation in scenario 2 can be modelled by rule 2.

Rule 1.   DeviceEvent(?d), has_associated_object(?d, door), takes_place_in(?d, kitchen), state_value(?d, open), Window(?w), located_in(?w, bedroom),Application(?a), has_application(?w,?a),curret_state(?a,on), swlrb:moreThan(sqwrl:count(?w), 1), → current_state(BedroomWindowsOpen, detected)

Rule 2.   DeviceEvent(?l), has_associated_object(?l, light), takes_place_in(?l, bedroom), state_value(?d, off), Window(?w), located_in(?w, bedroom),Application(?a1), has_application(?w,?a1),curret_state(?a1,on), swlrb:equals(sqwrl:count(?w), 0), Blind(?b), located_in(?b, bedroom),Application(?a2), has_application(?b,?a2),curret_state(?a2,on), swlrb:equals(sqwrl:count(?b), 0), Door(?d), located_in(?d, kitchen),Application(?a3), has_application(?bd,?a3),curret_state(?a3,on), swlrb:equals(sqwrl:count(?d), 1) → current_state(MainDoorOpen, detected)

4   Decision Making Using Markov Logic Network

The decision making module is the main component of the intelligent controller. When a situation is recognized, this module employs the high level knowledge in order to construct dynamically a decision model that takes into account the context and its degree of uncertainty. In this section we briefly describe the decision problem by influence diagram models and how it has been modelled by Markov Logic Network.

4.1   Modelling the Decision Making by Influence Diagrams

Influence diagrams [10] are probabilistic models used to represent decision problems. They extend Bayesian networks – composed only of state nodes – by the inclusion of two types of node: action and utility. An action node is a variable corresponding to a decision choice (e.g., turning the light on or warning the user). The state nodes represent the variables in the problem domain that are affected by the actions. Finally, utility nodes are variables that represent the utility value obtained as consequence of applying the decided actions. For instance, turning the light on at full intensity when the person is asleep would have a negative utility.

Formally, given a set of actions A and an assignment of choices $a \in A$, the expected utility EU for a is computed by:

$$EU(a) = \sum_X P(X|a, e)U(X) \qquad (1)$$

where X is a set of state nodes, $U(X)$ is the utility value of X and e is the evidence (e.g., the context). The process of finding the "best" decision consists of solving the Maximum Expected Utility (MEU) problem which demands to compute the EU of every possible assignment of $a_{best} = argmax_a EU(a)$.

Figure 2 shows an example of Influence Diagram, based on the scenario 1. In this case, the setting of action variables, represented by rectangular nodes, indicate which *lights* are operated and their *intensity*. Oval nodes are the state nodes, some of which are affected by the decision, while the others belong to the context (within the dashed area). Two variables influence directly the utility: the *comfort* of the inhabitant and the suitability of the activated *lights location* that ideally should be the same of the inhabitant. Note that this location is not easy to determine in some cases since the inhabitant could be moving in the SH while uttering the vocal order.

The interest of influence diagrams is essentially its ability to easily represent the structure of a decision problem and the dependencies between variables. However, it is limited to propositional variables while a decision model could benefit of relational knowledge (e.g., turning on a light *next to* the room of the dweller). Yet, first order rules, though very expressive, cannot make it possible for an expert to express uncertainty. To overcome these limitations, we propose to model the decision process by a Markov Logic Network.

4.2   Markov Logic Networks (MLN)

MLN [22] combines first-order logic and Markov Networks, an undirected probabilistic graphical model. A MLN is composed of a set of first-order formulas each one associated to a weight that expresses a degree of truth. This approach soften the assumption that a logic formula can only be true or false. A formula in which each variable is replaced by a constant is *ground* and if it consists of a single predicate it is a *ground atom*. A set of ground atoms is a *possible world*. All possible worlds in a MLN are true with a certain probability which depends on the number of formulas they agree with and the weights of these formulas.

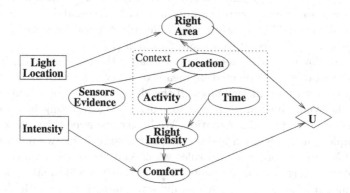

Fig. 2. Influence diagram for a decision after a vocal order is recognised

A MLN, however, can also have hard constraints by giving a infinite weight to some formulas, so that worlds violating these formulas have zero probability.

Let's consider F a set of first-order logic formulas, i.e. a knowledge base, $w_i \in \mathbf{R}$ the weight of the formula $f_i \in F$, and C a set of constants (in our case, input data). During the inference process [22], every MLN predicated is grounded and a Markov network $M_{F,C}$ is constructed where each random variable corresponds to a ground atom. The probability of a possible world $P(X = x)$ can then be estimated using equation 2.

$$P(X = x) = \tfrac{1}{Z} exp \left(\sum_{f_i \in F} w_i n_i(x) \right) \tag{2}$$

where $Z = \sum_{x' \in \chi} exp \left(\sum_{f_i \in F} w_i n_i(x') \right)$ is a normalisation factor, χ the set of possible worlds, and $n_i(x)$ is the number of true groundings of the ith clause in the possible world x.

Because computing Z involve grounding the whole network in each possible world, exact inference in MLN is intractable in most cases, so Markov Chain Monte Carlo methods are applied [22].

MLN models can be acquired by supervised learning which consists in two independent tasks: structure learning and weight learning. Structure can be obtained by applying machine learning methods, such as Inductive Logic Programming, or rules written by human experts. Weight learning is an optimisation problem that requires learning data. Weight learning can be achieve by maximizing the likelihood wrt a learning set x. If the ith formula is satisfied $n_i(x)$ times in x, then by using equation (2), the derivative of the log-likelihood wrt the weight w_i is given by equation (3).

$$\frac{\partial}{\partial w_i} \log P_w(X = x) = n_i(x) - \sum_{x'} P_w(X = x') n_i(x) \tag{3}$$

Where x' is a possible world in x. The sum is thus performed over all the possible worlds x' and $P_w(X = x')$ is $P(X = x')$ computed using the vector $w = (w_1, \ldots, w_i, \ldots)$. The maximisation of the likelihood is performed by an iterative process converging towards an optimal w. Unfortunately, the computing equation (3) is intractable in most cases. Thus, approximation method are used in practice such as the *Scaled Conjugate Gradient* [16].

Since a Markov network is more general than a Bayesian network, Influence diagrams can also be implemented by means of MLN [18]. Nath et al. [19] have proposed an algorithm that evaluates all the choices in a set of actions without executing the whole inference process for each choice resulting in an efficient way to estimate the optimal assignation. We have considered this approach suitable for implementing decision making in our framework for two main reasons: Firstly, MLNs are 1st order logical rules which can be stored in an ontological representation, using domain concepts in order to keep a standard vocabulary besides achieving decision model readability. Secondly, it deals with the uncertainty related to context variables.

A MLN for the influence diagram of Figure 2 can be defined as follows:

Predicate	Domain	Type
Intensity	{low,high}	Action
LightLocation	{bedroom,kitchen,toilet...}	Action
Comfort	{low,medium,high}	Utility
RightArea	{good,bad,acceptable}	Utility
Location	{bedroom,kitchen,toilet...}	State
Activity	{sleep,eat,clean,dress...}	State

Weight	Rule
3.35	$LightLocation(l) \land Location(l) \rightarrow RightArea(good)$
0.12	$LightLocation(l1) \land Location(l2) \land NextTo(l1,l2) \rightarrow RightArea(acceptable)$
2.44	$LightLocation(l1) \land Location(l2) \land l1! = l2 \rightarrow RightArea(low)$
1.46	$Activity(a) \land Agitation(a, degree) \land Intensity(d) \rightarrow Comfort(high)$
-0.79	$Activity(a) \land Agitation(a, d1) \land Intensity(d2) \land d1! = d2 \rightarrow Comfort(medium)$
-0.09	$Activity(a) \land Agitation(a, d1) \land Intensity(d2) \land d1! = d2 \rightarrow Comfort(low)$

Utility Value

U(RightArea(bad))=-2	U(RightArea(fair))=0	U(RightArea(good))=2
U(Comfort(low))=-3	U(Comfort(medium))=0	U(Comfort(high))=3

Evidence

NextTo(kitchen,bedroom)	NextTo(bedroom,study)	Agitation(rest,low)
Agitation(sleep,low)	Agitation(eat,low)	Agitation(tidy,high)
Agitation(hygien,high)	Agitation(dress up,high)	Agitation(communication,high)

This MLN is a template for constructing Markov network modelling an influence diagram. It must be constructed dynamically since the probability of context variables, location and activity, can not be known *a priori*. As shown Figure 3, once the decision module is triggered, it gets the evidences from the ontology instances that are used to ground the MLN and generates an influence diagram (actually a Markov network). This grounded network is then used to compute the action that maximize the expected utility using equation 4.

$$EU(a) = \sum_{x \in \{bad,fair,good\}} P(RightArea(x) \mid a).U(RightArea(x))$$
$$+ \sum_{x \in \{low,med.,high\}} P(LightLocation(x) \mid a).U(LightLocation(x)) \quad (4)$$

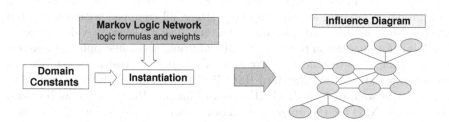

Fig. 3. Influence diagram construction by MLN grounding

4.3 Making Decision with Uncertain Information

As presented in Figure 1, contextual information, such as location and activity, results from an inference process. As such, contextual information is often uncertain and we assume such inferences to be provided with a probability measure. These uncertain results are the input evidence of the decision model. But, in the decision model, the expected utility is computed without taking the uncertainty of the evidence into account. For instance, if the activity recognition module gives the following activities with their probabilities: sleeping (.33), tidying up (.34) and resting (.33), the decision module will consider only the most probable activity and will possibly make a wrong decision. To account for the uncertainty in the evidence, we extended the approach by using the Jeffrey's rule [12] to estimate the probability of the best action. Based on this, the probability of a state node X (e.g., $RightArea$ and $LightLocation$), given an action a, is computed by equation 5:

$$P'(X) = \sum_{i=1}^{n} P(X \mid Activity_i, a).P(Activity_i) \qquad (5)$$

From equations 1 and 5, EU can then be estimated by equation 6. Note that $Activity$ is no more included in the set of contextual evidence e.

$$EU(a) = \sum_{X} \sum_{i=1}^{n} P(X \mid Activity_i, a, e).P(Activity_i).U(X) \qquad (6)$$

5   Experiments

The method was experimented in real situations in a smart home with 'typical' naive users and users with special needs interacting with the environment. This section describes the experimental set up and the results of the decision making for the 'typical' users and some preliminary feedbacks from the users with special needs.

5.1   Experimental Set Up and Collected Data

The experimental smart home is depicted Figure 4. It is a $32m^2$ flat including a bathroom, a kitchen, a bedroom and a study, all equipped with sensors and effectors such as infra-red presence detectors, contact sensors, video cameras (used only for annotation purpose), etc. In addition, seven microphones were set in the ceiling. The technical architecture of DOMUS is based on the KNX bus system, a worldwide ISO standard (ISO/IEC 14543), and include several other field buses as well, such as UPnP (Universal Plug and Play) for the audio video distribution, X2D for the opening detection (doors, windows, and cupboards), etc. More than 150 sensors, actuators and information providers are managed in the flat.

The experiments consisted in following a scenario of activities without constraints of time or the way of performing them. During the scenario, the participants had to utter several voice commands. A previous visit was organised so that the participants find all the items necessary to perform the activities. Many decisions were to be made by the decision module such as answering orders related to giving the time or closing the blinds. Due to space limitation,

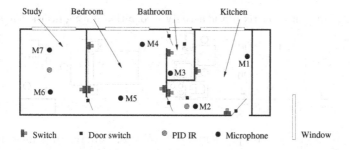

Fig. 4. The DOMUS Smart Home

we will focus the paper on context aware decisions. In this case, 4 situations were specifically considered when the user utters the voice order *"turn on the light"*. In each situation, two lights that can be turned on, one brighter than the other:

1. **Situation 1**. The user is sitting eating in the kitchen, the most adequate light is the light above the table.
2. **Situation 2**. The user is tidying up the bedroom, the most adequate light is the ceiling light.
3. **Situation 3**. The user is washing up the dishes in the kitchen, the most adequate light is the light above the sink.
4. **Situation 4**. The user is finishing her nap in the bedroom, the most adequate light is the bedside lamp.

Moreover, the two situations described in Section 1 related to forgetting to close a window or the front door where included in the scenario. Each time these situation were recognized, a warning message was generated.

15 persons (including 9 women) participated to the experiment to record sensors data in a daily living context. The average age of the participants was 38 ± 13.6 years (19-62, min-max). At the end of the study, 11 hours of data was recorded (50 minutes per experiment in average).

5.2   Results of the Decision Making

Despite the time devoted to the experiment, the dataset was insufficient to learn the weights of a MLN decision model. Thus, the training corpus for weight learning was the result of the simulation of 200 instances, most of which expressing the best location and intensity but also including contradictory configurations. For instance, if in most of the situation 1 cases, the best light is the one above the table, a ceiling light can also be acceptable and very rarely the one above the table is considered as a bad decision. The learned weights are the one of the model presented in Section 4.2. From these weights it can be understood that the best location is always preferred while an incorrect intensity is not a high risk for the comfort.

Table 1. Confusion matrix of the activity recognition during decision making

Target/Hit	Eat	Tidy	Dress	Sleep	Rest	Hygiene	Talk
Eat	9	6	0	0	0	0	0
Tidy	3	20	1	1	4	0	1
Sleep	1	2	1	10	1	0	0

Despite the scenario, the participants took some liberty and in some cases the warning situations were not recognized. The 15 instances of the warning situation 1 and 2 were recognized 8 and 5 times respectively. For each recognized situation, the intelligent controller acted immediately to deliver an appropriate warning message.

As discussed before, activity recognition is a difficult task which deliver uncertain information. In this paper, we focus strictly on the activity recognition during a voice command whose performance is presented in Table 1. There were 60 activity instances performed during voice command, they belong to: sleeping, eating and tidying up. However, our model has been trained to recognize seven activities (see [3] for more details). The most important confusion is between eating and tidying up. Both activity are performed in the kitchen and share many characteristics such as the noise produced by the dishes. The overall accuracy is of 65% which is a reasonable rate given the poverty of the information sources. This also shows the necessity of taking the activity uncertainty into account in the decision model.

Table 2 shows the overall correct decision rate for each situation. The second column shows the standard EU, for which the most probable activity is considered as true and others as false. In the third column, the EU is computed using equation 6. In practice, the uncertainty of the location was close to 100%, thus the uncertainty was mainly due to the activity recognition.

The worst performance is in the situation 1. This is mainly due to the confusion between eating and tidying up. However, the tidying up activity was well recognized and this explain the high accuracy for situation 2. Overall, the results with and without uncertainty are very close. They actually differs in only 5 instances out of 60. For instance, in the situation 3 for the participant 12, the activity recognition output was : hygiene(0.20), dressing (0.16), sleeping (0.28), and resting (0.17) while the ground truth was tidying up (0.08) in the

Table 2. Correct decision rate with and without activity uncertainty

Situation/Expected Utility	without uncertainty	with uncertainty
Situation 1	54%	54%
Situation 2	93%	100%
Situation 3	73%	86%
Situation 4	60%	53%
Total	70%	73%

kitchen [1]. In this example, there is a high uncertainty about the actual activity, but the most probable activities leading to a high intensity choice for the light, the controller did choose a high intensity despite the most probable activity was sleeping.

5.3 Preliminary Results from Experiments with the Aged and Visually Impaired Population

The method has also been applied in the same context but with aged and visually impaired people. The aim was both to validate the technology with this specific population and to perform a user study to assess the adequacy of this technology with the targeted users. In this experiment, eleven participants, either aged (6 women) or visually impaired (2 women, 3 men), were recruited. The participants were asked to perform 4 scenarios involving daily living activities and distress or risky situations. The average age was 72 years (49-91, min-max). During this experiment, 4 hours and 39 minutes of data was collected including the same sensors as the one previously described. All the participants went through a questionnaire and a debriefing after the experiment. At the time of writing, we are still analysing the results but overall, none of the aged or visually impaired persons had any difficulty in performing the experiment. They all appreciated to control the house by voice.

6   Discussion and Future Work

Dealing with context in pervasive environments involves treating uncertainty, imprecision, and modeling complex relational information; and so far, not a single method can overcome all these problems. Therefore, Ambient Intelligence projects must rely on the application of several methods sharing a common base and serving each one a specific purpose. Our proposed framework is an attempt towards this direction. The system we developed integrates several components that are devoted to specifics aspects of a smart homes. Thus, the whole framework covers the requirements of expressibility and uncertainty treatment.

Decision making by means of Markov logic networks presents many advantages. First of all, MLN relying on a formal logic representation which is particularly suited to Ambient Intelligent systems where knowledge is often represented by means of logic. When possible, this permits translation from one representation to another to perform, for instance, addition of relational knowledge as expert knowledge in the MLN structure learning. In this perspective, the use of a formal domain knowledge description and logic-based decision method could lead to a higher re-usability of the model in another smart home. Secondly, MLN, being a probabilistic model, can deal with uncertainty and make inference from a incomplete input.

---

[1] It must be emphasized that the activity recognition is performed using a sliding window. In this window several instances of activity can intersect, that is why a sleeping activity and an hygiene activity can both have a high probability

However, as most of probabilistic models, MLN requires a considerable amount of data to estimate the optimal parameters. Unfortunately, corpora on pervasive environments with annotated data useful for decision making is rarely available. Furthermore, to the best of our knowledge there is no available corpora for decision making from vocal orders. To overcome this limitation, we took benefit from the capacity of the MLN to handle a priori knowledge. It had been possible to acquire the structure from expert knowledge and to estimate the weights from a set of synthetic data. Though not ideal, given the difficulty and cost of acquiring training data in the smart home domain this way seems promising to alleviate the need of large volumes of training data of purely statistical methods.

The experiments carried out in a real SH platform with naive and targeted users has shown that our approach is promising both regarding decision making and the overall system. From this research, many studies can be conducted to improve the decision making. Given that decision data have been acquired, the a priori model could feed a learning with this reduced set in order to adapt the model to the specific home environment. Furthermore, information is uncertain in the smart home environment, thus the handling of the uncertain evidence must be generalised. Regarding knowledge representation, a tighter integration of the decision model with the ontology would be desirable. We consider very interesting the possibility to check for coherence of the decision model rules by means of an ontology reasoner. In general, this integration is not trivial as MLN rules are defined in first-order logic, while description logic and safe rules are only a subset of first-order logic.

References

1. Artikis, A., Skarlatidis, A., Portet, F., Paliouras, G.: Logic-Based Event Recognition. Knowledge Engineering Review 27(4), 469–506 (2012)
2. Badii, A., Boudy, J.: CompanionAble - integrated cognitive assistive & domotic companion robotic systems for ability & security. In: SFTAG 2009, Troyes, France, pp. 18–20 (2009)
3. Chahuara, P., Portet, F., Vacher, M.: Fusion of Audio and Temporal Multimodal Data by Spreading Activation for Dweller Localisation in a Smart Home. In: STAMI Series, Space, Time and Ambient Intelligence (2011)
4. Chen, L., Nugent, C.: Ontology-based activity recognition in intelligent pervasive environments. International Journal of Web Information Systems 5(4), 410–430 (2009)
5. De Carolis, B., Cozzolongo, G.: C@sa: Intelligent home control and simulation. In: International Conference on Computational Intelligence, pp. 462–465 (2004)
6. Filho, G., Moir, T.J.: From science fiction to science fact: a smart-house interface using speech technology and a photorealistic avatar. International Journal of Computer Applications in Technology 39(8), 32–39 (2010)
7. Gu, T., Pung, H.K., Zhang, D.Q.: A service-oriented middleware for building context-aware services. Journal of Network and Computer Applications 28(1), 1–18 (2005)
8. Hamill, M., Young, V., Boger, J., Mihailidis, A.: Development of an automated speech recognition interface for personal emergency response systems. Journal of NeuroEngineering and Rehabilitation 6 (2009)

9. Hitzler, P., Parsia, B.: Ontologies and rules. In: Staab, S., Studer, R. (eds.) Handbook on Ontologies, 2nd edn., pp. 111–132. Springer, Heidelberg (2009)
10. Howard, R., Matheson, J.: Influence diagrams. Readings on The Principles and Applications of Decision Analysis 1 and 2, 720 (1981)
11. Istrate, D., Vacher, M., Serignat, J.-F.: Embedded implementation of distress situation identification through sound analysis. The Journal on Information Technology in Healthcare 6, 204–211 (2008)
12. Jeffrey, R.C.: The Logic of Decision. University of Chicago Press (July 1990)
13. Klein, M., Schmidt, A., Lauer, R.: Ontology-centred design of an ambient middleware for assisted living: The case of soprano. In: 30th Annual German Conference on Artificial Intelligence, KI 2007 (2007)
14. Lecouteux, B., Vacher, M., Portet, F.: Distant Speech Recognition in a Smart Home: Comparison of Several Multisource ASRs in Realistic Conditions. In: Interspeech 2011, Florence, Italy, pp. 2273–2276 (August 2011)
15. Liao, H.-C., Tu, C.-C.: A RDF and OWL-based temporal context reasoning model for smart home. Information Technology Journal 6(8), 1130–1138 (2007)
16. Lowd, D., Domingos, P.: Efficient weight learning for Markov logic networks. In: Kok, J.N., Koronacki, J., Lopez de Mantaras, R., Matwin, S., Mladenič, D., Skowron, A. (eds.) PKDD 2007. LNCS (LNAI), vol. 4702, pp. 200–211. Springer, Heidelberg (2007)
17. Mileo, A., Merico, D., Bisiani, R.: Reasoning support for risk prediction and prevention in independent living. Theory and Practice of Logic Programming 11(2-3), 361–395 (2011)
18. Nath, A., Domingos, P.: A language for relational decision theory. In: International Workshop on Statistical Relational Learning, Leuven, Belgium (2009)
19. Nath, A., Domingos, P.: Efficient belief propagation for utility maximization and repeated inference. In: AAAI (2010)
20. Nishiyama, T., Hibiya, S., Sawaragi, T.: Development of agent system based on decision model for creating an ambient space. AI & Society 26(3), 247–259 (2011)
21. Portet, F., Vacher, M., Golanski, C., Roux, C., Meillon, B.: Design and evaluation of a smart home voice interface for the elderly — Acceptability and objection aspects. Personal and Ubiquitous Computing 17(1), 127–144 (2013)
22. Richardson, M., Domingos, P.: Markov logic networks. Machine Learning 62(1-2), 107–136 (2006)
23. Schilit, B., Adams, N., Want, R.: Context-aware computing applications. In: Proceedings of the Workshop on Mobile Computing Systems and Applications, pp. 85–90. IEEE Computer Society (1994)
24. Vacher, M., Istrate, D., Portet, F., Joubert, T., Chevalier, T., Smidtas, S., Meillon, B., Lecouteux, B., Sehili, M., Chahuara, P., Méniard, S.: The Sweet-Home project: Audio technology in smart homes to improve well-being and reliance. In: EMBC 2011, Boston, USA, pp. 5291–5294 (2011)
25. Wolf, P., Schmidt, A., Klein, M.: Soprano - an extensible, open aal platform for elderly people based on semantic contracts. In: 3rd Workshop on Artificial Intelligence Techniques for Ambient Intelligence, Patras, Greece (2008)

Towards Human Energy Expenditure Estimation Using Smart Phone Inertial Sensors

Božidara Cvetković[1,3], Boštjan Kaluža[1,3], Radoje Milić[2], and Mitja Luštrek[1,3]

[1] Jožef Stefan Institute, Department of Intelligent Systems,
Jamova ceta 39, 1000 Ljubljana, Slovenia
{boza.cvetkovic,bostjan.kaluza,mitja.lustrek}@ijs.si
http://ijs.dis.si
[2] University of Ljubljana, Faculty of Sports
Gortanova 22, Ljubljana, Slovenia
radoje.milic@fsp.uni-lj.si
http://www.fsp.uni-lj.si/
[3] Jožef Stefan International Postgradute Shool
Jamova ceta 39, 1000 Ljubljana, Slovenia
http://www.mps.si

Abstract. This paper is focused on a machine-learning approach for estimating human energy expenditure during sport and normal daily activities. The paper presents technical feasibility assessment that analyses requirements and applicability of smart phone sensors to human energy expenditure. The paper compares and evaluates three different sensor configuration sets: (i) a heart rate monitor and two standard inertial sensors attached to the users thigh and chest; (ii) a heart rate monitor with an embedded inertial sensor and a smart phone carried in the pocket; and (iii) only a smart phone carried in the pocket. The accuracy of the models is validated against indirect calorimetry using the Cosmed system and compared to a commercial device for energy expenditure SenseWear armband. The results show that models trained using relevant features can perform comparable or even better than available commercial device.

Keywords: human energy expenditure, physical activity, wearable sensors, embedded smart phone sensors, regression.

1 Introduction

Medical research has shown that a sufficient amount of physical activity has a positive impact on health and well-being regardless of the age [1–3], and that physical inactivity is one of the leading causes of death worldwide [4]. Although this is widely accepted as a fact, only a small fraction of the population is engaged in regular or sufficient exercise. The key reasons usually include lack of time and fast pace of life. This means that a persuasive technology that would encourage exercise could be greatly beneficial to many people. An important component of such a technology is a possibility to quantify the amount of physical activity

J.C. Augusto et al. (Eds.): AmI 2013, LNCS 8309, pp. 94–108, 2013.

performed during the day. Furthermore, the amount of physical activity can be used to manage the diet of both, a healthy individual or someone who suffers from dietary disease (e.g., diabetes). This raises the question of how can we unobtrusively measure the amount of physical activity.

The cost of physical activity is usually expressed in metabolic equivalents of task (MET), where 1 MET is defined as the energy expended at rest. MET values range from 0.9 (sleeping) to over 20 in extreme exertion. Various methods can be used to reliably estimate energy expenditure (EE). Direct calorimetry [5] measures the heat produced by human body while exercising. This is the most accurate method, but it can be used only in a controlled environment such as a laboratory. Indirect calorimetry [6] measures the carbon dioxide production and oxygen consumption during rest and steady-state exercise. This method can be used outside the laboratory, but it cannot be used in everyday life since its usage requires a breathing mask. Doubly labelled water [7] is a gold standard: it measures the amount of exhaled carbon dioxide by tracking its amount in water which is labelled by deuterium and oxygen-18. This method can be used in everyday life, but it measures the energy expended over longer periods of time and is rather expensive. Finally, the most affordable approach is a commercial wearable sensors such as inertial sensors embedded in armbands and other devices, which are moderately accurate and reliable. These can be used in everyday life and the EE estimation can be done over shorter periods of time.

Inertial sensors as motion sensors are already very popular in different domains such as gaming industry [8, 9], healthcare and medicine [10–12] and security [13]. Their accessibility, ease of use, and understandable concept of accelerometry help broadening its applicability domains on a daily basis. For instance, even running shoes can contain an accelerometer, while an average smart phone contains a wide range of sensors, including an accelerometer. The fact that many of us hardly leave our home without a smart phone made an important impact on development, realization and acceptance of novel smart applications.

This paper thus studies EE estimation using inertial sensors that are present in every commercial armband for EE estimation. It presents a machine-learning approach, and is concerned both with normal daily activities as well as exercise. We compare three sensor configuration sets: (i) a chest strap heart rate monitor and two standard inertial sensors attached at the thigh and chest; (ii) a chest strap heart rate monitor with an embedded inertial sensor and a smart phone carried in the pocket; and (iii) a smart phone carried in the pocket. The accuracy of the EE estimation models is validated against indirect calorimetry approach using the Cosmed system [14] and a commercial device for EE, the SenseWear armband [15]. SenseWear armband show to have the lowest error in free-living situations [16] among the popular physical activity monitors.

The goal of the paper is two-fold: (i) to compare three sensor sets from the one requiring the most dedicated devices, to the one requiring only what most people carry around, i.e., smartphone; and (ii) to present the methodology for the development of an accurate machine-learning model for the EE estimation that can be used on a variety of devices.

The rest of the paper is structured as follows. Section 2 presents the related work; Section 3 presents the sensors used for data collection presented in Section 4. Section 5 contains the details on data pre-processing and feature selection, while section 6 shows experimental results. Section 7 concludes the paper.

2   Related Work

There is a growing trend in development of smart-phone applications for health monitoring, fitness trainers and EE estimation, which is evident at the application markets for mobile platforms. These applications can be divided into two categories; those that use the accelerometer embedded in the smart phone to estimate EE based on the number of steps the user does over one day [17] (essentially pedometers); and those that estimate the intensity of the performed activity and thus the expended energy directly, for example, MyFitnessCompanion [18]. Pedometers can be used only to detect the ambulatory activities, such as walking or running, and not their intensities. MyFitnessCompanion application can detect the intensity, but it has one major shortfall: the user must manually define which activity is being performed. The EE estimation is afterward based on a predefined energy estimation values taken from the Compendium of Physical Activities [19].

Most of the methods based on machine-learning techniques estimate EE using wearable smart phone sensors and seek linear or nonlinear relations between the energy expenditure and the accelerometer outputs. The most basic methods use an accelerometer and a linear regression model. The estimation accuracy can be improved by multiple regression models [20] and complex features [21]. A regression method by Crouter et al. [22], which is currently among the most accurate approaches, uses an accelerometer attached to the hip. In the first step, it classifies a person's activity into sitting, ambulatory activity or lifestyle activity. In the second step, it uses a linear regression model for the ambulatory activity and an exponential regression model for the lifestyle activity. Sitting is always considered to have the energy expenditure of 1 metabolic equivalent of task (MET, 1 MET is the energy expended at rest). A drawback of this method is the exclusion of some important activities, such as cycling, and a larger EE estimation error contributed by the upper body, which is caused by sensor placed at the hip.

There are many available commercial devices, dedicated to EE estimation such as Actigraph [23] and Nike+ [24]. One of the most accurate is the SenseWear armband [15, 16] device, comprising a variety of sensors such as skin temperature detection, heat flux, galvanic skin response and accelerometer. EE estimation is based on activity predicted from the armband accelerometer and data analysis from other sensors. It is highly accurate in EE estimation during sports activities; however, it performs with lower accuracy in case of normal daily activities such as chores.

This paper present an approach with an additional regression model, which is based on the current user's activity in case when at least two sensors are used. The activity is automatically recognised using an activity-recognition classifier. The approach is demonstrated on three sensor configuration sets, including a single smart phone. In this case the activity is not used as one of the features.

The experimental results compare the proposed approach against SenseWear armband developed by Bodymedia [15], and the indirect calorimeter measurement performed by portable Cosmed $k4b^2$ [14].

3   Sensors

We considered five different sensors as shown in Figure 1: first, a wireless Shimmer inertial sensor [25] (Figure 1a); second, an inertial sensor integrated in the Zephyr bioharness chest strap citezephyr (Figure 1b), which also measured heart rate; third, an inertial sensor embedded in a smart phone, in our case a Samsung Galaxy SII smart phone [27] (Figure 1c). Fourth, reference energy expenditure values, which are used to develop and evaluate EE estimation models, were measured using a portable indirect calorimetery system Cosmed $k4b^2$ [14] (Figure 1d), which is considered a gold standard for EE estimation. And fifth, in addition to reference energy expenditure values, we used a commercial product SenseWear armband developed by Bodymedia [15] (Figure 1e) as another baseline for result comparison.

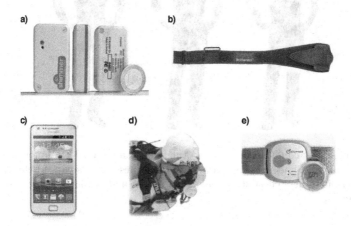

Fig. 1. Used sensors: a) a tri-axial Shimmer inertial sensor, b) a Zephyr bioharness chest-strap with tri-axial inertial sensor and hart rate monitor, c) a Samsung Galaxy SII smart phone, d) a gold standard portable indirect calorimetery Cosmed $k4b^2$ device and e) a SenseWear device for EE estimation

To study the feasibility of EE estimation using smart phone, we approached by gradually decreasing the number of used sensors and evaluating the accuracy of the machine-learning approach for EE estimation (explained in Section 6).

Particularly, we used three sensor configuration sets as shown in Figure 2. The full set consists of two tri-axial inertial sensors, one attached at the chest and the other at the thigh, and a heart rate monitor (Figure 2a). We assume that the full set should provide the lowest EE estimation error.

In the second, embedded set (Figure 2b), we replaced the dedicated inertial sensors with an embedded inertial sensors as follows: the inertial sensor on the chest is replaced with the inertial sensor embedded in the Zephyr chest strap, while the inertial sensor attached to the thigh is replaced with a smart phone containing an embedded inertial sensor. The embedded set is expected to perform the same or worse than the first one, since embedded sensors may contribute some measurement noise.

In the last sensor configuration, the smart-phone set, we removed the chest strap, and used a smart phone embedded inertial sensor only (Figure 2c). The smart-phone set is expected to achieve worse performance than the second configuration. We are interested if the EE estimation error is still in the range of acceptable values.

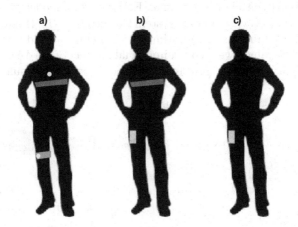

Fig. 2. Three sensor configuration sets: a) the full set, a tri-axial Shimmer inertial sensor attached to chest and thigh and a Zephyr bioharness chest strap, b) the embedded set, a Zephyr bioharness chest strap and smart phone, and c) the smart-phone set, only smart phone

4   Data Collection

A machine-learning approach requires a high quality dataset. For the purpose of EE estimation we must primarily have data with accurate EE values while performing different activities and secondly measurements of various sensors at the same time.

The dataset was collected in a controlled laboratory environment at the University of Ljubljana, Faculty of Sports. The laboratory was equipped with fitness equipment, such as treadmill and indoor bicycle, and a portable Cosmed $k4b^2$ system, which was used to measure reference EE values. The person being measured was supplied with all the sensors mentioned in Section 3; two Shimmer inertial sensors, attached at the chest and the thigh, a Zephyr bioharness, a SenseWear armband, a smart phone, carried in the right pocket downwards with screen towards the body, and the Cosmed system.

The person performed predefined scenarios presented in Table 4, which aim to capture the intensity and EE during free-living activities.

Table 1. Scenarios and activities performed by a person. The last column represents the average measured MET by Cosmed system.

Scenario	Atomic activities	Average MET
Lying	lying	1.2
Basic postures	sitting	1.15
	standing	1.21
	walking	1.37
	transition	1.97
Additional postures	allfours	2.22
	kneeling	1.45
	sitting	2.39
	standing	2.21
	leaning	1.85
	walking	2.75
Ofiice activities	sitting	1.17
Lying excersising	lying	2.12
Light chores	standing	1.68
	walking	2.02
Scrubbing the floor	kneeling	3.20
	allfours	3.03
Shoveling	standing	3.06
	walking	3.60
Walking	walking slowly (4 km/h)	3.02
	walking quickly (6 km/h)	4.54
Stationary cycling	cycling lightly	4.22
	cycling vigorously	6.30
Running	running slowly (8 km/h)	7.70

In more detail, the normal day scenarios are interpreted as follows:

- Lying scenario corresponds to sleeping period when the person's metabolic rate slows down.
- Basic postures scenario corresponds to a normal lazy day.

- Additional postures scenario corresponds to a dynamic day (playing with children on the floor).
- Office activities scenario corresponds to time at the office.
- Lying exercising scenario corresponds to stretching on the floor.
- Light chores scenario corresponds to cooking, serving food, washing dishes, folding/hanging laundry, shopping.
- Scrubbing the floor scenario corresponds to cleaning the floor on hands and knees.
- Shovelling scenario corresponds to digging and shovelling snow.

The sports activities, such as walking, running and cycling, were performed on a treadmill and a stationary bicycle under controlled speed. The EE in a specific scenario differs among activities, for example, standing in the basic posture scenario has EE of 1.21 MET, while standing in the shovelling scenario has EE of 3.06 MET. This indicates that if we can accurately (i) recognise the activity and (ii) detect the intensity, then we can reliably estimate EE, hence EE estimation error should decrease.

We recruited ten healthy people, eight males and two females with different fitness capabilities, to perform the scenarios presented in Table 4. Their body mass index (BMI) ranged from 20 to 28.9. Each person performed all the scenario activities while equipped with the sensors shown in Figure 1; only a single person did not carry the smart phone due to technical issues. The reference EE measured by Cosmed ranged from 0.9 MET to 12 MET.

5   The Methodology

5.1   Data Pre-processing

The collected data can be divided into two groups according to the modality. The first group corresponds to signals from inertial sensors; even-though it is collected from three devices (Shimmer, Zephyr, smart phone), it should be processed using the same mechanism. The second group corresponds to signals from heart rate sensor; this data is processed only if the sensor set configuration uses heart rate sensor).

The stream of data is collected from the connected devices and split into 10 seconds windows, each window overlapping with the previous one by one half of its length. For each overlapping window a set of features is computed. A single inertial sensor contributes 66 features, a heart rate monitor contributes one feature, and the recognised activity (by additional classifier) is considered as an additional feature. The reader is referred to [28, 29] for details on the activity recognition methods and adaptation of activity recognition. The heart rate feature is computed as an average heart rate in the time window.

Features computed from inertial sensor are partially adopted from Tapia [30] (43 features) and partially developed by us (25 features). Adopted features are: mean of absolute signal value, cumulative sum over absolute signal value, entropy, quartiles, variance, inter quartile range, Fourier transform features and mean crossing rate. Features developed by us are: signal peak count, cumulative sum over peak absolute value, cumulative sum over signal absolute value, cumulative sum over signal absolute value after band-pass filtering, cumulative square sum over signal absolute value after band-pass filtering, cumulative sum of square components, square of cumulative sum of components after band-pass filtering, velocity, kinetic energy, vector length, integration of area under vector length curve. In total, there are 136 features for full set and embedded set and 67 features for smart-phone set. These features form a feature vector, which if fed into a machine-learning algorithm to train a model.

5.2   Feature Selection

To filter out redundant features and to reduce calculation complexity we performed feature selection using ReliefF method [31], which returns the features ranked by its predictive power; the returned rank represents the importance of the feature. We proceeded with the first half of the features with a positive rank value, which were then used in the feature vector. The feature selection was performed for each sensor set configuration separately. Note, that feature selection in embedded set and smart phone set was performed with nine people only, since the smart phone data was missing for one person.

Full Set: the first five highest ranked features derived from inertial sensors are velocity (2 features), cumulative sum over peak absolute value (1), prevalent activity (1 feature), cumulative sum over signal absolute value (1 feature). The highest ranked feature is as expected the heart rate. The result is 68 highest ranked features, one from which is heart rate and one is prevalent activity. The prevalent activity can have one of ten values: lying, sitting, standing, standing leaning, allfours, kneeling, transition, walking, running or cycling.

Embedded Set: seven features were ranked negative and were discarded immediately leaving 129 features for selection. The cut of point left 64 features. Highest ranked features are quartiles (3 features) and peak count of thigh (1 feature) and prevalent activity. The prevalent activity can have one of seven values: lying, upright position, allfours, transition, walking, running or cycling. Heart rate feature is at seventh place.

Smart-phone Set: three features were ranked negative and were discarded immediately leaving 64 for the regression model. Since in this configuration we use only one sensor, none of the remaining features are discarded to have a comparable number of features to previous configurations. Highest ranked features are quartiles (4 features) and peak count (1 feature). This set does not contain feature of prevalent activity.

It is interesting to note that our developed features turned out to have better predictive power that the features developed by Tapia [30] in full set. Also at least one of our features were ranked in the first five in the embedded and smart-phone set.

Table 2 shows the number of features per sensor before and after feature selection for all the configuration sets.

Table 2. Number of features per sensor before and after feature selection

Sensors	Full set Before	After	Embedded set Before	After	Smart-phone set Before	After
Shimmer chest	67	39	-	-	-	-
Shimmer thigh	67	27	-	-	-	-
Zephyr inertial sensor	-	-	67	37	-	-
Zaphyr heart rate	1	1	1	1	-	-
Smart phone inertial sensor	-	-	67	25	67	64
Activity*	1	1	1	1	-	-
Total	136	68	136	64	67	64

5.3 The Approach

The main goals are: first, to build an effective model that can be used in each of the sensor configurations; second, to measure EE error; and third, to evaluate the feasibility of EE estimation using a smart phone.

The machine-learning approach, which is shown on Figure 3, comprises four steps. The first step is feature selection, while the second step selects the best performing algorithm. We compared the following six regression algorithms implemented in the Weka suite [32]: support vector regression (SVR), linear regression (LR), multilayer perceptron (MLP), M5-Rules (M5Rules), regression tree M5P (M5P) and regression tree REPTree (REPTree). The third step evaluates the models and analyses the distribution of mean absolute error. In case the error analysis shows that the model could be enhanced, the fourth step reconstructs and updates the regression model based on observation from previous step. When enhancement is not possible, we assume this is the final model. The experiment section reports on each configuration separately.

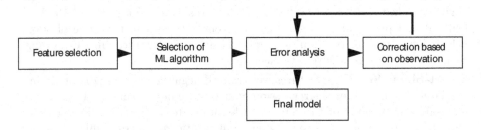

Fig. 3. The workflow of the development of the machine-learning approach

6   Experimental Results

For the experiment we collected the data described in Section 4 and processed as explained in Section 5.

The models are evaluated with two types of error measures. The first error measure is the mean absolute error (MAE) shown in Equation 1. It measures the absolute difference between the predicted and true value. The second error measure is the mean absolute percentage error (MAPE) shown in Equation 2. In contrast to MAE, it measures percentage of the error between the predicted and true value. We believe this error measure might be misleading, since errors are higher when the true value is low and lower when the true value is high; however, we report this measure to ensure comparability with other papers reporting it.

$$MAE = \frac{1}{n} \sum_{1}^{n} |MET_{true} - MET_{predicted}| \tag{1}$$

$$MAPE = \frac{1}{n} \sum_{1}^{n} \left| \frac{MET_{true} - MET_{predicted}}{MET_{true}} \right| \tag{2}$$

6.1 The Full Set

The full-set configuration dataset is described with the first 68 features ranked by the feature selection procedure described in Section 5.2. The performance comparison of different machine-learning algorithms is summarised in Table 4. Each column corresponds to MAE errors of a selected machine-learning approach, while each row corresponds to particular sensor set configuration. The results of the compared algorithms are obtained using 10-fold cross-validation with leave-one-person-out-approach. For example, the first row in Table 4, that is, full configuration, shows that the lowest MAE of 0.65 MET is achieved by support vector regression (SVR). Furthermore, Figure 4 shows the EE estimation error for the support vector regression model. The horizontal axis represents the true MET values, that is, the reference values obtained with Cosmed device, while vertical axis represents the estimated MET values, obtained with SVR model. We can observe that the predicted value is close to the true value. The highest error occurs in case of activities with EE from 2 MET to 8 MET. The highest error occurs in case of activities with the lowest intensity and the highest intensity.

This model alone is already more accurate than SensWear; however, the error analysis shows that the major error occurs in case of ambulatory activities such as walking, running, cycling and activity standing, thus can be improved. In our previous research [33], we observed that training per-class regression model for running and cycling contributes to lower EE estimation error. An improvement upon the error analysis includes training separate regression models for three activities, that is, running, walking and standing. This approach gives the final result, which is shown in Table 4. The MAE is decreased by 0.05 MET and the MAPE is decreased by 3 percentage points. The main insight from the error analysis is that it is beneficial to train separate regression model for individual activities.

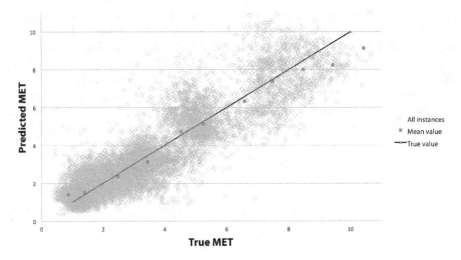

Fig. 4. Predicted MET vs. true MET for full-set configuration

6.2   Embedded Set

The embedded-set configuration dataset is described with the first 64 features ranked by the feature selection procedure. The results of the compared algorithms are obtained using 9-fold cross-validation with leave-one-person-out approach and are shown in the second row in Table 3. The lowest MAE is achieved using SVR. The SVR model outperforms the SensWear; however, the error analysis shows that running activity, if merged into a single regression model, can contribute to lower error.

A retraining of the independent model decreased MAE by 8 percentage point. The MAPE of the final model is higher, but still comparable to SenseWear's.

Figure 5 shows the EE estimation error for the embedded set model trained with SVR. It shows that the error is lower for activities with EE from 2 MET to 7 MET, while the error is higher for activities with the lowest intensity and the highest intensity.

6.3   Smart-Phone Set

The smart-phone set configuration dataset is described with the first 64 features ranked by the feature selection procedure. The results of the compared algorithms are obtained using 9-fold cross-validation with leave-one-person-out approach, which is shown in the third row in Table 3. The SVR outperformed other algorithms by training a model with MAE of 0.83 MET. The model outperforms Senswear's by 3 percentage points according to MAE, while MAPE of the final model is higher, but still comparable to SenseWeare's.

The error pattern is similar as in the previous configurations; however, in this case we cannot perform the adaptation procedure due to unknown activity (the activity recognition model did not perform with satisfactory results at this

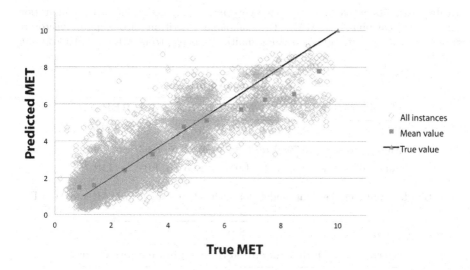

Fig. 5. Predicted MET vs. true MET for embedded-set configuration

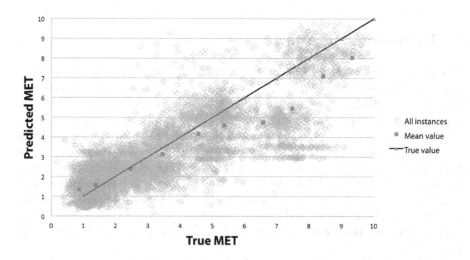

Fig. 6. Predicted MET vs. true MET for smart-phone configuration

point). The future work can focus on activity recognition using smart phone and using it to improve EE estimation.

Figure 6 shows the estimation error for the smart-phone set model trained with SVR. We can observe that the error is low only for the activities with low and moderate intensity from 1.5 MET to 6 MET. The error occurs for the activities with high-moderate and high intensity. MAE is lower than SenseWear's, while MAPE is higher, but still comparable to SenseWear's.

Table 3. Results of machine-learning algorithms for regression for each configuration. The error is calculated as MAE. The compared algorithms are: support vector regression (SVR), linear regression (LR), multilayer perceptron (MLP), M5Rules, M5P, REPTree.

	Algorithms					
Configuration	SVR	LR	MLP	M5Rules	M5P	REPTree
Full set	0.65	0.66	0.70	0.69	0.68	0.68
Embedded set	0.76	0.78	0.83	0.84	0.83	0.81
Smart phone set	0.83	0.88	1.04	1.05	1.04	1.01

Table 4. Results of the final models for each set presented in MAE and MAPE

	Set			
Error	Full	Embedded	Smart phone	SenseWear
MAE (MET)	0.60	0.68	0.83	0.86
MAPE (%)	26.71	33.57	33.97	33.53

7   Discussion and Conclusion

The paper analysed the feasibility of EE estimation during free-living activities using machine-learning, while using dedicated and smartphone inertial sensors. The study gradually decreased the number of sensors used, and evaluated the error for each of the following configurations: (i) the full set with two Shimmer inertial sensors (attached to the chest and thigh) and the heart-rate sensor from the Zephyr chest-strap, (ii)the embedded set with the embedded inertial and heart-rate sensors from the Zephyr chest strap, and the embedded inertial sensor from a smart phone, and (iii) the smart-phone set with the embedded inertial sensor from a smart phone. Additionally, the energy expenditure estimation was compared to a commercial device SenseWear, which also estimates energy expenditure and is currently one of the most accurate devices for free-living activities.

As expected, the best results were obtained using the richest sensor configuration, that is, dedicated inertial sensors and a heart rate sensor. The MAE for this configuration was 0.60 MET, which is 0.26 MET lower than MAE achieved by the SenseWear, while MAPE was lower by approximately 5 percentage points.

The second sensor-set configuration, which consists of embedded sensors placed at the same location as the sensors in the first configuration, achieved the MAE 0.08 MET higher than the first configuration, while still being lower than the SenseWear's by 0.18 MET. The MAPE increased and is comparable to SenseWear's MAPE.

The last sensor set configuration consists of a smart phone only, carried in the pocket. This configuration achieved the highest MAE and MAPE, thus confirming our hypothesis that a reduced sensor set cannot achieve top performance. However, the MAE and MAPE are approximately 0.03 MET lower and 0.5 percentage point higher than Senswear's, respectively. This result leads to the conclusion that smart phone inertial sensors can estimate the energy expenditure roughly as reliably as the current state-of-the-art commercial devices, while using fewer sensors and without requiring a dedicated device.

We used essentially the same methodology with all three sensor set configurations, and we are confident that this methodology can be used with other device as well, not only with dedicated sensors and smart phones. Considering the proliferation of sensors in everyday devices, this observation is increasingly relevant. The future work, apart from the research on features for energy expenditure, will focus on normalizing the smart phone orientation, so that the energy expenditure estimation will be equally reliable regardless of the orientation. Our plans also include and additional effort on activity recognition using only a smart phone, for which a proper orientation normalisation is particularly important. As demonstrated in richer configuration sets, when activities can be recognised with relatively high accuracy, the energy expenditure estimation models achieve lower error rates.

References

1. World health Organization, HEPA, http://www.euro.who.int/
2. Cooper, S.B., Bandelow, S., Nute, M.L., Morris, J.G., Nevill, M.E.: The effects of a mid-morning bout of exercise on adolescents' cognitive function. Mental Health and Physical Activity 5, 183–190 (2012)
3. Hamer, M., Stamatakis, E.: Objectively assessed physical activity, fitness and subjective wellbeing. Mental Health and Physical Activity 3, 67–71 (2010)
4. Kohl, H.W., Craig, C.L., Lambert, E.V., Inoue, S., Alkandari, J.R., Leetongin, G., Kahlmeier, S.: The pandemic of physical inactivity: global action for public health. The Lancet 380, 294–305 (2012)
5. Webb, P., Annis, J.F., Troutman Jr., S.J.: Energy balance in man measured by direct and indirect calorimetry. American Journal of Clinical Nutrition 33, 1287–1298 (1980)
6. Levine, J.A.: Measurement of Energy Expenditure. Public Health Nutrition 8, 1123–1132 (2005)
7. Speakman. J.: Doubly labelled water: Theory and practice. Springer (1997)
8. Nintendo Wii, http://www.nintendo.com/wii
9. EA Sports Active 2, http://www.ea.com/ea-sports-active-2
10. Lustrek, M., Gjoreski, H., Kozina, S., Cvetkovic, B., Mirchevska, V., Gams, M.: Detecting Falls with Location Sensors and Accelerometers. In: Proceedings of the Twenty-Fifth AAAI Conference on Artificial Intelligence and the Twenty-Third Innovative Applications of Artificial Intelligence, pp. 1662–1667. AAAI Press (2011)
11. Kaluza, B., Cvetkovic, B., Dovgan, E., Gjoreski, H., Gams, M., Lustrek, M.: Multiagent Care System to Support Independent Living. International Journal on Artificial Intelligence Tools (accepted for publication, 2013)

12. Aminian, K., Mariani, B., Paraschiv-Ionescu, A., Hoskovec, C., Bula, C., Penders, J., Tacconi, C., Marcellini, F.: Foot worn inertial sensors for gait assessment and rehabilitation based on motorized shoes. In: Annual International Conference of the IEEE Engineering in Medicine and Biology Society, EMBC, pp. 5820–5823. IEEE Press (2011)

13. Owusu, E., Han, J., Das, S., Perrig, A., Zhang, J.: ACCessory: password inference using accelerometers on smart phones. In: Proceedings of the Twelfth Workshop on Mobile Computing Systems and Applications, pp. 91–96. ACM, New York (2012)

14. Cosmed, http://www.cosmed.com/

15. SenseWear, http://sensewear.bodymedia.com/

16. Andre, D., Wolf, D.L.: Recent Advances in Free-Living Physical Activity Monitoring: A Review. J. Diabetes Sci. Technol. 1(5), 760–767 (2007)

17. ACCUPEDO, http://play.google.com/store/apps/details?id=com.corusen.accupedo.te

18. Leijdekkers, P., Gay, V.: User Adoption of Mobile Apps for Chronic Disease Management: A Case Study Based on myFitnessCompanion®. In: Donnelly, M., Paggetti, C., Nugent, C., Mokhtari, M. (eds.) ICOST 2012. LNCS, vol. 7251, pp. 42–49. Springer, Heidelberg (2012)

19. Ainsworth, B.E., Haskell, W.L., Whitt, M.C., Irwin, M.L., Swartz, A.M., et al.: Compendium of physical activities: An update of activity codes and MET intensities. Medicine and Science in Sports and Exercise 32, 498–516 (2000)

20. Heil, D.P.: Predicting activity energy expenditure using the actical activity monitor. Research Quarterly for Exercise and Sport 77, 64–80 (2006)

21. Bouten, C.V., Westerterp, K.R., Verduin, M., Janssen, J.D.: Assessment of energy expenditure for physical activity using a triaxial accelerometer. Med. Sci. Sports Exerc. 26, 1516–1523 (1994)

22. Crouter, S.E., Clowers, K.G., Bassett, D.R.: A novel method for using accelerometer data to predict energy expenditure. Journal of Applied Physiology 100, 1324–1331 (2006)

23. Actigraph, http://www.actigraphcorp.com/

24. Nike+, http://nikeplus.nike.com/plus/

25. Shimmer research, http://www.shimmer-research.com/

26. Zephyr Biohraness, http://www.zephyranywhere.com/products/bioharness-3/

27. Samsung Galaxy SII, http://www.samsung.com/

28. Kozina, S., Gjoreski, H., Gams, M., Lustrek, M.: Three-layer Activity Recognition Combining Domain Knowledge and Meta-classification. J. Med. Biol. Eng. (2013)

29. Cvetković, B., Kaluža, B., Luštrek, M., Gams, M.: Multi-Classifier Adaptive Training: Specialising an Activity Recognition Classifier Using Semi-supervised Learning. In: Paternò, F., de Ruyter, B., Markopoulos, P., Santoro, C., van Loenen, E., Luyten, K. (eds.) AmI 2012. LNCS, vol. 7683, pp. 193–207. Springer, Heidelberg (2012)

30. Tapia, E.M.: Using machine learning for real-time activity recognition and estimation of energy expenditure. Ph.D. Thesis, Massachusetts Institute of Technology (2008)

31. Robnik-Sikonja, M., Kononenko, I.: Theoretical and empirical analysis of ReliefF and RReliefF. Machine Learning 53, 23–69 (2003)

32. Hall, M., Frank, E., Holmes, G., Pfahringer, B., Reutemann, P., Witten, I.H.: The WEKA Data Mining Software: An Update. SIGKDD Explorations 11, 10–18 (2009)

33. Lustrek, M., Cvetkovic, B., Kozina, S.: Energy expenditure estimation with wearable accelerometers. In: 2012 IEEE International Symposium on Circuits and Systems (ISCAS), pp. 5–8. IEEE Press (2012)

Designing Personal Informatics for Self-reflection and Self-awareness: The Case of Children with Attention Deficit Hyperactivity Disorder

Juan Jimenez Garcia, Hilde de Bruyckere, David V. Keyson, and Natalia Romero

Delft University of Technology, Department of Industrial Design Engineering, ID-StudioLab,
Delft, The Netherlands
{j.c.jimenezgarcia,d.keyson,n.a.romero}@tudelft.nl,
h_debruyckere@hotmail.com

Abstract. A main challenge in designing for children with Attention Deficit Hyperactivity Disorder (ADHD) is to support the learning process of supressing undesired behaviour on daily routines by means of positive feedback and rewards. Personal Informatics (PI) is a model that supports capturing and integration of personal data to facilitate reflection and action that is used as a design platform to support behavioral learning. This paper presents a design-driven research study that illustrates the potential of PI to support self-awareness and self-reflection of ADHD children. Two design approaches are described which aim to support self-behavioral inhibition learning: (a) KITA, a Kinesiofeedback Toy for ADHD, being a Tangible User Interface that measures and assesses children's activity and provides them with feedback as to whether or not behavior is within appropriate limits; and (b) WRISTWIT, a Wearable device presenting information on attention and time for ADHD to increase on-task behavior. KITA and WRISTWIT were tested in the field with children as design means to implement PI to positively modify children behavior during daily school routines.

Keywords: Personal Informatics, children, Attention Deficit Hyperactivity Disorder, ADHD, Tangible User Interface, wearable, self-awareness, self-reflection, Empirical Research Through Design.

1   Introduction

ADHD is the most commonly diagnosed behavioral childhood disorder affecting 4% to 7% of children worldwide [1,2]. The main symptoms of ADHD are hyperactivity, inattention and lack of self-control [3]. When working in a class with little personalized supervision, children with ADHD easily loose their attention, start moving more, and stop working [4,5]. With their inability to focus for long periods and the need for stimulu, ADHD children rely on others to support positive behavior by providing external motivation [5]. When their attention has shifted they are often unable to get back to work without an external source telling or reminding them to do it [6].Therefore, the feedback they require has to be delivered at the moment in time

J.C. Augusto et al. (Eds.): AmI 2013, LNCS 8309, pp. 109–123, 2013.

the behavior is present, the point of performance. This makes it hard to treat since therapists, parents and teachers cannot be at each point of performance [5] and it also causes limitations in their independency. Two main behavioral aspects of ADHD that affect school periods were taken as the starting points to explore the role of Personal Informatics (PI) in supporting self-awareness and self-reflection for ADHD children.

The first aspect is related to the motor excess, as the most visible symptom, it is often the first indication parents and teachers detect in children. Over-activity is considered the most disrupting symptom in school setting. It affects their ability to focus on daily life activities, appointments, and goal-accomplishment, which could lead to social problems at home and with peers [1]. ADHD children express their emotions physically by showing unconscious high levels of arousal and energy expenditure. This characteristic requires behavioral interventions and medical therapies to decrease the symptoms. However, current solutions do not encourage children to learn how to self-control in a playful way [7,8,9]. As a result, many of these concepts are impersonal, and not particularly suitable for children to improve their learning experience of self-control and self-monitoring.

The second area focuses on the perception of time where a faulty sense of time awareness and management is seen as one of the underlying symptoms in ADHD [4]. As Barkley states, self-awareness across time is the ultimate yet nearly invisible disability afflicting ADHD individuals [4]. A deficit in time perception is also mentioned by Yang et al. (2007), suggesting that children with ADHD have a faster sense of time internally [10]. Therefore, future goals do not guide their present behavior, leaving them easily distracted by more immediate satisfaction in the here and now when a situation does not provide the immediate consequences or rewards. ADHD children are unable to estimate time spans and seem to feel no clear difference between small and large amounts of time. During classes where the child has to work independently this behavior is more evident. Their uncertainty about time, makes it difficult for them to independently adjust their behavior [10] ADHD children need support on-task behavior as well as support to get their attention back to class when being distracted. Motivation needs to be provided to increase their attention during the whole class.

Personal Informatics (PI) is an emerging area in the field of Human-Computer Interaction that facilitates people to collect and visualize personal relevant information for the purpose to support self-reflection and action for behavioral change [11]. Despite the importance of self-reflection in PI systems, most of the studies to date have been focused on supporting collection and representation of data with the implementation of new automated sensors, tools and attractive visualizations. In line with [12,13], the challenge in PI is the design of meaningful data towards in-depth self-awareness and self-reflection. Based on a review of current PIs, there are no systems that address the needs of children with specific health-related conditions such as Attention Deficit Hyperactivity Disorder in a specific context, such as during daily routines at school.

The following sections describe KITA and WRISTWIT as design studies, which were aimed at exploring the potential of collecting and displaying personal data to support ADHD children at school by facilitating self-awareness and self-reflection on-task behavior. The design and test of these prototypes were conducted by means of the Empirical Research Through Design (ERTD) process [14] in which design concepts were evaluated with teachers, parents and children to define the functional characteristics and the scope of the solutions through iterative design prototypes, which were tested with specific research variables embedded in the designs.

The design experiences described in this paper aims to inform the potential of designing and implementing supportive devices for ADHD, as well as to contribute to Personal Informatics by: (1) extending the challenge in developing devices that focus on the reflection stage as a core source for users to take action towards self-behavior modification, and (2) to provide insights in the design process of such systems with different prototypes iterations tested in-situ for health-related contexts.

2   KITA

Kinesiofeedback Toy for ADHD (KITA) is a behavioral technology device that aims to improve self-monitoring and self-control of kinetic behavior for children between 4-7 years old. Based on insights gained from context mapping techniques [15], observation sessions and mock-ups tested with children, it was found that they are emotionally attached to animals as friendly companions. Therefore, the final prototype is inspired by the design of a creature-like Tangible User Interface (TUI) (Fig 1a). KITA measures physical activity levels using an accelerometer and provides vibration feedback to inform the child that a predefined activity level threshold has been exceeded. A built-in agenda is used to adjust the threshold depending if it is class or break time. Monitoring of activity levels is reinforced during class time in form of a smiley face (Fig. 1b).

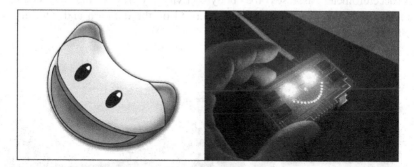

Fig. 1. KITA a) Cartoon-character concept; b) Prototype

2.1   Design and Implementation

Four main design phases led to the development of KITA. In the first phase, on-site observations of children with ADHD were conducted at a regular and a special school for ADHD children in Delft, The Netherlands. In both schools first, second, and third grade classes were observed. Children ranged in age from four to seven. At the special school De Bouwsteen Librijn, observations provided insights on how children and caregivers dealt with ADHD symptoms during class hours and breaks, while the regular school, De Horizon School, provided comparative information about how normal kids behave. Additionally, nine interviews were conducted with 2 specialists, 4 parents and 3 teachers at the special school, and with the teachers of the regular school. Later, a brainstorming session with 2 teachers and 3 design colleagues was conducted. The ideas from participants were helpful to open the possibilities of a toy/game in a form of "the perfect game for ADHD". Three design concepts were finally chosen and developed further through an iterative design process.

The third phase of development involved the test in laboratory of these design concepts with three ADHD children by means of three mock-ups. Each mock-up was related to a pre-defined game in which children had to accomplish specific tasks. The results provided a definition of the functional and non-functional parameters of a final design concept as follows: a) provide time out, reward desired behavior; b) support scheduled activities such as class time and play time; c) support real-time progress feedback; d) use a creature-like toy as a design concept; and e) a friendly companion wear it on the waist.

The fourth phase focused on defining behavior thresholds based on the data provided by an accelerometer. In order to define class-time related thresholds, a prototype with a 3-axis accelerometer was developed to support explorations at school (Fig. 2). Children used the device on their waist in the classroom while they were listening to the teacher and during self-study. This prototype was additionally used to define playtime related thresholds. A game was arranged with 10 children in the playground to observe the maximum levels they could get while playing with the device on their waist. Along with observations, the data analysis suggested kinetic behavior boundaries that were used as parameters to deliver feedback. The used of a 3-axis accelerometer assesses the body activity by registering the counts of movements in X,Y,Z axes. These counts depend on the duration and intensity of a single movement.

Fig. 2. Initial prototype. Collecting inertial data to define kinetic behavior thresholds during class time.

2.2   Final Concept and Prototype

The toy consists of two main parts: KITA, the creature companion, removable and portable (Figure 3), that aims to support self-control and self-monitoring by providing feedback on behavior progress; and its nest, a ball (Figure 3), addresses self-reflection by providing dynamic rewards.

After KITA' battery has been charged all night while placed in its nest, the child removes KITA from the ball and takes it to school. If the child wants to play with KITA afterwards, he needs to take care of it by letting KITA sleeps during class time. In this way, KITA will be happy and rested enough to play. When the device detects excess body behavior during class time vibration feedback is provided. Whether the child exceeds the defined number of activity counts during a preset time interval, or he remains in the defined activity threshold, KITA communicates the event to the child by means of its changing moody face. KITA's face involves two main parts: a) the eyes that help the child to be aware when is class time (sleeping state) and play time (awake state); and b) the smile that represents how the good/bad behavior of the child progresses overtime at school. The better the child behaves the wider is the KITA's smile. The visualization of the data as a smiley face facilitates self-monitoring on the go. The final prototype comprises in total 31 LEDs to represent KITA's face, a vibration motor, a rechargeable battery, a 3-axis accelerometer and an IR sensor to detect when KITA is placed in the ball to transfer the collected data to the ball (Fig. 3a).

Later at home, the child can place KITA in its nest. The ball reacts accordingly to the data assessed by KITA during the day. As a reward, the child is able to play with it using KITA's nest. The ball provides sounds and light feedback showing how happy KITA is after school (Fig. 3b). The amount of playtime is based on the assessment of kinetic behavior performed during school time. It is stated that ADHD children lack in bringing their over-arousal to normal levels when they have started an exciting activity [33]. Therefore, after playing for a while, KITA communicates to the child that it is getting tired, encouraging him to cool-down along, thus, reducing his arousal level. This feedback, enabled by a programmed microcontroller, aims to tutor the child to stop at the right time. KITA's nest comprises the micro-controller, a speaker, 8 LEDs, an IR sensor and a rechargeable battery.

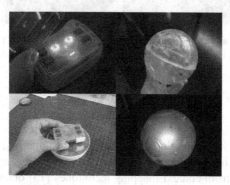

Fig. 3. KITA's main components: a) Left. KITA's face expressions and nest b) Right: rubber ball containing KITA's nest and providing sound and light feedback

2.3   Test and Summary of the Results

To evaluate how KITA elicited the intended behavior, two days of baseline measurement, were followed by two days of intervention with two ADHD children. In the baseline condition, the KITA display was concealed and measurements of children physical activity patterns were taken during class time (Fig. 4a). Raw data was collected registering how many peaks of high activity were detected during class time, in relation to the smile progress of KITA after each class session and the final smile at the end of the school day. Results of baseline and intervention were compared to detect behavioral change in relation to the displayed smile progress in KITA. Although the pilot test was short to draw conclusive results, initial findings showed an interesting trend in which children's activity level in class was reduced by 16% when using KITA.

After the tests, interviews were conducted with 2 teachers and the children that participated in the test to get insights about how they felt when using the prototype. Children reported to feel attached and curious about making KITA happier. Although children felt proud of having such a toy during class, further research is need to investigate to what degree the sense novelty of the toy may decrease over time, affecting children's sense of attachment with KITA.

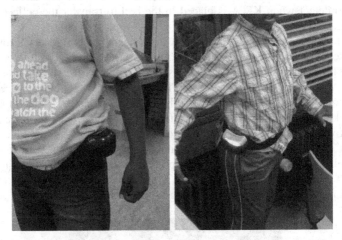

Fig. 4. a) Left, baseline and b) right, intervention. The device featured two different shields to hide and expose KITA's feedback capabilities.

3   WRISTWIT

WRISTWIT is a wearable device targeted at ADHD children between 8-12 years old to improve their ability to work independently by supporting sense of time and attention in classes, where the environment cannot provide this much needed support. With insights gained from context mapping techniques [15] observations and a focus group with children, the design concept resulted into a personal bracelet that provides information to the child. WRISTWIT is designed to increase on-task behavior by: (1)

increasing the sense of time, the bracelet displays time progress in a low-complex visual representation of 60 minutes by using 12 LED lights, each LED representing 5 minutes; and (2) increasing the level of attention, the device monitors body movement by means of an accelerometer alerting the child when he or she is inattentive.

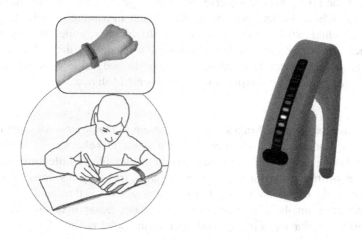

Fig. 5. WRISTWIT. Bracelet in use.

3.1   Design and Implementation

Exploring Time Perception in ADHD Children. The final concept of WRISTWIT was preceded by 2 explorative phases. The first phase consisted of observations and interviews that took place at two schools in The Netherlands to understand how ADHD behavior is specific to time in the school context. In total 7 observation sessions of 1 to 3 hours took place and 15 qualitative interviews were conducted with 8 teachers, 4 experts and 5 parents, giving the possibility to pose questions that arose during observations. Observations started at a regular elementary school in Delft, at the De Oostpoort. Two groups of children (age 8-10) and two groups (age 10-12) were observed during times in which at least one hour of independent study was required. Next, observations took place at a special elementary school, De Elsenburgschool, in Rijswijk for children with learning disabilities where 10-20% of children are diagnosed with ADHD. The researchers attended a regular class day with three groups with ages ranging from 8-9, 9-11 and 10-12. Later, in order to receive more in-depth information on time, attention and motivation, a focus group was conducted with 5 children. The qualitative information provided by sensitizing booklets used during the session was analyzed and categorized in quotes and themes with concluding statements that helped to define the requirements for WRISTWIT. When looking over the resulted insights, the need to help student's behavior by providing a sense of time and help focus attention was evident here. It was also found that children with ADHD work best with a qualitative over quantitative way of representing time.

Exploring Movement Measure by an iPhone App. In the second phase insights were gained on body movement as a measure to predict the child's attention. Three children participated in a test using the 3-axis accelerometer of an iPhone with the application Accelerometer Data Pro [16]. A consent form was provided before the session allowing the researchers to observe and videotape the tests. Before the test children wore the iPhone for an hour and a half without measuring in order to get used to it. Each child worked independently for 20 minutes while wearing the smartphone measuring movement of the non-dominant hand. The data of all axes provided by the accelerometer is combined to come to one value of movement, allowing the plotted graph to be compared with the observed behavior.

Findings from the Explorative Stages. The comparison of the observations and the measured activity lead to a classification of three types of behavior: 1) On-task behavior (e.g. working as required by the teacher), is measurable by little movement, whereas 2) clear off-task behavior (e.g. when the child trows up his arms or acts goofy) is seen with larger amounts of movement above a threshold and 3) intermediate behavior involves an amount of movement larger than on-task but smaller than off-task behavior (Fig. 6). Task that seem useful at first, for instance, getting up to get a book, are often used by children with ADHD as a form of inattention and looking for stimuli. Such activitiess, can be distinguished by longer performance of movement and a more frequent occurrence within a certain timespan. Two children showed on-task behavior the first 8 minutes and performed more intermediate and off-task behavior later, whereas the third participant displayed regular intermediate and off-task behavior from the beginning. The results showed that an off-task behavior or larger amounts of intermediate behaviors are often the start of more and consecutive off-task behaviors, confirming literature [6], and demonstrating that returning to on-task work by themselves is difficult to do. The types of behavior classified matched the amount of movement in 25 instances, in only 4 instances it did not.

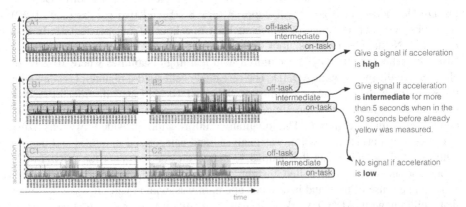

Fig. 6. Giving the signal at the right moment. Rules on when to give a signal based on movement and time.

3.2   Final Concept and Prototype

Therefore, WRISTWIT provides 4 visual feedback forms to support on-task behavior : a timer, a work signal, performance during class and score (Fig 7). When inattentive behavior is visible in an increased amount of restless body movements, the device provides feedback in the form of a work signal to get their attention back to work. The visual feedback is combined with vibration stimuli to make the child aware of their inattention.

To build up self-reflection moments and give children with ADHD the ability to link behavior to consequences, two additional forms of feedback are provided. Both are shown at the end of the class to ensure their attention to be on-task during class and create a motivating form of excitement. The performance of the class is shown at the end of each class by LEDs in the timer presenting a green, yellow and orange color-coding. It displays how the child behaved at which point in time: green for little movement and therefor attentive, yellow for less attentive and orange for even less. To keep the system positive red is not used (see Figure 7.c).

The amount of drop-shaped LEDs increases as the behavior is better. The drops, made up with 12 LEDs next to the LEDs from the timer, motivate the child to do better as it is something they desire to have: collect more of and share with others the results if wanted. The bracelet has a simple design that blends in with other bracelets children wear.

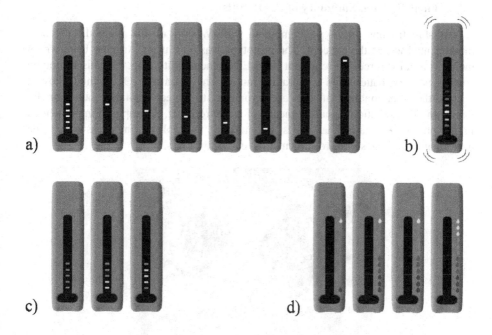

Fig. 7. WRISTWIT' feedback visualizations: a) timer b) worksignal c) performance d) score

Later at home, the child connects the bracelet to the computer and the drops collected on the bracelet are translated to an amount of water to nurture a plant (Fig. 8a). The amount of water represents the score of that day, more water means better behavior; the child can compare today's performance to other days of the week (Fig 8b).

Fig. 8. WRISTWIT additional software. a) Left, today, drops grow a flower; b) right, comparison between days.

3.3   Final Test and Summary of the Results

A semi-functioning prototype combined with Wizard of Oz method [17] was implemented to test the concept. The prototype was built using Arduino Uno, which included a color screen to represent the LEDs functionality (Fig. 8). This prototype comprises a 9V battery and a vibration motor. The Wizard of Oz method allowed testing the functionality of the accelerometer to detect off-tasks behavior by simulating the vibration signal by means of an IR-receiver. A strap was implemented in the prototype to attach all parts and make it wearable during class time. The performance and the score are shown at the end of the class.

Fig. 9. Prototype components. Battery pack, Arduino One and vibration motor.

To evaluate how well children understood WRISTWIT and how much it was useful in supporting on-task behavior, a two days test was conducted with three children (Fig. 10). The parents signed a consent form. Participants were scheduled to use the prototype twice on the first day and three times on the second day, but due to limited testing time one child only tested twice in total. Each test lasted 20 minutes and took place in a class in which all children work independently. Only the basics of the prototype and its functionalities were explained beforehand. Based on the knowledge gained from observations with children, the researchers observed the behavior of the child and used the remote to give a work signal when the child was distracted. After each test a short interview allowed the researchers to get insights about the child's experiences with the device. A final interview checked their full understanding of the product. The material was analyzed and categorized for each function.

Fig. 10. Prototype in test

The results from the movement measurement study and the prototype test showed that it is possible to use movement as a measure for inattention. It was reported that each signal was understood by the children at first instance and elicited the intended reaction. Children compared their performance with their score supporting self-reflection processes. Difficulties with the prototype, giving unintended work signals due to signal communication failures, showed that children were aware of it reporting that was not fair, displaying more awareness of their own behavior. By simply wearing WRISTWIT and having the timer worked as a reminder. All children were committed to work as long as the timer was on. Interestingly, one of them continued during the break because the timer feedback had not been triggered yet.

Interviews conducted with teachers, parents and children after the tests gave insights on how children felt using the prototype. Children expressed feeling proud of collecting the drops, eager to get more and knowing what to do to improve. The personal character of the product was appreciated by all of them. Parents and teachers believed the personal character of the product motivates children more than other external motivation provided by them. Although the feedback signals of score and performance were found to motivate children to reflect on their personal results in order to improve their behavior, more extensive research is needed to see if these initial findings apply to a wider sample of participants and for longer periods of time. A larger study is also needed to understand how a drop in active behavior during class increases attention towards on-task behavior.

4   Discussion

The design and evaluation of Personal Informatics solutions for ADHD children poses some challenges that are worth to discuss for the future development of KITA and WRISTWIT. The discussion addresses issues regarding the challenges of designing PI systems that go beyond the technicalities of collection, storage and data analysis and how these systems are conceived and tested in-situ.

4.1   Supportive Role: Facilitating Reflection

One of the biggest challenges in Personal Informatics is to provide meaningful information users can reflect upon in order to support self-awareness and self-reflection, to subsequently, encourage behaviour modification based on action. KITA and WRISTWIT share a common point: they support awareness and reflection by strengthening their roles on how the collected data from inertial sensors can be integrated and delivered to children with specific needs such as ADHD. As stated by [19], PI systems should be informative, effortless and simple to engage with. Low complexity interfaces have the potential to be more effective at motivating users in the long-term. KITA translates real-time physical behaviour data into a smiley face helping ADHD children to understand, in a way they had not thought about before, how their behaviour has short and long-term consequences. The progression of a bigger smile and awake/sleepy eyes facilitate self-monitoring progress in a friendly way. The use of a moody creature-like toy enabled children's level of engagement with the device. They stated that making his/her creature more and more happy was challenging and worth to try. On the other hand, WRISTWIT, provides data abstraction and visualizations facilitating the aspect of self-monitoring during on-tasks behaviours at school. Not only by measuring child's inattention by assessing excess of body movement, but even more important to visualize time progression in a simple way, WRISTWIT gives the opportunity for children to self-monitor time on the go and sustained interest over time. Moreover, the haptic characteristic of KITA as a creature-like toy, and WRISTWIT as a bracelet offered opportunities to initiate an immediate engagement with children, inviting them to explore. A sensing-based interaction with meaningful information can engage children in a new way of thinking and it can fit their natural way of learning by exploring and playing with the material world.

4.2   Personal Informatics in the Context: Designing and Testing In-situ

The challenge of Personal Informatics is to design solutions that will succeed in becoming part of people's daily routines in their living context. In order to find directions to address this challenge, both prototypes were developed and tested in-situ, with children, teachers and caregivers providing knowledge and personal preferences regarding ADHD treatment experiences. By means of several mock-ups and functional prototypes for both KITA and WRISTWIT, it was possible to explore what kind of information should be supplied that fits on the particular needs of

ADHD children, as well as define when this information should be delivered based on the requirements of a specific context such as the school. The studies during class time provided insights of their use. We discuss that these insights of testing in-situ two proof-of-concepts bring forward a more direct and relevant design considerations for Personal Informatics targeting ADHD children. Considering design and testing in-situ complements the role of KITA and WRISTWIT in addressing individual interest of 4-7 and 8-12 years old children facilitating their understanding of the provided feedback.

5   Conclusions and Future Work

Design and conceptualization process of the two prototypes discussed in this paper were derived from observations and interviews that took place in four schools. Witnessing class transitions between instruction, free and work time, exercise and play time provided information about how ADHD children behave during school, what they like to play, how teachers deal with burst of misbehaviors, as well as, information about time-awareness and constrains that a school setting could bring to children behavior. Next, in total 12 interviews with teachers, specialists, parents and children gave the possibility to pose questions that arose during observations. Researchers were interested in gaining insights about how children with ADHD experience rewards, restless periods, and time-awareness. Sensitizing booklets that enabled participants to provide more in-depth information followed these interviews. The material was analyzed and categorized in quotes and themes with concluding statements that helped researchers to define the design directions. First prototype iterations aimed to get insights into how body movement is a good measure to detect misbehavior and on/off-task behavior. In total 5 children participated in two tests. Two mock-ups, one designed for KITA using off-the-shelf accelerometer, and one more built specifically for WRISTWIT using an Arduino micro-controller. It is acknowledged that a higher number of testers are needed to be representative for a generalization in behavior change and self-awareness. However, the initial results open an interesting discussion about self-reflection in PI systems, it gave to the researchers rich insights about designing PI systems for a specific condition and context as ADHD, and it provided initial data that is possible to detect most of the behaviors right, and when the feedback signal can be given.

The design process of KITA and WRISTWIT was based on Empirical Research through Design process [14], User Centered Design methods and in-situ evaluations to inform the design of Personal Informatics devices for ADHD. The two experimental prototypes focused on integrating and visualize raw data of physical activity that fits in children's daily routines at school time. The design work demonstrates the potential for increasing children awareness with engaging feedback at the moment the child needs. ADHD behavior, reflected as activity patterns during the school day (KITA) or when time-based concentration is at risk, KITA and WRISTWIT, respectively, demonstrate the potential for ambient sensing technology and novel user-centered interfaces.

Acknowledgments. We are very grateful to the schools De Bouwsteen Librijn, De Horizon, De Oostpoort in Delft, and De Elsenburgschool, in Rijswijk for their support and interest, as well as the specialists, teachers, parents and children who actively contributed to the development and tests of these projects.

References

1. Szatmari, P.: The epidemiology of attention- deficit hyperactivity disorders. In: Weiss, G. (ed.) Attention-Deficit Hyperactivity Disorder, vol. 1, pp. 361–371. Saunders, Philadelphia (1992)
2. National Institutes of Health [NIH]. National Institutes of Health consensus development conference statement: Diagnosis and treat- ment of Attention Deficit/Hyperactivity Disorder (ADHD). Journal of the American Academy of Child and Adolescent Psychiatry 39, 182–193 (2000)
3. Barkley, R.A.: Attention-Deficit/Hyperactivity Disorder. In: Mash, E.J. (ed.) Child Psychopathology, pp. 75–143. Guilford Press, New York (2003)
4. Hallahan, D.P., Lloyd, J.W., Kauffman, J.M., Weiss, M.P., Martinez, E.A.: Learning Disabilities: Foundations, Characteristics and Effective Teaching, pp. 277–280 (2005)
5. GreatSchools.: Excerpts from his [Barkley's] lecture in San Francisco, CA on June 17, 2000 (2008) (retrieved April 6, 2012)
6. Fowler, M.: Increasing on-task performance for students with ADHD. New Jersey Education Association Review (2010)
7. AAPB, Applied Psychophysiology & Biofeedback, http://www.aapb.org
8. Klingberg, T., Fernell, E., Olesen, P., Johnson, M., Gustafsson, P., Dahlström, K., Gillberg, C., Forssberg, H., Westerberg, H.: Computerized Training of Working Memory in Children with ADHD – a Randomized, Controlled, Trial. J. American Academy of Child and Adolescent Psychiatry 44(2), 177–186 (2005)
9. Tryon Warren, W., Shick, T.G., Kazlausky, T., Gruen, W., Swanson, J.M.: Reducing Hyperactivity with a Feedback Actigraph: Initial Findings. Clinical Child Psychology and Psychiatry (2006)
10. Yang, B., Chan, R.C.K., Zou, X., Jing, J., Mai, J., Li, J.: Time perception deficit in children with ADHD. Brain Research 1170, 90–96 (2007), doi:10.1016/j.brainres. 2007.07.021
11. Ian, L., Anind, D., Jodi, F.: A stage-based model of personal informatics systems. In: Proceedings of the 28th International Conference on Human Factors in Computing Systems, Atlanta, Georgia, USA, April 10-15 (2010)
12. Pirzadeh, A., He, L., Stolterman, E.: Personal informatics and reflection: a critical examination of the nature of reflection. In: CHI Extended Abstracts 2013, pp. 1979–1988 (2013)
13. Munson, S.A.: Mindfulness, Reflection, and Persuasion in Personal Informatics. In: Personal Informatics Workshop, CHI 2012, May 6 (2012)
14. Keyson, D.V., Bruns, M.: Empirical research through design Proceedings And Conference Contributions. Empirical research through design. In: Proceeding of the Proceedings of the International Association of Societies of Design Research Conference (IASDR 2009), Seoul, Korea, October 18-22, pp. 4548–4557 (2009)
15. Visser, F.S., Stappers, P.J., Van der Lugt, R., Sanders, E.B.: Contextmapping: experiences from practice. CoDesign 1(2), 119–149 (2005)

16. Wavefrontlabs, Accelerometer Data Pro (retrieved October 27, 2012)
17. Kelley, J.F.: An iterative design methodology for user- friendly natural language office information applications. ACM Trans. Inf. Syst. 2(1), 26–41 (1984), doi:http://doi.acm.org/10.1145/357417.357420
18. O'Malley, C., Fraser, D.: Literature Review in Learning with Tangible Technologies. Nesta Futurelab series. Report 12 (2005), http://www.nesta-futurelab.org/research/reviews/reviews_11_and12/12_01.htm
19. Burns, P.J., Christopher, L., Shlomo, B.: Using Personal Informatics to Motivate Physical Activity: Could we be doing is wrong? In: CHI 2012 Workshop, vol. 1 (2012)

A Robotic Fitness Coach for the Elderly

Binnur Görer, Albert Ali Salah, and H. Levent Akın

Department of Computer Engineering, Boğaziçi University,
Istanbul, Turkey
{binnur.gorer,salah,akin}@boun.edu.tr

Abstract. The ultimate goal of ambient assisted living is to help elderly people live a healthy life in the convenience of their homes by making more intelligent technology bring them a set of required assistive tools. In this paper we describe a robotic fitness coach that learns a set of physical exercises from a professional trainer, and assists elderly subjects in performing these gestures. The gestures were selected from an actual training programme at an elderly care home. When demonstrating gestures, the robot performs the learned gestures to the best of its abilities, and while monitoring the elderly subject with an RGB-D camera, provides verbal guidance to complement the visual display, correcting gestures on the fly. We provide a detailed description of the training programme, the gesture acquisition, replication and evaluation algorithms, our solution to the robot stability problem, and a set of preliminary user tests to validate our approach.

1 Introduction

Ambient assisted living is a concept that summarizes the effort to create intelligent technologies to help elderly people live their lives without constant supervision from costly health personnel, as well as to improve their quality of life by offering solutions to typical problems related with age and its physical and social implications [1]. The primary goal in this enterprise is a preventive approach of healthcare for elderly, sometimes summarized by the concept of 'successful aging', where the subject retains and sustains its physical and mental well-being. Both physical and mental health require regular activity (possibly in form of regular exercises) for this purpose.

Performing regular physical exercise has well-known benefits for the elderly [2]. Through improvements in blood pressure regime, it helps reducing heart-related problems, most importantly helping the prevention of coronary heart diseases. As such, it makes sense to consider approaches to promote physical activities for the elderly. While there are findings that hospital-based rehabilitation is more effective than unsupervised home-based exercises [3], the introduction of smart technologies to supervise the latter may help in bridging the gap.

This paper proposes an approach to create a robotic fitness coach, and primarily concerns itself with the physical, rather than the mental fitness of the subject. Here, an early disclaimer is in order. A human fitness coach performs a series

J.C. Augusto et al. (Eds.): AmI 2013, LNCS 8309, pp. 124–139, 2013.

of complex tasks including assessing a subject's physical condition, creating a fitness program for the subject by taking into account a number of observed and known physical constraints, monitoring and adapting the program according to the progress and engagement of the subject (or the lack thereof), and performs all these while bearing responsibility for the health condition of the subject. We do not use the term 'coach' to incorporate all these functions, as many of which are beyond the abilities of current robotic and expert systems. The system we propose has the much more modest goal of assisting a real fitness coach in letting an elderly subject perform a given set of physical exercises.

The adaptation of the exercise program to the subjects individual needs requires expert knowledge. Once a set of individualized exercises are developed, the subject needs to perform these regularly over long periods. It is at this point where a robotic companion would play an important role, by monitoring the subject and its performance, as well as by motivating the subject through an engaging and fun interface. Subsequently, we propose two different modes of operation. In our application scenario, the robot learns the set of exercises from the physician or the fitness coach by observation and imitation. When in operation, the robot performs the exercises to the best of its abilities, and supervises the performance of the subject. Every once in a while, the fitness coach assesses and revises the exercise program. It is not practical to let a computer scientist encode new exercises into the coaching robot each time, so the robot should learn exercises automatically from the fitness coach. This part stands for the practical significance of our work. We facilitate the imitation system for gesture realization on real robot and investigate the applicability of this system for a robotic fitness coach by evaluating the user responses.

The first challenge in the proposed method is to analyse the coach's gestures automatically to form a good representation of the performed gesture. This is accomplished by the recently popularized RGB-D camera approaches to track the body of the coach. The second challenge is due to the fact that the robot possesses a different physical embodiment than the fitness coach (or the subject, for that matter) and hence is an imperfect intermediary interface. We discuss how the mapping of human gestures to the robot can be accomplished. The performance criteria for the robot's gesture are the stability and smoothness of the actual move, as well as the perceptual validity of the appearance of the robot.

The second operation mode of our application consists of exhibition of the learned gestures by the robot and providing vocal explanations about the performed motion. The challenge is to synchronise vocal explanation with the shown gesture so that both auditory and visual perception of the subject are kept active. The robot also gives vocal feedback on the success of the imitated gesture to correct it, if necessary.

This paper is structured as follows. In Section 2, we describe some related work in this area. Our proposed system is detailed in Section 3. Section 4 provides a list of most common exercises performed in training sessions for elderly. We provide initial results we have obtained with a working prototype, and report a set of preliminary user studies in Section 5, and conclude the paper with a discussion of the challenges and future directions envisaged for this work in Section 6.

2 Related Work

A social assistive robot (SAR) is a socially interactive robot whose primary goal is assistance [4]. Our approach is positioned in the related literature primarily as a SAR with non-contact assistance. There are a number of existing SAR systems [5], Marcel Heerink gives a detailed overview of these in [6]. Most of these systems focus on monitoring the elderly [7], or in helping them in their daily tasks. There are relatively few systems that target physical exercise applications. Rehabilitation robots that are created for physical training usually do not have a person-like embodiment [8], and lack the social aspect completely, which is found to be useful in elderly care scenarios [9].

Most existing systems for home based elderly physical training do not involve robots at all. An example is Respondesign's MayaFit Virtual Fitness Trainer, which uses Kinect-based motion analysis and a screen-based interface to guide subjects through physical exercises [10]. This system requires the precise specification of each gesture, and does not involve automatic imitation based learning. In [11] a web system is proposed for facilitating repetitive movement training. The subject is tracked with two cameras attached to a home PC.

Obviously, an embodied conversational agent (ECA) or a similar 3D avatar displayed on a screen would provide a much more realistic visualization of the target exercise. In [12] such a system was proposed. However, lacking physical and tangible embodiment, such a system may be at a certain disadvantage in terms of engaging the subject, when compared to a social robot. Indeed Fasola and Mataric have contrasted the user responses to physical robot and virtual robot in an exercising scenario, and found that the subjects rated the robot to be more engaging, enjoyable, and a better exercise partner [13]. In [14], the authors show that the mimicking tendency of the subjects are higher for real robot than virtual robot in a scenario of physiotherapy where the robot is utilized as an assistant to the physiotherapist.

In [15], a robotic exercise coach is proposed for chair aerobics, and the authors evaluate the motivational aspects of this scenario extensively. For instance, the robot always provides positive feedback on successfully completed exercises, and never gives negative feedback, because sustaining motivation over longer periods is one of the keys to building a successful system. One of the motivational factors the authors have used is providing numeric feedback on the task success, which 'gamifies' the experience, and makes it more engaging through the feeling of challenge.

In [16], a humanoid RoboPhilo robot is used in a physical exercise scenario that is similar to the one we propose. This robot has 20 degrees of freedom (DOF) that enable the turning movements of the head, waist, and thighs and joint movements of the limbs. In the proposed scenario, computer vision techniques are used to detect the face and hand positions, from which two gestures are detected: head turn, and hand raise, respectively. The robot gives vocal feedback when the gesture it performs is successfully imitated by the elderly. However, the feedbacks do not include any corrective information for the gestures which can not be imitated correctly by the elderly and they are provided for only two types of gestures.

For analysis of the gestures performed by the elderly, visual assessment is preferred to wearable sensors for ease of use. In [17], the robot compares the user's current arm angles to the pre-specified goal arm angles to determine whether an exercise is performed correctly, or not. A standard RGB camera is used for gesture analysis, and the visual analysis is performed against a uniform background which is not preferable for a daily use system such as robotic fitness coach. In this approach, there are no gesture-specific weights assigned to different joints, whereas in most physical exercises, the value and range of some angles are much more important than others.

Other approaches to exercising the elderly involve for instance the design of interactive games. Playful interaction for serious games is a recent area that is receiving more attention. Representative examples for physical exercise scenarios are given in [18] and [19]. A taxonomy of games for rehabilitation is given in [20].

3   Methodology

We use a robot, a Kinect, and a robotic simulator in the proposed scenario. The system works in two modes. In the first mode, the human coach 'teaches' the robot the desired exercise, and records the accompanying verbal description. In the second mode, the robot demonstrates the exercise to a subject, monitors and provides feedback on the performed gesture.

3.1   Gesture Learning from a Human Demonstrator

In our system, the human demonstrator is expected to perform the gesture in front of the robot, while marking the gesture boundaries via simple vocal commands such as "start" and "end". The robot is then expected to imitate the motion sequence performed between this interval, and store it for further reference. The visual input (i.e. the exercise performed by the human coach) is acquired with a Kinect camera, and the skeleton is extracted with the OpenNI software. The obtained joint angles are transformed to a set of corresponding Nao joint angles. The exercise is then assessed for the physical limits of Nao; if it involves stretching of limbs, or rotation of joints not available to the robot, the vocal assistance module is assumed to complement the system. At this moment, this is simply a recording (and replication) of the coach's vocal instruction (e.g. "...and stretch both arms"). Then the exercise plan is passed to the Webots simulation software, which assesses the stability of the gesture. If this check is not passed, joint angle positions are optimized to obey stability conditions in a way to produce minimal deviation from the desired appearance. Then the exercise is stored in a database

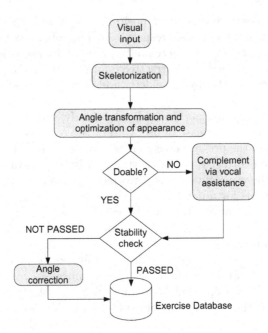

Fig. 1. Flowchart of the proposed system for gesture learning from a human demonstrator

for further reference. A flowchart is given in Figure 1 to summarize the proposed system.

Gesture Imitation. In order to map human gestures to the robot, the first challenge to be handled is to specify the embodiment differences between human and robot. Due to the anatomic differences, the robot is not able to imitate every motion of the human successfully. The Nao robot has a much smaller number of degrees of freedom than the human and the limits of each joint differs from the corresponding ones in humans. Hence, a robust mapping system is needed to allow the Nao to be able to imitate as many different motions as possible. We represent the gestures in terms of a 3D skeleton of joints and their connections.

We use two main criteria to determine the success of the gesture generated by the robot through the mapping system: the stability of the robot, and the similarity between the robot's motion and the human's motion, respectively. We use a simple approach for the similarity, and take the sum of absolute values of joint angle differences in the human and the robot. As mentioned earlier, a better approach would be to consult the physician about the relevance of each gesture component, for each gesture. That would, however, require explicit supervision. Another possibility is to let the fitness coach demonstrate each gesture multiple times, and discount joints that show high variance in their angle values. This in turn would require that the fitness coach is aware of this procedure, and exhibit such variance consciously.

The stability of the robot is a very important restrictive factor in exhibiting whole body motions. Especially raising a leg usually requires that the arms help in stabilizing the robot, lest it should fall. On the other hand, upper body motion imitation can be performed much more easily. Hence, the overall system should be evaluated separately for upper body motion and whole body motion imitation.

Upper Body Motion Imitation. The Nao robot has four degrees of freedom in its arm, which are shoulder pitch, shoulder yaw, elbow yaw, and elbow roll joints, respectively[1]. Humans also have the same number of DOF in their arms, but there are three of them in the shoulders and only one DOF is used for the elbow [21]. Hence, direct mapping from human arm joint angles to the Nao angles will not produce correct motions. To handle the difference in embodiments, a combination of inverse and forward kinematics is used.

We use an additional external RGB-D camera (i.e. Kinect) mounted on Nao's platform in this study. The positions of joints for the human skeleton are provided by the OpenNI software[2]. When the bones are treated as vectors whose initial and terminal points are defined by the two joint positions J_1, J_2 respectively, the angles between the bones and the XY, YZ and XZ planes give the angle ϕ of the joint J_1:

$$\phi = \arccos(|V|/|Proj(V_x)|)$$
$$x \in \{XY, YZ, XZ\}, V = \overrightarrow{J_1J_2} \tag{1}$$

The angle between the upper and the lower arm is found using the following formula:

$$\theta = \frac{V1*V2}{|V1|.|V2|} \tag{2}$$

where $*$ stands for scalar product of vectors, and $V1$ and $V2$ represent upper arm and lower arm, respectively. The same formula can be used for the angle between upper and lower legs.

These joint angles are first pre-processed to obey the limit angles of robot joint intervals. Afterwards, a Kalman filter, given in Eq. 3, is applied to eliminate the sudden changes in skeleton joint positions due to camera noise:

$$
\begin{aligned}
p &= p + q; \\
k &= p/(p + r); \\
x &= x + k*(m - x); \\
p &= (1 - k)*p
\end{aligned}
\tag{3}
$$

where p is estimation error covariance, q is process noise covariance, r is measurement noise covariance, k is the Kalman gain, x is the proposed value and m is the observed joint angle value.

For the upper body imitation case, the pre-processed shoulder pitch, shoulder roll and elbow roll angles from the human are directly usable in the robotic joints. For the elbow yaw joint, we need to approximate Nao's motion. In order to

---

[1] The more advanced versions of Nao also have a wrist joint, not used in this study.
[2] http://www.openni.org

achieve this, the position of the human hand is calculated by forward kinematics, using the first three determined joint angles. Denavit-Hartenberg notation is adopted for kinematic calculations. Table 1 shows the parameters for the right arm of Nao robot, where j_1, j_2, j_3 and j_4 stands for shoulder pitch joint, shoulder roll joint, elbow roll and elbow yaw joints, respectively. L_1 denotes the upper arm length, and L_2 denotes the lower arm length. In order to find the interpolated position of the hand of the robot using the shoulder pitch, shoulder roll and elbow roll joints, the transformation matrix is calculated using the Denavit-Hertenberg kinematic parameters of Nao [22].

Table 1. The Denavit-Hartenberg parameters for the right arm of Aldebaran Nao Humanoid Robot

i	α_i	a_i	Θ_i	d_i
1	$-\pi/2$	0	j_1	0
2	$\pi/2$	0	$\pi/2+j_2$	0
3	$\pi/2$	0	$\pi+j_3$	L_1
4	$\pi/2$	0	$\pi/2+j_4$	0
5	$-\pi/2$	L_2	0	0

The result is where the hand would be, if the shoulder yaw joint was in a neutral position. This position is measured in the 3D space relative to the shoulder. The spatial difference between this interpolated position and the real position of the hand needs to be compensated by the elbow yaw joint in the robot. Hence, the next step is to apply inverse kinematics to find the most suitable angle for the elbow yaw joint. Intuitively, the proposed approach tries to exchange the role of the shoulder yaw joint in the human with the elbow yaw joint in the Nao robot.

Fig. 2. The spatial difference between interpolated position and real position of the hand is compensated by the elbow yaw joint

Whole Body Imitation. There are few approaches where the gesture of the demonstrating human is transferred to a humanoid robot. Koenemann and Bennewitz implement a scenario where human gestures are transferred to a Nao robot, using an Xsens MVN motion capture system with inertial sensors attached to the body of the demonstrator [23]. Inverse kinematics is used to correct the transferred sensor positions for stability. They do not use this system in a particular application scenario.

In our system, the gesture is performed by a human demonstrator in front of the RGB-D camera and the joint angles, being derived by the external computer in real-time, are sent to the robot. Let A_h denote the joint angle vector for the human demonstrator. This vector will be mapped to a joint angle vector A_r for the robot. Two problems that we need to solve are the limited joint angle ranges of the robots (similarity) and the balance problems that arise during the performance of the gesture. For the latter, not only the center of mass of the robot needs to be maintained within the convex hull of the feet of the robot, but the time needed to interpolate between different gestures should also be taken into account: fast gesture changes can cause the robot to fall down, whereas the same gesture, performed slowly, may not. However, our application scenario of displaying gestures to the elderly permits the robot to move slower than the originally demonstrated gesture. Subsequently, we ignore speed-related instability here. Figure 3 shows examples from stable and unstable exercises.

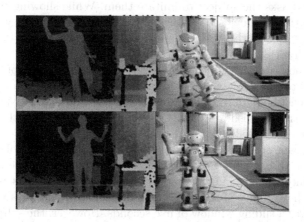

Fig. 3. Demonstration and imitation of two different exercises. The upper exercise is unstable, and if performed rapidly, can cause the Nao to fall, whereas the lower exercise is stable.

The whole body imitation problem is considered as a linear optimization problem in our proposed approach. There are two main requirements to be satisfied for a robot coach imitating a human, which are self-balance and maximum similarity with the human demonstrator, respectively. Our system tries to find joint configurations for the robot which have minimum difference from the ones collected from human and also satisfy balance constraints. Hence, the objective function we use is the minimization of the sum of the absolute differences between joint angles of the robot and the human demonstrator, subject to the stability constraint function that ensures that the ground projection of the center of mass of the robot lies within the support polygon of the robot. Moreover, ankle pitch angle of the foot in contact with the ground should be equal to zero minus of the sum of the related knee pitch angle and hip pitch angle, in order to satisfy the parallelism of the foot to the ground:

$$
\begin{aligned}
\min |A_h - A_r| \ & s.t. \\
\sigma(A_r) \quad & \in P(A_r), \\
\phi_{anklePitch} = & -\phi_{kneePitch} - \phi_{hipPitch}, \\
A_r^j \quad & \in [A_{min}^j \dots A_{max}^j], \quad \forall j = 1 \dots J,
\end{aligned}
\tag{4}
$$

where $\sigma(A_r)$ denotes the center of mass of the robot, and $P(A_r)$ is the convex hull of its feet support, both as functions of the joint angle vector A_r. The individual joints $j = 1 \dots J$ each should be within their respective minimum (A_{min}^j) and maximum (A_{max}^j) limits, at all times. To solve the optimization problem, we make use of COBYLA algorithm [24] from the NLOpt library [25].

3.2   Interaction with the Subject

In the second mode of the system, the robot performs the learned gestures to the subject and asks the subject to imitate them. While showing the motion, a verbal explanation of the gesture is also provided to the subject by the robot to make the perception of the gesture easier and to compensate for the differences between the physical embodiment of the robot and the human.

The robot monitors the subject during the exhibition of the motion and gives vocal feedback on the success of the imitation of gesture. The aim is to force the subject to repeat the performed gesture successfully and motivate the subject to continue with the exercise program. One challenge is to adjust the timing and the amount of verbal feedback in the exercise sequence.

In our approach, the feedback is given to the subject when the robot completes to demonstrate the gesture, and stays in the final posture of the gesture. The robot determines when the imitation of the gesture by the subject is terminated by analysing the stability of the subject, as indicated by the variances of all the joint angles over a sliding window of five seconds. However, the subject may not be able to perform the gesture simultaneously with the robot, or the performance speed may be different. The dynamic time warping algorithm is used to normalize gestures in time by stretching the shorter sequence. The feedback message is verbally given, but it is not pre-recorded. It is composed on the fly, by analysis of the imitated gesture. The joints that have high variance (called "gesture characterizing joint") are compared to the original stored gesture template, as performed by the coach. The feedback then consists of simple sentences such as "please raise your right arm up slightly" or "please spread the arms to both sides as much as you can", depending on the difference from the template. Each message consists of an action verb (e.g. "raise", "lower", "spread"), the target limb (e.g. "right arm", "both arms") and a modifier indicating the amount of correction (e.g. "slightly", "as much as you can"). Finally, the feedback text is converted to an audio file using a text to speech module, and played on the robot.

4 Taxonomy of Physical Exercises

Exercise motions are generally categorized into four classes, which are stretching and relaxation exercises, strength exercises, balance exercises and endurance exercises, respectively. The nursing home that helps us to observe the exercise session hosts seniors whose ages are generally above 75. These exercise sessions are held out three times a week and the same seniors participate in the sessions regularly. Hence, the exercises listed in Table 2 and Table 3 stand for the general and common exercises performed in a real senior fitness scenario. At this point, balance and endurance exercises will not be included for robotic coaching due to the risk of falling, and heart problems, respectively.

With the proposed pipeline of observation, skeletonization and angle matching, the Nao humanoid robot is able to perform six out of 16 stretching motions completely, and three motions partially. Stretching exercises help warming the muscles, protect against injury and allow a maximum range of motion for joints. Hence, these exercises require a muscle system to be exploited properly while being performed within certain minimum or maximum limit angles of joints. Human joints have a greater degree of freedom compared to Nao's joints, and some exercises fall beyond the robots capabilities.

Purely gesture based imitation success in strength exercises is higher. The Nao is able to perform five motions properly and eight motions partially, while four exercises are beyond its physical limits. The main problem in strength exercises is the constraints in the joint angle intervals. Figure 4 shows some exercises, fully learned and imitated by the Nao.

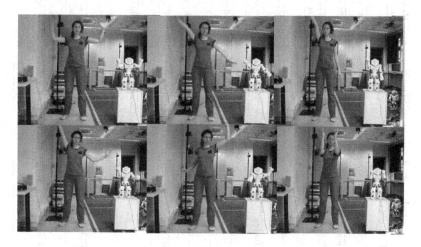

Fig. 4. Demonstration and subsequent imitation of several fitness exercises

The motions that the Nao is not able to perform are displayed with additional vocal assistance. Understanding motion characteristics such that stretching or strengthening may be a difficult task even for the humans; we observed some

Table 2. Analysis of Stretching and Relaxation Exercises Considering Nao Humanoid Robot

Stretching and Relaxation Exercises	Stance	Description	Robot Joints	Doability	Problems
1. Side lumbar stretching	Standing	One hand is on the lumbar, stretch the body using lumber to the side of that hand	Upper body joints + hip roll	Yes	
2. Lumbar spine relaxation	Standing	Arms are relaxed and swing around body, turn upper body around itself	Shoulder roll + hip pitchyaw	Yes	
3. Whole body stretching 1	Standing	One foot is on front a bit, bend over that foot and stand again by raising and stretching arms		No	Balance problem
4. Upper arm stretching	Standing	Reach the arms at back	Upper body joints	Yes	
5. Circular hip exercise	Standing	Hands on hips, one foot is moved to front, side and back to draw a half circle	Hip pitch and roll	Yes	
6. Upper body stretching	Sitting	Link the hands by raising arms horizontally, stretch upper body back and forth	Shoulder roll + hip pitch	Partially	Nao can not link his hands on front due to embodiment constraint in shoulder roll joints
7. Shoulder rolls	Sitting	Sit up, move shoulders up and down while breathing carefully		No	Nao does not have movable joints
8. Chest stretching 1	Sitting	Link the hands at back, stretch chest area		No	Shoulder joint angles' interval does not allow
9. Neck stretching	Sitting	Move the head back and forth, to the right and left	Head pitch and yaw joints	Yes	
10. Neck side stretching	Sitting	Gently tilt the head to the left and right in turn		No	No head roll joints available in Nao
11. Hand stretching	Sitting	Open and close the hand, spreading the fingers apart		No	Nao does not have motors for hands
12. Chest stretching 2	Sitting	Raise arms and place hands behind your head and stretch	Upper body joints	Partially	Linking okay, but no stretching, no movable shoulder joints
13. Standing quadriceps stretching	Standing	Bend your right knee, grasp your right ankle, gently pull up toward your bottom, repeat for left ankle	Whole body joints	Partially	Nao should tilt sidewards in order to balance itself.
14. Whole body stretching 2	Sitting	Extend one leg horizontally, stretch the upper body over this leg without bending knee		Partially	Nao's body length ratios are different from humans.
15. Back reach	Sitting	Exhale and gently move arms backward. Pause, then return to the start position	Shoulder roll+pitch	Yes	
16. Upper hind leg and back stretch	Sitting	pull the knee to the head level by lowering back		No	Upper body and upper leg lengths are not convenient, hip pitch joint interval is not large enough.

Table 3. Analysis of Strength Exercises Considering Nao Humanoid Robot

Strength Exercises	Stance	Description	Robot Joints	Doability	Problems
1. Knee extensions	Sitting	Make the legs horizontal to the floor by moving lower leg up and down from the knee	Knee pitch	Yes	
2. Back strength	Sitting	Upper arm is horizontal to the floor, lower arm makes 90 degrees with upper arm, link the arms at front then open towards to the back and close again		Partially	Nao can not link its hands in front because of shoulder roll joint constraints, but can bend the lower arm a bit to perform the motion
3. Shoulder circles	Sitting	Circle shoulders forward and backward		No	Nao does not have movable joints
4. Upper leg strength 1	Sitting	Raise both of the feet up slightly	Knee pitch	Yes	
5. Arm raising and side lumber strength	Sitting	Hold a ribbon, bend over hip to the floor, raise the upper body and arms to the cross side	Hip roll + upper body joints	Partially	Common hip pitch yaw joint does not allow to perform the motion as in human. However, hip roll joint is used to do a similar motion.
6. Upper inner leg strength	Sitting	Raise both feet up, open and close them in a lateral way	Hip pitch+hip roll+knee pitch	Yes	
7. Upper leg strength 2	Sitting	Pull the knee to the head level rapidly and extend leg without bending afterwards		No	Upper body and upper leg lengths are not convenient, hip pitch joint interval is not large enough
8. Ankle exercises	Sitting	Move ankle up and down	Ankle pitch	Yes	
9. Shoulder strength and abdominal region exercise	Sitting	Make the arms cross over each other on the knee (upper body tilted forward), stretch strongly to the back by raising arms up		Partially	Shoulder roll interval does not allow crossing the arms over each other
10. Ankle circles	Sitting	Extend knee and move foot in a circle	Knee pitch+ankle roll+ankle pitch	Partially	Nao does not have ankle yaw joints. Ankle pitch and roll joints are used to perform the motion
11. Lower hind leg strength	Standing	Hands on hips, move through heel to toe on one foot while the other is stable for self balance		Partially	Due to balance problem, the motion can not be performed smoothly while going through heel to toe
12. Upper hind leg strength	Standing	Hands on hips, move forward the legs from the hips	whole body joints	Partially	Due to balance problem, Nao tends to tilt sidewards
13. Shoulder and leg exercise	Standing	Bend knees, cross arms, then stand up while raising the arm up to the head level		Partially	Shoulder roll interval does not allow crossing the arms over each other
14. Hip side extension	Standing	Lift your leg to the side as high as comfortable, then return to the stand position again	Hip roll joint	Partially	Due to balance problem, Nao tends to tilt sidewards
15. Calf raises	Standing	Rise up on toes as high as you comfortably can		No	Balance problem
16. Hip extension	Standing	Extend your leg backward, keeping knee straight.	Hip pitch + knee pitch	Yes	
17. Sit to stand	Standing	Lean forward with bending knees and lower yourself towards the chair as if attempting to sit.		No	Balance problem

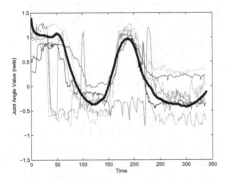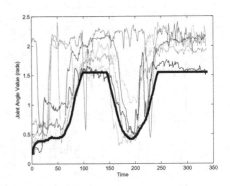

Fig. 5. Left Shoulder Pitch (left) and Right Elbow Roll (right) joint angle trajectories for one gesture. The trajectory of the coach is indicated with a bold line, and the individual subjects are indicated with thin lines. The values are shown without smoothing. In each case, only one subject displays an incorrect gesture.

elderly having difficulty in properly interpreting the instructions of the human coach. In order to correctly explain the action where needed, the Nao should provide qualitative markers, for instance "pull your knee to the head level", instead of saying "rotate the knee joint 10 degrees and set the hip pitch angle to -40 degrees". The definition and proper use of a set of highly explanatory and practical qualitative markers is at the moment left as a future work.

5   Experimental Study and Results

The proposed system was tested with eight people whose ages are between 25 and 35 in a preliminary user study. Ethical committee approval is pending for the study with a large set of elderly people in the nursing home. The exercise session performed by the robot contains five different gestures. Three of them are arm related exercises (arm stretching and relaxation exercises), while the remaining are leg strength exercises.

The subjects received a brief description about the overall scenario before starting the test. During the session, each gesture is explained verbally by the robot in the beginning of the gesture exhibition. The subjects were monitored during the session and skeleton joint angles were recorded to analyse how the subjects were synchronized with the robot and the performance of the subject in imitating the gesture accurately. Figure 5 shows angles for two different tracked joints (for all subjects) during two different gestures. The gold standard is the gesture performed by the coach, which is indicated by a bold line. Except for one subject, all subjects were able to perform these gestures correctly.

We have also assessed the interaction with a post-exercise study. The subjects were requested to fill out a survey to measure the effects of the system after the exercise session. The survey contains questions adapted to our scenario based on the the Game Experience Questionnaire (GEQ) that measures different emotional responses to a game-like experience [26]. We used questions related to positive and negative affect, flow, immersion and challenge. A 5-point Likert scale was used with 1 being the lowest score, and 5 being the highest. Each component is tested with five questions, which results in 25 questions in total, given in a random order to the subject. The results are given in Table 4. The designed system scores high on immersion and positive affect, and on a smaller degree on flow. The flow is affected by the lack of smoothness in the robot's gestures. The scores on challenge and negative affect are small, indicating an easy-to-use system.

Table 4. Results of user evaluation

Component	Mean	Standard Deviation
Positive Affect	3.625	0.7206
Negative Affect	2.2	0.6761
Flow	3.25	1.1301
Immersion	3.675	0.3694
Challenge	2.65	0.7151

6   Conclusions

Most assistive robotics research focuses on helping the elderly to perform daily tasks more easily (like intelligent wheelchairs or easily operated robotic arms), or to monitor the elderly to ensure their safety and well-being. Yet robotic solutions for improving the physical condition of the elderly can be very useful. We describe a method to teach a humanoid robot to perform physical exercises for the purpose of implementing a robotic physical exercise coach. We have observed an actual training program running in an elderly care facility, and provided a taxonomy of exercises. Our initial results reveal that one third of these exercises can be easily performed by the robot, one third can be partially performed, and one third requires some additional tricks to overcome the physical limitations in the robot. We use audio feedback to deal with these cases in particular.

At the moment, we are comparing the success of the robot in providing coaching by letting different groups of subjects observe either a human coach or the robot. The system then converts the performed gestures of the subjects into a skeleton representation, and compares joint angles to the ground truth (i.e. the angle representation of the human coach) to compare the two demonstration methods.

A proper assessment of an elderly assistance scenario requires monitoring of the elderly over long periods of interaction, as well as follow-up assessments, typically spanning one or two years of observations in total to get a thorough understanding of the physical implications [27]. We work with an elderly care facility, where the robotic fitness coach was warmly received by the inhabitants.

Our plans for near future include assessing interaction aspects for perceived usefulness, perceived ease of use, and for variables that relate to social interaction [28].

Acknowledgments. This research is supported by Bogazici University project BAP-6531 and BAP-7361.

References

1. Kröse, B., Oosterhout, T., Kasteren, T.: Activity monitoring systems in health care. In: Salah, A.A., Gevers, T. (eds.) Computer Analysis of Human Behavior, pp. 325–346. Springer (2011)
2. Nied, R.J., Franklin, B.: Promoting and prescribing exercise for the elderly. American Family Physician 65(3), 419–430 (2002)
3. Regensteiner, J.G., Meyer, T.J., Krupski, W.C., Cranford, L.S., Hiatt, W.R.: Hospital vs home-based exercise rehabilitation for patients with peripheral arterial occlusive disease. Angiology 48(4), 291–300 (1997)
4. Feil-Seifer, D., Mataric, M.J.: Defining socially assistive robotics. In: 9th International Conference on Rehabilitation Robotics, ICORR 2005, pp. 465–468. IEEE (2005)
5. Broekens, J., Heerink, M., Rosendal, H.: Assistive social robots in elderly care: a review. Gerontechnology 8(2), 94–103 (2009)
6. Heerink, M.: Assessing acceptance of assistive social robots by aging adults (2010)
7. Pineau, J., Montemerlo, M., Pollack, M., Roy, N., Thrun, S.: Towards robotic assistants in nursing homes: Challenges and results. Robotics and Autonomous Systems 42(3), 271–281 (2003)
8. Colombo, R., Pisano, F., Mazzone, A., Delconte, C., Micera, S., Carrozza, M.C., Dario, P., Minuco, G.: Design strategies to improve patient motivation during robot-aided rehabilitation. Journal of NeuroEngineering and Rehabilitation 4(3) (2007)
9. Wada, K., Shibata, T., Saito, T., Sakamoto, K., Tanie, K.: Psychological and social effects of one year robot assisted activity on elderly people at a health service facility for the aged. In: Proceedings of the 2005 IEEE International Conference on Robotics and Automation, ICRA 2005, pp. 2785–2790. IEEE (2005)
10. Barnes, P.A., Spooner, T., Dhabolt, J.L., Leighton, J.: Instructional gaming methods and apparatus. Patent A1 20090176581 (2009)
11. Sucar, L.E., Azcárate, G., Leder, R.S., Reinkensmeyer, D., Hernández, J., Sanchez, I., Saucedo, P.: Gesture therapy: A vision-based system for arm rehabilitation after stroke. In: Fred, A., Filipe, J., Gamboa, H. (eds.) BIOSTEC 2008. CCIS, vol. 25, pp. 531–540. Springer, Heidelberg (2009)
12. Bickmore, T.W., Picard, R.W.: Establishing and maintaining long-term human-computer relationships. ACM Transactions on Computer-Human Interaction (TOCHI) 12(2), 293–327 (2005)
13. Fasola, J., Matarić, M.J.: A socially assistive robot exercise coach for the elderly. Journal of Human-Robot Interaction 2(2), 3–32 (2013)
14. Lopez Recio, D., Marquez Segura, L., Marquez Segura, E., Waern, A.: The nao models for the elderly. In: 2013 8th ACM/IEEE International Conference on Human-Robot Interaction (HRI), pp. 187–188 (2013)

15. Fasola, J., Matarić, M.J.: Using socially assistive human-robot interaction to motivate physical exercise for older adults. In: Kanade, T. (ed.) Proceedings of the IEEE, Special Issue on Quality of Life Technology (2012)
16. Gadde, P., Kharrazi, H., Patel, H., MacDorman, K.F.: Toward monitoring and increasing exercise adherence in older adults by robotic intervention: A proof of concept study. Journal of Robotics, vol. 2011 (2011)
17. Fasola, J., Matarić, M.: Robot exercise instructor: A socially assistive robot system to monitor and encourage physical exercise for the elderly. In: Proc. of 19th IEEE International Symposium in Robot and Human Interactive Communication. Citeseer (2010)
18. Smith, S.T., Talaei-Khoei, A., Ray, M., Ray, P.: Electronic games for aged care and rehabilitation. In: 11th International Conference on e-Health Networking, Applications and Services, Healthcom 2009, pp. 42–47. IEEE (2009)
19. Doyle, J., Bailey, C., Dromey, B., Scanaill, C.N.: Base-an interactive technology solution to deliver balance and strength exercises to older adults. In: 2010 4th International Conference on Pervasive Computing Technologies for Healthcare (PervasiveHealth), pp. 1–5. IEEE (2010)
20. Rego, P., Moreira, P.M., Reis, L.P.: Serious games for rehabilitation: A survey and a classification towards a taxonomy. In: 2010 5th Iberian Conference on Information Systems and Technologies (CISTI), pp. 1–6. IEEE (2010)
21. Badler, N.I., Tolani, D.: Real-time inverse kinematics of the human arm. Presence 5(4), 393–401 (1996)
22. Denavit, J., Hartenberg, R.S.: A kinematic notation for lower-pair mechanisms based on matrices. Trans. ASME E, Journal of Applied Mechanics 22, 215–221 (1955)
23. Koenemann, J., Bennewitz, M.: Whole-body imitation of human motions with a nao humanoid. In: Proceedings of the Seventh Annual ACM/IEEE International Conference on Human-Robot Interaction, pp. 425–426. ACM (2012)
24. Powell, M.J.D.: Direct search algorithms for optimization calculations (1998)
25. Johnson, S.G.: The nlopt nonlinear-optimization package, http://ab-initio.mit.edu/nlopt
26. Norman, K.L.: GEQ (Game Engagement/Experience Questionnaire): A Review of Two Papers. Interacting with Computers (2013)
27. King, A.C., Rejeski, W.J., Buchner, D.M.: Physical activity interventions targeting older adults. American Journal of Preventive Medicine 15(4), 316–333 (2004)
28. Heerink, M., Kröse, B., Evers, V., Wielinga, B.: Assessing acceptance of assistive social agent technology by older adults: The Almere model. International Journal of Social Robotics 2(4), 361–375 (2010)

Digital Receipts: Fostering Mobile Payment Adoption

Edward Ho[1], Silviu Apostu[1], Florian Michahelles[1], and Alexander Ilic[2]

[1] ETH Zürich, Weinbergstrasse 56/58
8092 Zürich, Switzerland
{eho,fmichahelles}@ethz.ch, silviu.apostu@cdtm.de
[2] University of St. Gallen, Dufourstrasse 40a
9000 St. Gallen, Switzerland
alexander.ilic@unisg.ch

Abstract. Mobile payment adoption remains low. This paper presents a user-study that evaluates whether providing digital receipts in-store to customers could drive mobile payment adoption. Our results reveal that although our smart phone based payment and digital receipt processes took up to 60% longer than getting paper receipts and paying with cash, users perceived the digital receipt approach as fun, useful, and even time-saving. These insights may help drive adoption of mobile payment systems.

Keywords: Mobile Payment, Digital Receipt, Usability, Retail.

1 Introduction

The large adoption of smart phones has inspired retailers to explore new ways of in-store payment. While Google Wallet and others are already being deployed, the adoption of in-store mobile payment systems by consumers remain slow, blocking the emergence of new process changes enabled by pervasive computing. Latest studies show that consumers are quite satisfied with current payment instruments at the point-of-sale (PoS) [1]. We argue that instead of replacing one payment method by another, value added services are needed. In our approach, with each payment transaction the user will receive a full itemized receipt on their phone. From this data, context-driven applications ranging from personal money management to shopping suggestions can be derived. The consumer value of such applications has been validated stand-alone both in research [2] and in rising m-commerce solutions like mint.com, which has reached over one million downloads in Q1 2013; this paper explores how such applications arising from digital receipts could be leveraged to drive mobile payment adoption. To this end, we have developed a mobile application for digital receipts and conducted a user study in a near real-world supermarket environment.

2 Related Work

Researchers and practitioners have already explored separately the ideas of consumer empowerment applications, digital receipts, and payment - but combining all three has been rare. Krüger et al. [3] examined virtual shopping assistants embedded into several in-store artifacts. Bhattacharya et al. [4] evaluated customers' product recommendation

J.C. Augusto et al. (Eds.): AmI 2013, LNCS 8309, pp. 140–149, 2013.

and shopping assistance systems. These applications depend on having rich and rapidly available data about the user. In this vein, Mankoff [5] proposed a nutritional assistant solution by scanning paper receipts and deriving shopping recommendations accordingly. Following Apple in 2005, several practitioners and start-ups such as alletronic.com or lemon.com have started to provide receipts to customers digitally. Mobile payment, which offers an alternative to paying with cash, check, or credit cards by allowing the consumer to use his mobile phone at the check-out, has research mostly centered around the technical development and evaluation of new payment systems (summarized in [1]), and theories of mobile payment acceptance [6]. While there are various systems on the market[1] advertising the advantages for merchants of those systems, a research gap exists in identifying and evaluating the added value for consumers to adopt mobile payment solutions. Thus, the contribution of this paper is an approach that combines the information of digital receipts with a layer of applications built on top, to motivate users to adopt a new method of payment.

3   Concept of a Digital Receipt Solution

We developed a smartphone application in order to assess the level of acceptance of a digital receipt solution with subjects in a near real-world supermarket environment.

3.1   Text Formatting

A visual representation of each item on the receipt provides access to detailed information on each product. Fig. 1 shows a comparison between a traditional paper

Fig. 1. Paper *(left)* and digital receipt *(right)*

---

[1] E.g. Square (https://squareup.com/), Paypal (https://mobile.paypal.com), Gopago (http://www.gopago.com/).

receipt and the mobile digital receipt solution. The user can click on individual items to view a short description and nutritional information. As users might be also shopping for other members in the same household, the application's personalization is designed for the household level.

3.2 Value Added Solutions

On top of the digital receipt data, we envision applications were users get feedback about their shopping, can set shopping goals and spending limits, and receive related product recommendations. In our study, mock-ups of these functions were deployed which users could interact with. Since our evaluation dealt with the user perceptions of these functions at a high level, these features were not developed to be fully functioning, but rather at the level where the user experience during our test was close to reality.

4   Implementation and Study Setup

4.1   Implementation Details

The study followed a randomized repeated-measures design of two tasks. The independent variables were the method of obtaining a receipt and the digital receipt applications shown to the users. The dependent variables were task completion time and measures of user perception of the digital receipt applications via a questionnaire. In addition, we conducted short interviews with the subjects to collect also qualitative feedback. The study was run in a close-to-reality test supermarket. The test center has been setup by a supermarket chain for research on consumer responses to new technologies. This approach of conducting a user study in a retail laboratory is in line with related work in the field [5,6]. The mobile application was deployed on Samsung Nexus S phones running Google Android 2.3.3 with NFC capabilities for one of the receipt obtainment methods. Each subject used the same phone type and same software.

4.1.1   Digital Receipt Obtainment Method
For the independent variable, we varied among three methods of getting a receipt at checkout: a paper receipt, and two digital methods below.

2D Bar Codes. The user scanned a QR code that was generated on a POS screen facing the customer, to directly pick up the receipt data. QR codes have become standard method for phone users to acquire data and have sufficient data capacity to encode all required receipt data.

Near Field Communication (NFC). Here, the receipt information was contained in an NFC tag which the user touched with the smartphone to obtain the receipt information. We also simulated a "pay" function with the phone that is confirmed by inputting a personal code on the smartphone screen. Similar to the value-added solutions, only the user experience of payment was developed, rather than a "true" payment solution.

Once the receipt has been received by either method, the digital receipt indicates on the smartphone which products have been bought, in what quantity and for what price.

4.1.2   Users' Characteristics
The study was completed with a convenience sample of 12 users (3 of which were female). Ages ranged from 24-47 years with a median age of 26. Professions ranged from researchers, students and secretaries.

4.2   Evaluation Procedure

The study consisted of an introduction, an interactive demonstration task on the mobile phone, a shopping check-out task, and a follow-up questionnaire and validation interview to gather data about the two tasks (See Fig. 2). All users completed both tasks.

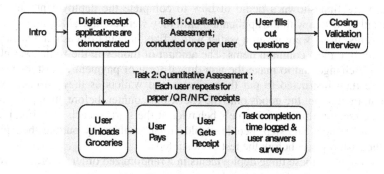

Fig. 2. Steps and tasks of the user study

4.2.1   Introduction
The introduction was read from a script. One experimenter guided the user, and the other observed. The guide explained the study's objective was to compare the perceived usefulness of different digital receipt applications and the digital receipt obtainment methods. We mentioned to each participant that we were comparing our designs and not evaluating their skills, to avoid biasing users into rushing through the tasks.

4.2.2   Task 1: Evaluation of Digital Receipts Applications
The objective of the first task was to determine the perceived value of digital receipts. Users were shown and walked through the ancillary functions and use cases of goal setting, history of spending, recommendation, past receipts, and check-out information features.

Then, users were allowed to interact and to become acquainted with the applications. They proceeded to the second task when they confirmed that they understood what was presented. After the users completed all iterations of Task 2 (see below), they were then given a set of questions to evaluate key functions and overall impressions of the presented digital receipt solution (i.e. the solution consisting of the app prototypes in Task 1 in combination with the payment schemes in Task 2).

4.2.3   Task 2: Evaluation of Digital Receipt Deployment in Store

The objective of this task was to compare three possible deployments of making payments and getting receipts at the point of sale:

1. **Cash Payment, Paper Receipt** - the user paid with the wallet we provided, and then received a paper receipt.
2. **Cash Payment, Digital Receipt by QR scanning** – the user paid with the wallet we provided, and then unlocked the phone, turned on the app, and retrieved the receipt by scanning the fixed QR code we provide on an adjacent screen.
3. **Phone Payment, Digital Receipt** – the user walked up to the NFC terminal, scanned the tag with the phone, entered a PIN code, paid and got the receipt in the same step.

Users were first shown a demo of how to complete the deployments and could subsequently practice with the application until they were comfortable.

Afterwards, users were given a wallet with a fixed amount of cash and a shopping basket with five most common items. The amount of money in the wallet was chosen to minimize change and to make the non-digital form of payment as fast as possible. They were then instructed to put their phones and wallets as they normally would have them, then to put the goods onto the check-out counter, before attempting to pay and get the receipt; this reset people's behavior at the start of each trial. In a pre-test we saw that without this step, people would violate realism by putting their phones next to the cash register before the test even started.

Users completed these three deployments in a randomized order, in order to reduce possible biasing effects of the task order on our dependent measures.

4.2.4   Measures and Instruments

Dependent measures were collected as follows: First, at the end of each deployment in Task 2, the task completion time was recorded. The task completion time started after the last grocery basket item was unloaded and stopped after the person received the receipt, resulting in the actual time to pay and to get the receipt. Additionally, we also needed to empirically evaluate how they accepted the overall system (i.e. the app prototypes in Task 1 in combination with the different payment schemes in Task 2) and their future intention to use it. We aimed for parsimony in our measurements, so to this end, we applied constructs from the original Technology Acceptance Model (TAM), widely used for empirically evaluating the end-user perception of the information systems [7]. The original TAM model contains constructs for "Intention to use", "Perceived Usefulness" and "Perceived Ease of Use", which suit our purposes. The TAM model has been since extended from its original form [8], for example, with constructs like "Computer Playfulness", which we included since our app might be perceived as enjoyable. In order to maintain a parsimonious survey and also to maintain only the most important items, we did not include other constructs from the TAM extensions. Users could rate their agreement with the statements on a 7-point Likert scale from 1="strongly disagree" to 7="strongly agree". In effect, users had to apply the TAM to these three use cases: (1) No app, with cash payment and paper receipt, (2) Digital receipt applications with cash payment and digital receipts by QR scanning and (3) Digital receipt applications with phone payment and digital receipts.

Secondly, after all iterations of Task 2 were completed, users were given a questionnaire with statements representing the main functions of the digital receipt solution as experienced by the users in Task 1. They were asked "How do you value the following statements about the presented solution?" and given 9 statements representing specific functions and use cases of the presented solution. Results were collected on a 7-point Likert scale. The order of all the questions was randomized. Finally, users were asked to record their age, profession and how often they shopped.

4.2.5   Final Interview

For qualitative feedback, we asked users about how much they spent in general on different product categories and what their shopping goals are; then we asked them what applications shown or additional functionalities would convince them to adopt the presented solution.

5   Results

5.1   Task 1: Evaluation of Digital Receipts Applications

During this task we collected users' opinions about "How do you value the following statements about the presented solution?" Of the nine statements, four lie prominently above a neutral answer (shown in Fig. 3), while two functions which do not rank so prominently are "I can receive recommendations about future purchases" and "I can see the opinions of other users about products".

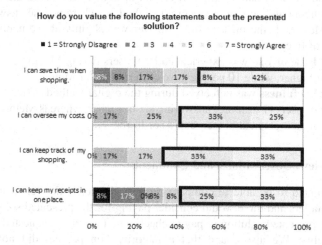

Fig. 3. User replies to "How do you value the following statements about the presented solutions?"; frequencies are presented, with four features perceived strongly positive.

5.2   Task 2: Evaluation of Digital Receipt Deployment at the POS

The results of Task 2 are the task completion times, measured for each of the different methods of paying and getting the receipt. We saw that users have different habits while checking out. Also, there are different approaches for handling both phone and wallet simultaneously: some users set one down while using the other, while others held both at the same time. Although this led to different check-out times between users, a one-way repeated-measures ANOVA proves the significant effect of the receipt/payment method on task completion time, $F(2,22) = 12.15$, $p < 0.01$. Mauchly's test did not show a violation of sphericity ($\chi2 (2) = 3.008$, $p = 0.22$).

When comparing between the three methods, the present method of cash & paper receipt ($\mu = 14.9s$, $\sigma = 5.3s$) was the fastest. Post-Hoc tests showed that in comparison with the present method, cash & digital receipt ($\mu = 28.3s$, $\sigma = 7.3s$, $p = 0.000$) and full digital payment & receipt ($\mu = 23.7s$, $\sigma = 6.6s$, $p = 0.014$) were slower and statistically significantly different. Meanwhile, the difference between the new methods was insignificant ($p = 0.611$).

5.3   Overall Evaluation of the Solution

The overall evaluation of the solution was embedded in the TAM responses. We can observe the following qualitative trends from the user's answers below:

Intention to Use was perceived positively and qualitatively similar between the present method of payment and getting the receipt (Method 1) and the fully digital method (Method 3); 9 users answered six or higher in both cases. For the cash payment and digital receipt method (Method 2), 7 users answered six or higher.

Computer Playfulness / Fun was experienced during both digital methods (Method 2 and 3) (with half of the answers six or higher) compared the present day method of payment and getting the receipt (Method 1), where no one answered six or higher. For Method 1, the most positive answer was slightly above neutral (5 users gave a rating of five).

Perceived Ease of Use was experienced by 9 users during Method 1 and 2 with a score of six or higher, while 10 people gave such ratings for Method 3.

Perceived Usefulness was perceived during the digital methods (Methods 2 and 3) by a majority of users (7 or more) answering six or higher, whereas Method 1 resulted in a majority of answers neutral (score of 4) or lower.

5.4   Interview, Observations, and Comments

Five users wanted to be able to compare product characteristics (e.g., price) across competing retailers and three would consider paying for the presented solution if they could use the presented solution to pay at check-out. Two users requested a shopping list functionality. We also found that a majority (ten people) did not have any awareness of how much they were spending on different categories, but would be interested in knowing.

6   Discussion

6.1   Added-Value versus Objective Time Savings

The task completion time recorded in Task 2 showed that acquiring a digital receipt could take at least 60% longer than a paper receipt. In spite of this, the digital methods received the highest TAM scores; users perceived the digital receipt methods more positive than paper receipts. Within the two digital methods, the perceived fun and usefulness were similar, even though the payment methods were different (cash versus simulated pre-pay). This implies that the underlying method of payment had little impact on user perceptions; rather it suggests the digital receipt applications boosted the acceptance of the digital payment methods. This result is consistent with previous findings that consumers are already satisfied with traditional payment instruments at the point-of-sale [1]; our result extends this by showing that digital receipt applications could motivate consumers to try other payment instruments.

Counter intuitively, users also perceived the digital receipt solution as being able to "save time when shopping". The mobile payment adoption literature emphasized fast checkout time [6] as a key driver for adoption; our results complements this by showing that that the added-value of a digital receipt can even overcome non-optimal checkout times. Studies in the consumer behavior literature on in-queue time perception [9,10,11] corroborate our results; studies have shown that the consumer perception of time during check-out could be influenced by external factors such as distractions or an engaging environment. Since our solution was perceived as fun by the users, it could be that it led to a perception of a shorter check-out time than it objectively was. Accordingly, our contribution increments the body of work on the consumer acceptance of mobile payment, by introducing a dimension of fun through digital receipts and their applications. Additionally, our work is also relevant to existing commercial solutions of mobile payment by providing insight on how to get users to accept mobile payment in general via value-added applications. We acknowledge that for a full scale roll-out, checkout times are of importance to the retailer and the proposed solution needs to be further improved. Regarding mobile payment, there needs to be an improvement in terms of operational speed. For receiving the digital receipt, there are already technologies for increasing the speed [12] so that a mass deployment would be feasible.

6.2   Important Digital Receipt Applications

The previous results suggested that offering value added applications to complement mobile payment led to positive evaluations of the overall system, which could foster mobile payment adoption. This empirical result is in line with correlational models of mobile payment acceptance [6]. We found that users prefer utilitarian functions; both ranking of statements and interviews indicate a strong preference for utilitarian functions in a digital receipt application, e.g. cost-tracking of purchases. Other desired functions were product comparison and the possibility to track and review one's own shopping habits. Instead of recommendations, some users proposed a subscription or reminder function which remains under user's decision and control. These desired functions were also consistent with the findings by Bhattacharya et al. [4] regarding preferred in-store mobile applications.

6.3   Limitations

Our study sampled user experience in a single moment in time in a close-to-reality setting; a longer period of time with a larger sample of users in the field is a next step. This can validate the extent of acceptance when people shop under stressful or tired conditions, and the impact of the increased check-out time.

7   Conclusions

By using in-store digital receipts on smart phones, we compared different checkout scenarios of receipt obtainment and payment methods. We built our own prototypical solution and tested it in a near real-world environment. Our study revealed that users perceive the digital receipt solution as fun and time-saving, even though it objectively took longer than the other methods. Retailers can use this insight as a stepping stone towards mobile payment adoption. It also opens up opportunity for new research on faster digital receipt obtainment and value-added receipt applications.

References

1. Dahlberg, T., Mallat, N., Ondrus, J., Zmijewska, A.: Past, present and future of mobile payments research: A literature review. Electronic Commerce Research and Applications 7(2), 165–181 (2008)
2. Kowatsch, T., Maass, W.: In-store consumer behavior: How mobile recommendation agents influence usage intentions, product purchases, and store preferences. Computers in Human Behavior 26(4), 697–704 (2010)
3. Krüger, A., Spassova, L., Jung, R.: Innovative Retail Laboratory — Investigating Future Shopping Technologies Innovative Retail Laboratory. i- Information Technology 52(2), 114–118 (2010)
4. Bhattacharya, S., Floreen, P., Forsblom, A., et al.: Ma$$iv€ – An Intelligent Mobile Grocery Assistant. In: Proceedings of the Eighth International Conference on Intelligent Environments (2012)
5. Mankoff, J., Hsieh, G., Hung, H.C., Lee, S., Nitao, E.: Using low-cost sensing to support nutritional awareness. In: Borriello, G., Holmquist, L.E. (eds.) UbiComp 2002. LNCS, vol. 2498, pp. 371–376. Springer, Heidelberg (2002)
6. Chen, L.: A model of consumer acceptance of mobile payment. International Journal of Mobile Communications 6(1), 32–52 (2008)
7. Davis, F.D.: Perceived Usefulness, Perceived Ease of Use, and User Acceptance of Information Technology. MIS Quarterly 13(3), 319–340 (1989)
8. Venkatesh, V.: Determinants of perceived ease of use: Integrating control, intrinsic motivation, and emotion into the technology acceptance model. Information Systems Research 11(4), 342–365 (2000)

9. Katz, K.L., Larson, B.M., Larson, R.C.: Prescription for the waiting-in-line blues: Entertain, enlighten, and engage. Sloan Management Review, 44–53 (1991)
10. Allan, L.G.: The Perception of Time. Perception and Psychophysics 26(5), 340–354 (1979)
11. Hornik, J.: Subjective vs. Objective Time Measures: A Note on the Perception of Time in Consumer Behavior. Journal of Consumer Research 11(1), 615–618 (1984)
12. Raffelsieper, M., Ilic, A., Keller, T., Fleisch, E.: Efficient Encoding and Transmission of Digital Receipts for mobile Commerce. In: 12th International Conference on Mobile Business (ICMB), Berlin, Germany

Exploring Persuasion in the Home: Results of a Long-Term Study on Energy Consumption Behavior

Patricia M. Kluckner[1], Astrid Weiss[2], Johann Schrammel[3], and Manfred Tscheligi[1,3]

[1] ICT&S Center, HCI & Usability Unit, University of Salzburg, Austria
{patricia.kluckner,manfred.tscheligi}@sbg.ac.at
[2] ACIN - Automation and Control Institute, Vienna University of Technology, Austria
astrid.weiss@tuwien.ac.at
[3] CURE - Center for Usability Research & Engineering, Austria
schrammel@sbg.ac.at

Abstract. This paper presents a seven-months field study on a persuasive ambient display in private households. The *FORE-Watch* aims at adjusting the consumption behavior of energy users in 24 multi-person households and persuading them to change their timing of consumption activities; half of them were shown a forecast of the occupancy rate of the local energy grid (i.e., grid status), and the other half were shown how much energy will be delivered by green sources such as windmills (i.e., green energy). Our qualitative and quantitative survey and the energy consumption data revealed that the grid status group showed a more constant behavior than the green energy, indicating that the more dynamic forecast presentation did not lead to the same type of behavior change as the static forecast presentation. Overall, the *FORE-Watch* aroused awareness, attention and interest through permanent presence, clear and simple information, and changed the energy consumption behavior of our participants.

Keywords: Ambient persuasive display, eco-feedback and management technology, long-term in-situ study, changing energy consumption, home.

1 Introduction

The efficient use of energy-providing systems in private homes is an important step towards reaching the overall climate goals and the transformation of our society's sustainable energy consumption. A promising approach to address this problem is the utilization of ambient technologies informed by the field of persuasion. This choice is based on the insight that a change in individual and collective attitude towards the environment will result in a necessary behavioral change to reach the goal sustainability. Persuasion for sustainability can be challenging since people are not always intrinsically motivated to adopt a more environmentally friendly lifestyle. Therefore, information of individual benefits needs to be provided additionally to the collectivist goal of "saving the planet". Improving the efficiency and management of domestic energy consumption is an important area to save energy. Providing customers with detailed feedback on their energy consumption supports them in

J.C. Augusto et al. (Eds.): AmI 2013, LNCS 8309, pp. 150–165, 2013.

changing their behavior towards CO2 reduction. Neustaeder et al. [21] provide insights about how families understand the relationship between everyday activities and energy consumption. Ambient displays have been identified as being especially suitable to communicate this kind of information to the end-user. Various systems providing ambient feedback on the current energy consumption (e.g., Choreflect [27], POEM [20], eMeter [17], or the well-known Energy AWARE Clock[1] have been developed so far. However, up to date, very few long-term studies in real households have been conducted, which try to understand the influences of such ambient displays over time (e.g., Smeaton and Doherty [31], Midden et al. [19], Staats et al. [32]).

Studying persuasive strategies in the field is a challenging endeavor in determining how to measure the persuasiveness of a system and to ensure that an attitude or behavior change is sustainable. In the framework of the PEEM project (Persuasive End-User Energy Management), the *FORE-Watch* (Forecast Of Renewable Energy - Watch) was developed [29] based on a user-centered design approach [12]. It is an ambient persuasive display, which gives users feedback on their energy consumption, including forecast of energy availability. Our aim is to influence the energy consumption behavior with regard to the timing of consumption activities; in other words to consume energy when the forecast presents it. To investigate if the interface can achieve this change, we installed the *FORE-Watch* in 24 private multi-person households and accompanied and monitored them for a period of seven-months.

After an overview of related research, we describe persuasive systems and studies for energy consumption behavior change, in addition to presenting the link between persuasion and change with user studies. In order to prove the usefulness of the *FORE-Watch*, we show the experimental development of our long-term study in-situ of private households. We present the results for attitudinal changes and behavior modification measured over a period of time and related results.

1.1   Ambient Persuasive Systems for Change

Many studies have investigated the possibilities to persuade people (i.e., feedback, commitment, rewarding, etc.) within the context of sustainability. A study to understand consumers' awareness of energy consumption in the home and to determine their requirements for an interface led to a three-stage approach to support electricity conservation routines: raise awareness, inform complex changes, and maintain sustainable routines [28]. Awareness and reflection of household tasks on inhabitants' contribution was investigated [27] and increased engagement through the distributed ambient persuasive display, named Choreflect. While researching visual signals to induce interaction, Kukka et al. [14] identified a behavior termed display avoidance that people reveal with interactive public displays.

Mobile phone applications are a comfortable way to achieve awareness of saving electricity. Applications can be a suitable means of changing human behavior. An investigation of a mobile tool, UbiGreen, for tracking and supporting green transportation habits was developed [8] to explore the use of personal ambient displays and to give users feedback about sensed and self-reported transportation behaviors. Driven by the spread of smart meters (e.g., Strengers [33, 34]) and energy

---

[1] http://www.tii.se/node/5984

monitors, research on portable and stationary energy consumption displays resulted [40] that the comparison between these monitors showed that users took both displays to identify high-power devices in their home whereby conserve energy. But after the initial survey, participants used the portable displays as stationary ones. A current eco-feedback technology design, the eco-end user application prototype POEM (Personal Office Energy Monitor) was presented by Milenkovic et al. [20]. Petkov et al. [25] tried to understand what feedback individuals find relevant for energy savings. They designed mock-up screens that provide eco-feedback catering towards different pro-environmental values and concerns, and asked users to evaluate them. The most respondents ranked the egoistic screen as highest. They show how environmental psychology could play a role in informing the design of persuasive applications that motivate energy saving behavior. Also, Massung et al. [16] offered new insights and recommendations on the pro-environmental design of systems that target groups and communities.

In [22] a theoretical foundation is offered for how to study Behavior Change Support System (BCSS) defining behavior change archetypes as well as design principles for such systems. A central cluster of work focused on Electricity Consumption Feedback and highlighted emerging energy system trends with strong relevance to HCI and interaction design, including smart grid, demand response, and distributed generation technologies [26]. They outlined a range of opportunities to engage emerging systems referring to experimental, behavioral, social, and cultural aspects; new areas move beyond, i.e., energy feedback displays, increase awareness, and motivate individual conservation behavior.

1.2   Studying Long-Term Change through Persuasive Systems

Summarizing the above-mentioned studies, a lot of work has already been done in order to influence consumption behavior with respect to energy. However, only little work exists on long-term persuasive effects of these persuasive systems. The idea to compare on-site social stairs vs. "Piano-Staircase" (each step plays a note) toward long-term behavior change was currently investigated [24]. The goal was to help users to activate intrinsic motivation and not to persuade or extrinsically motivate them to act or behave differently in that moment of time. However, their outcome could not present a solution of which trigger lead to intrinsic motivation.

Moreover, we want to mention three specific long-term studies in the energy sector similar to our research. We reference the current work of Smeaton and Doherty [31] as linkage between energy consumption and long-term data collection. In their experimental setup, 24 households were involved and they collected electricity consumption data over a period of 18 months. Four real-time intervention methods to impact the reduction of consumption were used. Due to the fact that we also used a display in our research, we focused on the results of their touchscreen display. Further interventions were an initial web page, e-mail rewards, and a web portal. First, background information was gathered and built up into an energy consumption behavior profile. Second, participants got the touchscreen application, which noted recorded savings. Results showed that thirteen regular households saved 14% in one month on average after receiving access to the desktop display, 9% two months later, 14% three months later, and 16% four months later. They concluded their work with the statement that a variety of feedback mechanisms and interventions may be needed in order to sustain user interest. The EcoTeam Program [32] is an intervention package that aims to target considerable number of behaviors and durable change in pro-environmental behavior. A detailed analysis of the three-year longitudinal study of behavior suggests that the interplay between the factors behavioral intention and habitual performance can predict participation before the study and the degree of social influence experienced during participation. A focus on the appraisal of climate risks and interactive approaches to influence energy consumption in households are mentioned [19]. They state that sustainable consumption is conceptualized as the result of various types of interactions between users and systems.

1.3   Research Gap

The information needed for appropriate actions is not presented in the context where it is needed most, i.e., when interacting with the home appliances or environment. Therefore, the feedback lacks a direct and tangible link to the consumers' behavior. Beyond self-monitoring, ambient displays made it easier for the user to reflect their behavior or attitude by arising unconscious aspects, such as our electricity consumption, to our awareness. These aspects give us the possibility to understand and react accordingly. An ambient/situated display can support reflection and allow adjusting reactions. Current studies of such displays frequently have shortcomings with regard to long-term effectiveness; initial results tend to wear off once the novelty effect is over. We clearly acknowledge the value and the need of short-term studies in order to improve the design of a system, e.g. [5] and to identify major issues (e.g., usability). There are few studies that investigate ambient persuasive displays in private households over a long period to get insights about attitude and behavior change. We claim that in order to gain an understanding how our persuasive systems need to be designed to have a sustainable persuasive interface, long-term field studies with actual representative users and mature deployed systems are required. We contribute an essential part to comprehend persuasion and sustainability.

Our research attempts to focus at improving the communication of energy feedback by seamlessly integrating it in the environment of the user and providing it where and when it is most useful and efficient. Such an integration of feedback could increase the comfort of the users, as no abstract translation and explicit attention towards achieving the goals is needed. Additionally, we provide forecast information to set a link between timing of activity and feedback information for maximum efficiency and conclusive traceability for the feedback values. The objective of our study is to research and develop new strategies and tools for the home context that provide energy-saving related feedback in a persuasive and unobtrusive way and, thereby, have the potential to help to reduce energy consumption without loss of comfort. We explore persuasive technologies to influence behavior towards optimized end-user energy management. Tailored persuasive approaches overcoming limitations of existing solutions have been developed, prototyped, and experimentally validated with real user in realistic long-term settings. Thus, we decided to conduct a seven-month study in 24 households, which is accompanied by several different questionnaires at various points of measurement to identify that aspects change after which period of time.

2   The FORE-Watch

The aim of our study was to explore if this eco-management technology, *FORE-Watch,* influences the energy consumption behavior, specifically with regard to the timing of consumption activities, either to consume energy when the grid status is high or when green energy is available, over a longer period of time. The *FORE-Watch* triggers energy consumption behavior through cues equipped with persuasive strategies. Our seven-months in-situ household study involved 24 running systems on tablets and installed smart meters in private homes. The study was accompanied by several different questionnaires at various points of measurement to identify if attitudes and behaviors are changing over time (*t*) and if so which aspects of the App caused the change. Moreover, we wanted to explore if the different forecast methods also impact how participants experience the *FORE-Watch* and its persuasive potential.

2.1   Design and Implementation

We want users to align their energy consumption with requirements from production and distribution within the grid. The design process was based on various sources, both theoretical (literature review) and empirical-based (user requirements and design experts). We decided to focus on the familiar and well-known system of the traffic light system with red, yellow, green, to adjust action. Due to the fact that this color code was recognized unconsciously and intuitively, there is little cognitive demand. Furthermore, the device is based on a kitchen clock and shows additional information to the time of day. The *FORE-Watch* consists of two views: the forecast and the feedback. Each view presents three cues equipped with persuasive strategies (see Fig. 1). The instruction of activities for the participants is as described. There are three colors: green represents a request of action (e.g., turning on the washing machine), yellow an action realization is not recommended, and red an action realization should be avoided. Darker shades represented unsuitable moments for action, while brighter shades depict a suitable moment for action to obtain a smooth transition. This color-triad also represents good, bad, medium performances based on the adjustment at the forecast and the KW/h-consumption. In the following we present each cue.

Clock. The clock displays the forecast of green energy/grid status profile of the next hour in detail per minute. The background information about the different forecast views is more complex. The colors indicate activities, but the composition of (1) static, dependent of the grid load patterns and (2) dynamic, dependent of the availability of the eco-electricity (windmills) are different. (1) Green means a lot of energy is available and convenient to consume the stream and perform action; yellow means there is a moderate amount and red reflects limited energy available. (2) Green means a lot of electricity is produced, unfavorable to consume the stream and perform action; yellow, medium level of energy; and red, there is little electricity produced.

Timeline. This timeline indicates the forecast of the next 24 hours. The kink of the axis indicates the current hour and divides the areas of *"today"* and *"tomorrow"*.

 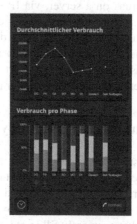

Fig. 1. Forecast view: Clock, timeline *"today"* and timeline *"tomorrow"* (left), and the feedback view: Average consumption, consumption per phase, and reward icons (right)

Average Consumption. The display shows the average electricity consumption (in KW/h units) over a week, the day before is labeled as *"yesterday"*. The dot represents the average from baseline start.

Consumption per Phase. This implies: How much energy to a certain red, yellow, or green zone of the clock was consumed in proportion to the KW/h consumption. It uses two modalities of feedback electricity consumption (1) bar chart, which is divided into a week (the day before is labeled as *"yesterday"*) and the average consumption from baseline start, and (2) reward icon for honor that are three levels of performances/adjustment of the forecast (gray-shades for good, very good, excellent).

2.2   Integration in the Home

In the following section, we present how the *FORE-Watch* was integrated in the private homes of our participants, explaining the interaction loops between the smart meter, the tablet on which the *FORE-Watch* was running, and the servers where data was stored. Furthermore, we explain how the color and feedback visualizations for seven days were calculated.

Forecast Data. The grid status data (*static forecast*) was provided daily by the energy consumption company. The data was computed according to a mathematical model by the usability research and engineering company. For the green energy group, the wind forecast (*dynamic forecast*) was used from the Norwegian Meteorological Service. For our purpose, the data of Salzburg/Austria were retrieved. This forecast is only available in a six-hour rhythm; the values were interpolated to get a fifteen-minute interval. For both conditions, data were sorted and transformed into color (top third assigned green, second third yellow, and final third red).

Feedback Data. The smart meters sent the consumption data of the customer to a database, which runs on a server, via IP gateway and cable modem (wireless). The consumption data from our cooperating energy consumption company, which was stored in a database on a server, sent this data to one of our servers and categorized it into phases. Thus, the consumption was immediately updated in that current color which is then displayed in the bar chart. At the end of the day, the totals for the various colors were compiled. In a similar procedure the trophies were developed.

3   The Long-Term Field Study

Our long-term study was set-up as a low-intrusive study with little researcher involvement. Therefore, we decided to start the field phase with kick-off workshops in which the participants were informed about the *FORE-Watch*, followed by the gathering of all attitudinal measures by the means of online surveys in which participants could conveniently fill in at home. At the end of the study, final reflection workshops were conducted with the participants in order to gather qualitative data, as well as give participants the opportunity to provide feedback. Moreover, the integration of the *FORE-Watch* in the smart meter architecture allowed us to constantly gather KW/h-data on the energy consumption behavior.

The following set of research questions synthesizing attitudinal change drives this exploratory household study. (1) Can an attitudinal (behavior) change be observed in the perception of the *FORE-Watch* depending on the various forecasts (static vs. dynamic)? (2) Can an attitudinal (behavior) change be observed in the perception of the *FORE-Watch* depending on the various points of measure?

3.1   Participants

A total of 28 users (24 energy consultants and four of their partners) participated in our seven-month study (M=44.85, SD=8.20 years; educational levels: 75.0% teaching/professional school, 10.7% high school/ a-levels, 10.7% college/university). The recruitment was done with consulting experts of the energy company. This procedure was efficient on the basis of the ongoing time and the effort to install the smart meter and the IP-Gateways; the predefined count of smart meters reduces the households that participate at the study. As a result, we got a more homogenous group (men, between 29-55 years), where we could calculate tendencies. We separated this group of 24 households into two parts with random distribution of the living space in square meter, the type of house (one-family house, apartments, and townhouse), and the number of household members. We made this separation because we used the possibility to integrate two forecast conditions: the dynamic one, which is the green energy profile, and the static one, which represents the grid status group.

3.2   Measurement

We used online surveys as evaluation of the *FORE-Watch* in various trials during the study to gather self-reporting data. These questionnaires gave us results about attitude and awareness change. The various types of questionnaires can be distinguished in two categories: (1) the *FORE-Watch* questionnaires include the Single-Cue Questionnaire (SCQ), and the Grouped-Cue Questionnaire (GCQ), and (2) the User Characteristic questionnaires (UCQs) with the General Questionnaires (GQs) the Profile Questionnaires (PQs), and the User Experience Questionnaires (UXQs). We used the UXQs to get an overview of the users' experience interacting with *FORE-Watch*, their motivation in different phases during seven-months, and their trust into the application. Moreover, quantitative data was collected through the integration of the *FORE-Watch* in the smart meter architecture that allowed us to constantly gather data on the energy consumption behavior (KW/h units). The UCQs consisted of a compilation of various sub-questionnaires. The advantage of these questionnaires was especially in their standardization and, thus, the repeated use monitored changes in attitude and self-evaluation to determine attitude changes. The frequency of measurement time points enabled us to include smaller setting changes within the study period, which would otherwise have remained hidden. This supports the measurement of long-term patterns of behavior and attitude in real environments.

3.3   Procedure

We started the field phase with kick-off workshops to inform participants about the *FORE-Watch* and to complete the following parts of the UCQs. The GQs: *Technic Affinity Questionnaire (TA-Q)* [11], *General Motivation Questionnaire (GMQs)*, the PQs: *Meyers-Briggs Type Indicator (MBTI)* [4], and *NEO Personality Inventory (NEO-FFI)* [3]. The study closed with final reflection workshops in order to gather qualitative data (recording) as well as to give participants the opportunity to give feedback. During the study, all measures were taken by the means of online surveys sent to fill in via web link (see Fig. 2). The UXQs were measured three times at twelve-week intervals over seven-months as well as the SCQ; the GCQ ten times at two-week intervals.

Fig. 2. Long-term data collection

In the following, we present in detail the UXQs. The *Intuitive Interaction (INTUI)* [35] is a tool for detecting various components of intuitive use and experience while their product usage. The *Positive and Negative Affect Scale (PANAS)* [38] detects the emotional state. The *Unified Theory of Acceptance and Use of Technology (UTAUT)* [37] is a tool that provide a unified theoretical basis from which to facilitate research on information system and technology adoption and diffusion. The *Technology Acceptance Model2 (TAM2)* [36] used the approach of behavioral intention and extend it with social influence and cognitive process variables. The *Attractiveness makes the Difference2 (AttrakDiff2)* [9] rates the user experience product perceptions and evaluations. We also used the *TRUST* [18] questionnaire, the *Need Scale* (NS) [10], and the Motivation Questionnaires (the Short *Scale of Intrinsic Motivation* (SIM) [39], the *Incentive Focus Scale* (AF-S)[2], the *Perceived Locus of Causality* (PLOCQ) [15], and the *Situational Intrinsic Motivation Scale* (SIMS)[15]).

4   Results and Interpretation

As mentioned before, the results of our long-term study (March-September 2012) are the online survey results of the UXQs, the procedure of the data analysis, and the results and implications of the attitudinal change of participants over time. With a 76% response rate, we achieved an excellent result, as 20% is an average common result for email based online surveys [1]. The recruitment of energy consultants as participant's maybe a reason for the high commitment and the fact that the *FORE-Watch* as intervention in the home was a constant reminder for study participation.

In the data analysis, our external project partner screened the KW/h-data of the forecast view and the feedback view. They analyzed the consumption data from smart meter with the access to the fifteen-minute consumption values of the users. All smart meter failures were adjusted. An assessment of displacement effects could be enabled per user by means of time differentiated in fifteen minutes intervals and were calculated by working days, Saturdays, or Sundays/holidays. For each of these intervals, a difference between current consumption and mean over seven-months was calculated. The data transfer of the forecast always ran stable, as it had a separate exchange of information cycle. Due to indirect monitoring, we could calculate that on average, the *FORE-Watch* was activated over 60% of the time. However, based on the missing consumption cycle or interruptions of the feedback data, we had to eliminate several item sets of the attitudinal questionnaire belonging to the feedback view. We used the following criterion for data exclusion. If the consumption signal was unstable less than five out of fourteen days, the data for this period of time was excluded as we defined that five consecutively days are a decent reference score. In order to identify whether or not a questionnaire had to be excluded, we compared the timestamp of the missing data with the questionnaire schedule. Then, we searched for the missing consumption data and checked if the person was on vacation or if response patterns could be identified in the data.

4.1   Findings on Attitudinal Change and Implications

We present selected findings of the UXQs, which give insight into the attitudinal change of our two user groups at three times of measurement. Our data was not normally distributed, therefore, we depict in Table 1 the bivariate correlation

---

[2] http://www.psych.uni-potsdam.de/people/rheinberg/
messverfahren/index-d.html

(Spearman) stratified by total group (TG): static and dynamic group (Mann-Whitney U-Test) and all significant effects (p) for all times of measurements ($t1$-$t3$).

No significant effects (all p's = >.05) during $t1$ to $t3$ in the total group and between the static vs. dynamic group were revealed at the Need Scale [10] and at three out of four Motivation Questionnaires[2] [15, 39]. Therefore, we conclude that participants responded similar to these questionnaires during the run of the always-on *FORE-Watch*.

Significant results could be identified for the **INTUI** questionnaire. The group answer differs in the scale *magical experience* at $t3$ (p=.047), whereas static has higher scores (Mdn=4.50; dynamic Mdn=4.00), i.e., the interaction with the product is seen as extraordinary and fascinating. The scale goes beyond the fulfillment of tasks. Implication: Eco-feedback and management products achieve their value not at the beginning of their usage; their interaction value rises after a period of time.

The analysis of the **PANAS** revealed at the scale *"How did you feel in the last days? (LD)"* and the scale *"How did you feel in general? (G)"* on $t1$ significant (p_{LD}=.009; p_{G}=.012), whereby the static reached higher scores (Mdn_{LD}=30.40; Mdn_{G}=34.30; dynamic Mdn_{LD}=19.10; Mdn_{G}=26.20). In both scales, the positive affect scale achieved higher scores as the negative affect scale. Therefore, the emotional state during the usage of the display was positive with the qualities: active, excited, attentive, enthusiastic, committed, excited, interested, strong, proud, and alert. Implication: Ambient persuasive displays obtain a positive effect over time.

For the *interest/enjoyment* scale of the **SIM** at $t1$, a significant difference could be identified (p=.034), whereby dynamic reached higher scores (Mdn=2.67; static Mdn =1.33). At the beginning of the study, the interaction with the *FORE-Watch* was more entertaining and interesting for the dynamic forecast group. Implication: The factors fun and enjoyment seemed to be a short-term phenomenon. Due to the fact that enjoyment and interest are very flexible, individual depended variables, and nearly impossible to sustain, flexibility in information presentation through updates could be the sustainable solution to maximize enjoyment and interest for a product.

The analysis of the **UTAUT** questionnaire revealed that at $t1$ the scale *effort expectancy* calculate a significant difference (p=.033), whereby dynamic reached higher scores (Mdn=19.25; static Mdn=16.50), meaning that they considered more effort to use the application than the static. This result was expected at the beginning of our study, as the forecast view of green energy is more dynamic than that of the grid status, which was clearer, more comprehensible, and easier to learn and to use at the beginning. Implication: Displays who present information in a dynamic way are more complex, require more attention, and take a longer time to pass to routine/habit.

At $t1$, the scale *behavioral intention to use the system* the groups differed significantly (p=.019), in which the static (Mdn=14.00) has higher scores (dynamic Mdn=10.67). That indicates that they presented a higher intention of long-term use. Implication: After short-term use, the static group recognizes a higher potential for long-term use of our ambient persuasive display. This may have caused due to the fact that they reached their routine behavior earlier, as their presented information is more periodic.

The rating for the scale *perceived usefulness* of the **TAM2** on $t1$ and $t3$ differed significantly (p_{t1}=.041; p_{t3}=.029). The static (Mdn_{t1}=9.67; Mdn_{t3}=11.17) had in both times of measurement higher scores (dynamic: Mdn_{t1}=8.67; Mdn_{t3}=7.00). The results depict that the static view shows an easier handling with the application, which indicated a higher perceived usefulness at $t1$ and at $t3$. In the mid-term, no differences

Table 1. User Experience Questionnaire: Significances

Questionnaire	Time	Scale	Total Group		Static & Dynamic			
	t		r_s	$p*$	U	z	$p*$	r
INTUI	3	Magical Experience	.42	.040	33.5	-1.99	.047	-.41
PANAS	1	Last Days	-.52	.006	32.5	-2.60	.009	-.51
	1	In General	-.50	.009	34.0	-2.52	.012	-.49
SIM	1	Interest/Enjoyable	-.41	.031	52.0	-2.12	.034	-.40
UTAUT	1	Effort Expectancy	-.43	.030	41.5	-2.13	.033	-.42
	1	Behav. Intention[1]	-.47	.015	37.5	-2.35	.019	-.46
TAM2	1	Perceiv. Usefulness[2]	-.41	.038	43.5	-2.04	.041	-.40
	3	Perceiv. Usefulness[2]	-.45	.025	38.0	-2.19	.029	-.44
	1	Output-Quality	-.51	.008	34	-2.54	.011	-.50
	2	Output-Quality	-.58	.002	27	-2.91	.004	-.57
	1	Result Demonstr.[3]	-.44	.026	40.5	-2.18	.029	-.43
AttrakDiff2	1	Pragmatic Quality	-.59	.001	25.5	-2.97	.003	-.58
	1	Attractiveness	-.60	.001	25.0	-3.00	.003	-.59
	1	Hedonic Qu.-S.[4]	-.70	.000	15.5	-3.49	.000**	-.68

* p = 2-tailed
** Highly significant
[1] Behavioral Intention to Use the System
[2] Perceived Usefulness
[3] Result Demonstrability
[4] Hedonic Quality - Stimulation

were detected. At the beginning of the usage, the interaction with the application is for both groups necessary to understand how it supports their decision and manage behavior. Implication: Perceived usefulness is an important aspect that underpins the success of our watch over time, as it is rated important not only short-term but also long-term. But, we also recognize that it plays no role any longer after three months. At the scale *output-quality* on *t1* and *t2*, the groups were significantly different (p_{t1}=.011; p_{t2}=.004); the static (Mdn_{t1}=5.50; Mdn_{t2}= 6.00) had in both times of measurement higher scores (dynamic Mdn_{t1}=4.50; Mdn_{t2}=4.50). At the beginning and in mid-term, the grid status group stated that they are satisfied with the quality of data and that the quality is generally very high. Implication: The data output should be presented in a high quality, balanced way. There were group differences in the positive sense about their opinion and attitude in short-term and mid-term. At the scale *result demonstrability*, the groups at *t1* differed significantly (p=.029), whereby the static (Mdn_{t1}=12.50) scored higher (dynamic Mdn_{t1}=10.75). This scale shows that the user has no difficulty to tell others about the results; it is easy to do or to explain the impact of the application, as well as that fact that the usage of the application is obvious. At the beginning of the study, the groups gain positive insights about the meaning of the FORE-Watch. They know about the background of the display and feel well informed about it. Implication: Knowledge about a product itself, background information, and 'sense-attributing' application as reduction or conservation of energy can be an indication for long-term usage.

For the scale *pragmatic quality* of the **AttrakDiff2,** the groups differed significantly in the rating (p=.003) at *t1*. The static (Mdn=29.86) had higher scores (dynamic: Mdn=25.71). This predicts that certain users may use it to achieve the specified goal, as to adjust action with effectiveness, efficiency, and satisfaction. The ratings of the product as simple, practically, and clearly is an indication that the *FORE-Watch* was very well accepted; there were group difference at short-term, which disappeared afterwards. Implication: Simplification and practical applications are well-known criteria for the success and efficiency of products. Significant results (p=.003) were presented for the scale *attractiveness*, whereby the static (*Mdn*=27.86) had higher scores (dynamic: *Mdn*=24.57) at *t1*; the application is among others considered nice, good, attractive, and inviting. Implication: Attractiveness is a strong component of the advertisement like "attractive products sell better." The success of an ambient persuasive display seems also to be depended on its attractiveness. For the subscale *hedonic quality - stimulation* significant differences between groups (p<.001) could be found at *t1*, for which the static (*Mdn*=28.57) had higher scores (dynamic *Mdn*=24.57). The group output presents that the App stimulated the human need of personal development, i.e., the impact of knowledge and skills is different by groups. The *FORE-Watch* is innovative. Implication: Ambient persuasive displays, which are convincingly innovative, have a higher potential of usage, as they show their actuality and novelty as well as their future view of our society.

After the presentation of the results in granularity, we can answer the research questions. In the perception of the *FORE-Watch*, we observed an attitudinal change between the various forecast groups and points of measurement. The green energy group rated the forecast presentation (and the feedback presentation) more positively as the grid status group. At the three times of measurement, the grid status group had higher scores, especially at *t1*, than the green energy group.

4.2   Behavioral Change

The analysis of the KW/h-consumption of the two experimental groups resulted that a low correlation between consumption behavior and the dynamic group exists; a weak trend is presented for the static group. This difference was expected since the dynamic group due to the different temporal dynamics of the forecast had more room for a maneuver. Moreover, the calculation of "consumption per phase" points out that behavioral change appeared to occur particularly in red phases. Shifting of activities occurs also into yellow and not only in green phases, which can be explained by the proximity in time. This shifting into yellow (adjacent) and non-green area maybe resulted in the fact that the time horizon for activity shifting is very short and depends on type of activity. This can possibly be explained by increased consumption in the yellow zone with a simultaneous reduction in the red zone. Furthermore, the absence of real-time consumption data, the non-presented data from the pre-phase of the study and the temporal periodicity of the forecast, the evidence of effects for the static group is particularly difficult. Over the period of seven-months, we analyzed the temporal periodicity (24 hours) of the forecast and, contrary to our expectations, we find out that the static forecast presented information more dynamic (s-curve with the peak around 11:00 a.m.) than the green energy/dynamic forecast itself. Belonging to the weekly forecast presentation, we saw recurring patters in the grid status group and slowly shifting and atypical timely accumulations.

However, there are some indicators for the coherence of the KW/h-data: (1) data is consistent with the qualitative information of the subjects, (2) data shows expected differences between dynamic and static group, and (3) there is a magnification of the effect during the operating hours of the devices.

5   Discussion

In sum, six out of ten questionnaires used over three different points of measurement revealed significant results, i.e., 12 out of 32 scales show answer differences by groups. Five out of ten questionnaires present significant results at the beginning of the study. All questionnaires showed significant differences between the groups at *t1* excluding the *INTUI,* which revealed significant results at the scale *magic experience* at *t3.* At these three times of measurement, the grid status group had in eleven out of fourteen scales higher scores than the green energy group. Interestingly, the results of the *TAM2* confirmed differences for two scales at two times of measurement, *perceived usefulness* presented significant differences between *t1* and *t3,* and *output-quality* depicted significant differences between *t1* and *t2.*

In the next section, we discuss our results for further research in the field of ambient displays and for the metering infrastructure and smart meters. Our qualitative survey revealed that the grid status group showed a more constant behavior on the basis of the considered answers than the green energy group, indicating that the more dynamic forecast presentation of the green energy did not lead to the same type of attitude change as in the grid status group. This result of the groups cohere with our assumption that the green energy group needed more time to be in touch with the *FORE-Watch,* i.e., to understand the presented information. Due to our energy consultants, we assume that other population groups need far longer to adjust their activity rhythm at the *FORE-Watch.* We suppose that the dynamic forecast group status caused a steeper learning curve and that the forecast is needed as a supportive tool in long-term use, as the availability of green energy does not follow a constant pattern. The grid status group could quickly learn the grid status forecast with the watch and, therefore, change their behavior sustainably (even without a forecast on the long run). Especially for the first time of measurement, the grid status group had higher scores in four out of five questionnaires than the green energy group. The green energy group presented various results regarding to the answers of the *INTUI* at the third time of measurement. In the mid-term and at the end of the study, the grid status group showed higher scores at the *AttrakDiff2.* These results indicated that the grid status group at the beginning of the study was more satisfied in using the App than the green energy group. At the end of the study, the acceptance increased for the grid status group and the intuitive use of the application for the green power group. Based on the questionnaires of motivation and the need scale, both seemed to be factors which are nearly independent and less connected to influence participants during the use of the *FORE-Watch.* At the issue of users' behavior change, we can emphasize a magnitude of the effect size over the seven-month in-situ study; there is small significant correlation by the dynamic group and the static group presents a tendency.

In summary, attitude change and behavior change took place: the grid status group had more attitude changes by the *FORE-Watch* at the beginning of the study as the green energy group. However, this fact changed, and disappeared at the end of the study. Overall, the green energy group rated the forecast presentation and the feedback presentation more positive than the grid status group and showed more behavior change. Altogether, the behavior change arose in the red phases as well as modifications occurred in the yellow and also green phases.

In comparison to similar approaches (e.g. Peeters et al. [24], Smeaton and Doherty [31], Staats et al. [32]), we also advocate that intervention tools lead to changes of attitude or behavior. We understand the *FORE-Watch* as a trigger to target durable change in pro-environmental behavior. We agree with the argumentation of Midden et al. [19] that sustainable consumption is conceptualized as the result of various types of interactions between users and systems, and argue that our App equipped with various strategies supports the user-system interaction every time. Our study showed that the overall concept of the *FORE-Watch* as ambient persuasive display was feasible for our participating households in a seven-month period of time, which leads us to the conclusion that it could sustainably change energy consumption behavior.

6   Conclusion

In general, our results presented that a lot of effects on user experience factors are relevant at the beginning of a study (short-term), but this effect decreases after seven-months. In long-term usage of the *FORE-Watch,* only the *TAM2* presents significant group difference on two scales at two times of measurement and the *INTUI* calculate significant differences between groups. Our results led us to the implication that the users showed relevant experiences at the first usage of the eco-technology and, if the usage were ongoing, the application would be integrated in daily life whereby other kinds of experiences occur and become important/essential for long-term sustainable change. As to answer our research questions, we can summarize that the user's attitude and behavior was modified during seven-months (three times of measurement) and between the groups justified in various forecasts.

With our work we contribute to the first long-term studies of user-centered developed persuasive ambient displays for home energy management. We can review that the variation of questionnaires was very fruitful in terms of methodology and give an extensive view of user's motivation, emotion, need, technology acceptance, and trust. The future step for this system include an in-depth investigation of persuasive cues that support the usage and promise to convey the desired behavior modification, without the interventions are experienced as intrusive or restrictive.

Acknowledgements. This work is part of the PEEM-Project (Persuasive End-user Energy Management) and funded by the Austrian Research Promotion Agency (FFG, grant 82550). It was supported by project partners Salzburg AG, and Center for Usability Research and Engineering (CURE).

References

1. Andrews, B., Nonnecke, D., Preece, J.: Electronic survey methodology: A case study in reaching hard to involve Internet users. Int. J. of HCI 16(2), 185–210 (2003)
2. Beale, R., Courage, C., Hammontree, M., Jain, J., Rosenbaum, S., Vaughan, M., Welsh, D.: Longitudinal Usability Data Collection: Art versus Science? In: Proc. CHI EA 2008 (2008)
3. Borkenau, P., Ostendorf, F.: NEO-FFI, 2nd version personality questionnaire (2008)

4. Briggs, K., Myers, I.: Developed (1989); German version: Bents, R., Blank, R. (1995)
5. Costanza, E., Ramchurn, S.D., Jennings, R.J.: Understanding Domestic Energy Consumption through Interactive Visualisation: a Field Study. In: Proc. UbiComp 2012 (2012)
6. Fogg, B.J., Eckles, D.: Mobile Persuasion: 20 Perspectives of the Future of Behavior Change. Stanford Captology Media (2007)
7. Froehlich, J., Dillahunt, T., Klasnja, P., Mankoff, J., Consolvo, S., Harrison, B., Landay, J.A.: UbiGreen: Investigating a mobile tool for tracking and supporting green transportation habits. In: Proc. CHI 2009, pp. 1043–1052 (2009)
8. Froehlich, J.: Promoting Energy Efficient Behaviors in the Home through Feedback: The Role of Human- Computer Interaction. In: Proc. HCIC 2009 Winter Workshop Boaster Paper (2009)
9. Hassenzahl, M., Burmester, M., Koller, F.: AttrakDiff: Ein Fragebogen zur Messung wahrgenommener hedonischer und pragmatischer Qualität. In: Ziegler, J., Szwillus, G. (hrsg.) Mensch & Computer 2003. Interaktion in Bewegung, pp. 187–196 (2003)
10. Hassenzahl, M., Diefenbach, S., Göritz, A.: Needs, affect, and interactive products – Facets of user experience. Interacting with Computers 22(5), 353–362 (2010)
11. Karrer, K., Glaser, C., Clemens, C., Bruder, C.: Technikaffinität erfassen – der Fragebogen TA-EG. In: Lichtenstein, A., Stößel, C., Clemens, C. (hrsg.) Der Mensch im Mittelpunkt technischer Systeme. 8. Berliner ZMMS Spektrum, Reihe 22, vol. 29, pp. 196–201 (2009)
12. Kluckner, P.M., Weiss, A., Sundström, P., Tscheligi, M.: Two Actors: Providers and Consumers inform the Design of an Ambient Energy Saving Display with Persuasive Strategies. In: First Int. Conf. on Behavior Change Support Systems (BCSS), Adjunct PERSUASIVE 2013, Position Paper, pp. 33–44 (2013)
13. Kluckner, P.M.: Improving long-term Persuasion for Energy Consumption Behavior: User-centered Development of an Ambient Persuasive Display for private Households. In: Adjunct PERSUASIVE 2013, Ext. Abstracts (2013)
14. Kukka, H., Oja, H., Kostakos, V., Goncalves, J., Ojala, T.: What makes you click: Exploring visual signals to entice interaction on public displays. In: Proc. CHI 2013, pp. 1699–1708 (2013)
15. Lonsdale, C., Sabiston, C.M., Taylor, I.M., Ntoumanis, N.: Measuring Student Motivation for Physical Education: Examining the Psychometric Properties of the Perceived Locus of Causality Questionnaire and the Situational Motivation Scale. Psychology of Sport and Exercise 12, 284–292 (2011)
16. Massung, E., Coyle, D., Carter, K., Jay, M., Preist, C.: Using Crowdsourcing to support Pro-environmental Community Activism. In: Proc. CHI EA 2013, pp. 371–380 (2013)
17. Mattern, F., Staake, T., Weiss, M.: ICT for green: how computers can help us to conserve energy. In: e-Energy 2010: Int. Conf. on Energy-Efficient Computing and Networking, Interdisciplinary Quarterly, vol. 16(1), pp. 98–105 (2010)
18. McKnight, D.H., Carter, M., Thatcher, J.B., Clay, P.F.: Trust in a specific technology: An investigation of its components and measures. Trans. Manag. Inform. Syst. 2(2), Article 12, 25 pages (2011)
19. Midden, C., McCalley, T., Ham, J., Zaalberg, R.: Using persuasive technology to encourage sustainable behavior. Sustainability WS PERVASIVE 2008 (2008)
20. Milenkovic, M., Hanebutte, U., Huang, Y., Predergast, D., Pham, H.: Improving user comfort and office energy efficiency with POEM (personal office energy monitor). In: Proc. CHI EA 2013, pp. 1455–1460 (2013)
21. Neustaeder, C., Bartram, L., Mah, A.: Everyday Activities and Energy Consumption: How Families Understand the Relationship. In: Proc. CHI 2013, pp. 1183–1192 (2013)
22. Oinas-Kukkonen, H.: A foundation for the study of behavior change support systems. J. Personal and Ubiquitous Computing (2012)

23. Pasch, M., Landoni, M.: Longitudinal assessment of a user experience evaluation tool for children. In: Proc. CHI EA 2012 (2012)
24. Peeters, M., Megens, C., van den Hoven, E., Hummels, C., Brombacher, A.: Social Stairs: Taking the Piano Staircase towards Long-Term Behavioral Change. In: Berkovsky, S., Freyne, J. (eds.) PERSUASIVE 2013. LNCS, vol. 7822, pp. 174–179. Springer, Heidelberg (2013)
25. Petkov, P., Köbler, F., Goswami, S., Krcmar, H.: Personalised Eco-Feedback as A Design Technique for Motivating Energy Saving Behaviour at Home. In: Proc. NordiCHI 2012 (2012)
26. Pierce, J., Paulos, E.: Beyond energy monitors: Interaction, energy, and emerging energy systems. In: Proc. CHI 2012, pp. 665–674. ACM Press (2012)
27. Reitberger, W., Kastenmiller, M., Fitzpatrick, G.: Invisible Work: An Ambient System for Awareness and Reflection of Household Tasks. In: Berkovsky, S., Freyne, J. (eds.) PERSUASIVE 2013. LNCS, vol. 7822, pp. 180–191. Springer, Heidelberg (2013)
28. Riche, Y., Dodge, J., Metoyer, R.A.: Studying always-on electricity feedback in the home. In: Proc. CHI 2010, pp. 1995–1998. ACM, NY (2010)
29. Schrammel, J., Gerdenitsch, C., Weiss, A., Kluckner, P.M., Tscheligi, M.: FORE-Watch - The clock that tells you when to use: Persuading users to align their energy consumption with green energy availability. In: Keyson, D.V., et al. (eds.) AmI 2011. LNCS, vol. 7040, pp. 157–166. Springer, Heidelberg (2011)
30. Shneiderman, B., Plaisant, C.: Strategies for Evaluating Information Visualization Tools: Multi-dimensional In-depth Long-term Case Studies. In: WS BELIV 2006 (2006)
31. Smeaton, A.F., Doherty, A.R.: Persuading Consumers to Reduce their Consumption of Electricity in the Home. In: Berkovsky, S., Freyne, J. (eds.) PERSUASIVE 2013. LNCS, vol. 7822, pp. 204–215. Springer, Heidelberg (2013)
32. Staats, H., Harland, P., Wilke, H.A.M.: Effecting Durable Change. Environment and Behavior 36(3), 341–367 (2004)
33. Strengers, Y.A.A.: Designing eco-feedback systems for everyday life. In: Proc. CHI 2012 (2012)
34. Strengers, Y.A.A.: Smart metering demand management programs: challenging the comfort and cleanliness habitus of households. In: Proc. OZCHI 2008, pp. 9–16 (2008)
35. Ullrich, D., Diefenbach, S.: Exploring the Facets of Intuitive Interaction. In: Ziegler, J., Schmidt, S. (eds.) Mensch & Computer, pp. 251–260 (2010)
36. Venkatesh, V., Davis, F.D.: A Theoretical Extension of the Technology Acceptance Model: Four Longitudinal Field Studies. J. Manag. Science 46(2), 186–204 (2000)
37. Venkatesh, V., Morris, M.G., Davis, G.B., Davis, F.D.: User Acceptance of Information Technology: Toward a Unified View. MIS Quarterly 27(3), 425–478 (2003)
38. Watson, D., Clark, L.A., Tellegen, A.: Development and validation of brief measures of Positive and Negative Affect: The PANAS scales. J. of Personality and Social Psychology 54, 1063–1070 (1998); German translation: Krohne, H.W., Egloff, B., Kohlmann, C.-W., Tausch, A.: Experimental study with the German version of "Positive and Negative Affect Schedule". Diagnostica 42, 139–156 (1996)
39. Wilde, M., Bätz, K., Kovaleva, A., Urhahne, D.: Überprüfung einer Kurzskala intrinsischer Motivation, pp. 31–45 (2009)
40. Yun, T.-J.: Investigating the impact of a minimalist in-home energy consumption display. In: Proc. CHI EA 2009, pp. 4417–4422 (2009)

Low-Power Ambient Sensing in Smartphones for Continuous Semantic Localization

Sînziana Mazilu, Ulf Blanke, Alberto Calatroni, and Gerhard Tröster

Wearable Computing Laboratory
Swiss Federal Institute of Technology Zürich, Switzerland
{sinziana.mazilu,ulf.blanke,alberto.calatroni,troester}@ife.ee.ethz.ch

Abstract. Extracting semantic meaning of locations enables a large range of applications including automatic daily activity logging, assisted living for elderly, as well as the adaptation of phone user profiles according to user needs. Traditional location recognition approaches often rely on power-hungry sensor modalities such as GPS, network localization or audio to identify semantic locations, e.g., *at home*, or *in a shop*. To enable a continuous observation with minimal impact on power consumption, we propose to use low-power ambient sensors – pressure, temperature, humidity and light – integrated in phones. Ambient fingerprints allow the recognition of routinely visited places without requiring traditional localization sensing modalities. We show the feasibility of our approach on 250 hours of data collected in realistic settings by five users during their daily transition patterns, in the course of 49 days. To this end, we employ a prototype smartphone with integrated humidity and temperature sensor. We achieve up to 80% accuracy for recognition of five location categories in a user-specific setting, while saving up to 85% of the battery power consumed by traditional sensing modalities.

1 Introduction

Location is one of the most common information types humans frequently use in their daily lives, either for navigation to a destination, geo-tagging images with visited spots, or for discovering points of interests on maps. It has been shown that location is a powerful cue for human activities [15] and gained popularity in activity recognition [10] or for learning daily routines automatically [9].

The notion of location has various meanings: it can be expressed in geographic coordinates, e.g., latitude and longitude, as human readable addresses such as street name and number, or as logical labels of the places, e.g., Central Park, the McDonald's around the corner [1]. Our understanding of location refers to routinely visited places in daily life. We refer to these as *semantic locations*, as introduced in [16]. Examples include someone's *home* or *office*, but also non-fixed locations such as commuting by *train*, or *in a shop*, which can map to different physical locations. This information can be fed into location-based services or applications, such as refined searches of places of interest, targeted advertisement, urban planning, analysis of user patterns or triggering user profiles on the handset.

J.C. Augusto et al. (Eds.): AmI 2013, LNCS 8309, pp. 166–181, 2013.

State of the art systems for semantic localization rely on modalities such as GPS [9], WiFi, Bluetooth beacons [4] or audio [5] [11]. While feasible for sporadic localization, their power consumption hinders continuous monitoring [3,14]. More power efficient approaches use triangulation with cell towers based on signal strength. Apple's iOS region monitoring service, for instance, makes use of this to continuously monitor if a user enters or exits a certain zone. However, localization is coarse in the range of 100s of meters of radius, even with good network coverage, and is designed for fixed geographic locations only.

Fig. 1. Recognizing semantic locations (e.g., home, train, office, shop, and outdoors) using low-power sensors from the phone: *atmospheric pressure, light, temperature,* and *humidity*

In this work, we propose an alternative path to identify routinely visited locations. We investigate ambient characteristics (i.e. barometric pressure, temperature, light, and humidity) for fingerprinting locations. Observation of such characteristics and their variations by a combined set of low-power ambient sensors can indicate whether a user is indoors or outdoors, distinguish between different indoor places or even indicate the means of transportation. For example, *home* or *office* are characterized by a location-specific pressure value ranges. Also, indoor places such as corridors or elevators are characterized by specific and constant light. To capture such characteristics continuously, we employ ambient sensors, i.e., pressure, light sensors, thermometers and hygrometers integrated in a commodity smartphone. With combinations of these sensors we capture a rich set of ambient characteristics that allows to recognize a variety of personalized semantic locations that are routinely visited. The sensor's low power profile allows us to minimize the power consumption. In addition, such sensors become lately embedded in commercially available phones, e.g., Samsung Galaxy S4. This gives the opportunity to assess the semantic location of the phone's user in a realistic and non-intrusive manner.

To study our hypothesis we collected a real-life dataset from five subjects during 49 days. Subjects recorded sensor data using a prototype phone during daily-life activities and they annotated their semantic locations. To study the feasibility of ambient fingerprinting for semantic localization, we formulate the semantic location recognition as a supervised machine learning task.

Our main contributions are as follows: (i) We implement a sensing and recognition platform allowing us to gather, visualize and analyze data from the sensors incorporated in customized smartphone, (ii) we recorded a large and naturalistic dataset from various users for testing the feasibility of our hypothesis, and (iii) we show the effectiveness both in terms of recognition performances and power consumption for ambient sensing for distinguishing typical daily locations visited by a user.

The remainder of this paper is structured as follows. In Section 2 we present the rationale for using ambient sensing data to do semantic location recognition. Section 3 reviews the state of the art in semantic localization and power-saving approaches for activity and context recognition. In Section 4 we describe the collected dataset. Further, Sections 5 and 6 present the experimental results on recognition performances and power consumption of the ambient sensors from the smartphone. Finally in Section 7 we discuss and conclude our work.

2   Multimodal Ambient Sensing for Semantic Localization

Our goal is to study whether we can recognize different semantic locations from a user's daily-life pattern using multimodal ambient sensing, such as temperature, humidity, pressure and light of the different locations. We postulate that semantic locations such as the *home, office, car, train, restaurant*, or *pub* that are visited by a person are defined by a specific combination of values from these sensors, and these combinations form the *fingerprint* of the location. For example, homes, offices, and even public transportation tend to have constant ranges of temperature and humidity, as they are equipped with air-conditioned systems set to maintain these ambient conditions constant. Restaurants and pubs tend to have higher temperature values than other living places, due to cooking or because they are crowded.

Our research question is: *Is multimodal ambient-based fingerprinting sufficient to discriminate between the locations?* As in [1] we believe that these fingerprints are not necessarily unique and can be shared between different places. Nevertheless, the ambient fingerprints of more general categories, e.g., *train, car, restaurant*, are expected to be sufficiently different, thus allowing to distinguish between them. Also, people have their own set of semantic locations, that are visited during the daily-life pattern. Thus for a user-centric approach, we need only the fingerprints of the places visited by that specific user.

To evaluate the informative power of the multimodal ambient sensing data, we formulate the semantic location recognition approach as a standard supervised machine learning task. To capture the ambient conditions for semantic localization we use light, barometric pressure, humidity, and temperature sensors embedded in a phone. We follow the same steps as in the case of an activity recognition problem solved with supervised machine learning techniques [17], and use data collected from the sensors and the annotated semantic locations to learn how to distinguish between the different locations. For that we follow the next steps: the acquired continuous data is segmented into non-overlapping time windows. We extract mean, standard deviation, min- and max-values for each of the four sensing modalities, and label them with their equivalent semantic location. The resulted feature vectors are then fed into a C4.5 classification tree to learn a discriminative model of the semantic locations. C4.5 was chosen because of its low computational complexity, which makes it appealing for a future deployment directly on the phone.

3   State of the Art

Location and Semantic Location. In [2] GPS data is used for mining semantic locations such as shopping malls and restaurants. However, continuous use of GPS localization is extremely power-hungry [3,14]. Furthermore, it relies on good GPS perception which can be inhibited when the phone is held in pocket or bag for example or fails completely for indoor locations. WiFi, GSM signatures and Bluetooth-based localization can replace or compensate GPS data [6] to automatically assess the personal semantic locations and daily routines of the user, but the frequency at which the Bluetooth module needs to be used might impact negatively the battery life [3]. Audio is a very rich source of information to capture a location's characteristics [5,11,19,20], but comes at significant battery drainage.

The idea of using small wearable devices with embedded sensors such as light, pressure, acceleration, audio and temperature to detect the context of an individual roots back to the work of Schmidt et al. [21]. Low-power sensing approaches like fingerprinting of room colors and sensing of pressure, light intensity, temperature and humidity have been considered [13], but always in addition to power-hungry modalities [1,8]. Pressure sensing has been used in isolation but only in a constrained setting of recognizing subway stations [23].

Ravi et al. [18] use the light properties of the indoor places, e.g., offices and corridors of a CS department for fingerprinting and indoor localization. Azyzian et al. [1] propose SurroundSense, a mobile framework to detect the logical indoor locations, e.g., Starbucks, McDonald's, by creating a fingerprint of each indoor location based on the data collected from ambient sound, light, color, or RF layout-induced user movement. Lane et al. [7] use accelerometer, light and temperature data for the so-called *ambient beacon localization* to distinguish different regions of mobile sensors. However, their evaluation relies on simulated data with a limited number of locations.

Power Saving. Wang et al. [22] propose a framework for energy efficient mobile sensing by using a hierarchical sensor management strategy to recognize the user states and detect state transitions. A minimum set of sensors are turned on to monitor the current state of the user, and a new set of sensors is triggered only when it is necessary to detect a state transition. The evaluation done on ten users over one week shows that their approach can increase the battery life up to 75%, while identifying the end-user activities. Yan et al. [24] seek to reduce the energy consumption on the mobile phones for continuously detecting locomotive activities by adapting the accelerometer sampling frequency manually creating groups of activities for each sampling rate. Lu et al. [12] propose Jigsaw, an engine for continuous sensing for mobile phones which are dynamically turning on/off the acceleration, GPS and audio sensors.

4   Dataset Collection

We gathered data from five subjects (S1 to S5): two graduate students and three employees working in different companies, two females and three males, with ages varying between 26 and 51 years. Except for two employees, all subjects exhibit a regular daily life, consisting of working, leisure time at home, commuting, or shopping.

4.1   Sensing Platform

We used a modified Samsung Galaxy Nexus phone, courtesy of Sensirion AG[1], with four ambient sensors integrated. Pressure and light sensors are incorporated off the shelf. In addition, temperature and relative humidity sensors have been integrated (see Fig 2(a)). For comparison to state of the art localization, we obtained location from Android location services and we gathered data from the microphone to compare to localization approaches based on audio. The data was recorded in the background by an Android application and stored locally, with each user visiting between 4 and 11 semantic locations.

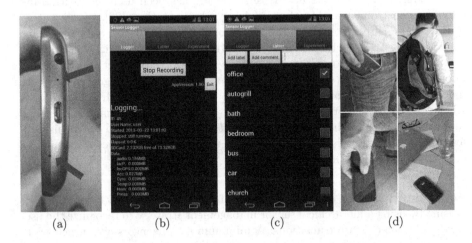

(a)   (b)   (c)   (d)

Fig. 2. (a) The modified Samsung Galaxy Nexus with added temperature and humidity sensors, (b, c) screenshots of the Android application for data gathering, and (d) an illustration of different phone wearing-contexts for a user during its daily-pattern (pocket, backpack, hand, table)

---

[1] http://www.sensirion.com

4.2   Data Recording

Subjects were asked to use the prototype phone for the data collection as if it was their own. This naturalistic usage resulted in different placements of the phone, e.g., different pockets, in the backpack, purse, on the table, on the couch. Variations of the placement occurred between different users as well as for single users, e.g., wearing the phone in the purse while commuting or wearing it in the trouser's pocket during work or putting it on the office desk. Users recorded data for at least five consecutive days. Additionally, arbitrary days within a month have been recorded. In total, we gathered 250 hours of data, during 49 days of sensor data from five users in realistic settings.

Table 1. User-annotated semantic locations

High level category	Semantic Location
Outdoors	general outdoors
Indoor public places	Opera, Theater, Cinema, Church, Shop, Department store, Mall, Pub, Restaurant, Cafeteria, Seminar room
Indoor personal places	Home (living room, office home, bedroom, bathroom, kitchen), Office (office room, meetings room, conference room), Friends home, Indoor (other)
Transportation	Tram, Train, Car, Bus, Funicular

4.3   Data Annotation

The Android application used for data recording offers user interfaces to label semantic locations. It contains a list of predefined categories, e.g. *home, tram, train, car*, but gives the option to add individual categories (Fig 2(c)). This allows to capture a personalized set of the semantic locations in which individual subjects reside. Table 1 contains the sum of all semantic locations grouped in categories that were labeled by all subjects during data collection. Subjects did not visit all the locations enumerated, but only a subset of locations visited on a week-pattern basis for each of them. In total we obtained labeled data for 26 categories of semantic locations. Users provided annotations in real-time when changing their location, resulting a total of about 1000 location changes. Annotations were not always provided at the exact time of location change. However, the users remained in the locations for a sufficient time and annotated data correctly, allowing to neglect this label noise.

5   Location Recognition Experiments

Each subject experienced an individual lifestyle with specific activities and semantic locations during the recording days. Also, the same semantic location category, e.g. *home, office*, had different ambient signatures for each subject, i.e., *home* category for S1 does not have the same ambient fingerprint as *home* category of S5. Therefore, we consider for the semantic-location recognition model a subject-dependent learning and classification scheme, as semantic categories are specific for each individual user.

5.1   Evaluation

We compare our approach based on low power sensors – temperature (T), humidity (H), pressure (P), light (L) – to two baseline approaches: (1) standard Android localization using GPS and WiFi/GSM fingerprinting, and (2) localization using audio data collected with the smartphone microphone. The time-series collected from the sensors are divided into non-overlapping segments of W seconds. For each window we consider latitude and longitude data obtained from Android's location manager, as standard localization data. For audio localization, we extract from the time-window 13 *Mel-frequency cepstral coefficients* (MFCC) channels, and for each MFCC channel we compute *mean* and *standard deviation* as features. An experimental evaluation of multiple window lengths $W \in \{5s, 10s, 15s, ...30s\}$, showed similar performance results for semantic location recognition. Therefore, we fixed the window size to $W = 10s$. For both baselines we use the same machine learning technique, i.e, C4.5 trees, as for our approach with low-power sensors. This paper does *not* aim to find the best performing algorithm for semantic localization for each type of sensor. Our objective is to investigate the feasibility of using ambient low-power sensors data from a smartphone for semantic location of the smartphone's user. Thus, we fixed the classifier to C4.5 trees throughout the remainder of the paper.

To evaluate the semantic location recognition performance, we conduct for each of the five subjects a *leave-one-recording-out* cross-validation. We report the accuracies averaged per category, so the semantic location in which the users reside in.

5.2   Visual Inspection of Ambient Sensor Data

Fig. 3 illustrates how data from ambient sensors in the phone characterizes several daily locations. It shows 90 minutes of continuous sensor data and the corresponding localization tracks collected from a phone. The subject wore the phone in the trousers pocket, used different transportation modes (*car, tram*) and visited typical locations during her daily life (*home, office, restaurant*). The variations of the sensor readings can be clearly seen during the location changes. The pressure is constant at the *home, office* and *restaurant* locations, since they lie at a certain altitude. Furthermore, temperature and humidity have different ranges across locations. The light intensity is informative at the beginning and at the end of this recording, since the phone was put on the table at home and in the office, yielding a characteristic light intensity, i.e., in the office there were neon tubes, whereas at home there were traditional, warmer light bulbs.

We observe that for each semantic location, the data variations contain discriminative information, that form a signature of various activities, e.g., when

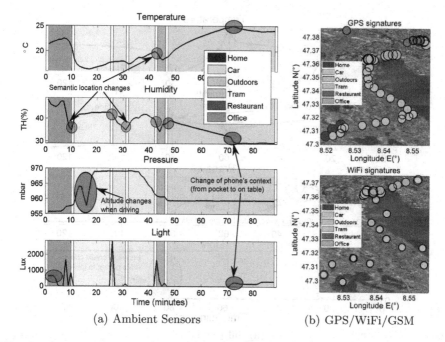

Fig. 3. An example of 90 minutes of multimodal data from (a) low-power ambient sensors from the phone (temperature, humidity, pressure, light), and (b) Android Location Service (GPS, WiFi/GSM). Semantic locations can be inferred from the data patterns (for ambient sensors) as well as directly from the physical coordinates

the phone's context changed from *in the pocket* to *on the table*, in the *office* location. Temperature and humidity data gives the same clues, and furthermore we can easily see the moment when the location changes. When in the *car* or *tram*, the pressure is varying, being dependent on the altitude and weather conditions, thus giving a clue on the moving semantic location of the user. Fig. 3(b) shows the physical coordinates, which were obtained by Android Location service – GPS, WiFi and GSM data. These location signatures are sufficient to provide information about the locations and the moving pattern of the user. However, GPS failed to acquire the satellites when indoors or even when the phone was placed in the pocket. Locations obtained from WiFi and GSM triangulation are partially imprecise, e.g., some coordinates are in the middle of the lake, while some others describe multiple semantic locations such as *home*, *outdoors*, and *car*. This can be only remediated by large temporal smoothing windows. Fig. 4 shows additional examples of multimodal ambient sensing data from two other subjects. In Fig. 4(a) data is collected from a user with a regular daily pattern that commutes in the morning. Again one can observe clear differences in temperature, humidity and pressure signatures between the fixed semantic locations, e.g., *home* and *office* and transportation, thus making it possible to distinguish between them and *outdoors* category. Light sensor data gives discriminative

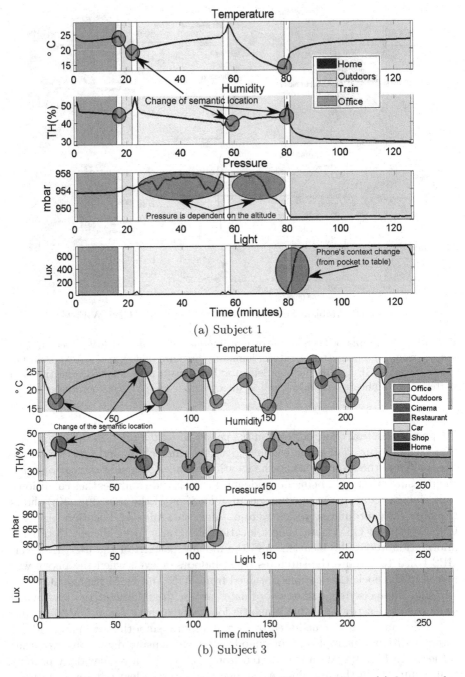

Fig. 4. Example of ambient sensing data from two different subjects: (a) from a subject with a fixed daily-pattern in the morning, and (b) from a subject with complex transitions over the day

information only in case of *office* location. Fig. 4(b) shows data from a user with a more complex daily-pattern, containing many transitions between the seven semantic locations. Still, we observe specific combinations for locations such as *cinema, office, restaurant* and *home*. For the *shop* category, respectively location, the data exhibits variation, as there are two distinct shops that are visited by the user. Furthermore, in temperature and humidity data are signatures of transition from one semantic location to another, e.g., from *car* to *outdoors, outdoors* to *shop, office* to *restaurant*. As in the previous figure, the light sensor data changes give information when the context of the phone changes, e.g., on the table, in the pocket.

Further, Fig. 5 presents a visualization example of the average temperature vs. the average humidity values for the dataset S1 with four semantic locations (*office, home, train* and *outdoors*) to which the *null category* is added. Same as before, the original time series was cut into windows of 10 seconds. We observe the data has a fibrous appearance, being clustered in threadlike series, corresponding to different recordings. Even if overlapping, data tends to form stable clusters corresponding to the different labeled locations. For example, *home* and *office* data formed two distinct, non-overlapping clusters. Although spread on a larger area, the *train*-category data is also grouped in a distinct cluster.

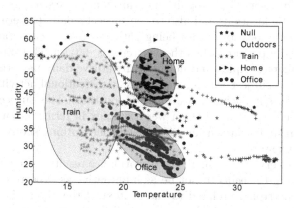

Fig. 5. A scatter plot with temperature vs. humidity for S1 dataset, with 5 semantic location categories

5.3   Overall Recognition Performances

Table 2 contains the overall semantic location recognition results for ambient sensors, audio, and physical location data gathered for each of the five subjects, with the locations specific for each user's weekly pattern.

For the multimodal ambient sensing we evaluate different subsets of data: TH (temperature and humidity data), THP (temperature, humidity and pressure), THL (temperature, humidity and light) and THPL (temperature, humidity, pressure and light). In case of low-power sensing models, the best results are obtained

Table 2. Average accuracies (%) over all categories for each subject dataset, for semantic-location detection, in case of using low-power sensing data (different subsets), audio data, and location data (GPS and WiFi/GSM coordinates), for $W = 10s$ windows

Subject	S1	S2	S3	S4	S5
TH	70	48.6	32.5	71.9	47.1
THP	69.5	**61.6**	**41.9**	**73.3**	**55.3**
THL	76.3	45	35.6	63.4	40.4
THPL	**80.3**	59.6	41.3	66.3	43.9
Audio	51	26.6	39.5	46.9	33.1
Location	55.5	40.7	38.7	61.4	38.6
Number of Semantic Locations	5	7	12	5	9

when using THP (for S2, S3, S4, S5) and THPL (for S1). For all subjects the ambient-sensors-based recognition methods outperform the recognition methods based on physical coordinates location and audio data, with up to 25% improvement, for the S1 dataset. The recognition performances are strongly linked to the number of semantic locations and also to the subject's daily pattern: S1 dataset has only 4 semantic locations, data being gathered from a corporate employee with a regular daily pattern. The other extreme is dataset S3, from a graduate student with a more complex and not often repetitive daily pattern – after the working hours, the subject was having different recreational activities, consisting of *cinema, theater, opera, shops* semantic locations. This subject visited 11 semantic locations and some of them were complex in terms of data variations - e.g., the *shop* includes data from different smaller clothing shops, department stores and grocery stores.

As a general observation from all the performance results on the five datasets, data from light sensor seems to not be as informative as expected. A reason is that light data is strongly related to the context of the phone, i.e., where the phone is placed, and not to the location visited by the user. For example, light information can be the same when the user visits *home, outdoors, train, car, office* personal locations, because the phone is located in the pocket, so light data obtained will have similar values, which will not help discriminate between the locations. So the best combination of ambient sensors to create a fingerprint range of visited locations are temperature, humidity and barometric pressure.

Low-power, audio and location-based recognition are equally affected by the label noise. Previous studies [9] showed that GPS is sufficient to provide information about outdoors locations. However, in these studies the GPS unit was attached to the user's hat or backpack for better accuracy. In our study we found that in a realistic setup, i.e. phone placed in the pocket or in bag, indoors, or even in the trains, the GPS did not produce any location data in 39% of the time, as only 45 out of 113 recordings were containing GPS data. When no data from GPS were available, we took into account the information from network localization. However, the coarse location estimation leads to the confusions and low recognition rate of semantic locations. In contrast our proposed set of ambient sensors does not suffer from signal loss and continuously acquires ambient parameters.

5.4   How Informative Is the Multimodal Ambient Sensing Data?

Fig. 6 contains the confusion matrices for the combinations of low-power ambient sensing data that performed best in detecting the semantic locations, for datasets S1 and S5. For S1 dataset, while *home* and *office* are well recognized, there are confusions for *train* and *outdoors*. The ambient sensing data converges in describing the fixed semantic locations, e.g., *home*, *office*, while transportation is strongly connected to the outdoors conditions. In case of dataset S5, most of the confusions appear between the indoor locations, e.g., *bathroom* is detected sometimes as *home* or *office*, *home* is mislabeled as *office*. Even if the ambient data describing the *home* and *office* locations is different, for this particular dataset the *home* category was under-represented compared with the *office*, thus resulting in these confusions. Similar to dataset S1, there are confusions between modes of transportation, i.e., *tram* and *train*.

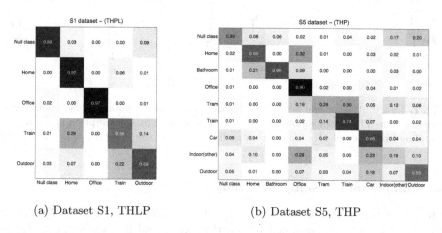

(a) Dataset S1, THLP   (b) Dataset S5, THP

Fig. 6. The confusion matrices for location recognition for datasets S1 and S5

The *indoor* category contains all the indoor data that was not included in the other semantic locations. Being a general category, indoor is often mislabeled as *outdoors, car,* or *office*. The ambient sensors measurements are different for each indoor location, therefore this category cannot be reliably detected.

6   Power Consumption Experiments

In this section we perform an analysis of the power consumption of the smartphone sensors. We begin with a rough estimation of consumption based on sensor datasheet figures. Then, we empirically study the battery drainage during data collection with different combinations of sensors.

6.1 Datasheet-Based Consumption Estimation

In Fig. 7 we plot the distributions of semantic localization accuracies reported to the power consumption of the sensing modalities. The horizontal axis shows a coarse estimation of the power consumption. We used the values provided in the datasheets by the sensor manufacturers for the prototype used in recordings. Surprisingly, using ultra-low-power sensors does not come at an expense of the performance detection, but it rather introduces more variance in the results. The THP combination appears to be the most stable one, having higher median and more compact distribution compared to all others. In theory this combination is up 180x less power-hungry than audio and location based recognition. However, the measurements do not include the computational effort for semantic location detection.

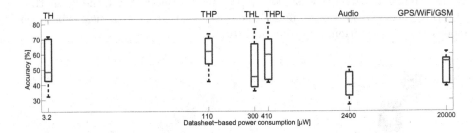

Fig. 7. Distribution of the accuracies for different sensor combinations versus power consumption. The boxes represent the 75th percentile. The consumption is given for a sampling frequency of 1Hz, apart from audio, where the sampling frequency is $16kHz$.

6.2 Empirical Consumption Study

The total power consumed during data gathering is $P_{total} = P_{sensor} + P_{gathering}$. P_{sensor} is the power consumed to run the sensor and its associated analog to digital converters. $P_{processing}$ is the power consumed while moving, storing and processing the data from the sensor. It includes the consumption of the processor, system memory, system storage and various system buses. In the previous section we took into account only P_{sensor}. For a more realistic evaluation, we have to include the second component. To this end, we monitor the battery level while running the data gathering application for the different combination of sensors used in the performance evaluation section.

The results are plotted in Fig. 8 for (a) the prototype phone with temperature and humidity sensor integrated, used during the recordings, and (b) the recently released Samsung Galaxy S4, which has the same humidity-temperature sensor integrated. For both phones, temperature-humidity, pressure and light sensors were set at the highest sampling rate from Android API, as they were used during the data gathering experiments. The audio data was gathered at $16kHz$. All the empirical battery consumption experiments were performed in similar settings as the data gathering for dataset S3. As expected, the most power hungry data were from GPS/WiFi/GSM and audio. Surprisingly for the THPL combination of sensors the battery consumption was similar as in case of audio and location data, but only for the Samsung Galaxy S4 phone.

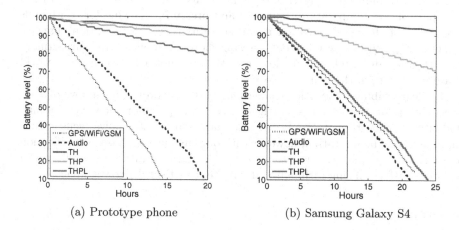

(a) Prototype phone   (b) Samsung Galaxy S4

Fig. 8. The measured battery level in case of collecting different sensor data combinations from (a) the prototype phone with temperature-humidity sensor integrated, and (b) a Samsung Galaxy S4 phone

However, in the previous performance analysis experiments for semantic location detection we concluded that light data is not informative enough to help to discriminate between different locations. So our target for power consumption analysis was the temperature, humidity and pressure (THP) combination. Still, with the other combinations that do not imply light sensor, we can save from 65% (THP) up to 85% (TH) of battery in case of Samsung Galaxy S4. We expect to increase the power savings when setting the ambient sensors to lower sampling rates in Android API.

In case of the phone prototype, for gathering all the ambient sensing combinations, we can save from 70% of battery (THPL) to around 85% (TH), when compared to gathering audio and standard location data.

7   Conclusion

Many mobile computing applications benefit from knowing the user's semantic location. In this work we study the feasibility of recognizing semantic locations from low-power ambient sensors embedded in phones. We gathered 250 hours of data from five subjects in a naturalistic setting during typical phone usage. In total 26 labeled semantic locations, e.g., *office, shop, church* have been annotated. Experimental results show that semantic location recognition with low-power ambient sensors can be an alternative to standard localization methods, i.e., GPS/WiFi/GSM and audio, while significantly reducing the power consumption and saving up to 65% of battery power for the THP sensor combination, and up to 85% for the TH combination.

Experiments show that the best combination of low-power ambient sensors to create discriminative fingerprints of locations visited by an user during a week-pattern are temperature, humidity and pressure. Allowing for continuous monitoring of the user's location it can serve as trigger for location changes, e.g., entering/exiting train, leaving/entering shop, for applications. Furthermore such triggers can be released for locations that are not attached to fixed world coordinates, e.g., in the train, in the car.

The clear visibility of location changes in the data is promising and we plan on investigating location changes as triggers. For example, more power-consuming modalities can be triggered only when a change in the low-power sensor data was observed. The limitation, however with our current supervised classification approach, is to require the user to annotate the data. In future research we will explore transfer learning techniques and make use of third party sources.

References

1. Azizyan, M., Constandache, I., Choudhury, R.R.: SurroundSense: mobile phone localization via ambience fingerprinting. In: International Conference on Mobile Computing and Networking, MobiCom (2009)
2. Cao, X., Cong, G., Jensen, C.S.: Mining significant semantic locations from gps data. Proc. VLDB Endow. 3, 1009–1020 (2010)
3. Carroll, A., Heiser, G.: An analysis of power consumption in a smartphone. In: Proceedings of the 2010 USENIX Annual Technical Conference (2010)
4. Eagle, N., Pentland, A.(S.): Reality mining: sensing complex social systems. Personal Ubiquitous Computing 10, 255–268 (2006)
5. Eronen, A.J., Peltonen, V.T., Tuomi, J.T., et al.: Audio-based context recognition. IEEE Transactions on Audio, Speech and Language Processing 14, 321–329 (2006)
6. Hightower, J., Consolvo, S., LaMarca, A., Smith, I., Hughes, J.: Learning and recognizing the places we go. In: Beigl, M., Intille, S.S., Rekimoto, J., Tokuda, H. (eds.) UbiComp 2005. LNCS, vol. 3660, pp. 159–176. Springer, Heidelberg (2005)
7. Lane, N.D., Lu, H., Campbell, A.T.: Ambient beacon localization: Using sensed characteristics of the physical world to localize mobile sensors. In: 4th Workshop on Embedded Networked Sensors in Cooperation with ACM SIGBED & SIGMOBILE, EmNets (2007)
8. Lester, J., Choudhury, T., Kern, N., et al.: A hybrid discriminative/generative approach for modeling human activities. In: International Joint Conference on Artificial Intelligence, IJCAI (2005)
9. Liao, L., Patterson, D.J., Fox, D., et al.: Learning and inferring transportation routines. Artificial Intelligence 171, 311–331 (2007)
10. Liao, L., Fox, D., Kautz, H.: Location-based activity recognition. In: Neural Information Processing Systems, NIPS (2005)

11. Lu, H., Pan, W., Lane, N., Choudhury, T., et al.: SoundSense: scalable sound sensing for people-centric applications on mobile phones. In: International Conference on Mobile Systems, Applications, and Services, MobiSys (2009)
12. Lu, H., Yang, J., Liu, Z., Lane, N.D., Choudhury, T., Campbell, A.T.: The Jigsaw continuous sensing engine for mobile phone applications. In: International Conference on Embedded Networked Sensor Systems, SenSys (2010)
13. Lukowicz, P., Junker, H., Stäger, M., von Büren, T., Tröster, G.: WearNET: A distributed multi-sensor system for context aware wearables. In: Borriello, G., Holmquist, L.E. (eds.) UbiComp 2002. LNCS, vol. 2498, pp. 361–370. Springer, Heidelberg (2002)
14. Paek, J., Kim, J., Govindan, R.: Energy-efficient rate-adaptive gps-based positioning for smartphones. In: Proceedings of the 8th International Conference on Mobile Systems, Applications, and Services, Mobisys (2010)
15. Partridge, K., Golle, P.: On using existing time-use study data for ubiquitous computing applications. In: International Conference on Ubiquitous Computing, Ubicomp (2008)
16. Pradhan, S.: Semantic location. Personal Technologies 4, 213–216 (2000)
17. Ravi, N., Dandekar, N., Mysore, P., Littman, M.L.: Activity recognition from accelerometer data. In: Seventeenth Conference on Innovative Applications of Artificial Intelligence, IAAI (2005)
18. Ravi, N., Iftode, L.: Fiatlux: Fingerprinting rooms using light intensity. In: Pervasive (2007)
19. Rossi, M., Tröster, G., Amft, O.: Recognizing daily life context using web-collected audio data. In: International Symposium on Wearable Computers, ISWC 2012 (2012)
20. Rossi, M., Feese, S., Amft, O., Braune, N., Martis, S., Tröster, G.: AmbientSense: A real - time ambient sound recognition system for smartphones. In: International Workshop on the Impact of Human Mobility in Pervasive Systems and Applications (PerMoby) 2013 (2013)
21. Schmidt, A., Beigl, M., Gellersen, H.-W.: There is more to context than location. Computers & Graphics 23, 893–901 (1999)
22. Wang, Y., Lin, J., Annavaram, M., Jacobson, Q.A., Hong, J., Krishnamachari, B., Sadeh, N.: A framework of energy efficient mobile sensing for automatic user state recognition. In: International Conference on Mobile Systems, Applications, and Services, MobiSys (2009)
23. Watanabe, T., Kamisaka, D., Muramatsu, S., et al.: At which station am I?: Identifying subway stations using only a pressure sensor. In: International Symposium on Wearable Computers (ISWC), pp. 110–111 (2012)
24. Yan, Z., Subbaraju, V., Chakraborty, D., et al.: Energy-efficient continuous activity recognition on mobile phones: An activity-adaptive approach. In: International Symposium on Wearable Computers, ISWC (2012)

Fast Adaptive Object Detection towards a Smart Environment by a Mobile Robot

Shigeru Takano[1], Ilya Loshchilov[2], David Meunier[2],
Michèle Sebag[2], and Einoshin Suzuki[1]

[1] Dept. Informatics, ISEE, Kyushu University,
819-0395 Fukuoka, Japan
{takano,suzuki}@inf.kyushu-u.ac.jp
[2] TAO - CNRS & Univ. Paris-Sud
LRI, Bat. 490, Univ. Paris-Sud,
F-91405 Orsay, France
ilya.loshchilov@gmail.com, {david.meunier,michele.sebag}@lri.fr

Abstract. This paper proposes a novel method to detect objects by a mobile robot which adapts to an environment. Such a robot would help human designers of a smart environment to recognize objects in the environment with their attributes, which significantly facilitates his/her design. We first introduce Lifting Complex Wavelet Transform (LCWT) which plays an important role in this work. Since the LCWT has a set of controllable free parameters, we can design the LCWTs with various properties by tuning their parameters. In this paper we construct a set of LCWTs so that they can extract local features from an image by multi-scale. The extracted local features must be robust against several kinds of changes of the image such as shift, scale and rotation. Our method can design these LCWTs by selecting their parameters so that the mobile robot adapts to the environment. Applying the new set of LCWTs to the images captured by the mobile robot in the environment, a local feature database can be constructed. By using this database, we implement an object detection system based on LCWTs on the mobile robot. Effectiveness of our method is demonstrated by several test results using the mobile robot.

Keywords: adaptive object detection, keypoint detection, on-board robot vision, visual words, lifting complex wavelet transforms.

1 Introduction

Recognizing objects in an environment with their attributes is an important first task for a designer of a smart environment. The task has been traditionally resolved by the designer manually, posing a considerable burden to him/her. Especially, it is necessary to estimate state attributes concerned with people and objects within the environment. These state attributes can be discriminative properties of the objects and the people, e.g., the object is still or moving, the person is walking or sitting. Typical conventional systems for ambient intelligence

J.C. Augusto et al. (Eds.): AmI 2013, LNCS 8309, pp. 182–197, 2013.
© Springer International Publishing Switzerland 2013

have been developed with the sophisticated sensing technologies [5] with various sensors embedded in objects and clothing of people in the environment. We have witnessed a significant progress of autonomous mobile robots in these years [4], [7]. It is natural to use such a robot to fulfill the recognition task.

In this paper, we argue that the adaptation to the environment of the mobile robot is the key to success. Our mobile robot acquires a set of local features from images captured in the environments. A local feature is defined as an image pattern which differs from its immediate neighborhood, e.g. corners, blobs, edges [12]. Generally a lot of various local features can be extracted from an image including several objects. Our adaptation significantly reduces the computation time of the robot so that it operates in real time.

Our approach is to detect objects using Content Based Image Retrieval (CBIR) [10], which is to judge whether an object is known or unknown by whether a similar image exists in a database. So far visual features such as color, shape and textures of images, have been used in the CBIR systems. The most studied topic the CBIR at present is to extract local features such as SIFT [6] and SURF [1]. Although it has become possible to run SIFT and SURF algorithm on an ordinary PC, it is still required to develop faster method for extracting local features for onboard root vision. The paper [7] also proposed a method for object recognition by a mobile robot. However, since this method assumes smart objects equipped with wireless sensors, it is time consuming and cannot be used when a wireless sensor network is unavailable.

Our object detection is based on Lifting Complex Wavelet Transform (LCWT) [11], which is complex wavelet transform (CWT) [3] with controllable free parameters. We call them lifting parameters. The LCWTs within the lifting parameters can be adjusted so as to adapt to the environment. This means that our robots can acquire the local features efficiently since the LCWT can be trained so as to increase the useful local features for the object detection in number and to reduce the other features.

In the paper [11] we have introduced a set of LCWTs which can extract multi-scale features of the image. They are comparable to Difference of Gaussian (DoG) images which are used to extract SIFT features. By virtue of a fast wavelet transform algorithm, our LCWT can be computed faster than the DoG images computed by applying 2D Gaussian filters. Moreover, we can reduce the computation of local features in each scale. The reason is that because we only compute multi-scale components of the LCWT in the case in which the first components are greater than a specified threshold, which are obtained by applying the initial CWT to the image. The LCWT components in each scale can be easily computed by adding lifting terms, which include the lifting parameters, to the initial CWT components.

Using the multi-scale LCWT components we can detect keypoints which are robust for several kinds of changes of the image. Our method obtains a feature vector of 128 dimension in each keypoint of the image, which are computed by using the oriented gradients around it. In order to build our CBIR system, we extract all feature vectors from training images captured by the mobile robot, and then cluster these vectors to form a vocabulary of visual words [9]. More recent works [8] successfully used k-means clustering but has difficulty in controlling the number of clusters. In this paper we use ϵ-mean clustering [2] to the set of feature vectors. Selecting ϵ parameter, we can tune the number of clusters which represent visual words. We expect that our CBIR system can retrieve similar images accurately as the entropy of the distribution of the feature vectors increases. Therefore we determine the lifting parameters so as to increase this entropy. Concretely we propose an algorithm for increasing the entropy based on genetic algorithm. The main contribution of our method is that the LCWTs can be designed so as to adapt to the environment for the mobile robot.

The outline of this paper is as follows. In Section 2, we give an overview of our adaptive object detection through CBIR using LCWT, and our robot architecture. Section 3 summarizes the LCWT and the multi-scale feature extraction. Section 4 presents algorithms for detecting and clustering of the keypoints in images, which are used in our CBIR system based on the LCWT, and shows how we design the adaptive LCWT to an environment. Section 5 contains experimental results. Concluding remarks and future work are given in Section 6.

2   Adaptive Object Detection for On-Board Robot Vision

2.1   Adaptive Object Detection

As noted above, our goal is to detect objects by a mobile robot adapting to the environment. We design the LCWTs so as to adapt to images captured in the indoor environment. We first apply the LCWTs to the training images, and then obtain the feature vectors. We next build the visual vocabulary by applying the ϵ-means clustering to the set of feature vectors.

The visual vocabulary can be evaluated by the entropy of distribution of these vectors. We train the LCWTs by the evolutionary algorithm so as to increase this evaluation. By using the trained LCWT our robot can extract the existing or new object in the indoor environment. Figure 1 illustrates an overview of our adaptive object detection.

2.2   Robot Architecture

Our robot moves in an indoor environment by two wheels and a supporting ball, and is equipped with a USB camera and an IR sensor. Since this camera and sensor can rotate from the left-hand side to the right-hand side and up and down by using three servos, our robot can capture images and measure the distance to obstacles in the area in front of the robot.

Our on-board robot vision is implemented on the Pandaboard, which is driven by the dual-core ARM Cortex-A9 OMAP4430, with each core running at 1 GHz, and equipped with 1 GB DDR2 RAM. A captured frame is in resolution of 320×240, and color depth of monochrome 8bit. The functions of robot vision can be operated on a Linux OS installed on the Pandaboard. Our mobile robot is shown in Fig.2.

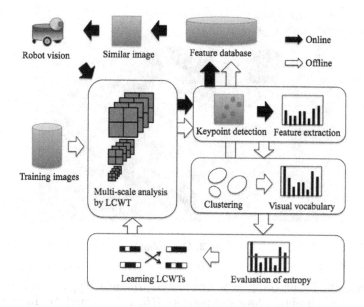

Fig. 1. Overview of adaptive object detection

3   Multi-scale Feature Extraction

In order to detect an object by robot vision, it is necessary to extract features fast from video frames captured by the mobile robot. This section introduces the LCWT [11] to extract multi-scale features of an image. The LCWT has controllable free parameters. We prepare a set of these lifting parameters for a multi-scale analysis of the image. Applying our LCWT to the video frames, we can obtain their multi-scale features fast.

3.1   Lifting Complex Wavelet Transform (LCWT)

Let us denote a set of complex wavelet filters by $\{h_k^{o,r}, g_k^{o,r}, h_k^{o,i}, g_k^{o,i}\}$ where h and g are lowpass and highpass filters, respectively. The superscript o means the initial filter, and r and i indicate that the corresponding filter are to obtain real and imaginary parts, respectively. Here we define a set of lifting complex wavelet filters $\{h_k^r, g_k^r, h_k^i, g_k^i\}$ as follows:

$$\begin{aligned}
h_k^r &= h_k^{o,r}, \\
g_k^r &= g_k^{o,r} - \sum_m s_m h_{k-m}^{o,r}, \\
h_k^i &= h_k^{o,i}, \\
g_k^i &= g_k^{o,i} - \sum_m s_m h_{k-m}^{o,i},
\end{aligned} \tag{1}$$

where s represents the lifting parameters.

Fig. 2. Our robot

Applying the lifting complex wavelet filters to image $C_{i,j}^1$ in row and column directions, we can obtain four components RR, RI, IR and II. In case of the RR, their LWTs are computed as follows:

$$C_{i,j}^0 = \sum_{k,l} h_k^r h_l^r C_{2i+k,2j+l}^1,$$

$$D_{i,j}^0 = \sum_{k,l} h_k^r g_l^r C_{2i+k,2j+l}^1,$$

$$E_{i,j}^0 = \sum_{k,l} g_k^r h_l^r C_{2i+k,2j+l}^1,$$

$$F_{i,j}^0 = \sum_{k,l} g_k^r g_l^r C_{2i+k,2j+l}^1.$$

Since the filter g^r includes the lifting parameters, we can rewrite the above LWTs as

$$C_{i,j}^0 = \hat{C}_{i,j}^0,$$

$$D_{i,j}^0 = \hat{D}_{i,j}^0 - \sum_m s_m \hat{C}_{i,j+m}^0,$$

$$E_{i,j}^0 = \hat{E}_{i,j}^0 - \sum_m s_m \hat{C}_{i+m,j}^0,$$

$$F_{i,j}^0 = \hat{F}_{i,j}^0 - \sum_m s_m \hat{D}_{i+m,j}^0$$

$$- \sum_m s_m \hat{E}_{i,j+m}^0 + \sum_{m,m'} s_m s_{m'} \hat{C}_{i+m,j+m'}^0,$$

where $\hat{C}^0$, $\hat{D}^0$, $\hat{E}^0$ and $\hat{F}^0$ are lowpass and three types of highpass components obtained by applying the initial filters to the input image C^1.

Similarly we can compute the LWTs in case of the RI, IR and II. The highpass components of six orientations can be computed by the combination of the RR, IR, IR and II [3].

$$\mathrm{Re}_{i,j} = \sqrt{RR_{i,j}^2 + II_{i,j}^2}, \tag{2}$$

$$\mathrm{Im}_{i,j} = \sqrt{RI_{i,j}^2 + IR_{i,j}^2}, \tag{3}$$

where $\mathrm{Re}_{i,j}$ and $\mathrm{Im}_{i,j}$ have each of 3 highpass components which differ in the feature of orientation. The paper [3] has shown that the robust features to the change of shift and rotation can be extracted by combining these components of the CWT. Finally we can obtain the robust features $H_{i,j}^0$ to the shift and rotation by summing these six highpass components of $\mathrm{Re}_{i,j}$ and $\mathrm{Im}_{i,j}$. In Fig. 3, we show an example of features obtained with LCWT.

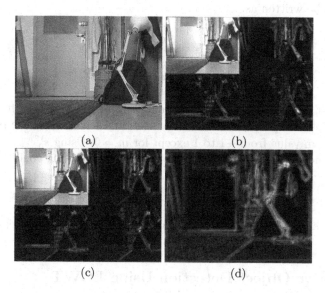

(a)   (b)

(c)   (d)

Fig. 3. An example of features obtained with LCWT: (a) input image, (b) LCWT of real parts, (c) LCWT of imaginary parts and (d) highpass components of LCWT

By iteratively applying the LCWT to the obtained each lowpass components C^0 in RR, RI, IR and II, a multi-resolution analysis can be conducted in the same way as the conventional wavelet transform. Therefore, we can obtain the lifting highpass components in each of resolutions $H_{i,j}^t, t = 0, -1, \cdots$ by using the LCWT, where t is an index that implies the resolution level.

3.2 Multi-scale Analysis Using LCWT

We must determine the parameters s_m in the LCWTs described in the previous subsection. In this paper we compute the set of the parameters so that the

LCWT can extract the multi-scale local features of an image. We first determine the length of a lifting parameter. Concretely, we use the property that the length of the lifting highpass filters (1) depending on the length of the parameters s_m. As the initial filters we use the complex wavelet filters proposed in [3]. In order to extract multi-scale local features from images, we introduce the following four kinds of parameters as

$$s_m^{(1)}, \ -1 \leq m \leq 1,$$
$$s_m^{(2)}, \ -2 \leq m \leq 2,$$
$$s_m^{(3)}, \ -4 \leq m \leq 4,$$
$$s_m^{(4)}, \ -8 \leq m \leq 8.$$

Using the parameters $s_m^{(\sigma)}$ $(\sigma = 1, \cdots, 4)$, we can construct four sets of the lifting complex wavelet filters $\{h_k^r, g_k^{\sigma,r}, h_k^i, g_k^{\sigma,i}\}$. The new highpass filters $g^{\sigma,r}$ and $g^{\sigma,i}$ can be written as

$$g_k^{\sigma,r} = g_k^{o,r} - \sum_m s^{(\sigma)} h_{k-2m}^{o,r}, \quad \sigma = 1, \cdots, 4,$$
$$g_k^{\sigma,i} = g_k^{o,i} - \sum_m s^{(\sigma)} h_{k-2m}^{o,i}, \quad \sigma = 1, \cdots, 4.$$

In the next section, we will propose a method to determine the lifting parameters for adaptive object detection. In this section, each of the lifting parameters has the random value from -1 to 1 except for $m = 0$. Using $s_0^{(\sigma)}$ $(\sigma = 1, \cdots, 4)$, we tune the new highpass filters so as to satisfy the following conditions.

$$\sum_k g_k^{\sigma,r} = 0, \quad \sum_k g_k^{\sigma,i} = 0, \quad \sigma = 1, \cdots, 4.$$

We assume that these highpass filters can extract the multi-scale features from an image.

4   Adaptive Object Detection Using LCWT

By tuning the lifting parameters, we can construct the LCWTs with various properties. In this paper, we concentrate to design the LCWT which can detect the local features from an image. We first introduce a keypoint detection algorithm using the LCWT. Each of the detected keypoints has a 128 dimensional vector each of which represents a feature based on the oriented gradients around it.

4.1   Keypoint Detection and Description by LCWT

As mentioned above, we can obtain the lifting highpass images $H_{i,j}^{t,\sigma}, t = 0, \cdots, -2,$ $\sigma = 1, \cdots, 4$, where t and σ represent the multi-level parameter and the mutli-scale parameter, respectively. We first extract the target point (i, j) as the candidate keypoints, if $H_{i,j}^{t,\sigma}$ is a local maximum or a minimum around the target point

(i, j). The extracted candidate keypoints include a lot of unstable points. We therefore eliminate such unstable points which have low contrast or are poorly localized along an edge.

First, for each of the candidates, an interpolation of the nearby data [6] is used to accurately determine its position. The interpolation of nearby data is done by using the following Taylor expansion of the lifting highpass images

$$H(\mathbf{x}) = H + \frac{\partial H}{\partial \mathbf{x}}\mathbf{x} + \frac{1}{2}\mathbf{x}^T\frac{\partial H}{\partial \mathbf{x}}\mathbf{x}, \tag{4}$$

where H and its derivatives are evaluated at the candidate keypoint (i, j), and $\mathbf{x} = (y, x, \sigma)$ is the offset from this point. We can obtain the subpixel keypoint position by computing the extremum of (4). If the location of the extremum $\hat{\mathbf{x}}$ is larger than 0.5 in any dimension, the extremum lies closer to the other candidate keypoints. In this case, we reject this target keypoint. Otherwise the offset $\hat{\mathbf{x}}$ is added to its candidate keypoint to detect the subpixel keypoint position. Here if $H(\mathbf{x})$ at the subpixel position is lower than a specified threshold, then we also reject this point due to its low contrast.

Next step, we estimate whether the remaining points are corners. The lifting highpass images will have large values along edges even if the candidate keypoint is not robust for noise. Therefore, we eliminate the candidates keypoints on edges of which positions are imprecise. For imprecise peaks in the lifting highpass image, the principal curvature across the edge would be much larger than the principal curvature along it. These principal curvatures can be obtained as eigenvalues of the Hessian matrix of the lifting highpass image, by the same approach as SIFT [6]. The final keypoints are selected by performing the above localization process to the candidate keypoints. Figure 4 illustrates examples of the detected keypoints by the LCWT.

We extract local features at each of positions of the selected keypoints. In this subsection, we compute a descriptor vector for each keypoint. First, each keypoint is assigned orientations based on local image gradient directions. The magnitude and direction calculations for the gradient are done for every pixel in a neighboring region around the keypoint in the lowpass components.

$$m(u, v) = \sqrt{f_u(u, v)^2 + f_v(u, v)^2}, \tag{5}$$

$$\theta(u, v) = \tan^{-1}\left(\frac{f_u(u, v)}{f_v(u, v)}\right), \tag{6}$$

where

$$f_u(u, v) = C_{u+1,v}^t - C_{u-1,v}^t,$$
$$f_v(u, v) = C_{u,v+1}^t - C_{u,v-1}^t,$$

where $C_{u,v}^t$ is a mean of the lowpass component in (2) and (3) of resolution level t.

We make an orientation histogram with 36 bins, each bin covering 10 degrees. Each sample in the neighboring window added to a histogram bin is weighted by its gradient magnitude.

Fig. 4. Example of detected keypoints by LCWT

The window size depends on the length of the lifting highpass filters corresponding to the scale of the target keypoint. The peaks in this histogram can be regarded as principal orientations. We therefore assign the peaks of this histogram to the keypoint.

Here a descriptor vector is computed based on the magnitudes and orientations which are sampled around the keypoint location by (5) and (6). In order to achieve orientation invariance, the coordinates of the descriptor and the gradient orientations are rotated relative to the orientation assigned at the keypoint. In each of 4×4 subregions of the region around the keypoint, the histogram with 8 orientation bins is created. Since there are $4 \times 4 = 16$ histograms each with 8 bins the vector has 128 elements. Finally the obtained vector is normalized to unit length in order to enhance invariance to affine changes in illumination.

4.2   Lifting Parameters for Object Detection

In our previous work [11], the lifting parameters are computed by using training images to be the desired response in each of levels and scales. This paper determines the effective lifting parameters for the object detection. We first prepare a set of training images which are captured by our mobile robot in an office. Applying the LCWT to these training images, we can obtain a set of feature vectors in the keypoints of all images. Using ϵ-means clustering [2], these feature vectors are classified into each cluster in which the Euclidean distance between any pair of feature vectors does not exceed a threshold ϵ. A pseudo code of the ϵ-means clustering is shown in Algorithm 1.

Algorithm 1. ϵ-means clustering

```
1 Input: ε, a threshold
2 Output: C, the result of clustering
3 C = ∅
4 for t = 1 to N_T
5    i(t) = argmin_{c_j ∈ C}{d(x_t, c_j)}
6    if (d(x_t, c_i) > ε) then C ← C ∪ (x_t, 1)
7    else N_i + +
8    end if
9 end for
```

The result of the ϵ-means clustering is evaluated by the entropy of the distribution.

$$-\sum_k p(k) \log p(k).$$

Here $p(k)$ is a normalized distribution in the cluster k, which can be computed as $p(k) = N_k/N_T$, where N_k is the number of keypoints in the cluster k, and N_T is the number of all keypoints of the training images.

We wish to determine the lifting parameters so as to increase the entropy of the distribution. We propose an algorithm for determining the lifting parameters based on the Genetic Algorithm (GA). In this paper, a set of the lifting parameters $s^{(\sigma)}$ ($\sigma = 1, \cdots, 4$) corresponds to an individual in GA, and is denoted with a binary array. We first choose the initial population of individuals. The initial lifting parameters are generated randomly by a method described in the previous subsection. We extract each distribution of feature vectors obtained by applying the LCWT with the set of parameters to the training images. Next, we evaluate the entropy of each distribution in that population. Here we repeat the following steps until a specified generation number N_g is reached.

1. Select the best-fit lifting parameters for reproduction.
2. Breed new lifting parameters through crossover and mutation operations (mutation probability $P_m = 0.01$).
3. Extract each set of feature vectors by applying new LCWTs to the training images.
4. Evaluate each entropy of the distribution obtained by using each of new LCWTs.
5. Replace least-fit population with new lifting parameters.

We show a pseudo code of the proposed algorithm in Algorithm 2.

In step 4 of Algorithm 2, we evaluate the result of clustering by using the following estimation:

$$\mathbf{e} = \frac{-1}{\log K} \sum_{k=1}^{K} p(k) \log p(k),$$

where K is the number of clusters. We can avoid increasing the number of clusters by virtue of this estimation.

Algorithm 2. Determining the lifting parameters based on the GA

1	**Input:** $\mathcal{P}$, an initial set of lifting parameters, P_m, mutation probability
2	**Output:** the best lifting parameters in $\mathcal{P}$
3	**for** $i = 1$ to N_g
4	$\quad$ $\mathbf{e} \leftarrow$ Evaluate($\mathcal{P}$)
5	$\quad$ $\tilde{\mathcal{P}} \leftarrow \emptyset$
6	$\quad$ **for** $j = 1$ to Size($\mathcal{P}$)
7	$\quad\quad$ $x \leftarrow$ Selection($\mathcal{P}, \mathbf{e}$)
8	$\quad\quad$ $y \leftarrow$ Selection($\mathcal{P}, \mathbf{e}$)
9	$\quad\quad$ $z \leftarrow$ Crossover(x, y)
10	$\quad\quad$ **if** (Random(0, 1) $< P_m$) **then**
11	$\quad\quad\quad$ $z \leftarrow$ Mutate(z)
12	$\quad\quad$ **end if**
13	$\quad\quad$ $\tilde{\mathcal{P}} \leftarrow z$
14	$\quad$ **end for**
15	$\quad$ $\mathcal{P} = \tilde{\mathcal{P}}$
16	**end for**

4.3 Adaptive Object Detection Algorithm

Recent works in object based image retrieval have been proposed using the similarity of visual words [10]. We also make visual vocabulary for detecting the existing objects in an indoor environment. Each cluster $c_i \in \mathcal{C}$ represents a visual word, which is generated by ϵ-means clustering in the previous section.

An image is represented as a bag of visual words by clustering each keypoint feature into each visual word. In order to evaluate the similarity between an input image Q and each of database images T, we use the following histogram intersection [10].

$$S(Q, T) = \sum_{k=1}^{K} \min(h_q(k), h_t(k)),$$

where h_q and h_t are the distribution of the visual words corresponding to the input image and each of the database images, respectively. Our adaptive object detection judges whether existing or new objects by whether similar images exist in the database. Our robot carries out the adaptively object detection online by providing in advance that each set of LCWTs is trained in each of environment.

5 Simulations

5.1 Clustering of Keypoint Features

We first prepared the training images in order to learn the set of LCWTs adapting to the indoor environment. The training images were captured by the robot while our robot was moving around in the experimental room. A training image is of size 320 × 240 pixels, and in color depth of monochrome 8bit. Since the IR sensor of our robot can be rotated from the left-hand side to the right-hand side, the robot can measure the distances between the robot and the obstacles in the front, left and right directions. The robot moves so that their distances do not exceed a set of corresponding thresholds, $T_f = 300$mm, $T_l = 200$mm and $T_r = 200$mm. The robot therefore is expected to be able to avoid the obstacles in the room. Our robot controller is shown in Algorithm 3.

Algorithm 3. Robot controller

```
 1 Input: T_f, T_l and T_r, thresholds for obstacle avoidance
 2 do
 3    measure the distances d_front, d_right and d_left
 4    if (d_front > T_f) then
 5       if (d_left > T_l & d_right > T_r) then
 6          capture a frame and then go forward
 7       else if (d_left < T_l & d_right > T_r) then turn right
 8       else if (d_left > T_l & d_right < T_r) then turn left
 9       else reverse
10       end if
11    else
12       if (d_left > T_l & d_right > T_r) then
13          capture a frame and then reverse
14       else if (d_left < T_l & d_right > T_r) then turn right
15       else if (d_left > T_l & d_right < T_r) then turn left
16       else reverse
17       end if
18    end if
19 loop until (robot receives a stop command)
```

Here we built the visual words by using 132 training images which include typical objects in the room. Figure 5 shows examples of the training images. We performed the ϵ-means clustering with $\epsilon = 2.0$ and trained the set of LCWT by using the proposed algorithm explained in the previous section. The entropies

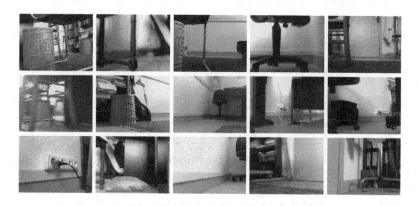

Fig. 5. Examples of the training images

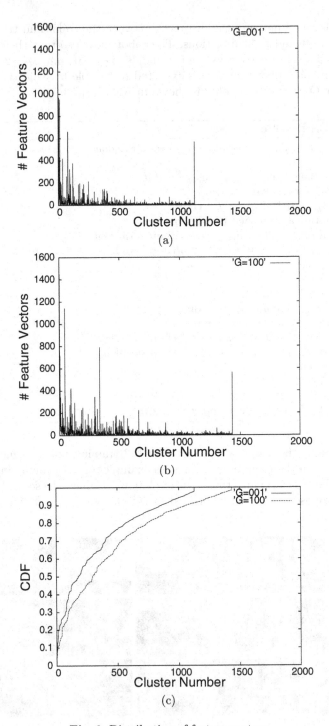

Fig. 6. Distribution of feature vectors

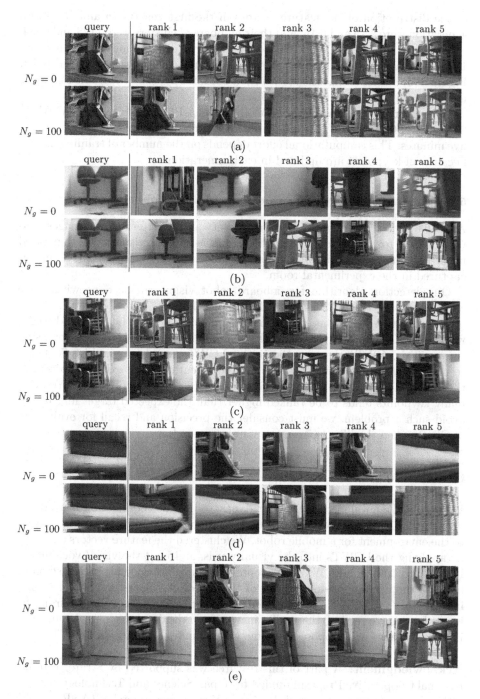

Fig. 7. Experimental results

of the distribution of the feature vectors in the first generation and the 100th generation were 5.75 and 6.15, and their numbers of clusters were 1128 and 1434, respectively. In Fig. 6 (a) and (b), we illustrate the distributions in the first and 100th generations, and Fig. 6 (c) shows their cumulative density functions (cdf). Figure 6 (c) indicates that the distribution obtained by using the trained LCWTs is statistically close to the uniform distribution.

We computed the visual words on the laptop PC with Intel Core i7 M640 2.80Ghz, 8.0GB of RAM. The computational time in each generation was about five minutes. This computational effort depends on the number of training images because all keypoints are updated in each generation.

5.2 Adaptive Object Detection by a Mobile Robot

Adaptive object detection by a mobile robot can be performed on images captured by our robot controller (Algorithm 3). By using the visual words generated in the previous subsection, we constructed the feature database from 3272 images captured in the experimental room.

Our detection algorithm for onboard robot vision can be done within one second by using the LCWTs trained in offline. Figure 7 shows examples of our object detection using the initial and the trained LCWTs. Our method works well for the CBIR effectively, since the target images are ranked higher by using the trained LCWTs than by the initial LCWTs, as shown in Fig. 7. These results indicate that our method can detect accurately the existing objects in the room. However the highly detailed image (e.g. rank 3 of Fig. 7 (a)) with many keypoints tends to be ranked higher than the expected target images. To avoid such a problem, we must consider the precision and recall for evaluation of CBIR, when the lifting parameters are computed.

6   Conclusion

We proposed a novel method for fast adaptive object detection for onboard robot vision by using the LCWT. Our method can design the LCWTs so as to adapt to the environment for a mobile robot. We clustered the feature vectors obtained by applying the LCWTs into the visual words, and built the visual vocabulary. In order to train the LCWTs we proposed the evolutionary algorithm so as to increase the entropy of distribution of these vectors. The experimental results indicate that the LCWT can be trained not only to extract local features from the image but also to retrieve the similar images from the database image accurately. In the future we will propose an online algorithm for learning the LCWT.

Acknowledgment. A part of this research was supported by Strategic International Cooperative Program funded by Japan Science and Technology Agency (JST) on the Japanese side and Agence Nationale de Recherches (ANR) on the French side. This work was partially supported by Grants-in-Aid for Scientific Research, JSPS (No. 23500183 and 24650070).

References

1. Bay, H., Tuytelaars, T., Van Gool, L.: SURF: Speeded Up Robust Features. In: Leonardis, A., Bischof, H., Pinz, A. (eds.) ECCV 2006, Part I. LNCS, vol. 3951, pp. 404–417. Springer, Heidelberg (2006)
2. Delarboulas, P., Schoenauer, M., Sebag, M.: Open-Ended Evolutionary Robotics: An Information Theoretic Approach. In: Schaefer, R., Cotta, C., Kołodziej, J., Rudolph, G. (eds.) PPSN XI. LNCS, vol. 6238, pp. 334–343. Springer, Heidelberg (2010)
3. Fauqueur, J., Kingsbury, N., Anderson, R.: Multiscale Keypoint Detection using the Dual-Tree Complex Wavelet Transform. In: Proc. IEEE Conference on Image Processing, pp. 8–11 (2006)
4. Frintrop, S., Rome, E., Christensen, H.I.: Computational Visual Attention Systems and their Cognitive Foundation: A Survey. ACM Transactions on Applied Perception (TAP) 7(1) (2010)
5. Ijsselmuiden, J., Grosselfinger, A.-K., Münch, D., Arens, M., Stiefelhagen, R.: Automatic Behavior Understanding in Crisis Response Control Rooms. In: Paternò, F., de Ruyter, B., Markopoulos, P., Santoro, C., van Loenen, E., Luyten, K. (eds.) AmI 2012. LNCS, vol. 7683, pp. 97–112. Springer, Heidelberg (2012)
6. Lowe, D.G.: Distinctive Image Features from Scale-Invariant Keypoints. International Journal of Computer Vision 60(2), 91–110 (2004)
7. Menegatti, E., Danieletto, M., Mina, M., Pretto, A., Bardella, A., Zanella, A., Zanuttigh, P.: Discovery, Localization and Recognition of Smart Objects by a Mobile Robot. In: Ando, N., Balakirsky, S., Hemker, T., Reggiani, M., von Stryk, O. (eds.) SIMPAR 2010. LNCS, vol. 6472, pp. 436–448. Springer, Heidelberg (2010)
8. Philbin, J., Chum, O., Isard, M., Sivic, J., Zisserman, A.: Object Retrieval with Large Vocabularies and Fast Spatial Matching. In: Proc. IEEE Conference on Computer Vision and Pattern Recognition (CVPR 2007), pp. 1–8 (2007)
9. Sivic, J., Zisserman, A.: Video Google: A Text Retrieval Approach to Object Matching in Videos. In: Proc. Ninth IEEE International Conference on Computer Vision (ICCV 2003), vol. 2, pp. 1470–1477 (2003)
10. Szeliski, R.: Computer Vision: Algorithms and Applications. Springer, New York (2010)
11. Takano, S., Suzuki, E.: New Object Detection for On-board Robot Vision by Lifting Complex Wavelet Transforms. In: Proc. Eleventh IEEE International Conference on Data Mining Workshops (ICDMW 2011), pp. 911–916 (2011)
12. Tuytelaars, T., Mikolajczyk, K.: Local Invariant Feature Detectors: A Survey. Foundations and Trends in Computer Graphics and Vision 3(3), 177–280 (2007)

On the Edge of a Virtual World – Investigating Users' Preferences and Different Visualization Techniques

Jarkko Vatjus-Anttila, Leena Ventä-Olkkonen, and Jonna Häkkilä

Center for Internet Excellence, University of Oulu,
P.O. Box 1001, 90014 Oulu, Finland
firstname.lastname@cie.fi

Abstract. This paper investigates how the edges of a limited size 3D virtual world model can be visualized. We compared five alternative visualization techniques by conducting downloading, post-processing and rendering measurements and evaluating the designs with a user study. Recommendations for UI designers working especially in the mobile computing domain are presented.

Keywords: Virtual worlds, user interfaces, user studies.

1   Introduction

Virtual worlds (VWs), or virtual environments, utilizing 3D graphics are familiar for large audiences mostly from game domain, e.g. from online games such as World of Warcraft. In addition to imaginary landscapes, increasing amount of work is done for creating 3D models and virtual world representations of our everyday environments e.g. for city architecture or interior design of apartments. Although 3D virtual worlds can be made to represent the real world exceedingly well, the models come with an inherent design challenge – they are limited in size.

Bringing the user to the edge of the virtual world model can create a visualization and user experience problem, and the model may appear e.g. to float in space, Figure 1. This is especially true for outdoor virtual world representations, where, contrary to indoor spaces, the walls do not create a naturally confined space. Moreover, especially with mobile devices, the processing power and data transfer capability set limitations. The graphics in the virtual world representations are often heavy for both of these requirements, and the technical feasibility and its effect on the user experience needs to be taken into account, when designing VW applications for mobile domain.

In the area of designing virtual world user interfaces (UIs), earlier research has examined, e.g., avatars [7], text readability in 3D games [4], and collaborative and shared space aspects [5]. In this paper, we examine the design challenge of visualizing the edges, or outer boundaries, of virtual worlds by examining the initial user perceptions as well as technical characteristics of alternative designs. To best of our knowledge, our paper is first one to address the topic of virtual world edges. Our research contributes novel knowledge for VW UX research, and can impact to the UI design of 3D virtual world applications especially for mobile devices.

J.C. Augusto et al. (Eds.): AmI 2013, LNCS 8309, pp. 198–203, 2013.

2   Studied Visualizations

For the study, five alternative visualizations demonstrating the edge of a 3D virtual world were created: A. Wall, B. Forest, C. Soil map, D Road map, E. Island, see Figure 1 A-E (for the 3D city model). These were selected to cover wide range of different visualizations used currently in games and other virtual world environments.

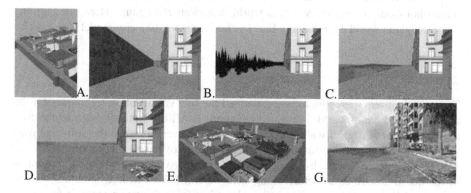

Fig. 1. Virtual world model, which appears to float in the space (top left), visualization types A-E created for virtual world edges, and example of the game world (G).

Technically, the process of loading 3D content into the client device, e.g. a PC or smart phone, can be split into three separate phases; first, the downloading phase, where all necessary 3D content is being downloaded from the remote service; second, post-processing phase, where the content is modified locally in the device if needed (i.e. content generation); and third, the actual rendering of the 3D scene.

Wall scenario encapsulates the 3D scene into fixed boundaries, which allows the client to utilize rendering optimizations to it, i.e. occlusion culling [8]. The *wall* was chosen as the simplest way to confine a limited area. The geometry of the 3D model of the wall is very simple, making the downloading time short and rendering simple.

Forest. Here, the terrain soil is used as the basis for a generated forest, and needs to be downloaded to match the real-world landscape. The 3D trees, selected to roughly match to the climate in Oulu, were generated from a single tree model, which was downloaded and multiplied in post-processing. Here, occlusion culling optimization is harder than with *wall* as the forest is sparse.

Soil Map. This scenario is based on the real world landscape, and is similar to the forest scenario but without the trees. Instead, a water simulation is generated to bring vividness to the view. No occlusion exists since there are no solid obstacles in the boundaries of the space. However, the terrain soil itself can be GeoMipMapped [1] to achieve better rendering performance in this scenario. The scenario can utilize the information from other geographical data sources.

Road map utilizes a very simple geometry under the city which then uses a single image to represent the city map for the user. Downloading wise the case is consuming not because of the geometry but the map details, which need to be high in order to give the clear enough view for the user. There is no need for post-processing.

In **Island** scenario, almost everything is created in the post-processing phase. In this game world type approach, the terrain soil is mathematically generated using perlin noise [6] and only its generation parameters are downloaded from the remote service.

Two alternative VW designs were presented: the 3D model of Oulu city, and a screenshot from an imaginary virtual world in Serious Sam game. Here, see Figure 1 G for the game world example and Fig. 1 C for corresponding city model.

3   User Study

To study the users' perceptions, we examined the five visualization techniques for the real world and game world, illustrated in Figure 1. All the pictures were demonstrating a street view from a walker's perspective. However, to make the soil- and road map visualizations more clear and understandable, an overview picture of a 3D world with its surroundings was also presented. Each alternative visualization was presented in the questionnaire as a picture along with 7-point Likert scale evaluation of pleasantness, following by an open question about justifying the given score or free comments. After five optional visualizations (which could be viewed simultaneously when assessing the designs), we asked users which visualization they liked most and least. This was repeated in both (3D model of the city of Oulu and imaginary 3D virtual world) cases. To avoid the bias, we counterbalanced the task so that half to the users started with the real world 3D model, half with the game world visualizations. Prior to the study, participants were shown a virtual walk around the 3D city model without any visualization of the VW boundaries, i.e. as in Figure 1 (top left). This was done with a tablet device.

Altogether 32 participants (11 female), aged 22-40 (average 28), took part to this study. As a background, 15/32 reported of playing computer games with a 3D virtual world. All participants lived in the city area and were familiar with the 3D city scene.

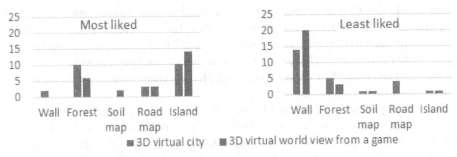

Fig. 2. Most liked (left) and least liked (right) visualizations (n=25)

The results for the most and least liked visualizations are presented in Figure 2 (25 answers in total). The most liked visualizations were the **forest** and the **island** for 3D city model, and the island for the game world. Also when participants assessed the pleasantness of the scenarios (7-point Likert scale), the island was considered most pleasant with both 3D virtual worlds. Average value of the pleasantness of the island visualization with Oulu 3D model was 5 (stdev 1,72) and with game view 4,97 (stdev 1,85).

The visualizations using the themes from the nature, such as forest, sea or mountains, were considered pleasant. The forest visualization was considered to be more realistic than some other versions, at least with the 3D city model: *"It's more like the real view, Oulu city is surrounded by the forest after all (#29)"*. From the comments it was evident that also the visualization of island was perceived to be a nature landscape. The sea view with a bit of a green grass was considered as relaxing: *"Nice view, tranquil, gives you a good feeling (#31)"*. Also the impression of wideness together with the sea was considered pleasant. *"I like the sea view and open areas (#10)."* Users were more unanimous when choosing the least liked scenario, see Figure 2. Nine of the 32 participants verbalized that the wall looked like a prison wall or made them feel like trapped. *"I feel like I am in prison. (#31)"* In addition, some users considered the wall to being simply boring and un-realistic: *"It is good to show boundary wall, but in practice no such walls exist, so there should be something else [visualized]. (#25)"*

The idea of the 3D virtual mirror world continuing from the edge in a format of a map was perceived interesting, but useless and unpleasant for the user on the perspective of a walker in the street. *Soil map* was seen realistic and giving true information from the environment, but again the visualization was not considered pleasant. On the other hand, some participants had difficulties in associating the *soil map* with the real world geography, but treated it as the imaginary *island* landscape.

4   Technical Measurements

To investigate the technical aspects and compare them with the user study results, we conducted downloading, post-processing and rendering measurements with the visualizations. These were done using a PC with Core I7-3770 Central Processing Unit (CPU). Downloading was done using local WCDMA/HSDPA network. Because the 3D city model was the same for all of the scenarios, it was not included in the downloading times, but instead we compared the delta between downloading times of the specific 3D assets for each scenario. Threading was not used and hence the post-processing started after the download phase was finished. Regular rendering optimizations, such as the occlusion culling, were performed. Rendering complexity was measured in terms of visible triangles and required drawcalls, which are both important performance factors. Each scenario was processed 50 times, and the results in the Figures 3 and 4 present an average for a single test run.

Figure 3 shows the download and processing times for each visualization. The lowest download time takes place with *island* scenario, which is evident since only a few parameter files were downloaded for the post-processing phase. *Wall* and *road map* visualizations are the second fastest due to their simple representation model. *Forest* and *soil map* visualizations took longer to download primarily for the terrain soil component. Post-processing affected the most in *island* scenario, since practically the whole visualization was generated from the scratch. In the *forest* scenario, the post-processing took care of the tree generation, which was much simpler that the terrain generation in the *island* scenario.

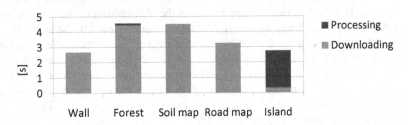

Fig. 3. Cumulative downloading and processing times for each visualization

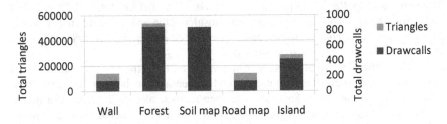

Fig. 4. Rendering complexity for each visualization

Figure 4 shows differences in the rendering complexity. The *wall* and *road map* visualizations were the simplest to render due occlusion culling opportunity (*wall*) and low geometry detail (*wall, road map*), which can be seen from both low triangle count and drawcall count. Forest and soil map visualization were both very heavy due to the terrain soil and no opportunity for the occlusion culling. In the forest scenario, there occurred some amount of occlusion, but its effect is neglected due to the added geometry in the forest itself. The benefit of the island scenario lies in the generation algorithm which was able to create dynamic level of detail [2] to the soil, which allowed the same surface area to be filled with less geometry. This is clearly a benefit of any generation algorithm, which can optimize the data to the client device.

5   Discussion and Conclusions

Based on our findings, it is recommended that the VW application designers should not go blindly towards the optimal technical solutions, but take into account the other factors that influence the user experience – here, the best option in technical sense, *the wall*, was the least preferred by the user study participants. On the other hand, the results indicate that it is possible to generate visualizations that are pleasant for the user but require small amount of downloaded data (*island*) or little post-processing (*forest*). This way, optimal solutions can be found for different technical settings. Based on our user study, we were able to derive the design recommendations for visualizing the outer boundaries of a 3D virtual world presented in Table 1.

Table 1. Desired characteristics for the visualization of 3D virtual world boundaries

Realistic	The design should fit to the VW environment and match with people's mental model of the physical world.
Natural	Themes from the nature, e.g. mountains, forests, water, are perceived pleasant
Open space	Rather use an open space, not narrow and closed
Pleasant to watch	Aesthetics plays a significant role in user perceptions
Provide additional information	Providing context information is appreciated in cases where that is possible.

The CPU used in the measurements was rather fast, and due to vast processing power does not compare to the mobile CPUs. Hence, the post-processing time appears fast. However, as we sought to explore the delta between the different techniques, we argue these results are reusable also for the mobile clients showing the scale of effect what to expect. Early research on location-aware mobile services studied in-the-wild has reported that the (too long) downloading times caused frustration for every participant (n=20) and was a central issue in resulting negative experiences with the service [3]. This aspect was not yet explored in the user study, but would be an interesting topic for the future user studies. We acknowledge that the laboratory setting for the user study does not necessarily fully reflect the user perceptions in the real life use context, and that the selected city (e.g. presence of the water) can influence to the perceptions. The results are preliminary, but nonetheless, we believe that they still provide interesting insight to the design challenge. Our plan for future work is to conduct a study *in situ* at the city center, with a mobile device.

References

1. de Boer, W.H.: Fast Terrain Rendering Using Geometrical MipMapping (2000)
2. Brown, R., Cooper, L., Pham, B.: Visual attention-based polygon level of detail management. In: Proc. GRAPHITE 2003, pp. 55–62. ACM, New York (2003)
3. Häkkilä, J., Isomursu, M.: User Experiences of Location-Aware Mobile Services. In: Proc. OZCHI 2005. CHISIG of Australia, Narrabundah, Australia (2005)
4. Jankowski, J., Samp, K., Irzynska, I., Jozwowicz, M., Decker, S.: Integrating Text with Video and 3D Graphics: The Effect of Text Drawing Styles on Text Readability. In: Proc. CHI 2010, pp. 1321–1330. ACM, New York (2010)
5. Liu, H., Bowman, M., Chang, F.: Survey of State Melding in Virtual Worlds. ACM Computing Surveys 44(4), Article 21 (April 2012)
6. Perlin, K.: An image synthesizer. In: Proc. SIGGRAPH 1985, pp. 287–296. ACM, New York (1985)
7. Wagner, D., Billinghurst, M., Schmalstieg, D.: How real should virtual characters be? In: Proc. ACE 2006. ACM, New York (2006)
8. Wonka, P., Schmalstieg, D.: Occluder Shadows for Fast Walkthroughs of Urban Environments. Computer Graphics Forum 18(3), 51–60 (1999)

Semantics-Driven Multi-user Concurrent Activity Recognition

Juan Ye and Graeme Stevenson*

School of Computer Science, University of St Andrews
juan.ye@st-andrews.ac.uk

Abstract. This paper presents a novel knowledge-driven approach to recognising multi-user concurrent activities in smart home environments. Capturing these concurrent activity patterns is challenging in that it usually requires detailed application-/user-specific specifications, or needs a large amount of data to build sophisticated models. The proposed approach is founded upon the use of a generic ontology model to represent domain knowledge, which is independent of particular sensor deployment and activities of interest. It leverages the hierarchical structure of domain concept ontologies and applies well-established hierarchy-based techniques to enable automatic segmentation of real-time sensor traces and supports matching finely grained sensor data to coarsely constrained activities. We empirically evaluate our approach using a large-scale real-world dataset, achieving an average accuracy of 86%.

1 Introduction

Recognising human activities in a sensor-instrumented environment is an important task in ambient intelligent environments. Earlier works mainly focus on identifying activities for a single user [20], however there are often multiple residents living in the same environment, performing different tasks *concurrently*. Distinguishing these activities is essential to the development of customised context aware applications in a real-world setting [5].

Recognising multi-user concurrent activities is challenging due to interwoven sensor traces and the numerous, flexible, and complicated ways of human conducting activities simultaneously. Sophisticated data-driven techniques have been designed to capture concurrent activity patterns [10], which usually leads to heavy computation and a craving for training data, and thus is unsuitable for real-time recognition. These learned models are also at risk from being overfitted to the training data, which is very likely to be different from the data at later real-time running. Few knowledge-driven techniques [18] have been applied, however the detailed specifications might only be specific to certain environments or users, thus not scalable to a wide range of deployment.

To address the above problems, we propose a general unsupervised approach for recognising multi-user concurrent activities. We think from a new direction:

* This work has been supported by the EU FP7 project "SAPERE - Self-aware Pervasive Service Ecosystems" under contract No. 256873.

J.C. Augusto et al. (Eds.): AmI 2013, LNCS 8309, pp. 204–219, 2013.

we consider one of the most important and pre-requisite processes toward recognising concurrent activities to be the automatic segmentation of a real-time *sensor trace* – composed of a sequence of raw sensor events – into semantically meaningful parts, each of which is assumed to correspond to one of the concurrent activities. Then we recognise each activity from segmented fragments by treating it as the single activity recognition problem.

Our approach falls into the knowledge-driven category, however, the main difference from existing techniques is that we use the generic ontologies (e.g., WordNet and the top-level ontology [21]) and necessary conditions to constrain activities which will result in more certain knowledge and require much less knowledge engineering effort. The top-level ontology model formally explores the universal hierarchical structure in all types of domain concepts, inspired by which we adapt two well-established hierarchy-based techniques to enable sensor trace segmentation and activity recognition. First of all we utilise the Wu's conceptual similarity measure [19] to study the similarity between sensor events based on their semantics annotated in the ontological model and use the similarity to segment a sensor trace. To recognise activities, we employ the Pyramid Match Kernel (PMK) which is an effective technique in supporting approximate matches between two sets of hierarchical concepts and has been widely used in recent image-based object detection and matching studies [22]. We extend the PMK for matching sensor events to activities, because the original PMK formula does not suit mapping sensor events to ontological activity description; e.g., the activity profile specified in the activity ontology and raw sensor events might not share the same level of abstraction and the domain concept ontologies are not uniformly hierarchical. We validate our segmentation and recognition algorithms using a large scale real-world dataset. Through comprehensive experimental studies, we demonstrate both the effectiveness and flexibility of our proposed algorithms.

The rest of the paper is organised as follows. Section 2 reviews the recent techniques in recognising interleaved and concurrent activities. Section 3 presents a generic ontological model to represent sensor events, objects, and locations, based on which we explore the semantics between sensor events and segment a sensor trace into fragments. Section 4 introduces an activity ontology that describes necessary conditions on an activity, and applies the PMK technique to support activity recognition. We evaluate our technique on a real-world data set in Section 5 and conclude the paper with future research directions in Section 6.

2   Related Work

Activity recognition, one of the main research topics in ambient intelligence [2], aims to identify users' daily activities from observed sensor readings. Different data-, knowledge-driven, and hybrid techniques are proposed in the literature, among which Hidden Markov Models (HMMs) have not only demonstrated promising accuracies in recognising single-user sequential activities [9] but also are presented as one of the most popular techniques in recognising interleaved and concurrent activities.

Patterson et al. [16] employ the HMM to recognise interleaved activities of a morning routine using RFID data. Having experimented with various HMMs, they conclude that using a HMM with a single state for each activity performs best and increasing model complexity does not necessarily improve the recognition accuracy. Modayil et al. [13] propose an *interleaved HMM* that aims to capture inter- and intra-activity dynamics. It recognises activities based on the last object used by the subject. This technique performs well in recognising certain interleaved activities and can, to a certain degree, deal with sensor data noise.

Gong et al [3] developed a dynamically multi-linked HMM to interpret group activities from video data involving multiple objects in a noisy outdoor scene. The model is based on the discovery of salient dynamic interlinks among multiple events using dynamic probabilistic networks. Nguyen et al. [14] employ the hierarchical HMM (HHMM) in a general framework to recognise primitive and complex behaviours of multiple people. A unified graphical model is constructed to incorporate a set of HHMMs with data association.

Hu et al. [8] propose a novel probabilistic framework for multi-goal recognition where both concurrent and interleaving goals can be recognised. The technique used is skip-chain conditional random fields (SCCRF), within which concurrent and interleaved goals are derived by adjusting inferred probabilities through a correlation graph. The SCCRF is computationally expensive when a large number of skip edges are involved. To prevent the recognition accuracy from deteriorating, every partial model of the interleaved activities has to be observed during the training phase. Hence the SCCRF requires a large amount of training data because there are many different ways to interrupt and resume an ongoing activity. As mentioned in [10], both HMMs and CRFs are more suitable for purely sequential activities. To recognise interleaved and concurrent activities, these techniques need to be extended or integrated with other techniques, which usually encounters the problems of heavy computation and of craving for training data.

Helaui et al. [7] build composite activity models using the Markov Logic Network, a statistical relational approach to incorporate common sense background knowledge. Gu et al. [5] present an unsupervised technique based on *emerging patterns* with sliding time windows to recognise interleaved activities. This technique calculates complex activity scores based on mined activity-feature sets as well as correlation scores between the activities. Our approach also uses feature relevance to segment the boundary of adjacent activities, however we apply a more formal knowledge-driven approach to segment real-time sensor traces solely based on the semantic similarity of raw sensor events, without the need for extra activity knowledge.

In knowledge-driven approaches, ontologies are one of the most popular [6,17,15]. Chen et al. [15] present an ontological mode to represent smart home activities and relevant context. The approach is motivated by the observations that ADLs are daily routines full of common-sense knowledge providing rich links between the environment, events, and activities. The domain and prior knowledge is valuable in creating activity models, avoiding the need of large-scale dataset collection and training. More recently, Saguna et al. [18] combine ontological and spatiotemporal modelling and reasoning to recognise interleaved and concurrent activities. However their approach requires detailed understanding and thorough investigation of the activity related specifics to successfully build long-term solutions. Although our approach shares the same motivation, we use the more certain must-have knowledge rather than provide a complete specification for each activity; thus, we can reduce the amount of knowledge engineering effort and as well as the bias from experts.

3 Sensor Semantics and Segmentation

This section describes the sensor and the associated domain ontologies based on which we introduce a semantic measure on evaluating the similarity between raw sensor events. Following on, we illustrate an algorithm to segment a real-time sensor trace into coherent fragments.

3.1 Domain and Sensor Ontologies

Central to our technique is a general ontological model that consists of four main components: Object, Location, Sensor, and Activity. Among them, the object and location ontologies are general (also called *domain ontology* in this paper) in that they represent concepts of an application domain or in a certain environment. By linking the sensor and activity ontologies to these two, we can make sense of raw sensor data and infer activities from them.

The object ontology (OO) describes the type-of relationships between household objects. For example, a *cup* is a type of *crockery*, denoted *cup* ⊑ *crockery*. To make the OO as general as possible, we extract it from WordNet [12], which

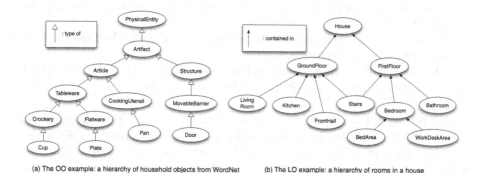

(a) The OO example: a hierarchy of household objects from WordNet   (b) The LO example: a hierarchy of rooms in a house

Fig. 1. The domain Object and Location ontologies

is a hierarchical lexical system where words are organised by semantic relations in terms of their meaning. Figure 1 (a) shows a part of the OO[1].

The location ontology (LO) describes the `containment` relationships between locations in terms of their spatial layout. Figure 1 (b) presents an example of room layouts in an ordinary house in the form of a lattice. A house consists of two floors, connected by a set of stairs.

The sensor ontology (SO) represents sensors and sensor events. A sensor event is usually represented in a tuple $se = (st, sId, val)$, indicating at the time st a sensor whose id is sId reports a value val. The sensor id refers to a sensor, which has a type (e.g., energy, object use, or temperature) and can be linked to an attached object and an installed location. Both objects and locations are instances defined in OO and LO. The sensor value can be abstracted into high-level terms (such as the status of the object like 'open' or 'close', or a particular property of an environment 'hot' or 'cold').

3.2 Semantic Similarity and Segmentation

Based on the conceptual models described in the above section, we will discuss *semantic similarity* with which to automatically segment a *sensor trace* that is composed of a sequence of sensor events.

Definition 1. Let se_i and se_j be two sensor events. The **semantic similarity** between them is defined as

$$sim(se_i, se_j) = (sim_T(st_i, st_j), sim_S(sId_i, sId_j)), \tag{1}$$

$$sim_S(sId_i, sId_j) = \frac{sim_C(so_i, so_j) + sim_C(sl_i, sl_j)}{2}, \tag{2}$$

where

- st_i (st_j), sId_i (sId_j), so_i (so_j), and sl_i (sl_j) are respectively the timestamp, sensor id, object that the sensor is attached to, and the location where the sensor is located.
- The sim_T is the time similarity function that compares the time distance between the sensor events.
- The sim_S is the sensor similarity function that normalises the conceptual similarity functions sim_C on their objects and locations.

The conceptual similarity function is built on the algorithm proposed by Wu et al. [19]. The idea is to find the least common subsumer (LCS) of the two input concepts and compute the path length from the LCS up to the root node. The LCS is the most specific concept that these two concepts share as an ancestor.

---

[1] For brevity, we omit intermediate terms.

Definition 2. Let c_1 and c_2 be two concepts organised in one hierarchy. The **conceptual similarity** measure between them is calculated as:

$$sim_C(c_1, c_2) = \frac{2 \times N_3}{N_1 + N_2 + 2 \times N_3},$$

where N_1 (N_2) is the path length between c_1 (c_2) and the LCS node of c_1 and c_2, and N_3 is the path length between the LCS and the root.

When c_1 equals to c_2, their LCS node is itself and the similarity is 1.0. When c_1 is semantically far from c_2, their LCS node can be close to the root in the hierarchy, which makes N_1 and N_2 large and N_3 small, so the similarity is close to 0. Therefore, the larger the similarity measure, the closer the two concepts. Taking an example from Figure 1, the conceptual similarity between a *cup* and a *plate* is $\frac{2*3}{2+2+2*3} = 0.6$, while the similarity between *cup* and *door* is $\frac{2*1}{3+4+2*1} = 0.22$.

The time similarity function sim_T can exist in two forms: fine- and coarse-grained. Since the timestamps on each sensor event can be represented in numeric values, its fine-grained form is calculated as

$$sim_T(st_1, st_2) = min(1, 1 - \frac{|st_2 - st_1|}{T_{max}}), \tag{3}$$

where T_{max} is the maximum range of the time under consideration. For example, if we consider daily activities we set the T_{max} to be 24 hours (equally 86,400 seconds). If there exists a hierarchy of temporal concepts similar to the object or location concepts, then its coarse-grained form is calculated as Definition 2. In this paper, we take the fine-grained form, because the time hierarchy can be application specific, which violates the generality principle. However, we note this as a future research direction.

Example 1. In this example, we calculate the semantic similarity between the sensor events se_1, se_2 and se_3 in Figure 2. The location and object concepts refer to the LO and OO in Figure 1.

- se_1 and se_2: their time similarity is $1 - \frac{10}{86400} = 1$ using Equation 3; their sensor similarity is $(0.22 + 0)/2 = 0.11$ using Definition 1.
- se_2 and se_3: Similarly, their time similarity is $1 - \frac{25}{86400} = 0.9997$ and their sensor similarity is $(0.22 + 0)/2 = 0.11$.
- se_1 and se_3: their time similarity is $1 - \frac{35}{86400} = 0.9996$ and their sensor similarity is $(0.6 + 1)/2 = 0.8$ where the location similarity between these two sensors is 1.

In the above example, based on the similarity measures between these three sensor events, we can intuitively observe that the sensor events se_1 and se_3 should be grouped together, and se_2 should be partitioned from the former two.

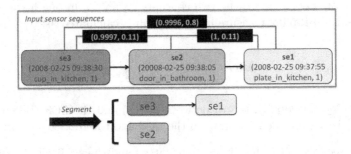

Fig. 2. Segmenting a sequence of interwoven sensor events based on their semantic similarity

This sequence could suggest that there are two users: one is cooking in the kitchen, while the other is using the bathroom. This example introduces our idea of *automatic segmentation* of sensor traces that record concurrent activities; that is, dividing a sequence of raw sensor events into segments, each of which is composed of sensor events that are semantically similar, intuitively corresponding to one of the concurrent activities.

Algorithm 1 illustrates the segmentation process. During the process, we maintain two lists: a *confirmed* list L_c that stores all the segmented sequences that are distant from the time of the current sensor event and will no longer be concatenated with other sensor events, and a *tentative* list L_t that records the unfinished sequences that are likely to be concatenated with new sensor events.

Algorithm 1. Automatic segmentation of a real-time sensor trace

Data: $SEQ = \langle se_1, se_2, \ldots, se_n \rangle$: a sequence of incoming sensor events
(θ_T, θ_S): the time and sensor threshold pair
Result: L_S: a list of segmented sequences
initialise(L_c);
initialise(L_t);
foreach $se \in SEQ$ **do**
    found = false;
    if *(!L_t.isEmpty)* **then**
        for $i = 1$ **to** L_t.size **do**
            $se_i = L_t.get(i).last$;
            $(sim_T, sim_S) = sim(se, se_i)$;
            if $sim_T \leq \theta_T$ **then**
                $L_c.add(L_t.get(i))$;
                $L_t.remove(i)$;

            else if *(!found && similarityCheck($sim_T, sim_S, \theta_T, \theta_S$))* **then**
                $L_t.add(se)$;
                $found = true$;

    if $!found$ **then**
        $formList(se)$;
        $L_t.add(se)$;
return L_c;

Given an incoming sensor event, se, we calculate the similarity measure between it and the previous sensor event in each sequence in the tentative list L_t; that is, $(sim_T, sim_S) = sim(se, se_i)$, $1 \leq i \leq m$, where m is the size of L_t, and se_i is the last sensor event in the ith sequence. If there exists a sequence i such that the similarity $sim(se, se_i)$ satisfies the given time and sensor thresholds θ_t and θ_s, the new event se will be joined with the sequence i as $\langle \ldots, se_i, se \rangle$. If the current se is different from all the sequences in L_t, then a new list $\langle se \rangle$ will be formed and added to L_t. That is, each sequence in L_t suggests one of the concurrent activities; and the number of sequences in L_t implies *how many* concurrent activities are ongoing.

During the process we also check whether any list i in the tentative list should be moved to the confirmed list by assessing the time similarity sim_T. If the similarity is too small, the list is distant from the current time and will be unlikely to be further linked with any new sensor events; in this case it will be moved to the confirmed list L_c. In the end, the segmentation result is $L_c = \{\langle se_1, se_2, \ldots, se_{k^1} \rangle, \langle se_{k^1+1}, \ldots, se_{k^2} \rangle, \ldots, \langle se_{k^{m-1}+1}, \ldots, se_n \rangle\}$, where $k^i(1 \leq i \leq m - 1)$ is the last index in the ith segmentation. Since the input sensor sequence records the concurrent activities, it is highly likely that there exists two sequences that are temporally contained or overlapping.

4   Activity Ontology and Recognition

After segmenting real-time raw sensor traces into fragments, we need to infer an activity for each fragment. This section describes an activity ontology that defines a profile with *time*, *location*, and *object* constraints. The activity recognition process is to find the activity whose profile best matches the current sensor fragment using the Primary Match Kernel (PMK) technique.

4.1   Activity Ontology

In the activity ontology (AO) we constrain each activity with *time*, *object*, and *location* conditions. Generally there are two types of conditions to constrain activities: *sufficient* and *necessary*. A sufficient condition is the most common type that has been used in knowledge-driven activity recognition techniques. If a sufficient condition is satisfied, then an activity is occurring. An example rule on the activity 'sleep' is:

person_in_bedroom ∧ *bed_is_accessed* ∧ *time_is_night*
∧ *light_in_bedroom_low* ∧ *door_in_bedroom_closed*
⇒ *user_is_sleeping.*

However, sufficient conditions are usually user-specific, over-detailed and do not always hold. In the above example, a user could sleep while leaving the bedroom's door open, or leaving the light on. Contrastingly, a necessary condition restricts what must hold when a user performs an activity, meaning that if an activity is occurring, then its necessary condition must hold. In other words, if the condition does not hold, then it is impossible that the user is performing activity. In the AO, only the necessary conditions are specified on activities.

We consider two types of *time* conditions: *occurring* time – when the activity usually occurs and *duration* – how long this activity typically lasts. For example, we place the constraint that the activity 'prepare breakfast' should occur in the morning (6am - 12am), and that the activity 'bath' should last more than 5 minutes. The *object* and *location* condition specifies what object the user must access to in order to perform this activity and where this activity must occur. To note that the necessary conditions that we specify here should be general knowledge in the sense that most people will execute the activity in this way. A summary of necessary conditions on the 'prepare breakfast' activity is presented as follows.

Activity	Occurring Time	Duration	Location	Object
prepare breakfast	[6am - 12am]	30min	kitchen	{cooking utensil, tableware}

As we can see, compared to the sufficient condition, the necessary condition is more certain and concise. The object and location conditions are defined on concepts in the domain ontologies OO and LO. Thanks to the existence of the OO and LO hierarchies, we can specify the conditions using *more general* concepts rather than listing each specific concept. For example, we could directly constrain the objects for the 'prepare breakfast' activity on cooking utensil or tableware, without the need of enumerating each concrete entity like a cup, plate or pan.

4.2   Pyramid Match Kernel and Activity Recognition

Activity recognition is done by finding an activity whose necessary condition *best matches* the currently segmented sensor traces. Here we employ the PMK technique [4], which is used to find an approximate correspondence between two sets of hierarchical concepts. PMK has been successfully utilised in recent image-based object detection and matching studies [22].

The principle of PMK is described as follows [11]: let X and Y be two sets of vectors in a D-dimensional feature space. Pyramid matching works by placing a sequence of increasingly coarser grids over the feature space and taking a weighted sum of the number of matches that occur at each level of resolution. At any fixed resolution, two points are said to match if they fall into the same cell of the grid; matches found at finer resolutions are weighed more heavily than matches found at coarser resolutions. More formally, let H_X^ℓ and H_Y^ℓ denote the histograms of X and Y at a resolution ℓ, so that $H_X^l(i)$ and $H_Y^l(i)$ are the numbers of points from X and Y that fall into the ith cell of the grid. The number of matches at ℓ is given by the histogram intersection function: $\mathcal{I}^\ell = \mathcal{I}(H_X^\ell, H_Y^\ell) = \sum_{i=1}^{N} min(H_X^\ell(i), H_Y^\ell(i))$, where N is the total number of cells at a level ℓ along each dimension, which is $N = 2^{D\ell}$.

Since the number of matches found at a coarser resolution ℓ includes all the matches found at the finer level $\ell + 1$, the matches at coarser levels involve

increasingly dissimilar features. To address this issue, PMK penalise matches at
the coarser level by associating the matches at each level ℓ with a weight $\frac{1}{2^{L-\ell}}$,
which is inversely proportional to the cell width at that level. Thus we come to
the formula: $K^L(X,Y) = \mathcal{I}^L + \sum_{l=0}^{L-1} \frac{1}{2^{L-\ell}}(I^\ell - I^{\ell+1})$.

Given the above, we next adapt PMK to support semantic matching between
the conditions in activities and sensor data. To prepare, we translate each activity's necessary condition into a D-dimensional vector V, where each dimension
represents a dimension of constraint (i.e., Location, Object, and Time). Correspondingly, we construct a set S of D-dimensional vectors extracted from a sensor
segment. For a cell i at a resolution level ℓ in a dimension d, we consider a value
falling into the cell if the value is more specific to the value corresponding to the
cell. Since each element in an activity vector could be composed of a set of values,
we call the activity element falling into a cell if any of its values falls into the cell.

Instead of employing uniform grids for each feature space, we use the conceptual hierarchies of the OO and LO presented in Figure 1. Thus, the match
degrees at each resolution level ℓ will be penalised by a new weight $\frac{1}{c_\ell^{L_d-\ell}}$, where
c_ℓ is the maximum width at ℓ. The final match degree between a sensor trace
and an activity profile is the summed degree at each resolution level in each
dimension, which is formally defined in Definition 3.

Definition 3. Let V be a D-dimensional activity profile and S be a set of D-
dimensional vectors extracted from a segment of sensor traces. The matching
degree between V and S is calculated in the following formula.

$$pmk\_match(V,S) = \frac{\sum_{d=1}^{D}(\mathcal{I}^{L_d} + \sum_{l=0}^{L_d-1} \frac{1}{c_\ell^{L_d-\ell}}(I^\ell(d) - I^{\ell+1}(d))))}{|S| \times D};$$

$$\mathcal{I}^\ell(d) = \mathcal{I}(S^\ell(d), V^\ell(d)) = \sum_{i=1}^{N(\ell)} \sum_{j=1}^{size(S^\ell(d))} \delta(i, S_j(d), V^\ell(d))$$

$$\delta(i, S_j(d), V^\ell(d)) = \begin{cases} 1, & \text{if both } S_j(d) \text{ and } V^\ell(d) \text{ fall into the cell } i \\ 0, & \text{otherwise.} \end{cases}$$

where L_d is the number of resolution levels in a dimension d, $N(\ell)$ is the number
of cells, and $size(S^\ell(d))$ is the size of values in the sensor segment S at a level
ℓ in the dimension d.

Example 2. We present a concrete example of calculating the match degree
between a sensor segment and the 'sleep' activity. We extract *time, location,*
and *object* data from a 3-length sensor segmentation as follows: $T = (23:12:38,$
$23:13:02, 23:13:04)$, $L = (BA, WDA, BA)$, $O = (Bed, Chair, Bed)$, where BA
and WDA represent a bed and work desk area in a bedroom (as shown in
Figure 1). The matching degree at these dimensions are calculated as follows.

Dimension	Constraint	PMK Degree
Occurring time	[8pm, 12pm], [0am, 8am]	3
Location	BA	2.5
Object	Bed	2.5

For the occurring time, we assume there is no hierarchy for temporal concepts, so we simply match the sensing time to the range, and the matching degree here is 3. Given the location constraint as the bed area (BA), the unpenalised match degrees from the coarsest level 0 to the finest level 3 respectively are 3, 3, 3, and 2. Then we penalise the match degrees by the weight and get the final result: $(0 + 0 + 1 * 1/2 + 2) = 2.5$. The match degree on the object dimension can be similarly calculated as 2.5. Then the total normalised match degree for this sensor fragment to the 'sleep' activity is $(3+2.5+2.5)/(3*3) = 0.89$.

The recognition of an activity is done by matching the extracted feature set from a sensor segment to each activity's conditions. The activity that achieves the highest score is the inferred result.

5   Experiment and Evaluation

We evaluate our *segmentation* and *recognition* algorithms on a well-known real-world dataset. To the best of our knowledge, there are few available multi-user datasets that are well annotated in the smart home community. After careful selection[2], we adopted the 'Interleaved ADL Activities' (IAA) dataset from the CASAS smart home project [1]. This dataset was collected in a smart apartment testbed hosted at Washington State University during the 2009-2010 academic year. The apartment was instrumented with various types of sensors to detect user movements, interaction with selected items, the statuses of doors and lights, consumption of water and electrical energy, and temperature, resulting in $2,804,812$ sensor traces. With the variety of sensors, number of sensor traces, length of the collection period, and the availability of the environment knowledge, we consider IAA as suitable to evaluate our technique.

The apartment housed two people, *R1* and *R2*, who performed their normal daily activities during the collection period. Within the AO described in the earlier section, each activity is constrained by the time, location and object conditions. In this dataset, we find that these activities do not have explicit temporal features; e.g., the sleeping activity is rather than defined as a proper night sleep, but as the user lying on the bed even for a few seconds. To be consistent with our knowledge engineering principle: only consider confident conditions when specifying an activity, we do not place any temporal constraints on the activities. The only objects used in this dataset is the equipment in the kitchen (e.g., the burner), which is only relevant to the 'meal preparation' activity. Therefore, we focus our constraints on the location. For example, the activity 'R1_Wander' is constrained to be in resident R1's bedroom, the activity 'R1_Sleep' is constrained to be in resident R1's bed area, and the activity 'Meal_Preparation' is constrained to the kitchen and using the burner object. The annotated activities along with their recorded occurrence time and location constraints are summarised as follows.

---

[2] Lists of Home Datasets: http://boxlab.wikispaces.com/List+of+Home+Datasets

Activity	Time(in hour)	Location Constraint
R1_Sleep	1053.97	R1's bed area
R1_Work	123.44	R1's work desk area
R1_Wander	1.47	R1's bedroom
R2_Sleep	1335.57	R2's bed area
R2_Work	99.87	R2's work desk area
R2_Wander	0.62	R2's bedroom
Meal (Preparation)	34.05	kitchen
Hygiene	83.83	bathroom
Bath	14.84	bathtub
Home	2.3	fronthall

In the end, the object ontology contains 20 instances and the location ontology contains 15 instances, on which we define 83 sensors, and 10 activities. We note that these ontologies are quite small for recognising activities in a real world smart home environment. Complement to such small size of knowledge in activity recognition is a novel use of hierarchy-based similarity measure and pattern recognition.

We note that in this paper we do not intend to distinguish behaviour for multiple users if they are semantically ambiguous; for example, 'R1_Meal_Preparation' and 'R2_Meal_Preparation' are treated together as one activity 'Meal_Preparation', while 'R1_Sleep' and 'R2_Sleep' are considered individually because they have explicit location semantics. The reason is that capturing the behaviour patterns for each individual user in performing the same activity is very challenging, which not only poses the risk of under- or over-specifying due to expert bias but also requires expressive logical language to specify and computationally expensive inference engine to process. Such knowledge is usually better discovered through sophisticated data mining and machine learning techniques [14]. One of our future goals is to combine our technique with such techniques to distinguish finer-grained interleaved activities. This paper focuses on demonstrating the effectiveness of using a very limited amount of more certain and less subjective knowledge in detecting multi-user concurrent activities with explicit semantic implications.

5.1   Parameter Selection

In terms of segmenting a real-time sensor trace, we have mentioned two parameters in Algorithm 1: *sensor* and *time* semantic thresholds. We set the semantic similarity threshold to be 0.5. In terms of the time threshold, we set a time distance d and the threshold $\theta_T = 1 - \frac{d}{T_{max}}$, and if $sim_T(st_1, st_2)$ in Formula 3 is below θ_T (i.e., their time distance is over d), then we dissect the corresponding sensor events se_1 and se_2. Here we propose another way to set the time threshold, called a Tuned Time threshold Configuration mechanism (TTC). The principle of TTC is to tune the time distance by taking the sensor similarity into account:

$$d'(sim_S) = \frac{d}{10^{1-sim_S}}.$$

Compared to setting the uniform time threshold configuration (*UTC*), TTC is a more flexible way to balance both the time and sensor thresholds. The intuition is that the sensor events reported in close proximity should be tied up, even though they are not highly similar; this is useful in detecting activities that have coarser constraints. For example, the 'R1_Wander' activity is constrained on R1's bedroom that spatially contains both the bed and work areas, which are defined as the location constraints on the 'R1_Sleep' and 'R1_Work' activities respectively. Using this tuned threshold, we could gather sensor traces that were spread over the room but whose timing gap was close, potentially implying that R1 is wandering. On the other hand, as the sensor threshold is roughly set, we could use this increasingly tighter time constraint to dissect sensor events whose semantics are not very close. For example, we could dissect sensor traces for the sleeping and working activities if the timing gap between the traces was not close enough.

5.2   Evaluation of Segmentation

We consider a segmentation algorithm to work well if it can partition the whole sensor trace into a much smaller number of fragments while still able to detect wherever there is a boundary between interleaved and concurrent activities. Therefore the performance of segmentation is measured using two parameters: (1) *partition percentage* – the percentage of the number of the segmentations over the total size of sensor traces and (2) *accuracy* – the percentage of boundaries between activities that is successfully detected. More specifically, a detection is considered successful and counted if the time at the detected segmentation (either start or end time) dst is within the range of the boundary time (again, either start or end time of an activity) rst; i.e., $dst \in [rst - tt, rst + tt]$, where tt is the time tolerance that is set to be 2 minutes in our experiment.

The evaluation result is presented in Figure 3, where we compare the performances of the above TTC and UTC mechanisms. As presented in Figure 3, our segmentation algorithms can partition a large sequence of sensor events into a much smaller number of fragments (whose partition percentages vary from 25% to 2%). The detection accuracy is close to 1, indicating we can detect the boundary successfully. Combined with both these measures, we can conclude that our algorithm is able to select and combine sensor events that resemble one activity and separate sensor events that correspond to different activities.

5.3   Evaluation of Recognition

After segmentation we use the recognition algorithm to infer the most likely activity for each segment. Figure 4 presents the overall accuracies of recognising single and concurrent activities. In the *IAA* dataset, there is 44% of the time that more than one activities are being simultaneously performed by different

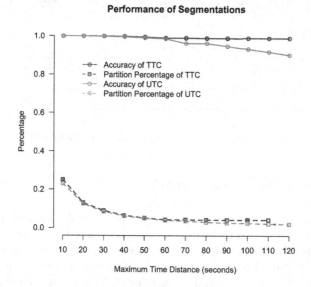

Fig. 3. Partition percentages and accuracies of segmentation

users, and the accuracy of recognising these activities is 95%. The reason that the accuracy of recognising concurrent activities is higher than that on single activity is that most of time we recognise more than one activities. There are times that the activities have been inferred while there is no corresponding activity recorded in the ground truth.

Single Activity		Concurrent Activity		Overall Accuracy
Proportion	Accuracy	Proportion	Accuracy	
56%	82%	44%	95%	86%

Fig. 4. Proportion and accuracies of single- and concurrent-activities in *IAA*

Figure 5 presents the confusion matrix of recognising the activities in *IAA*, where each figure is read as the percentage of predictions over actual occurrences. The result shows that the recognition algorithm can accurately recognise the activities with explicit constraints. For example, the 'Meal', 'Bath', 'Home' activities have distinguished location constraints that are exclusive from any other activities, so they are very well recognised. In contrast, the 'Wander' and 'Hygiene' activities are less well recognised since they are specified with coarser-grained constraints.

	R1_Sleep	R2_Sleep	R1_Wander	R2_Wander	R1_Work	R2_Work	Meal	Hygiene	Bath	Home
R1_Sleep	0.931	0.103	0.074	0	0	0	0	0	0	0
R2_Sleep	0	0.672	0	0.125	0	0	0	0	0	0
R1_Wander	0.069	0.164	0.852	0	0	0	0	0	0	0
R2_Wander	0	0.017	0	0.75	0	0	0	0	0	0
R1_Work	0	0.014	0.074	0	1	0	0	0	0	0
R2_Work	0	0	0	0.125	0	1	0	0	0	0
Meal	0	0	0	0	0	0	1	0	0	0
Hygiene	0	0.011	0	0	0	0	0	0.962	0	0
Bath	0	0.017	0	0	0	0	0	0.038	1	0
Home	0	0	0	0	0	0	0	0	0	1

Fig. 5. Confusion matrix for recognising the activities in *IAA*

6   Conclusion and Future Work

This paper presents a novel approach to combining ontologies with recent advances in semantic matching techniques to recognise daily human activities. The technique benefits from generality, low engineering effort, and no requirement for training data. We have demonstrated the effectiveness of our technique in segmenting sensor traces online, and recognising multi-user concurrent activities. The technique works well on activities that have explicit semantics, but is limited in its ability to distinguish coarsely constrained activities from similar but more finely constrained activities. In the future, we will explore other derivative PMK functions to tackle this problem.

Also the current segmentation algorithms work well on object use sensors such as motion sensors or RFID, and we will look into how to formally define correlations between different types of sensors so that we can segment other types of sensor data. Additional areas of future research will focus on distinguishing the individual user participating in a common activity, and extending our ontological model with time series analysis techniques and machine learning techniques; that is, using the frequency and gap of sensor events to characterise the temporal features of different users performing the same activity.

References

1. Cook, D., Schmitter-Edgecombe, M.: Assessing the quality of activities in a smart environment. Methods of Information in Medicine 48, 480–485 (2009)
2. Cook, D.J., Augusto, J.C., Jakkula, V.R.: Ambient intelligence: Technologies, applications, and opportunities. Pervasive and Mobile Computing 5(4), 277–298 (2009)
3. Gong, S., Xiang, T.: Recognition of group activities using dynamic probabilistic networks. In: ICCV 2003, Washington, DC, USA, pp. 742–749 (2003)
4. Grauman, K., Darrell, T.: The pyramid match kernel: Efficient learning with sets of features. J. Mach. Learn. Res. 8, 725–760 (2007)
5. Gu, T., Chen, S., Tao, X., Lu, J.: An unsupervised approach to activity recognition and segmentation based on object-use fingerprints. Data Knowl. Eng. 69(6), 533–544 (2010)

6. Gu, T., Wang, X.H., Pung, H.K., Zhang, D.Q.: An ontology-based context model in intelligent environments. In: CNDS 2004, pp. 270–275 (January 2004)

7. Helaoui, R., Niepert, M., Stuckenschmidt, H.: Recognizing interleaved and concurrent activities: A statistical-relational approach. In: PERCOM 2011, pp. 1–9. IEEE Computer Society, Washington, DC (2011)

8. Hu, D.H., Yang, Q.: Cigar: concurrent and interleaving goal and activity recognition. In: Proceedings of the 23rd National Conference on Artificial Intelligence, AAAI 2008, vol. 3, pp. 1363–1368. AAAI Press (2008)

9. Kasteren, T.L.M., Englebienne, G., Kröse, B.J.A.: Human activity recognition from wireless sensor network data: Benchmark and software. In: Chen, L., Nugent, C.D., Biswas, J., Hoey, J. (eds.) Activity Recognition in Pervasive Intelligent Environments. Atlantis Ambient and Pervasive Intelligence, vol. 4, ch. 8, pp. 165–186. Atlantis Press, Paris (2011)

10. Kim, E., Helal, S., Cook, D.: Human activity recognition and pattern discovery. IEEE Pervasive Computing 9(1), 48–53 (2010)

11. Lazebnik, S., Schmid, C., Ponce, J.: Beyond bags of features: Spatial pyramid matching for recognizing natural scene categories. In: CVPR 2006, pp. 2169–2178. IEEE Computer Society, Washington, DC (2006)

12. Miller, G.A.: Wordnet: a lexical database for english. Commun. ACM 38(11), 39–41 (1995)

13. Modayil, J., Bai, T., Kautz, H.: Improving the recognition of interleaved activities. In: Proceedings of the 10th International Conference on Ubiquitous Computing, UbiComp 2008, pp. 40–43. ACM, New York (2008)

14. Nguyen, N.T., Venkatesh, S., Bui, H.: Recognising behaviours of multiple people with hierarchical probabilistic model and statistical data association. In: Proceedings of the British Machine Vision Conference, pp. 126.1–126.10 (2006)

15. Okeyo, G., Chen, L., Wang, H., Sterritt, R.: Dynamic sensor data segmentation for real-time knowledge-driven activity recognition. Pervasive and Mobile Computing (2012)

16. Patterson, D.J., Fox, D., Kautz, H., Philipose, M.: Fine-grained activity recognition by aggregating abstract object usage. In: ISWC 2005, pp. 44–51. IEEE Computer Society (2005)

17. Riboni, D., Bettini, C.: Context-aware activity recognition through a combination of ontological and statistical reasoning. In: Zhang, D., Portmann, M., Tan, A.-H., Indulska, J. (eds.) UIC 2009. LNCS, vol. 5585, pp. 39–53. Springer, Heidelberg (2009)

18. Saguna, Zaslavsky, A., Chakraborty, D.: Recognizing concurrent and interleaved activities in social interactions. In: DASC 2011, pp. 230–237 (December 2011)

19. Wu, Z., Palmer, M.: Verbs semantics and lexical selection. In: ACL 1994, Stroudsburg, PA, USA, pp. 133–138 (1994)

20. Ye, J., Dobson, S., McKeever, S.: Situation identification techniques in pervasive computing: a review. Pervasive and Mobile Computing 8, 36–66 (2012)

21. Ye, J., Stevenson, G., Dobson, S.: A top-level ontology for smart environments. Pervasive and Mobile Computing 7, 359–378 (2011)

22. Yu, T.-H., Kim, T.-K., Cipolla, R.: Real-time action recognition by spatiotemporal semantic and structural forests. In: Proceedings of British Machine Vision Conference, Aberystwyth, UK, pp. 1–12. British Machine Vision Association (2010)

Part II

Landscape Track

Personalized Smart Environments to Increase Inclusion of People with Down's Syndrome

Juan Carlos Augusto[1], Terje Grimstad[2], Reiner Wichert[3], Eva Schulze[4], Andreas Braun[3], Gro Marit Rødevand[2], and Vanda Ridley[5,*]

[1] Middlesex University, School of Science and Technology, London, UK
[2] Karde AS, Oslo, Norway
[3] Fraunhofer Institut fr Graphische Datenverarbeitung, Darmstadt, Germany
[4] Institut fur Sozialforschung, Berlin, Germany
[5] Down's Syndrome Association, London, UK
j.augusto@mdx.ac.uk, {terje.grimstad,gro.marit.rodevand}@karde.no,
{reiner.wichert,andreas.braun}@igd.fraunhofer.de,
e.schulze@bis-berlin.de, vanda.ridley@downs-syndrome.org.uk

Abstract. Most people with Downs Syndrome (DS) experience low integration with society. Recent research and new opportunities for their integration in mainstream education and work provided numerous cases where levels of achievement exceeded the (limiting) expectations. This paper describes a project, POSEIDON, aiming at developing a technological infrastructure which can foster a growing number of services developed to support people with DS. People with DS have their own strengths, preferences and needs so POSEIDON will focus on using their strengths to provide support for their needs whilst allowing each individual to personalize the solution based on their preferences. This project is user-centred from its inception and will give all main stakeholders ample opportunities to shape the output of the project, which will ensure a final outcome which is of practical usefulness and interest to the intended users.

Keywords: Down's Syndrome, Inclusion, Activities Supporting Independence and Integration.

1 Introduction

We live in a world that generates technical advances and creates innovation at a very fast pace. However neither these advances and innovation reach all, nor they reach all in the same way. There are substantial groups of citizens in our

* The authors would like to acknowledge other members of the POSEIDON consortium: Riitta Hellman from Karde AS, Sheila Heslam from DSA-UK, Rita Lawrenz and Cornelia Bartelniewoehner from ADS-Germany, Lars Thomas Boye and Knut Eilif Husa from Tellu AS, Lars Brustad from NNDS-Norway, Susanna Laurin from Funka Nu, Tony Cook, Rui Loureiro and Gill Whitney from Middlesex University.

J.C. Augusto et al. (Eds.): AmI 2013, LNCS 8309, pp. 223–228, 2013.
© Springer International Publishing Switzerland 2013

society which have not been considered the focus of those developments and as a consequence can benefit only marginally, at the best of cases, from access to the services that most of the society enjoy.

Our project POSEIDON (PersOnalized Smart Environments to increase Inclusion of people with DOwn's syNdrome), focuses on the task of bringing some of the latest technological advances to increase inclusion in our society of a specific group of citizens: people with Down's Syndrome (DS)and tries to answer questions posed in the AAL community before about inclusion and the role of AAL beyond the current focus on supporting independence for the elderly [1, 2].

Common characteristics for people with Down's Syndrome include [3–6]:

- Relative strengths in: some aspects of visual processing, receptive language, and nonverbal social functioning.
- Relative weaknesses in: gross motor skills and expressive language skills
- People with DS sometimes: find transitions difficult, need prompts / reminders as they go about their daily lives, benefit from structure and routine as a way to cope with the complexity of the world, they need a little more time to process information and have difficulties with time because it is quite an abstract concept.

Our solution will aim at giving priority to preferences like these to create technology that is appealing and useful to them. People with DS (along with their relatives and other potential users) will be given the opportunity to co-design a solution along the project and we believe this will increase the chances of producing a solution which is really useful for the intended beneficiaries.

Our project gathers the direct participation of companies, research centres and Down's Syndrome Associations primarily from Germany, Norway and the UK. However the consortium is willing to gather the opinion and attract participation of all EU countries and possibly from other parts of the world as well.

2   The POSEIDON Approach

This overarching goal will be achieved by empowering first and foremost people with DS however this support will also be available to those who interact with them on a daily basis (family, carers, friends, and service providers). Although there are some technological products in the market, these are very limited and specialized on narrow services, without integrating and leveraging all the potential available by todays technology and expertise. Some of the challenges people with Down's Syndrome face:

- Access to education and the support provided is very limited
- Fewer opportunities are given to people with DS to find employment
- Most people with DS find it harder to access and maintain social networks
- Sedentarism can result in health problems for people with DS
- Public information is often in formats that are not easily accessible for people with DS (e.g. bus timetables)
- Reading and writing can be more difficult for people with DS

POSEIDON will aim to provide a technological infrastructure to foster the development of services which can support people with Down's Syndrome and, to some extent, also those who interact with them on a daily basis. The infrastructure will be illustrated with the creation of a system providing services supporting inclusion based on static and mobile smart environments to empower people with DS in different daily life situations. These services will provide evidence and guidance on how technology can help people with DS to be more integrated within their society through education, work, mobility and socialization.

This project cannot eradicate all of the problems that people with DS may experience; however, POSEIDON will provide an added layer of support that will facilitate their immersion in usual daily life activities as most of the population experiences it. The project will create extra support for people with DS. It is not intended that the project leads to a reduction in human contact. Instead, POSEIDON offers information and guidance to encourage decision-making and independence. This is achieved through devices which will provide the infrastructure for a Smart Environment and software which will provide the Ambient Intelligence needed to guide them and support them on interacting with the complex real world. Part of these Smart Environment and Ambient Intelligence is available in the market and part will be created new specifically to support people with Down's Syndrome or those with similar preferences and needs. See figure 1 below. The static devices (Interactive Table and Virtual Reality Set) will be used at specific locations, for example at home, school or work, whilst the users will have access to the inclusion services everywhere and all the time through the tablet. Notice the main users are people with DS but their family, school teachers, employers, bus drivers, and other people interacting with them will also be able to use the static and mobile devices with different interfaces and benefits.

Each individual is different but overall citizens with Down's Syndrome may require some level of extra support in a variety of situations. We cannot address

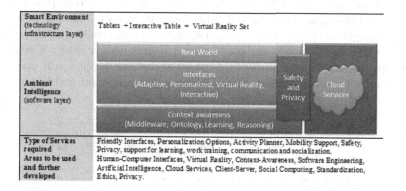

Fig. 1. Summary of infrastructure and its use within POSEIDON

all possible situations in this project but we aim to consider a few which are related to some of the core challenge areas they face: education, socialization, wellbeing, and mobility. We will use a scenario describing a day out as a guide and inspiration for our project: going from home to school or work, and from there to a place for socialization, e.g., to the cinema or restaurant and then back home (see figure 2 below).

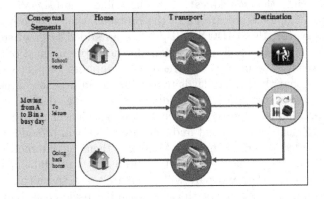

Fig. 2. Supporting mobility in POSEIDON

Different situations require different levels of support. There is availability of the system at all times (this is indicated in figure 3 in yellow) but in specific, safer and better known contexts that support is specialized and context-aware: safer at home (indicated in green) and not necessarily so safe at other places (indicated in orange). Transitions between environments/situations increase the potential for problems (including safety when travelling from one place to another) so support should be higher (indicated in red) in those situations. The new inclusion services should not replace humans, the system can be used to empower people with DS and encourage them to make their own decisions in different situations. At different places the person with DS can be with someone else ready to bring support when needed, for example, a travel companion, a tutor, a coach, or a relative, but the inclusion services provided by our project will open new opportunities for a person with DS to choose what to do next and how.

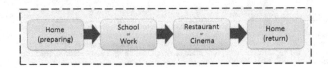

Fig. 3. Scenarios to be considered in POSEIDON

3   Projected Technological Infrastructure

Our system will be supported with a combination of devices and software specifically designed for people with DS and those who interact with them. The technological infrastructure has three main components

1. a display with a computer where Virtual Reality (VR) can be produced;
2. an interactive table which is under development by Fraunhofer and on
3. a tablet PC.

These developments will be based on previous research and innovative solutions created by some of the partners of the POSEIDON consortium [7, 8].

The technology can help to increase participation in education, work, socialization, and greater freedom of mobility. The tablets, VR set and interactive table can provide support for planning tasks and for learning, they are all interconnected maximizing their potential and availability of services. All of these naturally will vary case by case and we will get different degree of success but the project will be the first of this kind and of this scale that we are aware of, and, as such it can produce a tangible product as well as important insights which will nurture future developments.

Different contexts will require different inclusion services dictated by the intended natural preferences of a place: eating, sleeping, playing games at home, learning at school, doing exercise in the gym, etc. The system should be at all times aware of where the person is and what may be useful. We can achieve this level of consciousness and autonomy by the system thanks to the sensors, interfaces, planners and other technologies available. The consortium possess knowledge and experience on developing intelligent and context-aware software but here there are some interesting challenges posed by the characteristics of the main users: Will it be more efficient a system that is self-adapting all the time to make available services according to the context or will the frequent changes of the interface be more confusing than helpful for a person with Down's Syndrome? These and other practical questions and challenges on making sure the platform serves the users properly will be taken into consideration. The POSEIDON system will aim at meeting several desirable features of universal design and inclusion:

– as flexible as possible: it adapts to the user, it learns from its more frequent uses and learns to anticipate needs,
– as clever as possible, to (a) retrieve information which is context-aware and to (b) restructure its look according to the context
– multiregional: language translations for different countries
– across ages: it has to be personalized for children, teens, adults and elderly
– across ability: it has to be tailor-made for the intellectual capability of the user
– across platforms: work in tablets from at least three different providers (e.g. Samsung, Apple and Toshiba), which means the system should be portable across a variety of Operating Systems like Android, IOS and perhaps more

4   Conclusions

We live in an era where old assumptions and stereotypes are increasingly challenged. We are tackling the limitations on inclusion that society impose over people with DS, and we aim at creating technology which can facilitate their development at similar levels than others. POSEIDON gathers the expertise of companies leading technological innovation, academic organizations with deep technical knowledge in the area of assistive technologies and Intelligent Environments as well as on leading organizations to support people with DS.

This consortium is aiming to develop infrastructure to support people with DS, their circle of family and friends, as well as other sectors of our society (educators, job managers, etc.) so that we can create a more inclusive society where we aim to emphasize people's capabilities instead of focusing mostly on the assumed limitations. Each individual is unique and hence our project will aim to gather from the individuals which are their preferences and needs as well as to create a system which can be personalized by the users.

We understand this is the start of a long journey as there has not been comprehensive projects with this focus before and at the same time we know there are difficulties ahead, however we start this journey with the hope at the end of it we would have paved the way for innovative technological developments to support a more inclusive society.

References

1. Augusto, J.C., Huch, M., Kameas, A., Maitland, J., McCullagh, P., Roberts, J., Sixsmith, A., Wichert, R. (eds.): Handbook of Ambient Assisted Living. AISE Series, vol. 11. IOS Press (2012)
2. Augusto, J.C.: AAL4DS (Can AAL Technology Help People with Down's Syndrome to Live Better Lives?). In: Proceedings of AALForum 2012 (Tomorrow in Sight: From Design to Delivery), Eindhoven, The Netherlands, September 26, pp. 79–83 (2012)
3. Fidler, D.J.: The Emerging Down Syndrome Behavioural phenotype in Early Childhood: Implications for practice. Infants and Young Children 18(2), 86–103 (2005), http://depts.washington.edu/isei/iyc/fidler_18_2.pdf
4. Jarrold, C., Purser, H., Brock, J.: Short-term memory in Down syndrome. In: Alloway, T.P., Gathercole, S.E. (eds.) Working Memory and Neurodevelopmental Conditions, pp. 239–266. Psychology Press, Hove (2006)
5. Brigstocke, S., Hulme, C., Nye, J.: Number and arithmetic skills in children with Down syndrome. Down Syndrome Research and Practice (2008), http://www.down-syndrome.org/reviews/2070/reviews-2070.pdf
6. Courtney, T., Pahl, J., Karrim, S.: Employment in Down Syndrome. In: Proc. of 11th World Down Syndrome Congress, Capetown, South Africa, August 15-17 (2012)
7. Kamieth, F., Dähne, P., Wichert, R., Villalar, J., Jimenez-Mixco, V., Arca, A., Arredondo, M.: Exploring the Potential of Virtual Reality for the Elderly and People with Disabilities. In: Kim, J.-J. (ed.) "Virtual Reality", January 1. InTech (2011)
8. Rødevand, G.M., Hellman, R.: Young and Enthusiatic: ICT-based IADL-Training. Down Syndrome Quartely 13(1), 8–13 (2011), http://www.karde.no/DSQ_Rodevand_etal_paper.pdf

Living Lab and Research on Sustainability: Practical Approaches on Sustainable Interaction Design

David V. Keyson, Abdullah Al Mahmud, and Natalia Romero

ID-StudioLab, Faculty of Industrial Design Engineering,
Delft University of Technology, 2628 CE Delft, The Netherlands
{d.keyson,a.almahmud,n.a.romero}@tudelft.nl

Abstract. Living labs can be understood as the ability to bring user, technology and business into an open innovative development process that establishes real life environments. In this paper we describe our ongoing works on sustainable interaction design on energy saving and trading in which local residents are involved. The SusLabNWE (Sustainable Living Lab North-West Europe) project aims to resolve territorial challenges related to industrial competitiveness and sustainability in North West Europe. We present two projects in which local residents in the Netherlands were engaged in sustainable innovation in the context of the SusLabNWE project.

Keywords: Living lab, sustainable interaction design, sustainability.

1 Introduction and Background

Living lab infrastructure provides a means to observe social practices, involving technical artifacts in the process of everyday use, both in real households and in a living lab test facility [3, 8]. Taking social practices of new products into account is key to successful adoption of innovations, since too often products designed for environmental efficiency under given circumstances are misused, resulting in unintended less sustainable outcomes [7]. Undertaking the complexity of social practices entails the engagement of local residents as an extended peer community closely involved in the research and development of new innovations. Therefore, the need for an adequate research and design infrastructure and methodologies are essential. This paper highlights the challenges that SusLabNWE is confronting, including the need for a common infrastructure and methodologies to a) involve local residents in all steps of the design process and b) integrating sensing and subjective data from sustainable living studies. In the following section the SusLabNWE infrastructure and proposed design methodologies are introduced. Following this, two case studies to illustrate initial steps of the approach followed to engage local residents in interaction design for sustainability are described.

1.1 Sustainable Living Lab North West Europe (SusLabNWE)

SusLabNWE (www.suslabnwe.eu) is a national and international infrastructure of living labs that enables innovation processes in which users and other actors actively

J.C. Augusto et al. (Eds.): AmI 2013, LNCS 8309, pp. 229–234, 2013.

participate in the development, testing, and diffusion of new products, services and system solutions. Insights on human practices are collected in existing homes, which serve as input for the development of concepts and prototypes in collaboration with the extended community, and finally implemented in existing homes as well as in living laboratories for long and short-term studies on sustainable living. SusLab provides a context in which residents become an extended peer community in the innovation process that can interact with and report on sustainable innovations, while sharing practices with other households and stakeholders. Central to the project is the development of user centered design research methodologies and measures for in situ studies which can provide insights into the usability and adoption of sustainable innovations for industry, public and academia sectors. The main goal of SusLab is to create a unique new infrastructure where insights, co-development and validation of sustainable products, services, legislation and combinations of these take place directly with users in the complexity of their living environment and daily practices. To validate the infrastructures and methods, several pilot studies are ongoing across regions focusing on energy management and comfort in relation to heating and cooling.

In the Netherlands, the SusLab living lab called 'Concept House' acts as a communication and interaction platform for the innovation developments in the neighborhood of Heijplaat, Rotterdam. Stakeholders include present and future inhabitants, designers/architects, city planners, project developers, and the building and installation industry. A common research platform is created to accommodate qualitative and quantitative measures based on a wireless sensing infrastructure with cloud based database (Fig. 1).

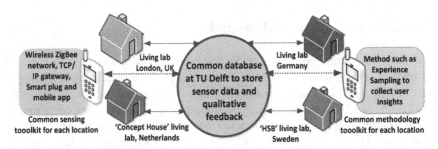

Fig. 1. The general architecture of the common research platform of SusLab

1.2   User Involvement in Sustainable Interaction Design and SusLabNWE Approach

The involvement of users in the design and evaluation process of sustainable technologies is fundamental in developing usable and acceptable products and services though the integration of the end-users remains a difficult task [1, 9]. Based on the living lab approach, the potential customers and other stakeholders are involved in all stages of product development lifecycle. It has been argued that the same users should participate in all the different stages of the design process [13]. 'Returning participants' are often involved as they can provide more effective feedback, as they already have a relatively deep understanding of the application's concepts.

Feedback captured directly from household inhabitants aims to provide a holistic and ecological understanding of home practices considering peoples' values and preferences. Home practices embrace momentary experiences that affect individuals' feelings regarding a specific situation [11]. Insights of momentary experiences related to home practices are expected to inform the design of sustainable home technologies from the perspective of the inhabitants and contextualized to when and where relevant practices take place. To bring insights on daily life experiences into the design of sustainable innovations it is expected to help the introduction and acceptance of new practices into people's life. Therefore part of SusLab research activities involves the development of appropriate methods to capture momentary experiences. Considering the value of Experience Sampling Method (ESM) [5] to capture in-situ experiences on a moment-to-moment basis, SusLab contributes with the development of adapted ESM methods to be implemented in existing homes and research houses.

With the goal of setting up a living lab infrastructure, including use of existing homes and a network of research houses, SusLab builds on the EU Living Lab project (http://www.livinglabproject.org/). Within the 'Living Lab' project, a 'Three-Tier Model' of research was developed, consisting of (a) insight research involving the study of current practices in existing homes, (b) studies in prototype houses equipped with innovative products and services focused on sustainable living, and (c) field testing, in which research prototypes are up-scaled such that existing homes can be equipped with innovative sustainable technologies. The three-tier approach also enables local communities to take part in design driven studies via early insights studies in their homes, participate in the development and test of innovations in a research house and experience the new products and services. In this manner localized comparative studies can be conducted in which research houses serve as an incubator and catalyst for increasing the chance of adoption of sustainable innovations in the homes of the users. SusLab exploits methods used in existing living lab projects such as described in [1, 3, 8, 9] and also adapts/develops new methods for sustainable interaction design which are unique.

2   Current Projects

In the following section two on-going projects are presented to illustrate the potentials of the sensing and methodology toolkit.

2.1   Project 1: Engaging Local Communities and the SusLab Living Lab

In a recent study local residents of the living lab at Heijplaat, Rotterdam, the Netherlands were engaged in the design of an energy feedback system called Ampul [12]. Ampul (Fig. 2-left) is a mobile application that aims to bring people closer to their consumption of energy and to stimulate their own production by solar cells. Ampul aims to connect local or small-scale energy production, such as solar energy, with people's domestic environment and their daily life activities in a meaningful and natural manner. An extension of the Ampul (http://131.180.117.131:8088/suslabnwe.php)

has been created (Fig. 2-right) to demonstrate the production and consumption of energy at the 'Concept House'.

In the first phase of the project user involvement, motivations, and their attitudes towards energy production and consumption at their homes has been explored. In the second phase, the emphasis was on designing user involvement in a living lab situation. A participatory field study was conducted with participants from six households (each family stayed two days and two nights) from the neighbourhood in the living lab 'Concept House'. The participants were asked to treat the house as if it was their own and to perform daily living activities while using Ampul. An offline tool, 'situated prompts' [10], was implemented to capture participants in situ experiences with the device. Participants were positively surprised by the use of Ampul and the effects it had on their feelings and decisions which eventually helped to further improve the Ampul design. The opportunity to conduct insight research with local communities and the use of participatory design approach by bringing the local communities in the living lab strengthen the final design of Ampul.

Fig. 2. The Ampul prototype [12] (left), extension of the Ampul concept (right) where solar panel production of the 'Concept House' is shown in green and total electricity consumption is shown in red

2.2 Project 2: Rolling Out SuslabNWE Solutions to Local Communities

One of the steps in the living lab approach is testing the new design solutions in the context of daily life situations. Towards this goal, we have designed an application to inform users about their daily energy performance and consumption behaviors. The application is called Equarium which has been designed, developed and tested in the 'Concept House' living lab and will be validated in a longitudinal field study in local Dutch houses.

The Equarium interface relies on the metaphor of a dynamically changing ecosystem to which a variety of energy parameters can be mapped. As the name suggests, the Equarium is a visualisation of an aquarium with flora and fauna. The Equarium is designed to provide users with a rich visualization, which not only stimulates them, to increase their energy performance but also engage them by means of an engaging fish character (Fig. 3-left). In previous research a game based approach was found to be an effective means to shape energy consumption behavior [4].

Detailed energy performance and energy saving tips can be provided via conversational dialog box. Based on a mixed user initiative design, the fish can indicate it has information by flapping a fin or the user can tap the screen to receive energy related tips which are either locally generated or remotely sent to the fish. For example the fish can ask subjective questions to gather user related performance data. Underlying simple data displays provide more detailed information. As the user demonstrates eco-efficient behavior, such as use of solar energy at peak times, the water may become more clear and additional living organism and objects may appear in the Equarium. The Equarium receives information from plug (Fig. 3-right) units equipped with energy sensors and ZigBee transceivers communicating with a ZigBee to Wi-Fi gateway and smart meter if available. The smart plugs enable appliance-level home monitoring and on/off control of devices.

Fig. 3. Example of Equarium^{TM} feedback (left) and custom smart plug (right) [6]

3   Discussion

In this paper the SusLab infrastructure and methodology to facilitate the engagement of the local communities in a design process was outlined. The 'living lab' concept which is central to SusLab can be generally understood as the ability to bring user, technology and business into an open innovative development process that establishes real life environments. The concept supports long-term cooperation, co-creative research and development by involving at an early stage the user in the innovation process for 'sensing, prototyping, validating and refining complex solutions in multiple and evolving real life contexts [1,8]. The long-term cooperation between researchers, companies and end users distinguish this concept from other approaches, which revert to traditional methods. In this regard heterogeneous empirical methods have been applied to studying behavior and media usage [2]. In addition to the technological aspects, SusLab allows insight into the human dimension of technology, which is of paramount importance for a successful societal deployment of new sustainable technologies. A positive societal impact can be achieved by integrating citizens' needs, requirements and feedback into R&D [2, 8], supported by the three-tier model as mentioned before. A maximum impact can be achieved by ensuring cooperation among the partners in a living lab infrastructure such as SusLab project. A longer term goal is to expand SusLab which is currently focused on North West Europe, into a wider network of living labs and common infrastructures and methodologies for field testing in Europe.

Acknowledgments. We thank project partners (www.suslabnwe.eu) and participants for their cooperation. We would also like to acknowledge the contribution of Jaap Rutten, Robet Stuursma and Marcus de Hoogh, Robe Luxen and Martin Havranek.

References

1. Bergvall-Kåreborn, B., Holst, M., Ståhlbröst, A.: Concept Design with a Living Lab Approach. In: Proc. of HICSS 2009, pp. 1–10. IEEE (2009)
2. Eriksson, M., Niitamo, V.-P., Kulkki, S., Hribernik, K.A.: Living Labs as a Multi-Contextual R&D Methodology. In: Proceeding of the International Conference on Concurrent Enterprising (2006)
3. Følstad, A.: Living Labs for Innovation and Development of Information and Communication Technology: A Literature Review. eJOV 10, 99–131 (2008)
4. Geelen, D.V., Keyson, D.V., Boess, S.U., Brezet, J.C.: Exploring the use of a game to stimulate energy saving in households. Journal of Design Research 10(1-2), 102–120 (2012)
5. Hektner, J.M., Schmidt, J.A., Cziks zentmihalyi, M.: Experience Sampling Method: Measuring the quality of everyday life. Sage (2007)
6. Keyson, D.V., Al Mahmud, A., de Hoogh, M., Luxen, R.: Designing a Portable and Low Cost Home Energy Management Toolkit. In: Proc. ANT/SEIT, pp. 646–653 (2013)
7. Liedtke, C., von Geibler, J., Baedeker, C.: The sustainability living lab as a reflective user-integrating research infrastructure. In: 3rd International Conference on Sustainability Transitions, pp. 206–222 (2012)
8. Niitamo, V.-P., Kulkki, S., et al.: State-of-the-art and good practice in the field of living labs. In: Proceedings of the 12th International Conference on Concurrent Enterprising: Innovative Products and Services through Collaborative Networks. Milan, Italy (2006)
9. Ogonowski, C., Ley, B., et al.: Designing for the living room: long-term user involvement in a living lab. In: Proceedings of the SIGCHI Conference on Human Factors in Computing Systems, pp. 1539–1548. ACM (2013)
10. Romero, N., Al Mahmud, A., Beella, S., Keyson, D.: Towards an Integrated Methodology to Design Sustainable Living Practices. In: Augusto, J.C., Wichert, R., Collier, R., Keyson, D., Salah, A.A., Tan, A.-H. (eds.) AmI 2013. LNCS, vol. 8309, pp. 299–304. Springer, Heidelberg (2013)
11. Roto, V., Law, E., Vermeeren, A., Hoonhout, J.: White paper (eds.): User Experience White Paper. Outcome of the Dagstuhl Seminar on Demarcating User Experience, Germany (2011)
12. Rutten, J.: Designing Ampul: exploring future prosumer interactions. Master thesis in Industrial Design Engineering, Delft University of Technology (2013)
13. Sleeswijk Visser, F., Visser, V.: Re-using users: cocreate and co-evaluate. Personal and Ubiquitous Computing 10(2-3), 148–152 (2006)

Intelligent Decision-Making in the Physical Environment

David Lillis, Sean Russell, Dominic Carr,
Rem W. Collier, and Gregory M.P. O'Hare

CLARITY: Centre for Sensor Web Technologies,
School of Computer Science and Informatics,
University College Dublin, Ireland
{david.lillis,sean.russell,dominic.carr,rem.collier,gregory.ohare}@ucd.ie

Abstract. The issue of situating intelligent agents within an environment, either virtual or physical, is an important research question in the area of Multi Agent Systems. In addition, the deployment of agents within Wireless Sensor Networks has received some focus also.

This paper proposes an architecture to augment the reasoning capabilities of agents with an abstraction of a physical sensing environment over which it has control. This architecture combines the SIXTH sensor middleware platform with the ASTRA agent programming language, using CArtAgO as the intermediary abstraction.

1 Introduction

The environment in which an agent is situated is considered to be an essential component of Multi Agent Systems (MASs) by many researchers. An environment provides the surrounding conditions for agents to exist, in addition to providing an exploitable design abstraction upon which a MAS can be developed [1]. As this notion has gained traction, a number of solutions have been proposed to allow environment abstractions be provided for agents.

This paper considers how agents can be provided with an abstraction of a physical environment by leveraging physical sensors. This includes access to sensor data and information about the structure of the sensor network itself. This allows agents to make intelligent decisions about which sensors must be enabled or disabled according to application demands, which sensor data is required and at what frequency, and other decisions relevant to the application domain.

Previous examples of incorporating agents into sensor networks typically concentrates on in-network intelligence, where lightweight agents are deployed on computationally constrained sensor motes in order to perform such tasks as power management [2], adaptive application development [3] and optimisation [4]. This work rather focuses on agents as means not only to make intelligent decisions based on sensor data but also to manage the sensor network itself.

Section 2 outlines some motivations for undertaking the integration discussed in this paper. Sections 3 and 4 respectively discuss the technologies chosen in implementing a solution and the proposed architecture for realising this. Finally, Section 5 presents the conclusions and future work.

J.C. Augusto et al. (Eds.): AmI 2013, LNCS 8309, pp. 235–240, 2013.

2   Motivation

The integration of component frameworks and intelligent reasoning, realised through the use of MASs, has been investigated both as a means of controlling the framework itself and as a method of incorporating intelligent behaviours within an application itself [5]. The use of intelligent agents to maintain these aspects of an application built upon such a component system is desirable as it provides an accessible means for quickly altering the behaviour of the system.

Of particular interest is the integration of generic reasoning systems within Sensor Web middleware. This would provide a coupling between an environment, typified by heterogeneous sensor networks, and intelligent reasoning. One application within which this combination would prove useful is Waste Augmentation and Integrated Shipment Tracking (WAIST) [6], which aims to use a myriad of sensing devices to monitor and validate the legal transportation of waste materials by licensed hauliers. The SIXTH sensor middleware (discussed in Section 3) provides the means of collecting and routing the data from heterogeneous sensors such as GPS, acceleration, light and contact sensors, but does not provide an easy mechanism for the addition or modification of intelligent behaviours.

A typical usage of such a system would be to analyse incoming GPS data. A simple agent could generate an event whenever the speed of a truck falls below a certain threshold, thereby recording all stopping locations. This event could be visualised for the end-user, further analysed by another agent to isolate and remove short stoppages such as traffic lights etc. Other additions could include activating a number of high intensity sensors within a truck when it stops (allowing the conservation of energy when the truck is in motion), or generating events when a truck stops in particular locations such as known dumping sites.

3   Technologies

3.1   Sensor Middleware

SIXTH is a Java-based Sensor Web Middleware incorporating sensed data from diverse data sources both physical and cyber. Through the adaptor layer abstraction, the middleware can be connected with any data source that is accessible programmatically. Examples of physical data samples include those from Wireless Sensor Networks composed of SunSpots, Waspmotes, Shimmers and smartphones. In the case of cyber data, this has been collected from sources such as Twitter, Xively, Foursquare and Facebook.

In terms of physical sensors, an *adaptor* typically wraps a particular sensor network. For example, in the case of SunSPOT motes, an adaptor would run on a machine connected to the SunSPOT base station. This would be responsible for providing access to multiple *sensor nodes* (individual SunSPOT motes), each of which may contain numerous *sensors* (e.g. light sensor, accelerometer). SIXTH exposes its resources to applications through lightweight interfaces such as those responsible for the receipt of possibly filtered sensor data streams, the interface for the interception of sensor and sensor node status alerts and one allowing the recipient to see (re)tasking conducted by other entities upon resources.

The (re)tasking of sensor nodes is conducted via the Tasking Service, which routes the request to the pertinent adaptor for execution. A request to change the behaviour of a sensor or the entire sensor node is encapsulated within a Tasking Message, for instance the application might wish to decrease the rate at which temperature is being sampled in response to a steady reading. A Tasking Message, if accepted as valid, is translated by an adaptor's Message Wrapper implementation, which performs transformation into a native messaging format for that platform and is then passed to the sensor node.

The architecture of SIXTH is discussed in greater detail in [7]. As SIXTH is an OSGi-based system implemented by means of various component bundles, the current research is partially motivated by previous work done in the area of the management of component-based systems using intelligent agents [5].

3.2   Environment Abstraction

In terms of work in the area of Agent Programming Languages (APLs), the two most well-known environment layer technologies are the Environment Interface Standard (EIS) [8] and the Common Artifacts for Agents Open framework (CArtAgO) [9]. Of these two standards, EIS follows the more traditional view of environments as it implements an interface that models the environment layer as a set of entities. The state of these entities is modelled as a set of beliefs (percepts) and they may be manipulated through a pre-defined set of actions. EIS promotes an opaque view of an environment where the implementation of the actual entities is hidden. Additionally, the set of percepts and actions generated by those entities is specified only in supporting documentation. CArtAgO operates in a similar way, by modelling the environment as a set of artifacts (equivalent to an entity in EIS) that can be manipulated by performing operations (equivalent to an action). Artifact state is modelled as a set of named observable properties that store Java objects. Changes in the observable properties result in the generation of custom events that are passed to the agent layer (e.g. property added, property updated, etc.). In contrast with EIS, CArtAgO is not opaque, and the developer is able to see the implementation of the artifacts and in fact contribute additional artifacts where appropriate.

From a deployment perspective, there are significant differences between the two approaches: in its current incarnation, EIS environments are loaded from the local file space using a dedicated (and inaccessible) Java ClassLoader. This makes EIS difficult to integrate into other technologies, such as OSGi that are also designed to manage ClassLoaders and which advocate that all resources for a deployment should be enclosed within one or more bundles. While it is possible to modify the EIS interface to be OSGi-sensitive, it would require the creation of a new version of EIS that may not be compatible with current EIS-enabled agent toolkits. Instead, the standard EIS approach in such scenarios is either to make the EIS environment into an ad-hoc remote client (e.g. [10]) or to completely embed the system within the EIS environment implementation.

CArtAgO does not suffer from this issue and can be easily integrated into OSGi as a dedicated bundle. A further benefit of CArtAgO is its built-in support for a distributed runtime. This means that any agent toolkit that supports CArtAgO can interact with artifacts deployed using OSGi even if the agents themselves cannot be deployed using OGSi.

3.3   Agent Programming Language

The agent-layer technology used in this paper is ASTRA: an implementation of AgentSpeak(L) [11] APL that is based on Jason operational semantics [12]. ASTRA was chosen because it represents a new breed of APL that provides minimal runtime mechanisms and as such can be easily integrated with other technologies, such as OSGi. ASTRA also has a number of other features, including static typing, support for multiple inheritance, and language level integration with CArtAgO and EIS.

4   Integration

Figure 1 shows a proposed architecture for the integration of ASTRA and SIXTH. For the purposes of clarity, only those elements of SIXTH that are relevant to this integration are shown. Agents interface directly with the CArtAgO layer, which provides access to the components and services provided by SIXTH.

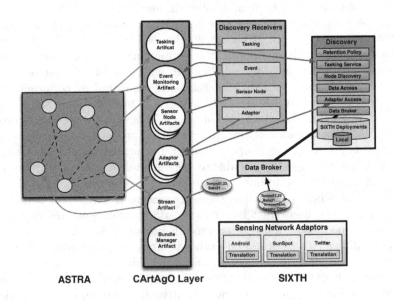

Fig. 1. Proposed integration architecture

The principal artifact types provided by the CArtAgO layer are as follows:

Tasking Artifact. Allows agents to reconfigure sensors by means of tasking messages (e.g. to adjust the sampling frequency). However, it is also possible that sensors can be tasked through other non-agent applications. Thus the Tasking Artifact will also notify interested agents whenever a sensor responds to any tasking message, so that the agents can maintain a correct model of the behaviour of the underlying sensor network.

Event Monitoring Artifact. Agents also require notification about changes in the middleware. For example, this may occur whenever a sensor node is added, removed, fails or becomes uncontactable.

Sensor Node Artifacts. Numerous sensor nodes will typically be attached to a running SIXTH instance. When a notification is received to inform the CArtAgO layer about the presence of a new sensor node, a Sensor Node Artifact is created to model that sensor node and the sensors it contains. The collection of Sensor Node Artifacts that is created serves as an abstraction of the sensor network itself that the agents can use in their process of reasoning about the network.

Adaptor Artifacts. In a similar way to the Sensor Node Artifacts, each Adaptor that is loaded into the SIXTH deployment is also modelled as an individual artifact.

Stream Artifact. Responsible from receiving sensor data from the SIXTH Data Broker and making it available to interested agents. This data is forwarded by the Data Broker whenever sensor data received from the sensors attached to the SIXTH deployment matches queries that the Data Broker has received.

Bundle Manager Artifact. As SIXTH is based on OSGi, its various services and subsystems are implemented by way of individual bundles that can be loaded, unloaded, started and suspended during runtime. This allows for dynamic configuration of the SIXTH system as a whole, to activate necessary services and deactivate those that are no longer required. The Bundle Manager Artifact allows the ASTRA agents to interact with the OSGi runtime to perform this bundle management.

Although this paper focuses primarily on physical sensors, it should be noted that the abstraction discussed above can also accommodate cyber sensors, which are treated in the same way as physical sensors under the SIXTH philosophy. These capture information from virtual sources such as web services.

5 Conclusions and Future Work

The architecture described here allows agents to firstly build an accurate model to represent the structure, capabilities and functioning of the underlying sensor middleware. In addition, it provides them with the ability to dynamically alter the behaviour of the sensors by sending tasking messages, change the structure of the middleware by loading and unloading OSGi bundles as appropriate to the requirements of the agent application. The nature of CArtAgO is such that this implementation is not restricted to the use of intelligent agents written in the

ASTRA APL. The abstraction provided by CArtAgO can be leveraged by any APL or agent framework into which CArtAgO support has been integrated.

A prototype of the architecture shown in Figure 1 has been developed. The next stage of this research will involve a full evaluation to ascertain the usability and effectiveness of this integration.

Acknowledgements. This work is supported by Science Foundation Ireland under grant 07/CE/I1147 and by the Irish Environmental Protection Agency (EPA) (Grant No. 2008-WrM-Ms-1-s).

References

1. Weyns, D., Omicini, A., Odell, J.: Environment as a first class abstraction in multiagent systems. Autonomous Agents and Multi-agent Systems 14, 5–30 (2007)
2. Tynan, R., Muldoon, C., O'Hare, G.M.P., O'Grady, M.J.: Coordinated intelligent power management and the heterogeneous sensing coverage problem. The Computer Journal 54(3), 490–502 (2011)
3. Fok, C.L., Roman, G.C., Lu, C.: Agilla: A mobile agent middleware for self-adaptive wireless sensor networks. ACM Transactions on Autonomous and Adaptove Systems (TAAS) 4(3), Article 16 (2009)
4. Farinelli, A., Rogers, A., Petcu, A., Jennings, N.R.: Decentralised coordination of low-power embedded devices using the max-sum algorithm. In: Proceedings of the 7th International Joint Conference on Autonomous Agents and Multiagent Systems, pp. 639–646 (2008)
5. Lillis, D., Collier, R.W., Dragone, M., O'Hare, G.M.P.: An Agent-Based Approach to Component Management. In: Proceedings of the 8th International Conference on Autonomous Agents and Multi-Agent Systems (AAMAS 2009), Budapest, Hungary (May 2009)
6. Russell, S., O'Grady, M.J., O'Hare, G.M.P., Diamond, D.: Monitoring and Validating the Transport of Waste. IEEE Pervasive Computing 12(1), 42–43 (2013)
7. O'Hare, G.M.P., Muldoon, C., O'Grady, M.J., Collier, R.W., Murdoch, O., Carr, D.: Sensor Web Interaction. International Journal on Artificial Intelligence Tools 21(02), 1240006 (April 2012)
8. Behrens, T., Hindriks, K.V., Bordini, R.H., Braubach, L., Dastani, M., Dix, J., Hübner, J.F., Pokahr, A.: An Interface for Agent-Environment Interaction. In: Collier, R., Dix, J., Novák, P. (eds.) ProMAS 2010. LNCS, vol. 6599, pp. 139–158. Springer, Heidelberg (2012)
9. Ricci, A., Viroli, M., Omicini, A.: CArtAgO: A Framework for Prototyping Artifact-Based Environments in MAS. In: Weyns, D., Van Dyke Parunak, H., Michel, F. (eds.) E4MAS 2006. LNCS (LNAI), vol. 4389, pp. 67–86. Springer, Heidelberg (2007)
10. Behrens, T., Dastani, M., Dix, J., Hübner, J.F., Köster, M., Novák, P., Schlesinger, F.: The Multi-Agent Programming Contest. AI Magazine 33(4), 111 (2012)
11. Rao, A.S.: AgentSpeak (L): BDI agents speak out in a logical computable language. In: Perram, J., Van de Velde, W. (eds.) MAAMAW 1996. LNCS, vol. 1038, pp. 42–55. Springer, Heidelberg (1996)
12. Bordini, R.H., Hübner, J.F., Wooldridge, M.: Programming multi-agent systems in AgentSpeak using Jason. Wiley-Interscience (2007)

An Intelligent Hotel Room

Asterios Leonidis[1], Maria Korozi[1], George Margetis[1],
Dimitris Grammenos[1], and Constantine Stephanidis[1,2]

[1] Foundation for Research and Technology – Hellas (FORTH) - Institute of Computer Science,
N. Plastira 100, Vassilika Vouton, GR-700 13 Heraklion, Crete, Greece
[2] University of Crete, Department of Computer Science
{leonidis,korozi,gmarget,gramenos,cs}@ics.forth.gr

Abstract. This paper presents an innovative application of ambient technology in the domain of tourism and leisure that aims to improve the quality of services offered by the hospitality industry. The main objective is to formulate an ambient ecosystem that observes its surroundings using non-invasive technology and adapts its behavior, in real-time, to deliver "intelligent" and personalized services to the occupants of a guest room. Towards that direction, the proposed system aims to leverage the disadvantages of being away from home and offer a unique user experience.

Keywords: smart hotel, ubiquitous environment, natural interaction, ambient intelligence.

1 Introduction

The rapid advancements in the domain of ICT and the emergence of mobile networks have broadened technology's reach to extend beyond the scope of working environments. The concept of "The Disappearing Computer"[24] is gaining wider attention, as major manufacturers continuously introduce innovative home appliances that blur the line between fantasy and reality. These are the same appliances that people have been using for decades, however, today they integrate smart features that aim to simplify and automate daily activities. Every appliance is no longer a simple device that performs certain tasks, but rather an interconnected, technologically-enhanced peer, that can interact, share information or control other appliances to satisfy users' needs.

The list of the currently available smart features is limited, yet indicative of those to come: smart ovens and refrigerators, sophisticated surveillance systems, etc. It is apparent that the era of technological convergence is approaching through a wealth of commercially available smart appliances and holds great potentials, including new ways to improve the quality of life of various user groups (e.g., the elderly, people with disabilities, etc.). Home automation is only the tip of the iceberg though; smart technologies can enhance virtually every domain of human activities. This paper presents an innovative application of ambient technology in the domain of tourism and leisure that aims to improve the quality of services offered by the hospitality industry.

J.C. Augusto et al. (Eds.): AmI 2013, LNCS 8309, pp. 241–246, 2013.

When travelling, people must cope with unfamiliar environments, where they must learn how to get around and do simple things that are taken for granted at home (e.g., buy a bus ticket) [8, 9, 22]. The proposed system leverages the disadvantages of being away from home and offers a unique user experience by redefining the way people stay and interact with a guest room [10]. A technologically augmented guest room observes its surroundings and adapts its behavior, in real-time, to deliver "intelligent" and personalized services without compromising the privacy of its guests. In order to support privacy, non-invasive observation methods are applied to collect the contextual data that drive the decision making process.

2   Related Work

The tremendous evolution of the computer technology (e.g., microprocessors, mobile networks and devices, social media, etc.) has inevitably brought much attention from the research community to the domain of Ambient Intelligence. These technological advancements made available the necessary tools to materialize the concept of "Disappearing Computing" and improve the quality of people's life by introducing novel applications, ranging from "simple" technologically-augmented artifacts to pervasive and ubiquitous environments where the technology disappears in the surroundings and seamlessly supports daily activities. In the past few years numerous studies and novel applications have outlined the potentials of ambient intelligent across various domains, including education and edutainment [2, 15], cultural heritage [12], products promotion and marketing [11], and as expected home automation.

In particular, in the domain of home automation the available systems share a common objective: monitor the environment (directly or indirectly) and assist users to perform their daily activities. Monitoring relies either solely on computer-vision technologies through wall- or ceiling- mounted cameras [4], or on a combination of cameras with additional sensors (e.g., microphone arrays, motion detectors, etc.) [6, 16] for improved efficiency. But monitoring is not sufficient; the purpose of smart environments is use the collected data to infer which actions should be taken [5] to facilitate user activities. To that objective, every system includes a proprietary context model for representing the environment, the actors and the activities, which is used by the appropriate inference engine to determine the actions to be executed. All approaches have in common that they build their models using ontologies to benefit from their expressive power and the available inferencing engines [7, 21].

However, the field of smart home research is still in its infancy and the relevant literature is sparse [1]. The majority of the aforementioned approaches are mainly applicable in closed environments where the users have enough time to configure and get used to these new interaction schemes. On the other hand, the hospitality industry, despite being an excellent application domain for Ambient Intelligence technologies, has not received the same level of attention. Numerous studies have shown that sooner or later it will have to increase the adoption rate of new technologies to satisfy the new generations of techsavvy tourists of the 21st century, who will have different requirements than their predecessors [14] and will demand innovative services [25].

As the hospitality industry becomes more competitive and industry professionals are strengthening their efforts to find competitive advantages in order to gain and retain guests [3], this work aims to bridge the identified technological gap by proposing a solid infrastructure that delivers "time-using" services [1] that not only facilitate daily activities [13], but also improve the quality of the services already offered by hotels to their guests [23] and the society in general [17].

3   System Overview

The Intelligent Hotel Room (iHR) provides a ubiquitous attentive environment [1] that constantly monitors the activity and location of people and objects within it, and uses this information to control technology in anticipation of the guests needs. To this end, various technological devices and software agents are incorporated in the physical environment to form an ambient ecosystem, that observes its surroundings and adapts its behavior in real-time to deliver "intelligent" and personalized services to its guests. The main iHR components (Figure 1: The major components of the intelligent Hotel) are presented in the following sections.

3.1   Intelligent Hotel Room Infrastructure

The iHR Infrastructure includes the Room Automation Facility and the Multi-Sensorial Network. The Room Automation Facility is the core electrical and mechanical infrastructure that feeds the Room Manager with data (section 3.2) and controls and monitors the available devices and facilities (i.e., lights, blinds, door, HVAC, etc.). The X10[1] standard was selected, as it constitutes a retrofitting solution that can easily support existing installations with minimal changes.

The Multi Sensorial Network, on the other hand, is a collection of pervasive wireless analog and digital sensors that monitor various environmental aspects (e.g., temperature, luminance, etc.), track user location, log user actions and exchange data using the XBee[2] protocol. In the context of the hospitality domain, binary sensors were the only viable solution for monitoring, since guests' privacy would be severely compromised if vision-based tracking methods were used. Moreover, to minimize network traffic, the Multi Sensorial Network constantly monitors the environment, but only notifies the Room Manager when an interesting event occurs (e.g., a person enters the room).

3.2   Intelligent Room Control

Room Manager. It is the core component of the iHR that monitors the environment and user actions in order to extrapolate potential habits and adapt room's behavior accordingly. The collected data are stored in a custom-built ontology, whereas a

---

[1] X10: Industry standard protocol for communication among electronic devices.
[2] XBee: A family of form factor compatible radio modules.

backward-chaining inference engine is used to evaluate heuristic rules and determine which actions should be taken. The developed ontologies include data that represent both contextual information and interaction history. The contextual information store data regarding: (i) the current state of the room (e.g., number of guests, pending requests for room services, etc.), (ii) the state of each space (e.g., occupancy of the bathroom), (iii) description and state of every electronic appliance (e.g., lights, TV, etc.), and constitute the conditionals that determine the next actions. The interaction history stores the events that are exchanged between the software agents and the hardware components due to user activity (e.g., motion was detected, a device has been switched off, etc.) and constitute the triggers that initiate the decision making process.

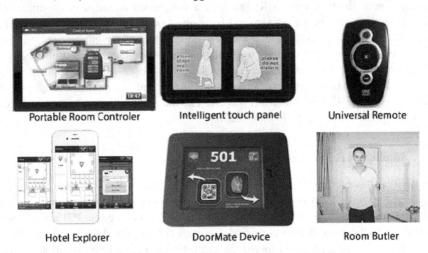

| Portable Room Controler | Intelligent touch panel | Universal Remote |
| Hotel Explorer | DoorMate Device | Room Butler |

Fig. 1. The major components of the intelligent Hotel Room

Intelligent Devices. Various smart devices integrated in the environment ease interaction with the room facilities and the request of the available hotel services. A "Universal Remote" can control every electronic appliance in the iHR (e.g., lights, blinds, etc.) using a limited amount of input buttons to reduce complexity. Its realization requires the installation of infrared receivers near the supported devices, which can be embedded within decorative elements to leave the hotel's aesthetics unaffected.

On the other hand, hotel service request or cancellation is simplified through natural and seamless interaction. In particular, an intelligent laundry hanger automatically requests the laundry service when a laundry bag is detected, while an intelligent touch panel mounted next to the room's entrance knob lets the guests easily request for the cleaning service before leaving their room by touching the respective area. Whenever a service is requested, the respective notification is propagated to (i) the Hotel Monitor application to facilitate the supervision and administration by the hotel stuff and (ii) the DoorMate device to inform the cleaning service accordingly.

The DoorMate is technologically-enhanced room label with a twofold role: on the one hand it presents the current state of a room (e.g., occupied, Do-not-Disturb, etc.) and the pending room service requests, and on the other hand it controls room access. In terms of access control, three alternatives are supported: (i) it interoperates with the existing card-based access systems, (ii) it incorporates a fingerprint reader that can recognize registered fingerprints of either clients or hotel employees, and (iii) it uses a camera to scan virtual keys (e.g., QR Codes).

Finally, as an alternative to the aforementioned ambient controls, guests can use the Portable Room Controller application to manipulate and configure room facilities and services through intuitive touch-based graphical user interfaces.

Room Butler. It is a 3D character, deployed on a TV, who welcomes the guest upon arrival and provides a mini tutorial about the features of the room. Besides the introductory presentation, the butler communicates with the guests to (i) assist them when necessary, (ii) inform them about any requests completed during their absence (e.g., the laundry was picked up), (iii) provide feedback for several user actions (e.g., when the client places the laundry on the hanger the Butler acknowledges that), (iv) alert them in case of an emergency, (v) advise them before leaving the room (e.g., remind the guest to carry an umbrella) and (vi) entertain them during special occasions.

Hotel Explorer. It is is an in-house navigator that localizes the user through 2D Barcodes (QR Codes) and calculates the shortest path between two given locations.

4   Conclusion and Future Work

The main objective of this work was to highlight the promising potentials of ambient technology in the hospitality industry, to improve the quality of the offered services and deliver unique travelling experiences. To this end, this paper has presented an intelligent hotel room which incorporates various technologically-augmented artifacts, devices and software agents and forms an ambient ecosystem that carefully observes its surroundings and adapts its behavior in real-time to deliver "intelligent" and personalized services to its guests.

Currently, the intelligent hotel room is installed in-vitro, in a fully-featured simulation laboratory. In the next few months, a pilot in-vivo installation is planned in a hotel where a full-scale user-based evaluation will be conducted. The evaluation is planned to include dozens of guests of different ages and technological backgrounds, where typical daily activities will be observed to: (i) assess the efficacy of the reasoning methodology, and (ii) determine how guests use the system in real-life situations. The evaluations findings are foreseen to extend the currently implemented rule set and improve the usability of the various applications. Additionally, relevant topics are being investigated for future upgrades, such as speech and gesture interaction, and the provision of a personalized system that recommends local events and activities.

References

1. Aldrich, F.K.: Smart homes: past, present and future. Inside the Smart Home 1, 17–39 (2003)
2. Antona, M., Leonidis, A., Margetis, G., Korozi, M., Ntoa, S., Stephanidis, C.: A student-centric intelligent classroom. In: Keyson, D.V., et al. (eds.) AmI 2011. LNCS, vol. 7040, pp. 248–252. Springer, Heidelberg (2011)

3. Berezina, E., Cobanoglu, C.: Importance-performance analysis of in-room technology amenities in hotels. In: Information and Communication Technologies in Tourism 2010, pp. 25–37. Springer, Vienna (2010)
4. Brdiczka, O., Crowley, J.L., Reignier, P.: Learning situation models in a smart home. IEEE Systems, Man, and Cybernetics, Part B: Cybernetics 39(1), 56–63 (2009)
5. Cetina, C., Giner, P., Fons, J., Pelechano, V.: Designing and prototyping dynamic software product lines: Techniques and guidelines. In: Bosch, J., Lee, J. (eds.) SPLC 2010. LNCS, vol. 6287, pp. 331–345. Springer, Heidelberg (2010)
6. Chen, H., et al.: Intelligent agents meet semantic web in a smart meeting room. In: 3rd International Joint Conference on Autonomous Agents and Multiagent Systems, pp. 854–861. IEEE Computer Society (2004)
7. Cook, D.J., et al.: MavHome: An agent-based smart home. In: 1st IEEE International Conference on Pervasive Computing and Communications (PerCom 2003), pp. 521–524. IEEE (2003)
8. Crouch, G.I., Perdue, R.R., Timmermans, H.J., Uysal, M.: Building Foundations for Understanding the Consumer Psychology of Tourism, Hospitality and Leisure. In: Consumer Psychology of Tourism, Hospitality and Leisure, vol. 3, ch. 1, p. 1 (2004)
9. Fridgen, J.D.: Environmental psychology and tourism. Annals of Tourism Research 11(1), 19–39 (1984)
10. Gilbert, D.C., Morris, L.: The relative importance of hotels and airlines to the business traveller. International Journal of Contemporary Hospitality Management 7(6), 19–23 (1995)
11. Grammenos, D., Margetis, G., Koutlemanis, P., Zabulis, X.: 53.090 virtual rusks = 510 real smiles using a fun exergame installation for advertising traditional food products. In: Nijholt, A., Romão, T., Reidsma, D. (eds.) ACE 2012. LNCS, vol. 7624, pp. 214–229. Springer, Heidelberg (2012)
12. Grammenos, D., et al.: Macedonia from fragments to pixels: A permanent exhibition of interactive systems at the archaeological museum of thessaloniki. In: Ioannides, M., Fritsch, D., Leissner, J., Davies, R., Remondino, F., Caffo, R. (eds.) EuroMed 2012. LNCS, vol. 7616, pp. 602–609. Springer, Heidelberg (2012)
13. Hagras, H., et al.: Creating an ambient-intelligence environment using embedded agents. IEEE Intelligent Systems 19(6), 12–20 (2004)
14. Kelley, B.: American Generation Y and The Hotel of 2030 (2012)
15. Korozi, M., et al.: Ambient educational mini-games. In: International Working Conference on Advanced Visual Interfaces, pp. 802–803. ACM (2012)
16. Nijholt, A., Zwiers, J., Peciva, J.: Mixed reality participants in smart meeting rooms and smart home environments. Personal and Ubiquitous Computing 13(1), 85–94 (2009)
17. Nizic, M.K., Karanovic, G., Ivanovic, S.: Importance of intelligent rooms for energy savings in the hotel industry. Tourism and Hospitality Management 14(2), 323–336 (2008)
18. Rutishauser, U., Joller, J., Douglas, R.: Control and learning of ambience by an intelligent building. IEEE Transactions on Systems, Man and Cybernetics, Part A: Systems and Humans 35(1), 121–132 (2005)
19. Sari, R.: Exploration of Travel Experience (2011)
20. Staab, S., et al.: Intelligent systems for tourism. IEEE Intelligent Systems 17(6), 53–64 (2002)
21. Streitz, N., Nixon, P.: The disappearing computer. Communications of the ACM 48(3), 32–35 (2005)
22. Waldhör, K., Freidl, C., Fessler, F., Starha, G.: RESA-An Automated Speech Based Hotel Room Booking Call Centre Agent. In: Information and Communication Technologies in Tourism 2007, pp. 1–10. Springer, Vienna (2007)

Part III

Doctoral Colloquium

Harnessing Mathematics
for Improved Ontology Alignment

Chau Do and Eric J. Pauwels

Centrum Wiskunde & Informatica, 1098 XG Amsterdam, The Netherlands
{do,eric.pauwels}@cwi.nl

Abstract. Given a domain of interest, an ontology provides a formal specification of the concepts and relationships in this domain. An alignment identifies a semantic connection between the concepts and relationships of ontologies purporting to describe the same knowledge. The majority of approaches to ontology alignment take a general view and rely on terminological and structural techniques to handle the widest possible class of ontologies. Due to the fuzzy nature of concepts and the variations in their representations, this matching process is often complicated. One area that should provide a more solid foundation for comparison is mathematical concepts. Mathematical concepts are covered by numerous ontologies, making them a potentially important basis for comparison. One part of this doctoral work is to investigate the potential of using mathematical concepts to improve ontology alignment.

Keywords: MathML, ontology matching, ontology alignment, units.

1   Introduction and Motivation

Ontologies are used in several areas such as multi-agents, knowledge bases and the semantic web for better representation of knowledge domains. Although a few popular ontologies exist, there is no widely accepted general ontology used by everyone. Typically, ontologies are developed independently resulting in heterogeneous representation of concepts and relationships. Consider for example, software agents on the semantic web. When they attempt to collect information to perform some task, they will encounter data represented using different ontologies. In order to make sense of the data and recognize how they are related to each other, a translation is required. Clearly, these translations are crucial to interoperability.

A translation is referred to as an ontology alignment. An alignment is a set of correspondences, where each correspondence represents a relationship (equivalence, disjointness, subclass etc.) between the entities of the two ontologies. Entities can be classes, properties (relationships) or individuals (instances of the classes) and so on. A correspondence can also include a confidence measure, typically between $[0, 1]$ which is dependent on the comparison method.

Until now, many approaches to ontology alignment use a combination of lexical and structural comparison. Some variations to these approaches include using

J.C. Augusto et al. (Eds.): AmI 2013, LNCS 8309, pp. 249–254, 2013.

a word database (e.g. WordNet, UMLS) for additional information. More complicated approaches using machine learning have also been proposed. Regardless, each has been met with limited success, prompting the need for alternative methods.

The rest of the paper is structured as follows: in section 2, a description of our general idea and a summary of the current work is provided. Section 3 gives a summary of related work. Section 4 provides a discussion on the current work and future directions.

2   General Idea

As opposed to taking a general alignment approach to deal with ontologies from any domain, we chose to focus on ontologies containing mathematical concepts. These include ontologies from the fields of engineering, science and math, to name a few. The basic idea is to use these mathematical concepts as a basis for comparison. General concepts can be ambiguous at times, making their comparison fuzzy. Math concepts on the other hand, have a structure to them making the comparison more straightforward. With this general idea in mind, we investigated units of measurements in ontologies to see if this approach would work. This is described in the following section.

2.1   Units of Measurement

We looked at three ontologies containing units of measurement: 1) Quantities, Units, Dimensions and Types (QUDT) [1], 2)Semantic Web for Earth and Environmental Terminology (SWEET) version 2.2 [2] and 3) Ontologies of units of measure (OM) version 1.8 [3]. The first two ontologies, QUDT and SWEET, were originally developed by different labs in NASA. OM was developed at Wageningen UR - Food & Biobased Research. All three are RDFS/OWL ontologies. This is only a brief summary of this work, see [4] for more details.

The goal was to align the units in each ontology by taking advantage of their mathematical properties. The theory goes as follows: suppose we have two ontologies Ω_1 relating concepts $\alpha, \beta, \gamma, \ldots$ (this is denoted as $\Omega_1 = \{\alpha, \beta, \gamma, \ldots\}$) and a second ontology $\Omega_2 = \{\xi, \eta, \zeta, \ldots\}$. Let us assume that we are given as prior knowledge that concept α in Ω_1 is equivalent to concept ξ (denoted here as $\Omega_1 : \alpha \leftrightarrow \Omega_2 : \xi$), as well as $\Omega_1 : \beta \leftrightarrow \Omega_2 : \eta$. If we are able to determine that $\gamma = \alpha/\beta$ and also that $\zeta = \xi/\eta$ (i.e. some mathematical relationship) then we can confidently infer the previously unknown match $\Omega_1 : \gamma \leftrightarrow \Omega_2 : \zeta$. From this, we need to determine the following a) What is the minimum prior knowledge? and b) Given a concept, how do we obtain its mathematical information?

Regarding question 1, it was noticed that units have a convention where they can be expressed in some combination of the seven SI base units: *meter, kilogram, second, kelvin, mole, candela, ampere*. So a unit can be broken down to a conversion multiplier, conversion offset and some combination of these base units. This is seen in equation 1, where a represents the conversion multiplier,

b the offset and n and d represent the composing units that this unit can be broken down to.

$$unit = a \times \frac{[n_1^{x1}][n_2^{x2}][n_3^{x3}]...}{[d_1^{y1}][d_2^{y2}][d_3^{y3}]...} + b \qquad (1)$$

Therefore the minimum prior knowledge is an alignment of the base units. This can be supplied by a user or obtained through other methods.

The second question involves extracting information from the ontologies themselves. Referring back to equation 1, it is necessary to obtain the conversion multiplier and offset as well as the composing units. One obstacle discovered when analyzing these ontologies is that while the information for equation 1 is present, it is represented in very different ways. Since RDFS/OWL ontologies have no restriction on how to represent mathematical concepts, their representation is inconsistent. In order to overcome this problem, it was decided to use MathML to represent these units. This representation provides a better basis for comparison. Figure 1 shows the general steps in our proposed alignment process:

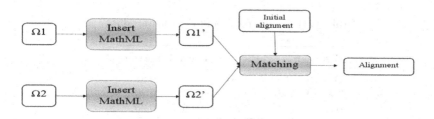

Fig. 1. Two ontologies have MathML representing their units inserted into them. The modified ontologies are then compared and the units are matched in the final alignment.

The first step involves generating MathML from the information contained in the ontologies and then inserting it into the ontologies. The complexity of this step depends on the ontology and the difficulty in extracting the necessary information. For example in OM, *tesla* has a property *dimension* with a value *magnetic_flux_density-dimension*, which further breaks down to the dimensions of time, electric current and mass (i.e. base units). QUDT represents the dimension and conversion data differently for *tesla*. Although each ontology represents its units differently, within each ontology there is a logical structure to how they are organized. For example, the property *dimension* in OM can be used to find the dimensions of other units. We discovered that there are only a handful of patterns within each ontology which must be recognized. In this manner, it was possible to semi-automatically generate and insert the MathML.

The matching step of figure 1, takes the modified ontologies, the initial alignment and compares the units based on the MathML. First the MathML code is extracted. Only units with corresponding MathML code are compared. The simplest comparisons are made first with the conversion offset and multiplier. When these are equal, the next step is to look at the units. Since these units can be expressed in intermediate units and not the base units themselves, it is necessary to check if they can be broken down first. For example, lets assume in OM *tesla* is given as $T = N/(A{\times}m)$ and in QUDT as $T = kg/(A{\times}s^2)$. If *tesla* were to be described in terms of *newton (N)* in both ontologies and *newton* has already been matched, then no breakdown is required. Otherwise a search is done for *newton* (already checked units are stored in memory) and if found, T will be modified to $T = (kg{\times}m)/(A{\times}m{\times}s^2)$ in the OM ontology. The next step, reduce dimensions, checks if there are the same units in the denominator and numerator and reduces them, resulting in $T = kg/(A{\times}s^2)$. Finally the units are compared with reference to the initial alignment, which shows that *tesla* in OM is equivalent to *tesla* in QUDT. The alignment generated by the matching, consists of these unit equivalences.

The resulting alignment was measured against a reference alignment, which was made manually. The precision, recall and F-measure were calculated and can be seen in table 1. These metrics are measured using the Alignment API version 4.4, which takes into consideration the semantics of alignments (see [5]).

Table 1. Precision, recall and F-measure values

Alignment	Precision	Recall	F-Measure
OM-QUDT	0.81	0.95	0.87
SWEET-QUDT	0.77	0.97	0.86
SWEET-OM	0.82	0.99	0.90

As a point of reference, the highest F-measure produced by the matchers participating in the Ontology Alignment Evaluation Initiative (OAEI) competition from 2007-2010 was around 0.86 [6]. The recall values are very good, indicating that the aligned units output by the matcher correspond well to those in the reference alignment. The precision values, while good could be better. Looking closer, there are two main causes of the lower precision: 1) mathematically equivalent but conceptually different units and 2) incorrect information in the ontologies. The former refers to units such as *hertz (1/s)* being equivalent to *becquerel (1/s)*.

3   Related Work

Many ontology matching systems have been proposed, some of which are summarized in [6], [7]. Despite the different approaches, most are based on terminological and structural methods. Terminological methods refers to the use of lexical comparisons of the labels, comments and/or other annotations of each entity. Structural comparisons look at for example similarities in the hierarchy of the ontology structure or the corresponding neighbors of matched entities. Semantic methods can also be applied for verification of matches or building on initial matches. These methods include looking at the range of values, cardinality, the transitivity and symmetry of the entities [8]. Many of the systems are generic matchers, while some have more inclination towards specific areas (e.g. medical).

Incorporating MathML into ontologies has been done before. For example, the Systems Biology Ontology (SBO) from the European Bioinformatics Institute [9] incorporates subject related equations using MathML. However, other than representing equations, the MathML is not being used further. More interesting usages of MathML can be seen in the Systems Biology of Microorganisms initiative, which has the aim of producing computerized mathematical models representing the dynamic molecular process of a micro-organism [10]. Within this initiative, SysMO Seek is an assets catalogue representing information such as models, experiments, and data. MathML is used to represent the mathematical models [11]. Another notable area where MathML and ontologies merge, is the OntoModel tool. Utilized for pharmaceutical product development, Onto-Model allows for model creation, manipulation, querying and searching. It uses a combination of Content MathML and OWL. The former is used to represent the mathematical equations and the latter is used for the ontologies that represent the mathematical models and other related information [12]. While SysMo Seek and OntoModel use MathML to represent mathematical equations/models, the MathML is not used to align ontologies as we proposed in our work.

4   Next Steps

The work outlined in section 2.1 was a step towards using mathematics as a basis of comparison. The next step involves expanding this approach to other mathematical concepts. It was necessary in our approach to insert MathML, because there are no standard rules in ontology development for representing math. We recognize that this approach has its limitations and may be tedious when expanding to other mathematical concepts. Previous work focusing on the integration of MathML/OpenMath with RDFS/OWL ontologies has been done (see [13], [14]). The general goal is to incorporate the two areas such that pre-existing tools (e.g. reasoners, computational algebra systems) can be used. Until now there has been no widely accepted way of doing this. However, we believe this is more of a standardization issue and any solution would have to be widely used before we could take advantage of it. In view of this, we plan to explore other approaches which do not rely on the usage of MathML. In general, we are exploring several approaches that could clarify the following areas:

1. Detecting mathematical concepts within ontologies
2. Obtaining additional information regarding the mathematical structure of these concepts
3. How to match the mathematical concepts given the information obtained
4. How to build upon these matches to match non-mathematical concepts

Mathematical concepts have an inherent structure as well as rules and conventions. Using them as a basis for comparison can simplify the difficult problem of ontology alignment as we have shown in our work to date.

Acknowledgements. The authors gratefully acknowledge financial support by CWI's Computational Energy Systems project (sponsored by the Dutch National Science Foundation NWO).

References

1. Hodgson, R., Keller, P.: QUDT - Quantities, Units, Dimensions and Data Types in OWL and XML, http://www.qudt.org/ (accessed on November 14, 2012)
2. NASA: Jet Propulsion Laboratory: Semantic Web for Earth and Environmental Terminology (SWEET), http://sweet.jpl.nasa.gov/ (accessed on November 14, 2012)
3. Rijgersberg, H., Wigham, M., Broekstra, J., van Assem, M., Top, J.: Ontology of units of Measure (OM), http://www.qudt.org/ (accessed on November 14, 2012)
4. Do, C., Pauwels, E.J.: Using mathML to represent units of measurement for improved ontology alignment. In: Carette, J., Aspinall, D., Lange, C., Sojka, P., Windsteiger, W. (eds.) CICM 2013. LNCS, vol. 7961, pp. 310–325. Springer, Heidelberg (2013)
5. Euzenat, J.: Semantic precision and recall for ontology alignment evaluation. In: Proc. 20th International Joint Conference on Artificial Intelligence (IJCAI), pp. 348–353 (2007)
6. Shvaiko, P., Euzenat, J.: Ontology matching: state of the art and future challenges. IEEE Transactions on Knowledge and Data Engineering (2012)
7. Choi, N., Song, I.Y., Han, H.: A survey on ontology mapping. ACM Sigmod Record 35(3), 34–41 (2006)
8. Euzenat, J., Meilicke, C., Stuckenschmidt, H., Shvaiko, P., Trojahn, C.: Ontology Alignment Evaluation Initiative: Six Years of Experience. In: Spaccapietra, S. (ed.) Journal on Data Semantics XV. LNCS, vol. 6720, pp. 158–192. Springer, Heidelberg (2011)
9. The European Bioinformatics Institute: Systems Biology Ontology, http://www.ebi.ac.uk/sbo/main/ (accessed on December 10, 2012)
10. Bechhofer, S., Buchan, I., De Roure, D., Missier, P., Ainsworth, J., Bhagat, J., Couch, P., Cruickshank, D., Delderfield, M., Dunlop, I., et al.: Why linked data is not enough for scientists. Future Generation Computer Systems (2011)
11. Lange, C.: Ontologies and Languages for Representing Mathematical Knowledge on the Semantic Web. Semantic Web Journal 4(2) (2013)
12. Suresh, P., Hsu, S.H., Akkisetty, P., Reklaitis, G.V., Venkatasubramanian, V.: OntoMODEL: ontological mathematical modeling knowledge management in pharmaceutical product development, 1: conceptual framework. Industrial & Engineering Chemistry Research 49(17) (2010)
13. Robbins, A.: Personal website, http://straymindcough.blogspot.de/2009/06/semantic-mathml.html (accessed on July 24, 2013)
14. Wenzel, K., Reinhardt, H.: Mathematical computations for linked data applications with openmath. In: Joint Proceedings of the 24th Workshop on OpenMath and the 7th Workshop on Mathematical User Interfaces (MathUI), p. 38 (2012)

On Combining a Context Recognition System and a Configuration Planner for Personalised Ambient Assisted Living

Lia Susana d.C. Silva-López, Jonas Ullberg, and Lars Karlsson

Center for Applied Autonomous Sensor Systems, Örebro University, SE-70182 Sweden
{lia.silva,jonas.ullberg,lars.karlsson}@oru.se

1 GiraffPlus System

This abstract describes how a context recognition system and a configuration planner can interact to enable personalised activity monitoring in apartments with different features. The two systems are developed to supporting independent living of senior citizens (primary users) by monitoring their daily interaction with the environment. For this purpose, networked non-intrusive sensors that senses motion, power usage, and pressure are used, in addition relevant physiological parameters such as heart rate and blood pressure are measured on demand. The system allows social interaction and timely involvement of family and caregivers, and is being developed within the European Commission FP7 project GiraffPlus [2]. The GiraffPlus system also contains a telepresence robot and an interface for caregivers and medical specialists (secondary users), to personalise and visualise data, alarms, and reminders for events of interest that have been permitted by the senior citizen. The environment is modelled as a collection of state variables that represent the layout of the apartment, position and motion of individuals and items (e.g. person1 in bedroom, book1 on table in bedroom), status of items in the apartment (e.g. light on/off, door open/closed), or physiological parameters (e.g. heart-rate of person1, weight of person1). Values of state variables are directly observable through sensors, or indirectly derivable from other state variables. There are also purely computational processes that refines sensed data to various levels of abstraction.

Now, consider an apartment with networked sensors (glucose, motion), actuators (alarms) and programs, as illustrated in the right hand side of Figure 1. Different apartments may be equipped with different sensors at different positions, have different layout and furniture, and all of the former can change position or be updated over time. In this way, the set of activities that are monitored and they way in which they are inferred varies between homes and can change over time. A configuration planner is being developed in order to enable activity monitoring under such varying conditions. The purpose of the configuration planner in the GiraffPlus project is to provide the context recognition with the data it requires for recognizing the activities requested by the users. When the physical setup of the apartment is represented in a domain along with the types of data the sensors handle, the effects of actuators, and the programs available for data processing, a configuration planner can be requested to obtain information or have desirable effects into the environment, by generating information flows from

J.C. Augusto et al. (Eds.): AmI 2013, LNCS 8309, pp. 255–260, 2013.

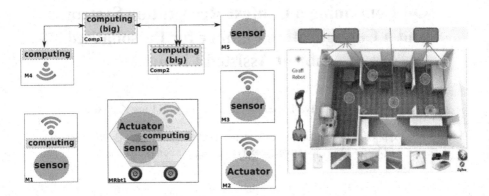

Fig. 1. An example of GiraffPlus apartment. The figure shows a schematic view of interconnected devices and the location of sensors and a robot in the home.

sensors and sequences of activations of programs and actuators. The different components of the GiraffPlus system have been implemented and integrated, and tested in a laboratory setting. We are currently evaluating the GiraffPlus system in six apartments of elderly persons. The result of this evaluation, both in terms of input from users and in terms of technical functions, will be used for further refinement of the system in an incremental fashion, at later stages the system will be deployed in fifteen apartments in Italy, Spain and Sweden.

2   Configuration Planner

The configuration planner allows separating descriptions of sensors and programs from descriptions of activities, which in turn allows the system to perform inferences in different apartments with different setups, in which elements are added, removed, or fail by *automatically* adapting to them. A **functionality instance** represents a program that either operates on a sensor or actuator, or processes data from and/or delivers data to other functionalities. In Figure 1, we represent devices by the information they sense (sensors in M1, M3, M5 and MRbt1), their actuating capacities (actuators in M2 and MRbt1), or by how they process information (computing elements may run programs). Functionalities are allowed to represent elements from different devices.

A **configuration** is a set of functionality instances to execute, a mapping of outputs of those functionalities to inputs of other functionalities in the same set, and mapping of causal dependencies and execution order constrains between them. Configurations involve activating elements to have an effect in the environment, providing programs with data from sensors, and even alternating combinations of performing effects and feeding programs with information. In a **fully admissible** configuration, no requirements of any functionality instance of the configuration are unsatisfied, and no effect threatens a condition for another functionality instance.

The representation for our planner is based on the work of Lundh et al. [7], and the planner is inspired by partial-order planning and more particularly UCPOP [11]).

Differences emerge from the interaction of information and causal requirements. In addition to single-task robots in [9, 3], our configuration planner is also capable of handling functionalities with more than one task, as long as the different tasks do not conflict with each other during execution. Moreover, our approach does not require the specification of hierarchical task networks as in [7], allowing every potentially useful source of information and causal effects to be considered when building a configuration, as opposed to only the ones foreseen when modelling the functionalities in a device. Finally, when coupled with an execution monitoring process, our approach can also be used for repairing failed configurations [6], since it searches in the space of partial configurations that are satisfied until admissibility, given a set of initial state variable assignments, a set of functionality instances, and the damaged configuration as a goal.

Our algorithm starts with an initial configuration to be refined until a solution is found. The initial configuration contains a functionality instance and its requirements as the requested goal, and initial execution order constraints imposed by the effects of a functionality instance in which the initial state is encoded, and by the goal functionality. The initial plan is refined by adding new functionalities, or using existing ones, in order to satisfy requirements of the present functionalities. The planner satisfies a causal requirement of a functionality f by the causal effect of another functionality f' that comes before in time, and satisfies an information requirements of f by the information output of functionality f' at the same time. Causal requirements and effect may interfere, and in such cases temporal constraints between the functionalities can be added in order to avoid that interference.

2.1 Tested Heuristics

For guiding search, our planner can use one (or several) heuristics for pruning, a heuristic for ordering the search front according a criteria, and another heuristic to select a requirement to satisfy first. We refer to this combination of heuristics as a *heuristic chain*. The idea is inspired on combining value ordering (choosing the next node to satisfy) and variable ordering (choosing the next unsatisfied link to satisfy) heuristics in constraint satisfaction problems. So far we have studied local information heuristics that use a histogram built with the frequencies of the sources provided by every available functionality instance, and a histogram with the frequencies of the requirements of the partial configuration. Sources and requirements are associated in bins that share the same property and format, of separate histograms. We have also used the Rho heuristic [5], which branches into the children that maximize the solution density of a problem by choosing the requirement with most and/or the tightest constraints.

3   Context Recognition

The context recognition system represents the states of the sensors and the inferred activities as intervals on different timelines. The model that describes the causal relationships between the states of the sensors and the inferred activities is provided as a set of quantitative Allen's interval algebra [1] constraints that are posted between intervals representing sensor readings. For instance, the rule: Cooking Equals Stove ∧

Cooking During Kitchen (cooking implies the stove being on during presence in the kitchen) defines how an activity, in this case the activity Cooking, can be inferred from intervals representing sensed data. This approach to context recognition was first described by Ullberg et al. [12] and then subsequently extended by Pecora et al. [10]. However, in prior work it was found that, although constraints taken from Allen's interval algebra provides a convenient way to describe relations, small deviations in how the raw sensory data is interpreted and placed on the timelines can prevent activities from being inferred and in some cases produce false positives. One possible way of overcoming this is by allowing constraint violations to some degree, for instance by using fuzzy Allen's interval constraints [8]. However, this former approach requires thresholds on the likelihood of inferred activities, which is not always possible to determine.

The context recognition in the GiraffPlus project handles the problem by performing temporal inference on multiple intervals contextually, admitting several interpretations of sensor and activity timelines. That is, each sensor reading is represented as a set of flexible temporal intervals rather than one. The former approach to context recognition is described in [13] where it is compared to the Chronicle recognition approach to context recognition proposed by Dousson and Maigat [4], in which Allen's interval constraints are also used.

The implementation of the context recognition system is implemented as three separate modules; preprocessing, inference and extraction. The preprocessing module fetches samples from the centralized data storage (which contains data from several homes) and generates a set of possible timeline candidates from them. The inference module takes these sets of timelines and uses temporal rules to propagate the constraints on the timelines, producing a set of possible activity timelines. Finally the extraction module inspects the set of activity timelines and extracts a single timeline that can be used by the rest of the system, for instance by visualizing the daily activities to a caregivers or to raise an automatic alarm.

4   Interactions between the Context Recognition and the Configuration Planner

The context recognition provides goals in the form of *entity . property . format* to refer to information to obtain in the form of a state variable, an when a *value* field is added to the request, the goal refers to changing the value of the state variable. For instance, if we wanted to ask the configuration planner to find a configuration in order to know in which room of the apartment a person is, we could do it with *person . location . rooms*. Similarly, if we wanted to move a robot the room in which the person is located, we could do it with *robot*1 *. location . rooms = person . location . rooms*, and if we wanted to move the robot to a particular position in the house, we could do it with *robot*1 *. location . coordinates* = (33.5,44.2). The context recognition can add additional goals on the fly. After receiving a goal, the configuration planner searches in the space of possible partial configurations until a fully admissible configuration that satisfies the goal is found. When a configuration is found, functionalities can be executed with the help of an execution monitoring algorithm.

5   Ongoing Work on Incorporating Preferences into the System

We are currently working on expanding the interaction of both systems so that they can support preferences when generating goals, when searching for ways of satisfying the goal, and when modelling the requirements of the functionality instances.

The preferences may come from the primary user, the secondary user, the context recognition, and the domain designers. Preferences coming from primary users usually involve permissions and express how comfortable or not is the senior citizen with certain ways of monitoring their health and activities, as well as for allowing certain services or not, and under which circumstances. Preferences coming from secondary users involve which activities and situations are of most importance for the system to keep track of, and which physiological signals too. Preferences coming from the context recognition can involve relations between how desirable are certain types of information sources in order to perform certain inferences, so richer goals can be formulated to maximize the chance of obtaining good information sources. Preferences coming from domain designers are used to describe how each program, sensor and actuator works on the system. For instance, preferences can be used to express the fact that a functionality that works as a thermostat will work as long as it has all information inputs with the temperatures of the rooms of the house, and it would *prefer* that all doors and windows are closed. If for receiving a guest a door needs to be open, that would still be fine and the configuration running a thermostat does not need to stop. It will be possible to state that the configuration may no longer be as reliable. However, if all thermometers fail, the configuration may stop, since the hard" requirements ceased being satisfied.

Preferences will enrich resource handling: to sense blood sugar, shall we use data from the sensors a person is wearing, shall we ask the person to take a test on a glucometer that uses expensive stripes and also measures ketone concentrations but hurts the finger more, or shall we ask the person to use the simple glucometer with cheaper stripes?. Preferences will allow the planner to get more "adequate" configurations: the planner should avoid a configuration in which something uncomfortable for the senior citizen could happen, except perhaps for a life-or-death scenario. Preferences can also be used to express richer goals for the whole system: in the representation for a device, requirements can be expressed in terms of preferences e.g. a service can now state that it prefers to use the information gathered by the pressure sensor in the bed, rather than the information gathered by the movement sensor in the bedroom, in order to determine the amount of sleep that a person had. Preferences will be used to express reliability of functionalities according to the different ways in which they can be satisfied, which will be of help to have a better functioning and more dependable system e.g. it would make it possible to express that a thermostat functionality is more reliable if the condition "door in bedroom == closed" holds. Preferences can be used to express data quality as a function of how preferable are the sources that are being used to satisfy the requirements of a functionality instance. Our current challenge is to incorporate all of the former ways of working with preferences, and to be able to interact with the preferences stated by the context recognition and the users.

References

[1] Allen, J.F.: Maintaining knowledge about temporal intervals. Communications of the ACM 26, 832–843 (1983), http://doi.acm.org/10.1145/182.358434

[2] Coradeschi, S., Cesta, A., Cortellessa, G., Coraci, L., Gonzalez, J., Karlsson, L., Furfari, F., Loutfi, A., Orlandini, A., Palumbo, F., Pecora, F., von Rump, S., Stimec, A., Ullberg, J., Östlund, B.: Giraffplus: Combining social interaction and long term monitoring for promoting independent living. In: 6th International Conference on Human System Interactions, HSI (2013)

[3] Di Rocco, M., Pecora, F., Sivakumar, P.K., Saffiotti, A.: Configuration planning with multiple dynamic goals. In: Proceedings of the AAAI Spring Symposium on Designing Intelligent Robots, Stanford, California (2013)

[4] Dousson, C., Maigat, P.L.: Chronicle recognition improvement using temporal focusing and hierarchization. In: Proceedings of the 20th International Joint Conference on Artifical Intelligence, IJCAI 2007, pp. 324–329. Morgan Kaufmann Publishers Inc., San Francisco (2007), http://dl.acm.org/citation.cfm?id=1625275.1625326

[5] Gent, I., MacIntyre, E., Presser, P., Smith, B., Walsh, T.: An empirical study of dynamic variable ordering heuristics for the constraint satisfaction problem. In: Freuder, E.C. (ed.) CP 1996. LNCS, vol. 1118, pp. 179–193. Springer, Heidelberg (1996)

[6] Gritti, M., Broxvall, M., Saffiotti, A.: Reactive self-configuration of an ecology of robots. In: Proceedings of the ICRA 2007 Workshop on Network Robot Systems (2007)

[7] Lundh, R., Karlsson, L., Saffiotti, A.: Autonomous functional configuration of a network robot system. Robotics and Autonomous Systems 56(10), 819–830 (2008)

[8] Mansouri, M.: Constraint-Based Activity Recognition with Uncertainty. Master's thesis, Örebro University, School of Science and Technology (2011)

[9] Parker, L.E., Tang, F.: Building multirobot coalitions through automated task solution synthesis. Proceedings of the IEEE 94(7), 1289–1305 (2006)

[10] Pecora, F., Cirillo, M., Dell'Osa, F., Ullberg, J., Saffiotti, A.: A Constraint-Based Approach for Proactive, Context-Aware Human Support. Journal of Ambient Intelligence and Smart Environments (2012) (accepted)

[11] Penberthy, J., Weld, D., et al.: Ucpop: A sound, complete, partial order planner for adl. In: Proceedings of the Third International Conference on Knowledge Representation and Reasoning, pp. 103–114. Citeseer (1992)

[12] Ullberg, J., Loutfi, A., Pecora, F.: Towards Continuous Activity Monitoring with Temporal Constraints. In: Proceedings of the 4th Workshop on Planning and Plan Execution for Real-World Systems at ICAPS 2009 (2009)

[13] Ullberg, J., Pecora, F.: Propagating temporal constraints on sets of intervals. ICAPS Workshop on Planning and Scheduling with Timelines, PSTL (2012), files/papers/UllbergPecora-ICAPS12-WS-PSTL_v2.pdf

Towards Automatic Detection of Missing Referred Documents during Meetings

Hugo Lopez-Tovar and John Dowell

University College London

Abstract. Business meetings are often informed by and make reference to documents, however not every document that a meeting wishes to consult will already be present. We propose the concept of a smart meeting room capable of detecting when the meeting talks about a document and determining whether that document is already present. We report a preliminary interview-based study into the experience of attending meetings where documents are missing. A subsequent study investigated how observers of meetings are able to judge whether a document being talked about is currently present. This indicates the specific capabilities required by an intelligent assistant system able to detect references to missing documents. We describe an experimental investigation into one such capability involving visually tracking hands and printed documents in a video recording of a meeting.

Keywords: Ambient Intelligence, Intelligent Assistant, Computer Supported Cooperative Work, Smart Rooms, Meetings.

1 Introduction

Organisations are cooperative systems, with the capacity for processing high levels of information and with huge need for decision making [1]. Moreover, it is considered that their success is strongly determined by their ability to process information [2] and make good decisions. Organisations procedures frequently require such information and decisions to be stored in digital documents for future access. Most of this decision making and exchange of information happens in meetings [3], often by referring to documents. Because it is commonly not possible to anticipate in advance all documents that will need to be referred to at a meeting, there is significant need to consult documents that are not currently present. This need is related to specific episodes and therefore is transitory.

The concept of the smart meeting room integrates an Intelligent Assistant (IA) agent capable of recognising when a meeting refers to a document that is not currently available to the participants, in order to understand the needs and then be in the position of taking further action (i.e. retrieving such document from a repository and providing it).

J.C. Augusto et al. (Eds.): AmI 2013, LNCS 8309, pp. 261–266, 2013.

2   Background and Motivation

Information Management (IM) is concerned with collecting and distributing information in a business environment, and therefore the same should be for meetings as well. The dramatic increment in the size of repositories, as well as the speed and accuracy of information retrieval improves the IM capability, which is fundamental to develop other business capabilities such as process management and performance management [4].

By considering IM inside the meeting room, we engage with the field of Ambient Intelligence (AmI), which deals with the conversion of our surrounding environment into a sensitive and adaptive technology that responds to our actions [5]. Cook et al [6] provide a survey on the technologies and applications of this field among which appears the workplace and its smart meeting rooms, for which efforts have been directed to develop specific technologies (e.g. intelligent sketch-boards [7]) as well as to design models that bring everything together (e.g. context ontologies for creating context-aware computing infrastructures [8]).

This concept of the smart meeting room, integrates IA agents, which aim to help in tasks such as schedule management [9], information search, or even email organisation [10]. Other more ambitious efforts have intended to focus in meetings as multi-party interactions addressing multiple tasks for which one of the most celebrated is CALO Meeting Assistant [11], by capturing and interpreting meeting conversations and activities and, as appropriate, retrieving relevant information.

We can group meeting IA in two main classes: memory and participation [12]. The most common example of memory assistants are meeting browsers which have the objective of providing rich navigation of recorded meetings for posterior reviews [13,11]. This is the area of research where reference to documents [14,15] is most studied. On the other hand, the participation assistants are online systems that have a direct real-time interaction with the meeting participants, such as recommender systems [16,17] and document providers [18]. The most relevant work on technology for information provision in meetings has been conducted by the Automatic Content Linking Device (ACLD) [19], as a recommender system, constantly monitoring speech and providing documents and internet links to related information based on the topic identified from automatic speech recognition.

3   Rationale

3.1   Problem Statement

To develop and demonstrate the concept of a personal assistant agent for a smart meeting room capable of detecting when participants on a meeting make reference (implicitly or explicitly) to a document not currently present, we must first explore how and how well people observing a meeting are able to judge whether a document is being talked about and whether that document is currently present. The high and low level features used to infer their judgements must be collected for analysis, in order to identify what techniques replicate better to such human 'capture', and 'understanding', to finally implement and evaluate them.

3.2 Contribution

While previous research in the context of automatic provision of documents to meetings has focused on suggesting topic related documents, this study focuses the efforts to a more intelligent understanding of the meeting needs to provide only required documents, reducing overwhelm and distraction produced by a substantial amount of irrelevant suggestions.

4 Study on Meetings and Their Documents

The study started with interviews to four subjects with experience on meetings, with the aim of freely obtaining relevant information about meetings and how documents relate to them and to their performance and productivity. The following hypotheses emerged which confirmed the desirability of the research topic and provided a high level orientation for its development:

- Productivity is measured against the meeting goals, while efficiency is in consideration of the fluency and coordination of the meeting itself.
- Although reading a required document means there is a distraction which could affect the meeting efficiency in that moment, the overall productivity is improved.
- The decision to be distracted by reading a document depends on both the relevance of the ongoing discourse and the relevance of the document.

Subsequently, an experiment has been produced to identify what cues and features from the scene are relied on by observers to make judgements about reference to documents and their availability, and to verify if there is a tendency to a consistent view across the participants. The experiment is conducted making use of crowdsourcing techniques, requesting participants to watch and judge meeting video episodes from the AMI corpus [20]. The results show that determining if there is a reference to a document is basically inferred from the conversation, while detecting whether the document is available or not, is balanced between the verbal, non-verbal behaviours and visual elements being present. As the number of such relevant indicators increases, the tendency to judgement consistency rises as well.

To analyse the participants conversation, their behaviour and the elements present during the meeting, from multimodal signal (i.e. audio and video) captured in a smart room, requires initially audio and video low-level analysis, generating a transcript of the conversation and an understanding of where are the participants and significant elements located during the meeting. Subsequently, a high-level analysis will allow to understand the participants conversations, behaviours and interactions with significant elements.

5   Practical Experiment

As a practical demonstration of the problem complexity, an experiment has been executed implementing video processing and recognition techniques using openCV libraries, aiming to track participants hands and visible printed documents (i.e. papers) as a preparation of detecting participants interaction with printed documents (e.g. grabbing, handing over). To expose the complexity of this task, the IB4010 session from the AMI corpus has been chosen, specifically the right camera, which includes complex paper manipulation, several occlusions and different elements of same color leading to confusion (Fig. 1(a)).

The required techniques include multiple object detection and tracking in a video recorded from a static camera on a known scenario facilitating the background removal by a simple subtraction from each video frame. In case the background is unknown, a gaussian background subtraction can be implemented [21], which consider non-changing areas (during the last n frames) as background.

(a)   (b)

Fig. 1. AMI video screenshots. a) Object detection and tracking difficulties. b) Detection and Tracking output.

Once the foreground has been isolated, areas of interest are extracted by color detection in HSV color space to break the correlation between hue and light. This step is performed as two separate filters, one for skin and one for papers. The color ranges used are heuristically determined, but can as well be learned from a set of training videos. From the areas of interest, contours are extracted and bounding boxes are approximated to them. Each bounding box encloses a detected object. Each one of them must be tracked, which means finding its corresponding detected object in consecutive frames. This is achieved by considering that the object's new position falls into a close location given by a gaussian distribution, meaning that the closest a new object is found in the next frame, the more likely it is that it corresponds to the object we are tracking. Figure 1(b) shows the output of the detection and tracking implementation, where boxes are the identified objects (blue for hands, green for papers) and circles are ground truth labels. Note that the bounding boxes and circles areas are not meaningful, only their center to indicate location.

To evaluate the multiple object tracking performance, the CLEAR MOT Metrics [22] has been followed, which provides both tracking accuracy and precision measures. Table 1 shows the evaluation results.

Table 1. Evaluation results. a) Tracked object. b) Multiple Object Tracking Precision shows the average precision error in location detection. c) Missing rate refers to the objects not detected. d) False Positive Rate tells how many of the detected objects were incorrect. e) Mismatches count the number of object incorrectly matched during tracking. f) Multiple Object Tracking Accuracy intuitively express a tracker's overall strengths combining the previous ratios.

Object	MOTP	Miss rate	FPR	Mismatches	MOTA
Hand	8.7 pixels	12.0%	32.0%	0	56.0%
Paper	6.1 pixels	4.67%	37.4%	0	57.94%

6 Conclusions and Future Work

Very little research has been done into how technology can improve meetings by just-in-time provision of missing documents. The more extensive efforts related to this task are meeting browsers in the act of providing related media during off-line revision. Since information provision in real time means dealing with interruption, it should be minimal by providing only relevant referenced and missing documents rather than continuously suggesting related documents as other approaches do.

Preliminary interviews demonstrated the close relationship between the relevance of document use, meeting interruption and its performance and productivity, demonstrating the need of a solution considering all these factors together. Practical experimentation evidenced the complexity of the problem being addressed by this study, confirming it as an interesting and challenging issue.

Future work will explore techniques for the different features collected from the initial study, focusing on those techniques that balance accuracy and speed allowing real-time execution. Finally, a validation experiment of the generated system will be executed to assess how well the system produce judgements in comparison to humans.

References

1. March, J., Simon, H.A.: Organizations. University of Illinois (1958)
2. Daft, R.L., Lengel, R.H.: Information richness. A new approach to managerial behavior and organization design. Technical report, DTIC Document (1983)
3. Rienks, R., Nijholt, A., Reidsma, D.: 18 Meetings and Meeting Support in Ambient Intelligence (2006)

4. Mithas, S., Ramasubbu, N., Sambamurthy, V.: How information management capability influences firm performance. Mis Quarterly 35(1), 237–256 (2011)
5. Aarts, E., Wichert, R.: Ambient intelligence, pp. 244–249 (2009)
6. Cook, D.J., Augusto, J.C., Jakkula, V.R.: Ambient intelligence: Technologies, applications, and opportunities. Pervasive and Mobile Computing 5(4), 277–298 (2009)
7. Adler, A., Davis, R.: Speech and sketching for multimodal design. In: ACM SIGGRAPH 2007 Courses, p. 14. ACM (2007)
8. Preuveneers, D., et al.: Towards an extensible context ontology for ambient intelligence. In: Markopoulos, P., Eggen, B., Aarts, E., Crowley, J.L. (eds.) EUSAI 2004. LNCS, vol. 3295, pp. 148–159. Springer, Heidelberg (2004)
9. Myers, K., Berry, P., Blythe, J., Conley, K., Gervasio, M., McGuinness, D.L., Morley, D., Pfeffer, A., Pollack, M., Tambe, M.: An intelligent personal assistant for task and time management. AI Magazine 28(2), 47 (2007)
10. Segal, R.B., Kephart, J.O.: Mailcat: an intelligent assistant for organizing e-mail. In: Proceedings of the Third Annual Conference on Autonomous Agents, pp. 276–282. ACM (1999)
11. Tur, G., Stolcke, A., Voss, L., Peters, S., Hakkani-Tur, D., Dowding, J., Favre, B., Fernández, R., Frampton, M., Frandsen, M., et al.: The calo meeting assistant system. IEEE Transactions on Audio, Speech, and Language Processing 18(6), 1601–1611 (2010)
12. Ehlen, P., Fernandez, R., Frampton, M.: Designing and evaluating meeting assistants, keeping humans in mind. In: Popescu-Belis, A., Stiefelhagen, R. (eds.) MLMI 2008. LNCS, vol. 5237, pp. 309–314. Springer, Heidelberg (2008)
13. Popescu-Belis, A., Lalanne, D., Bourlard, H.: Finding information in multimedia meeting records. IEEE Multimedia 19(2), 48–57 (2012)
14. Popescu-Belis, A., Lalanne, D., et al.: Reference resolution over a restricted domain: References to documents. In: ACL 2004 Workshop on Reference Resolution and its Applications, Barcelona, Spain, pp. 71–78 (2004)
15. Mekhaldi, D., Lalanne, D., Ingold, R.: A multimodal alignment framework for spoken documents. Multimedia Tools and Applications 61(2), 353–388 (2012)
16. O'Connor, M., Cosley, D., Konstan, J.A., Riedl, J.: Polylens: a recommender system for groups of users. In: ECSCW 2001, pp. 199–218. Springer (2002)
17. Porcel, C., Tejeda-Lorente, A., Martínez, M., Herrera-Viedma, E.: A hybrid recommender system for the selective dissemination of research resources in a technology transfer office. Information Sciences 184(1), 1–19 (2012)
18. Popescu-Belis, A., Boertjes, E., Kilgour, J., Poller, P., Castronovo, S., Wilson, T., Jaimes, A., Carletta, J.: The AMIDA automatic content linking device: Just-in-time document retrieval in meetings. In: Popescu-Belis, A., Stiefelhagen, R. (eds.) MLMI 2008. LNCS, vol. 5237, pp. 272–283. Springer, Heidelberg (2008)
19. Popescu-Belis, A., Yazdani, M., Nanchen, A., Garner, P.N.: A speech-based just-in-time retrieval system using semantic search. In: Proceedings of the 49th Annual Meeting of the ACL, pp. 80–85. Citeseer (2011)
20. AMI-Project: AMI meeting corpus, http://corpus.amiproject.org/
21. Lee, D.S.: Effective gaussian mixture learning for video background subtraction. IEEE Transactions on Pattern Analysis and Machine Intelligence 27(5), 827–832 (2005)
22. Keni, B., Rainer, S.: Evaluating multiple object tracking performance: the clear mot metrics. EURASIP Journal on Image and Video Processing 2008 (2008)

Part IV

Demos and Posters Track

SHIP-Tool Live: Orchestrating the Activities in the Bremen Ambient Assisted Living Lab

(Demo)

Serge Autexier, Dieter Hutter, Christian Mandel, and Christoph Stahl

German Research Center for Artificial Intelligence (DFKI), Bremen, Germany
{serge.autexier,dieter.hutter,christian.mandel,christoph.stahl}@dfki.de

Abstract. Developing ambient intelligence for a smart home living lab is a complex task. We present the SHIP-tool to define ambient intelligence processes on an adequate level of abstraction. Based on the representation of the environment in a formal logical description, communication from and to the environment is via updates of the logical description. Processes are built from basic actions to update the current logical descriptions and include means to monitor the evolution of the environment in a temporal logic formalism. The SHIP-tool implements the process language and serves both for simulation and execution of sample ambient intelligent services in a real smart home living labs also presented in the paper. Two showcases have been realized: a night surveillance service and a transportation assistance. The demonstration consisted of showing both showcases both simulated in a desktop VR environment and remotely controlling the real smart home living lab.

1 Introduction

Smart homes typically comprise a variety of different systems such as sensors, devices, machines or vehicles. Such systems range from rather primitive ones like light sensors or remotely controllable light switches, to more sophisticated ones like gesture recognition systems or autonomously driving vehicles. To realize an intelligent environment making intelligent use of such systems is a major task as it has to go all the way up from the protocols connecting these systems on a technical level to sophisticated services mediating between different activities running in multiple parallel processes. The focus of this work is on the development of such processes for smart homes, which provide specific assistance, while observing the behaviour of the components, devices and individuals and taking actions via specific rules. The solution implemented in the SHIP-tool (see [2]) is the logic based modeling of the environment and a rule-based process language with rules, conditionals as well as behaviour monitors based on derived properties of the environment rather than only on the states of devices and sensors.

The contribution of this paper is to describe an instantiation of the SHIP-tool showcasing two assistance services developed for the Bremen Ambient Assisted Living Lab (BAALL) with autonomously driving wheelchairs. Section 2 describes

J.C. Augusto et al. (Eds.): AmI 2013, LNCS 8309, pp. 269–274, 2013.
© Springer International Publishing Switzerland 2013

(a) Living Room with kitchen, doors open   (b) Bedroom with Desk, doors closed

Fig. 1. Smart home living lab serving as test environment

the smart home living lab, the 3D-model of it used for visualization in simulations and the SHIP-tool. The scenarios demonstrated at the 2013 conference on Ambient Intelligence (AmI-13, www.ami-13.org) are presented in Section 3.

2   The Setting

The Bremen Ambient Assisted Living Lab (BAALL, cf. Fig. 1) is an apartment suitable for the elderly and people with disabilities. On $60m^2$ it includes all standard living areas, i.e. kitchen, bathroom, bedroom, and living room. Besides the usual control of light, shades and heating, the lab features five electric sliding doors to let the wheelchairs pass through. The lab also includes height-adaptable furnishing (bed, kitchenette and shelves, washing basin, WC) to suit the needs of wheelchair users.

The wheelchairs are standard electric wheelchairs upgraded with sensors and actuators to assist safe driving (braking, automatic obstacle avoidance) as well as autonomous navigation to known destinations. These augmented wheelchairs are called *Rolland* and have been developed under the hypothesis that there is only one wheelchair in the flat. While operating more than one wheelchair is safe, the wheelchairs not being aware of each other poses the problem of running into deadlock situations.

When developing processes for the BAALL and the wheelchairs, test runs of the processes with the real wheelchairs and devices in real-time is limiting and always poses the risk of costly hardware damage in case of software errors. Hence we have implemented a virtual simulation environment (see also Fig. 2.(a)) based on [3]. The modeling toolkit provides the necessary objects for lights, doors, and height-adaptable furniture visualized in 3D. Lamps are visualized as cones that appear either black (off) or bright yellow (on) and the sliding doors appear either open or closed. The toolkit also implements a simplified motion model to animate the virtual wheelchairs. The interactive simulator has been implemented in two

(a) Physical small-scale model of the environment (1:20)

(b) 3D Visualization Modell

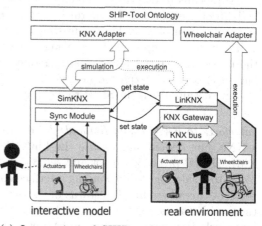

(c) Integration of SHIP-tool, interactive model and real environment via the same adapter components mediating between ontological description and simulated/real state

Fig. 2. Physical small-scale model and 3D model as interactive simulation model and architecture of the integration between SHIP-tool, interactive model and real environment

different instances that share the same code base: a desktop VR environment (Fig. 2.(a)) and a physical small-scale model (Fig. 2.(b)).

The SHIP-tool [2] is an attempt to provide an environment to develop assistance processes orchestrating available heterogeneous devices in a smart home on a high-level of abstraction. It implements a process language and interface components connecting, among others, to the BAALL, the Rolland wheelchairs and the 3D-visualization tool. It thus provides an implementation, simulation, and execution environment for ambient intelligent processes. It uses Description Logic (DL) to represent the states of the environment and any state change of the real environment gives rise to a change of the logical representation. Vice-versa every change on the logical representation triggers changes in the real environment. The bidirectional communication between the real environment and its logical representation is realized in interface components described further below.

Processes based on basic actions to change the logical representation are defined in a dynamic description logic language (DDL). Using a logical representation allows to formulate actions and conditionals over complex, derived properties of the system state while avoiding the burden to have to maintain consistently basic and derived information in each update. Moreover, using a logical representation provides a clean principle to separate the technological protocol layer to communicate with the integrated systems from the design of the assistance services.

As a means to describe behaviors over the evolution of the environment, the SHIP-tool uses a linear temporal logic formalism over Description Logic properties of the ontologies. The monitoring consists of observing a specific behavior over environment updates. Integrating success and failure of the observation into the process semantics allows one to monitor the evolution of the environment and react on a non-expected behavior.

More details about the SHIP-tool and its underlying principles are given in [2].

Interfaces to BAALL and Rolland. All devices in the BAALL are controlled by a KNX bus system and we use the LinKNX[1] interface on top of it (based on XML/HTTP protocol) to get and set the status of the KNX actuators. On the SHIP-tool side, the corresponding interface component *KNX Adapter* is an independent thread reading the status of the actuators every second and comparing them with the last status. Upon change, it updates the logical representation by translating the change into an ABox-update which is subsequently applied. Vice-versa, each ontology update communicated to the interface component is analysed wrt. if the status of some KNX actuator is affected and if so, sets its status via the LinKNX interface.

The interface component to the Rolland wheelchairs is the *Wheelchair Adapter* communicating with these over sockets using an dedicated XML protocol. The wheelchairs initially communicate their route graphs consisting of symbolically named positions and their coordinates in the 2D-coordinate system of the flat and the directed edges between these positions. The logical representation only includes the symbolic names of the positions and which wheelchair is at which position. Afterwards the wheelchairs constantly communicate their 2D-positions obtained by self-localization as well as their orientations. That information is used to determine the position of the wheelchair in the logical representation. Vice-versa, new targets can be send off to the wheelchairs using the symbolic names and the wheelchairs start driving to the corresponding position. In the logical representation, we represent the position of the wheelchair, its current route and which positions are cleared for the wheelchair. Upon each ontology update, the wheelchair adapter queries the ontology whether it has new target position to drive to and which has been cleared for it. If so, the corresponding command is sent to the wheelchair. When the wheelchair arrives at destination, or is unable to move any further because of an obstacle, it sends a corresponding information, and only then, the logical representation of the wheelchair's position is updated.

The 3D-visualization software is used to simulate the BAALL and the wheelchairs operating in it. It implements a LinKNX-like protocol (SimKNX) which allows to connect with the SHIP-tool via the same KNX Adapter interface as the real BAALL. However, it has additional virtual actuators for the wheelchairs and the virtual persons, which status are positions and allows for animating the movement from one position to another and mimicking the behaviour of the real wheelchairs.

---

[1] http://sourceforge.net/apps/mediawiki/linknx/

This setup is crucial to switch from simulation mode to controlling the real BAALL: switching consists simply of connecting to a different host and port, no other adaptations are required. Having the possibility to test the developed assistance processes first in the simulation and then being able to easily connect to the real BAALL was extremely useful.

3   Demonstration Scenarios

3.1   Night Surveillance

The first scenario illustrates how the SHIP-tool is used to enforce several general directives regarding the setting of doors and lights inside the flat. It realizes a night surveillance service, where at night time, doors are automatically closed. If persons move around in the flat and open doors, the doors are automatically closed again after a short delay. In case of an emergency such as a fire alarm, the above rules are superseded by emergency rules saying that doors have to be kept open and the whole flat has to be illuminated in order to support the evacuation of the flat. Internally each directive is encoded as monitor rules that are active as long as the desired property holds and fail once the property is violated. As a consequence, the failure of a monitor rule typically activates a process that takes care of the violated property; e.g. it closes the open door during night or opens the door if an emergency happens.

3.2   Transportation Assistance Service

The second scenario illustrates the orchestration of various autonomous processes within the SHIP-tool. The setting is that there are is more than one Rolland wheelchair independently operating in the flat. Initialized with the transportation request a wheelchair computes its own route based on an built-in abstract map of the flat. The wheelchairs themselves comprise a safety-mechanisms that avoids collisions and enables the wheelchair to pass narrow doorways or corridors. Since the wheelchairs do not know about the existence nor about the routes of other wheelchairs there is still a high risk that they block each other in the narrow flat causing a deadlock situation. The SHIP-tool orchestrates the wheelchairs: it knows about the geometry of the flat and is constantly updated on the actual positions and goals of the wheelchairs. Based on this information the SHIP-tool takes care that the doors that have to be passed by the wheelchairs are open and the lights along the route are switched on when driving at night. It computes a schedule in which order the individual wheelchairs can pass particular segments of their routes and informs the wheelchairs when they are actually allowed to enter the next segments of their routes. This schedule has to be recalculated whenever a new transportation request is filed. Internally, a monitor waits for changes in the transportation requests or changed positions of the wheelchairs to initialize a re-computation of the schedule. While in general the status and the updates of the world are represent in logic (DL, [1]), the computation of the schedule is done in a functional programming language. In- and output of the scheduler are translated from their logical representations (ABoxes) to abstract datatypes and vice versa. This allows us to use an efficient functional programming language to implement complex functions while we still operate on a logic representation of the world in which we can reason about implicit consequences of explicitly stated facts. For instance, moving a wheelchair implies that the person sitting in the wheelchair will also move. This *ramification* is done implicitly when performing an ABox-update (i.e. a change of the actual status).

4   Conclusion

This paper presented the demonstration setting of the SHIP-tool as an implementation, simulation, execution and platform for assistance processes in intelligent environments. The SHIP-tool has been used to realize two ambient services in the BAALL shown in Fig. 1 (p. 270). Videos documenting these two scenarios are available from the SHIP-tool website

http://www.dfki.de/cps/projects/ship/shiptool.

References

1. Autexier, S., Hutter, D.: Constructive DL update and reasoning for modeling and executing the orchestration of heterogenous processes. In: Eiter, T., Glimm, B., Kazakov, Y., Krötzsch, M. (eds.) Informal Proceedings of the 26th International Workshop on Description Logics, Ulm, Germany, vol. 1014, pp. 501–512. Technical University of Aachen, RWTH (July 2013)
2. Autexier, S., Hutter, D., Stahl, C.: An implementation, execution and simulation platform for processes in heterogeneous smart environments. In: Augusto, J.C., Wichert, R., Collier, R., Keyson, D., Salah, A.A., Tan, A.-H. (eds.) AmI 2013. LNCS, vol. 8309, pp. 3–18. Springer, Heidelberg (2013)
3. Laue, T., Stahl, C.: Modeling and simulating ambient assisted living environments – A case study. In: Augusto, J.C., Corchado, J.M., Novais, P., Analide, C. (eds.) ISAmI 2010. AISC, vol. 72, pp. 217–220. Springer, Heidelberg (2010)

CAKE – Distributed Environments for Context-Aware Systems

Jörg Cassens[1], Felix Schmitt[2], and Michael Herczeg[2]

[1] Institute for Mathematics and Applied Informatics,
University of Hildesheim, Samelsonplatz 1, 31141 Hildesheim, Germany
cassens@cs.uni-hildesheim.de
[2] Institute for Multimedia and Interactive Systems,
University of Lübeck, Ratzeburger Allee 160, 23562 Lübeck, Germany
{schmitt,herczeg}@imis.uni-luebeck.de

Abstract. In this paper, we introduce the distributed Context Awareness and Knowledge Environment CAKE. The design objectives for CAKE were to develop a system that is flexible enough to be used in different application domains, that supports re-use of components with the help of a well-defined plugin-system and application programming interface and that caters for privacy concerns by giving users access to personal context aware environments that share information selectively with other users' context aware environments. We describe related work on context middleware and the niche CAKE is targeting. We also argue for taking privacy concerns into account and outline how our framework addresses such issues. The concepts behind CAKE are introduced, and we describe how reasoning engines based on different paradigms can be put to work together in our framework. A first take on end-user programming is outlined and a prototypical implementation of the system presented.

Keywords: Context Awareness, Context Middleware, Distributed Systems.

1 Introduction

We have previously developed a framework for ambient intelligent systems [16,17], but its architecture had two main shortcomings. The first one was a lack of flexibility and versatility with regard to how the system interacts with sensors and actuators, and the second one was a lack of ability to deal with user concerns about privacy. These shortcomings are a result of the genesis of the project: it started as a system to support coordination and communication in small teams of knowledge workers.

To target the original application domain, we developed a centralized architecture that supported the whole team, and we introduced specific protocols for communicating with sensors and actuators based on the Extensible Messaging and Presence Protocol (XMPP)[1]. From a technical point of view, this meant that every sensor and actuator had to either implement the whole stack up to the XMPP-layer, including

---

[1] http://xmpp.org/

J.C. Augusto et al. (Eds.): AmI 2013, LNCS 8309, pp. 275–280, 2013.

having its own XMPP-ID (or JID, for Jabber ID), or that they had to be connected to an aggregator driving the specific sensor or actuator. This was not a problem for teams of knowledge workers, since we could assume that the user's PC would be used to connect "dumb" devices with the central hub, but it placed an increasing burden on the development of novel input and output devices for different application domains.

The centralized hub and spoke architecture introduced another set of problems. While it was not unreasonable for small teams where the members trusted each other, it became increasingly clear both from our own experience and the literature [3,12,14] that users might not accept to share raw sensor data with a centralized architecture where they had no control on how this data was to be used.

Therefore, it was decided to design a new framework building upon the lessons learned with the existing system, eliminating the weaknesses identified while retaining its strengths. The latter part is also the reason for not abandoning our own framework completely in favor of one of the existing middleware solutions.

2   Related Work

The goal of the AmbieSense project [11] is to provide an "ambient landscape" where personal, mobile computers connect to so-called context tags in the environment in order to access context parameters. The devices can also make use of net-based information services. Communication and coordination of different personal devices is not the main focus.

The ASTRA project [15] realizes a pervasive awareness system where personal pervasive systems are connected to deliver information about the state of users to each other. ASTRA provides means for end-user development in the form of rule sets that define what information is shared and how one's own environment reacts to changes in other users' environments. Privacy is a core aspect in ASTRA, but local reasoning capabilities are limited.

UbiCollab [5] is a toolkit that supports collaboration in ubiquitous environments, e.g. using mobile phones. It is a mature platform for developing mobile and ubiquitous applications with a strong focus on CSCW-aspects.

The Integ Smart Home System [13] uses a wireless, ad-hoc sensor network to allow users to control their homes over the internet. The application domain and the solutions to connect sensors and actuators via abstracted interfaces are very relevant for our own work. However, the collaboration support is not very elaborated, and underlying reasoning mechanisms seem to be restricted to a rule-based system.

The POSTECH U-Health Smart Home project [9] targets ambient assisted living, another interesting application domain. U-Health also uses abstraction techniques to access different system types. When it comes to connecting different environments, the main focus is the ability to notify help personnel in case of emergencies. U-Health exhibits learning capabilities to adapt to its users.

Ambient Dynamix [1] is a framework for connecting mobile applications and websites with sensors and actuators in the real world. An interesting feature of Dynamix is the concept of a context firewall, which allows different applications to limit access to contextual information on a fine-grained level. The main focus lies on services for mobile phones, and not so much on context reasoning.

3   Concept and Vision

The analysis of the literature combined with our own lessons learned lead to the following goals, which became central to the development of the new system:

1. **Flexibility** with regard to **sensors** and **actuators**: it should be comparatively easy to connect new devices with the system, both for developers and users:
   (a) It should be easy for developers to write new software components, and
   (b) users should be able to easily and safely add such components by their means.
2. **Flexibility** with regard to the **reasoning engines** that can be used, in order to utilize different reasoning paradigms based on their suitability for the task at hand.
3. **Reusability** of sensors and actuators across different domains, where applicable.
4. A **decentralized** architecture that would allow every user to run his or her own context-aware environment to address concerns about sharing raw data.
5. Further addressing **privacy** concerns by allowing for fine-grained and coarse-grained control of who can access what information.
6. **Feature parity** with the existing system when it comes to sensors, actuators, reasoners and simulators.

4   Design and Architecture

In this section, we describe the basic design and architectural features of the new system called CAKE (Context Awareness and Knowledge Environment). It is a distributed system that allows every user to run his or her own CAKE instance and grant other instances only access to selected raw or processed data. In the domain of team coordination, for example, the user might give other team members access to limited information only, while providing personal friends with more information from the same CAKE instance [16].

CAKE is a modular system, based on a strict separation of concerns, where the different modules are only loosely coupled. The system is implemented predominantly in JAVA. CAKE encompasses four different modules, as described in the following.

Plugin-Management. This module allows adding and removing sensor and actuator plugins at runtime. It abstracts sensor data according to CAKE's knowledge model. A plugin provides connectivity for a specific sensor or actuator. The API demands a manifest describing the plugin, a description how to calibrate the attached device, the update rate and a unique ID plus version information. Plugins can be published in a repository to be searched for and downloaded by other CAKE instances. Calibration information can be used to calibrate sensors or actuators from inside the running CAKE instance. For security reasons, each of the plugins runs in its own sandbox.

Logic. The logic module represents the known state of the world and connects the different reasoning engines to work on and transform the information known. CAKE uses a whiteboard to assemble all the information the system has about the world and the state of its reasoners. The whiteboard has been inspired by multi-agent black-boards [4], but it does not support the whole functionality needed for multi-agent systems, like for example the control shell. Sensor values are written on the white-board, and the different reasoners can subscribe to changes of these values. Results of the reasoning process are again written onto the whiteboard. Those results can be aggregated to "virtual sensors" which again can serve as input to other reasoners, or the results can be used to change the state of actuators. Per default, information on the whiteboard is only available to the CAKE instance where it runs, but it can selectively be made accessible by other CAKE instances.

The world model used by the whiteboard is described in terms of an RDF graph, but the system is agnostic with regard to the reasoning paradigms used by the different reasoners. Attached reasoning engines can read the state of the whiteboard through the RDF graph or via JAVA methods. Updates can, for now, only be done via JAVA methods. The reasoners can add to the ontology that describes CAKE's world model by supplying additional RDF graphs. Reasoners that work on RDF representations can be added directly. Developers of reasoners using different paradigms have to provide a mapping of their internal representation and the corresponding RDF model. A myCBR-based[2] case-based reasoner is being integrated.

A simple reasoner based on production rules [7] is built into the system. Users can use this reasoner to develop their own production system, where they define how actuators should react based on different sensor parameters. This provides basic end-user development capabilities. However, making users define what basically are complex, hierarchical if-then rules has poor transparency for non-expert users. Therefore we are looking into other paradigms for end-user development as well.

Communication. The communication module provides a REST interface [6] for the graphical user interface and connects to other CAKE instances through XMPP. For the GUI part, it is possible to configure actuators or sensors, define new rules and add or modify users, groups and permissions. Users who are given access to local data are represented by their XMPP-ID (or JID). Specific XMPP-extensions to facilitate connecting different context-aware systems have been developed and make it possible to connect to CAKE instances from other types of systems as well.

GUI. The web-based GUI-component adds user-facing administrative capabilities such as user and group management, plugin management and the definition of production rules as a means of end-user programming of context reasoners. The idea is that the CAKE system can be deployed similarly to routers or modems: small appliances that come with the necessary connectivity and are set up by the end user.

---

[2] http://mycbr-project.net/

5   Conclusions and Further Work

Looking at how CAKE interfaces with its environment, the first goal of *flexibility* for developers with regard to *sensors* and *actuators* is supported by a plugin architecture that helps developers to write software components to access new sensors and actuators. Flexibility for end users is supported by the integrated web GUI. Here, users can not only perform administrative tasks like adding and removing sensors and add, change or remove users and groups who are allowed to access one's own CAKE instance, but also define basic production rules to perform end-user development.

In order to support the second goal of retaining *flexibility* with regard to *reasoning* about context, the integrated whiteboard architecture allows for different application-specific and general-purpose reasoners to access sensor information, change the state of actuators and put processed information back onto the whiteboard for use by other reasoners or sharing with other CAKE instances.

The third goal, *reusability,* is supported by the ability to make plugins available to others and install and configure new plugins at runtime. Reusability of reasoners is, for the time being, supported in a limited way. Reasoners can only be added or changed when the system is not running, and updates from the reasoners are limited to the JAVA object interface and cannot be done through manipulating the RDF graph.

CAKE instances can be run by individual users or groups, and the integrated networking components make it easy to connect several instances so that e.g. members of work teams can get access to their peers' interruptibility status. Authorization and authentication of different instances are handled by the underlying XMPP layer. This fulfills the fourth goal of designing a *distributed system*.

Privacy issues, concerning the fifth goal, are handled by each instance through user and group management, where different users or groups can get fine- or coarse-grained permissions to access information or raw data. However, this approach does not scale very well, and issues such as minimizing asymmetry in information flow [8] can only be addressed by introducing meta-reasoners that monitor the information flow. Further work in this direction, like adding the ability to add proxies for privacy [10], has to be conducted.

Finally, the sixth goal of *feature parity* with the existing system has not been reached yet. Several sensors and actuators from previous incarnations are not available, and not all reasoners have been ported. However, we hope that we will able to port those entities on a case by case basis, if the existing solutions prove worthwhile to keep. This is especially true of our own simulation environment [2].

Acknowledgments. The authors wish to thank their students for their contributions in designing and implementing CAKE: David Bouck-Standen, Tim Dubbels, Bjørn Eberhardt, Eva Jehle, Sandro Kock, Alexander Schulze and Daniel Wilken.

References

1. Carlson, D., Schrader, A.: Dynamix: An open plug-and-play context framework for Android. In: 3rd International Conference on the Internet of Things (IOT), pp. 151–158. IEEE, New York (2012)
2. Cassens, J., Schmitt, F., Mende, T., Herczeg, M.: CASi – A Generic Context Awareness Simulator for Ambient Systems. In: Paternò, F., de Ruyter, B., Markopoulos, P., Santoro, C., van Loenen, E., Luyten, K. (eds.) AmI 2012. LNCS, vol. 7683, pp. 421–426. Springer, Heidelberg (2012)
3. Consolvo, S., Smith, I.E., Matthews, T., LaMarca, A., Tabert, J., Powledge, P.: Location disclosure to social relations: why, when, & what people want to share. In: Proceedings of the SIGCHI Conference on Human Factors in Computing Systems, pp. 81–90. ACM, New York (2005)
4. Corkill, D.D.: Blackboard systems. AI Expert 6(9), 40–47 (1991)
5. Divitini, M., Farshchian, B.A., Samset, H.: UbiCollab: collaboration support for mobile users. In: Proceedings of the 2004 ACM Symposium on Applied Computing, pp. 1191–1195. ACM, New York (2004)
6. Fielding, R.T.: Architectural styles and the design of network-based software architectures. PhD Thesis, University of California, Irvine (2000)
7. Giarratano, J.C., Riley, G.D.: Expert Systems: Principles and Programming. Brooks/Cole Publishing Co., Pacific Grove (2005)
8. Jiang, X., Hong, J.I., Landay, J.A.: Approximate information flows: Socially-based modeling of privacy in ubiquitous computing. In: Borriello, G., Holmquist, L.E. (eds.) UbiComp 2002. LNCS, vol. 2498, pp. 176–193. Springer, Heidelberg (2002)
9. Kim, J., Choi, H., Wang, H., Agoulmine, N., Deerv, M.J., Hong, J.W.-K.: POSTECH's U-Health Smart Home for elderly monitoring and support. In: IEEE International Symposium on a World of Wireless Mobile and Multimedia Networks (WoWMoM), pp. 1–6. IEEE, New York (2010)
10. Kofod-Petersen, A., Cassens, J.: Proxies for Privacy in Ambient Systems. Journal of Wireless Mobile Networks, Ubiquitous Computing, and Dependable Applications 1(4), 63–75 (2010)
11. Kofod-Petersen, A.: A Case-Based Approach to Realising Ambient Intelligence among Agents. PhD Thesis, Norwegian University of Sci. and Tech. (2007)
12. Lederer, S., Manko, J., Dey, A.K.: Who wants to know what when? Privacy preference determinants in ubiquitous computing. In: CHI 2003 Extended Abstracts on Human Factors in Computing Systems. ACM, New York (2003)
13. Mantoro, T., Ayu, M.A., Elnour, E.E.: Web-enabled smart home using wireless node infrastructure. In: Proceedings of the 9th International Conference on Advances in Mobile Computing and Multimedia, pp. 72–79. ACM, New York (2011)
14. Nissenbaum, H.: Privacy in Context: Technology, Policy, and the Integrity of Social Life. Stanford University Press, Palo Alto (2009)
15. Romero, N., Markopoulos, P., van Baren, J., de Ruyter, B., Ijsselsteijn, W., Farshchian, B.: Connecting the family with awareness systems. Personal and Ubiquitous Computing 11(4), 299–312 (2006)
16. Ruge, L., Kindsmüller, M.C., Cassens, J., Herczeg, M.: How About a MATe for Awareness in Teams? In: Proceedings of Context 2011, pp. 58–69. Springer, Heidelberg (2011)
17. Schmitt, F., Cassens, J., Kindsmüller, M.C., Herczeg, M.: Mental Models of Ambient Systems: A Modular Research Framework. In: Beigl, M., Christiansen, H., Roth-Berghofer, T.R., Kofod-Petersen, A., Coventry, K.R., Schmidtke, H.R. (eds.) CONTEXT 2011. LNCS, vol. 6967, pp. 278–291. Springer, Heidelberg (2011)

Energy Expenditure Estimation DEMO Application

Božidara Cvetković[1,2], Simon Kozina[1,2],
Boštjan Kaluža[1,2], and Mitja Luštrek[1,2]

[1] Jožef Stefan Institute,
Department of Intelligent Systems,
Jamova ceta 39, 1000 Ljubljana, Slovenia
{boza.cvetkovic,simon.kozina,bostjan.kaluza,mitja.lustrek}@ijs.si
http://ijs.dis.si
[2] Jožef Stefan International Postgraduate School
Jamova ceta 39, 1000 Ljubljana, Slovenia
http://www.mps.si

Abstract. The paper presents two prototypes for the estimation of human energy expenditure during normal daily activities and exercise. The first prototype employs two dedicated inertial sensors attached to the user's chest and thigh and a heart rate monitor. The second prototype uses only the accelerometer embedded in a smart phone carried in the user's pocket. Both systems use machine learning for the energy expenditure estimation. The focus of the demo is the convenience of using a smart phone application to provide the user with real-time insight into his/hers current status of the expended energy and also for on-the-spot encouragement based on the status. The evaluation and validation of both systems were done against the Cosmed indirect calorimeter, a gold standard for energy expenditure estimation and against the SenseWear, a dedicated commercial product for energy expenditure estimation.

Keywords: human energy expenditure, physical activity, wearable sensors, embedded smart phone sensors, smart phone application.

1 Introduction

It is widely accepted that sufficient physical activity can have a positive impact on one's life [1]. Regardless of this fact, only small fraction of the modern population dedicates time to sufficient exercise. Physical inactivity is becoming one of the main premature death causes [2]. This calls for a quick and smart solution.

To motivate people to increase their physical activity, it is important to quantify it first. The intensity of physical activity or the expended energy (EE) is usually expressed in a unit called metabolic equivalent of task (MET), where 1 MET corresponds to the energy at rest. The MET values range from 0.9 for sleeping to over 20 for extreme exertion. To accurately measure the EE, one has to use methods such as direct calorimety [3], which measures the produced

J.C. Augusto et al. (Eds.): AmI 2013, LNCS 8309, pp. 281–286, 2013.

body heat, indirect calorimetry [4], which measures the amount of carbon dioxide production and oxygen consumption using the breathing mask, and doubly labelled water [5], which measures the exhaled carbon dioxide by tracking its amount in water labelled with deuterium and oxygen-18. None of these methods can be used in everyday life to continuously monitor the EE, moreover they are very expensive. Wearable sensors do not have these problems, although they are somewhat less accurate.

Inertial sensors are very popular in different domains [6–8] due to their accessibility and understandable concept of accelerometry. An average smart phone contains an inertial sensor and today we hardly leave our home without it. As a result, we can observe a growing trend in development of mobile applications that use sensor data for monitoring.

Mobile application markets already offer a number of application for EE estimation. These applications either estimate the EE based on the number of steps the user does over one day [9] (essentially pedometers), or estimate the intensity of phone movement caused by the activity [10]. The weakness of pedometers is that they can be used only to detect the ambulatory activities such as walking or running. Applications that detect the intensity of the activity usually require the user to manually define which activity is being performed.

EE estimation is also a popular topic in the research community. Recent papers by Pande et. al. [11] report good results on estimation using smartphone data, personal information and artificial neural network. However, this paper presents EE estimation for walking up and down the stairs, standing and walking. This is only a subset of activities a person performs during a normal day. Other papers are also limited to a small subset of activities.

This paper present two prototypes: the first one uses two commercially available accelerometers and a heart rate monitor, and the second one uses only the accelerometer embedded in a smartphone. We compare these two prototypes against the gold standard Cosmed [12] indirect calorimeter and Senswear [13], a dedicated EE estimation device. The activities performed by the user are normal daily activities such as office work, cooking, cleaning, light exercising and sports activities such as lying, walking, running, cycling. A prototype application running on a smart phone provides helpful tips and encouragements to the user in addition to the EE estimation.

2   Human Energy Expenditure Estimation Systems

We considered five different sensors as shown in Figure 1: a) a wireless tri-axial Shimmer accelerometer [14]; b) an accelerometer and heart rate monitor integrated in the Zephyr Bioharness chest strap [15], which also measured heart rate; and c) an accelerometer embedded in a smart phone, in our case a Samsung Galaxy SII [16]. The reference energy expenditure values, which were used to develop and evaluate the EE estimation models, were measured using d) Cosmed $k4b^2$ portable indirect calorimeter [12]. Finally, we used e) SenseWear, a commercial EE estimation armband developed by Bodymedia [13] as another result for comparison.

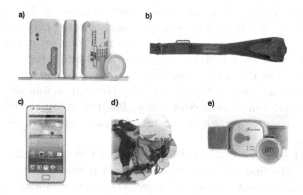

Fig. 1. Sensors used: a) Shimmer accelerometer, b) Zephyr Bioharness chest strap, c) a Samsung Galaxy SII smart phone, d) portable indirect calorimeter Cosmed $k4b^2$ and e) SenseWear EE estimation device.

Both prototypes use machine learning for the estimation of the EE, therefore a high quality dataset was collected for this purpose. The data was collected in a laboratory using all the sensors mentioned above. The laboratory was equipped with fitness equipment, such as treadmill and indoor bicycle. The person being measured performed a scenario containing activities ranging from lying to running, and from office work to shovelling, with the intention to collect a wide sample of typical daily activities and exercise. The scenario was performed by ten healthy people.

2.1 Energy Expenditure Estimation Using Dedicated Sensors

This system uses two types of sensors: two tri-axial accelerometer placed on the chest and thigh, and a heart rate monitor. Data from all the sensors are collected in real time using a dedicated APIs and software provided by the manufacturers. Sampling frequency of the accelerometers is 50Hz, while the heart rate monitor returns one hart rate measure per second. The data is received by a Java client running on a PC. The client pre-processes the data using a low-pass and a band-pass filter.

The activity recognition is performed every two seconds. The preliminary tests [17] showed that a 2-second window size for the sliding window is a reasonable trade-off between the duration of the activities and the recognition delay. The stream of collected data is split into 2-second time windows. For each time window, 41 features are computed. This feature vector is then passed to the machine learning model which was computed from the data gathered during the experiments using the Random Forest algorithm, as implemented in the Weka suite [18]. The machine-learning model is trained to classify following ten activities: lying, sitting, walking, standing, running, allfours, kneeling, leaning, transition and cycling. Evaluation of the classification model used for activity recognition has achieved a classification accuracy of 92.0 %.

The estimation of the EE is performed every 10 seconds. The stream of collected data is split into 10 seconds windows, each window overlapping with the previous one by one half of its length. For each window a set of features is computed. The features form a feature vector that is fed into a regression model for the estimation of the EE. The feature vector consists of one heart rate feature, the prevalent activity provided by the activity recognition module and 68 other features calculated from the accelerations. The regression model was trained with the support vector regression machine-learning algorithm as implemented in the Weka suite.

The evaluation of the machine learning model was done using two types of error measure. The first error measure is the mean absolute error (MAE). Absolute error is the absolute difference between the predicted and true value. The second error measure is the mean absolute percentage error (MAPE). It measures the ratio between the absolute error and the true value. SenseWear MAE is 0.86 MET and MAPE 33.53%. This system outperformed the SenseWeare with MAE of 0.60 MET and MAPE 26.71.

2.2   Energy Expenditure Estimation Using Smart Phone

This prototype uses the accelerometer embedded in the smart phone, and runs entirely on the phone. The smart phone should be carried in the right pocket downwards with screen towards the body, although the prototype works in other orientations as well but with a lower accuracy.

Similar to the previous prototype, the estimation of the EE is performed every 10 seconds from the stream of data split into 10 second overlapping windows. For each window a set of features is computed. The feature vector consists of 64 features calculated only from the accelerations. The machine-leaning algorithm of choice was again support vector regression. This prototype does not have the activity recognition module, due to orientation problems of the smart phone.

The prototype using smart phone outperformed SenseWear according to MAE, 0.83 MET, and was a bit worse according to MAPE, 33.97%.

3   Demo

The demo application with the prototype EE estimation systems using dedicated sensors can be seen in Figure 2 a). The left part of the application is the activity recognition graphical interface, where the system has recognised current activity as running. The middle part is the estimation of EE, where we can observe the predicted MET value (as well as the true MET value when the application is running offline on data with gold standard EE measurements from the indirect calorimeter) and some statistics of the prediction.

The smart-phone prototype can be seen in Figure 2 b). The user interface shows the current status on how much energy was expanded until current time point. It also shows the daily goal and how much energy should be burned by now. It contains a graph of average hourly EE for the current day. In addition

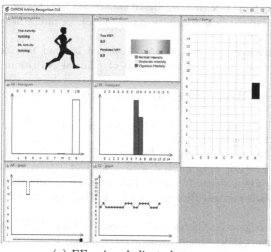
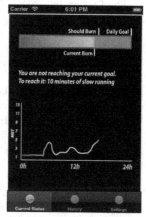

(a) EE using dedicated sensors.   (b) EE using smartphone.

Fig. 2. User interface for estimation of EE when using dedicated sensors a) and when using smartphone sensors b)

to the EE estimation, the prototype contains an encouragement module, which encourages the user to achieve the daily goal.

For encouragement module, the user has to provide his/hers weight, height, age and gender. Based on these information the basal metabolic rate (BMR) is calculated. BMR equals to the number of calories the body would burn if a user would stay in bed all day and is defined as follows: $bmr_{male} = 10*weight + 6.25*height - 5*age + 5$ and $bmr_{female} = 10*weight + 6.25*height - 5*age - 161$

In the demo application, the expected daily consumption equals to BMR plus 1000 calories. This is a rough estimate of how much calories a user should burn during one day and is used only in a prototype version of the application. At each time point we can determine the calories burnt by metabolic processes and by movement (with EE) and if the user will reach the daily goal by the end of the day. If the goal will not be reached, the application warns the user and proposes one of the predetermined exercises and the duration in order to achieve the daily goal. If the daily goal is surpassed the application rewards the user. The application computes the amount of snacks the user can consume and remain in the scope of the daily goal.

References

1. Cooper, S.B., Bandelow, S., Nute, M.L., Morris, J.G., Nevill, M.E.: The effects of a mid-morning bout of exercise on adolescents' cognitive function. Mental Health and Physical Activity 5, 183–190 (2012)

2. Kohl, H.W., Craig, C.L., Lambert, E.V., Inoue, S., Alkandari, J.R., Leetongin, G., Kahlmeier, S.: The pandemic of physical inactivity: global action for public health. The Lancet 380, 294–305 (2012)

3. Webb, P., Annis, J.F., Troutman Jr., S.J.: Energy balance in man measured by direct and indirect calorimetry. American Journal of Clinical Nutrition 33, 1287–1298 (1980)

4. Levine, J.A.: Measurement of Energy Expenditure. Public Health Nutrition 8, 1123–1132 (2005)

5. Speakman, J.: Doubly labelled water: Theory and practice. Springer (1997)

6. Nintendo Wii, http://www.nintendo.com/wii

7. Aminian, K., Mariani, B., Paraschiv-Ionescu, A., Hoskovec, C., Bula, C., Penders, J., Tacconi, C., Marcellini, F.: Foot worn inertial sensors for gait assessment and rehabilitation based on motorized shoes. In: Annual International Conference of the IEEE Engineering in Medicine and Biology Society, EMBC, pp. 5820–5823. IEEE Press (2011)

8. Kaluza, B., Cvetkovic, B., Dovgan, E., Gjoreski, H., Gams, M., Lustrek, M.: Multiagent Care System to Support Independent Living. International Journal on Artificial Intelligence Tools (accepted for publication, 2013)

9. ACCUPEDO, http://play.google.com/

10. Leijdekkers, P., Gay, V.: User Adoption of Mobile Apps for Chronic Disease Management: A Case Study Based on myFitnessCompanion®. In: Donnelly, M., Paggetti, C., Nugent, C., Mokhtari, M. (eds.) ICOST 2012. LNCS, vol. 7251, pp. 42–49. Springer, Heidelberg (2012)

11. Pande, A., Zeng, Z., Das, A., Mohapatra, P., Miyamoto, S., Seto, E., Henricson, E.K., Han, J.J.: Accurate Energy Expenditure Estimation Using Smartphone Sensors. In: ACM Wireless Health (2013)

12. Cosmed, http://www.cosmed.com/

13. SenseWear, http://sensewear.bodymedia.com/

14. Shimmer research, http://www.shimmer-research.com/

15. Zephyr Biohraness, http://www.zephyranywhere.com/products/bioharness-3/

16. Samsung Galaxy SII, http://www.samsung.com/

17. Zbogar, M., Gjoreski, H., Kozina, S., Lustrek, M.: Improving accelerometer based activity recognition. In: Proc. 15th Int. Multiconf. Inf. Soc., pp. 167–170 (2012)

18. Hall, M., Frank, E., Holmes, G., Pfahringer, B., Reutemann, P., Witten, I.H.: The WEKA Data Mining Software: An Update. SIGKDD Explorations 11, 10–18 (2009)

Enabling a Mobile, Dynamic and Heterogeneous Discovery Service in a Sensor Web by Using AndroSIXTH

Levent Görgü, Barnard Kroon, Abraham G. Campbell,
and Gregory M.P. O'Hare

CLARITY: Centre for Sensor Web Technologies
University College Dublin
Ireland
{leventgorgu,abey.campbell,gregory.ohare}@ucd.ie,
barnard.kroon@gmail.com

Abstract. Achieving the vision of Ambient Intelligence, a world where devices adapt and anticipation our needs without intervention, requires a device to connect to multiple sensors to achieve this goal. One solution to this goal is to create a sensor web between sensors. This proves to be challenging due to the range of devices, different application requirements and is compounded by the fact that devices with their corresponding sensors can be mobile. Therefore a sensor web also requires the ability of heterogenous sensors to be discovered dynamically. This paper seeks to address the challenge of discovery by demonstrating how this can be achieved using a lightweight discovery service developed for this paper. AndroSIXTH aims to improve network middleware SIXTH with discovery services and extend its abilities to mobile networks. To illustrate the functionality of AndroSIXTH discovery service and its importance to the creation of Ambient Intelligent applications, a case study will be examined that demonstrates how through a seamless discovery service, an Augmented Reality environment can be created and used for maintenance and deployment of sensors for an Ambient Intelligent environment.

1 Introduction

Giving a device awareness of its environment is the first step in allowing it to make intelligent decisions without a user needing to intervene. With the growing number of available sensors within our environment this ability appears to becoming reality but questions still remain on how these sensors can be discovered and used by devices in their proximity. One of the most intriguing solutions to this problem is the concept of a *sensor web* [1] , this paradigm has become the basis of SIXTH [2], which is a Java-based network middleware which builds upon the paradigm of the creation of a unified interface by which a variety of sensor types can be utilised. The SIXTH support extends not only to traditional networks, wireless sensor networks (WSN), but also to Cyber sensors. AndroSIXTH

J.C. Augusto et al. (Eds.): AmI 2013, LNCS 8309, pp. 287–292, 2013.

targeted to improve and expand SIXTH capabilities to mobile sensor networks and Android environment.

Where SIXTH was only allowing primitive local discovery, discovering sensors on the current sixth deployment only, improved AndroSIXTH discovery service facilitates the implementation of a dynamic discovery which allows the creation of a mobile Sensor Web. This service is achieved by the implementation of network discovery which can discover other SIXTH deployments in the network and the sensors on their deployments. After this, local discovery is reimplemented and combined with network discovery in the AndroSIXTH discovery service. JmDNS is used to solve the "pre-known ID" problem by allowing devices to get dynamic ip/port, start advertising and listening for other devices. This enabled "zero configuration" networking within AndroSIXTH. The implementation of AndroSIXTH is comprised as OSGi bundles and based on both the OSGi framework and Android environment. AndroSIXTH discovery service targets ad-hoc networks of Android devices, their embedded sensors, non-android devices and Bluetooth sensors.

The paper will first give a short outline on the current approaches in developing sensor webs and the discovery services they depend on. With that perspective, a discussion can take place on the novel approach AndroSixth takes to discovery in utilising android based smart phones for the creation of a mobile sensor web which can integrate multiple heterogenous devices. This mobile sensor web allows for multiple potential future ambient intelligent scenarios, but one important scenario will be highlighted. Thus this paper will introduce a brief case study to discuss how utilising AndroSIXTH will allow for the development of an application that can aid in the maintenance and deployment of sensors for an Ambient Intelligent environment.

2   Related Work

There have emerged a number of approaches for building a Sensor Web which include systems such as SOCRADES[3], Sensor Network Services Platform[4] and Global Sensor Network (GSN)[5]. However no standardised way has emerged for different networks to expose their underlying sensors to the web which will explicitly help discovery mechanisms. At the forefront of solving this problem is the Open Geospatial Consortium's (OGC) Sensor Web Enablement (SWE) initiative[6]. The aim of the SWE is to allow web accessible sensors by using standardised data formats and interfaces. The 52 North Sensor Web framework[1] provides implementation of the SWE. However the uptake and implementation of SWE has been slow, largely due to the complex and verbose XML schema that is associated with the services exposed by SWE. NASA's Sensor Web 2.0[7] combines the SWE with a RESTful[2] approach but how the SWE standards are mapped to RESTful interfaces is unclear.

---

[1] http://52north.org/swe

[2] REST: REpresentation State Transfer. This is a communication paradigm based on using stateless communications using the HTTP transfer protocol.

In parallel to these developments, discovery mechanisms for mobile ad hoc networks has been an important area of research for sensor networks. As the sensor web is intrinsically Multi-hop, the most important developments have been discovery mechanisms such as the Konark SGP [8] protocol. The approach of AndroSIXTH to discovery combines the approaches taken by MOBI-DIC [9] and DICHOTOMY [10] protocols. An outline of this approach is discussed in the next section.

3 Handling Mobile Discovery within AndroSIXTH

AndroSIXTH aim to generate a discovery service to help solve the mobility and heterogeneity problem that exists in a mobile sensor web. AndroSIXTH discovery service maintains a single common interface for Network Discovery services which built on top of the OSGi Services paradigm. The modular approach of OSGi, Android and SIXTH allows AndroSIXTH to be extendible which actually enables the non-Android devices to connect to an AndroSIXTH network. AndroSIXTH communication technologies and discovery abilities are structured into OSGi Services, modules or components which are almost entirely plug and play. SIXTH allows seamless addition and removal of these services without requiring additional effort from the Android application.

There are two communication protocols that are provided by AndroSIXTH discovery service. First one is the RESTful Discovery service which uses the RESTful communication paradigm between different SIXTH deployments. The second service is the Streaming Discovery service which uses a Java socket connection over TCP/IP to communicate. These communication methods are not limited to TCP/IP communications and implementations that build on other communication methods such as using a uPNP, Bluetooth or even Zigbee are also possible. Both RESTful and Streaming discovery implementations rely on JmDNS[3] to facilitate "zero configuration" IP networking and node discovery. JmDNS is a Multi-cast DNS discovery service, and is fully compatible with Apple's Bonjour. Handling node discovery with JmDNS allows AndroSIXTH to avoid the use of a centralised look up and registry mechanisms. AndroSIXTH discovery service can notify SIXTH deployments in the network and allows for the subscription of discovery events such as the addition or removal of Sensors and Services. This is accomplished without being required to manually configure addresses or rely on central servers. The primary service at present is the ability to submit Queries to remote SIXTH Deployments, and thus receive Sensor Data updates.

The creation of AndroSIXTH allows SIXTH to move away from the approach of other WSN implementations that require and rely on at least one static node in the network to establish the tasks like registering services, etc. between nodes and to be able to support them being mobile. Thus these systems are part of a specific sensor network deployment and allow mobility only at system level. AndroSIXTH does not need any static/fixed node in the network.

---

[3] http://jmdns.sourceforge.net/

The final innovation of AndroSIXTH comes from the abstraction abilities of its underlying SIXTH middleware. Sensor nodes and sensors are abstracted and kept away in an Android-SIXTH Adaptor for AndroSIXTH. This enables the rapid creation of adaptors for any new or old device and also for any new or old communication technology/protocol. AndroSIXTH discovery services are also all hidden behind in an Android-SIXTH Gateway Library and they can be reused or extended to other communication technologies such as Bluetooth or UPnP. An illustration for the architectures of the applications used in case study can be seen in Figure 1. With this brief outline of how AndroSIXTH handles Mobile Discovery complete, the next section will outline the use of AndroSIXTH in a case study to highlight its abilities.

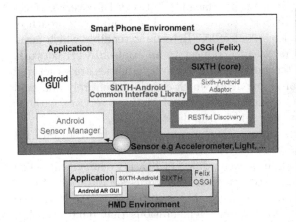

Fig. 1. Outline of the Case Study applications in both the Smart phone and HMD environments

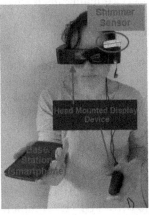

Fig. 2. The mobile sensor web generated for user by AndroSIXTH

4 Case Study

AndroSIXTH allows the creation of a mobile sensor web which through its discovery service can connect with sensors dynamically as a user enters and exits the range of a given sensor. This ability offers unique possibilities for future ambient intelligent applications and services. A case study was developed to explore how sensors could be maintained and deployed within an ambient intelligent environment. As most sensors in ambient intelligent environments are designed to be ubiquitous, checking if they are functional or if they have been deployed correctly prove a difficult task. For example the placement of a temperature sensor may require a precise placement.

Using the combination of an Android based smartphone (Galaxy Nexus), tablet (Nexus 7), Head Mounted Display device (BT-100) and a Bluetooth Shimmer, a mobile sensor web was created (see Figure 2) that allowed the creation of an Augmented Reality application. An Augmented Reality application that can allow its user to view the real world through a transparent display with additional virtual information superimposed on their field of vision.

This application enables a user to check by entering a room and looking at a sensor to see if it is functioning. An overview of the case study is given in Figure 3. This case study also demonstrates the ability of a mobile sensor web as the HMD used is sensor deficient and can only function as an Augmented Reality device by using a Shimmer to provide it with orientational information. This data must be streamed to the HMD and to create an AR application, this data must be provided in real time.

When a smartphone running AndroSIXTH enters into a room, it starts discovering any sensors within it. It then queries these sensors for their data and displays this information to the user through the HMD. This discovery is achieved through the RESTful discovery as the data does not need to be updated in real time unlike the data from Shimmer providing the AR interface. For this case study the locations of the sensors are previously known to the application but in future versions of AndroSIXTH, location tracking methods will be used to generate this information in an ad hoc fashion. To illustrate how this information is visualised for the user, Figure 4 shows the view from a WASP temperature sensor from the perspective of a user. This brief outline of this case study is a simple but effective demonstration of the potential of the AndroSIXTH discovery service and in general the potential for a mobile sensor web.

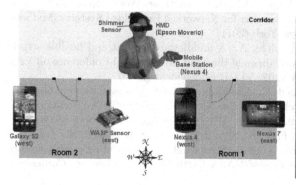 

Fig. 3. Overview of the Case study environment   **Fig. 4.** Sensor view on HMD

5 Conclusions

This paper illustrates how a robust, flexible sensor discovery and communication mechanism may be realised through harnessing, augmenting and improving a pre-existing middleware framework into mobile computing context. Embedding AndroSIXTH within SIXTH onto Android devices allowed using these devices for real time raw data communications and useful information support within the network with zero configuration IP networking. AndroSIXTH

Gateway Library and AndroSIXTH Adaptor were implemented to achieve full integration between SIXTH and Android. This library and adaptor has been released under a non-commercial licence (http://sixth.ucd.ie). To demonstrate AndroSIXTH capabilities an Augment Reality based application was developed to demonstrate how AndroSIXTH can support a unique approach to the task of maintaining and deploying sensors in Ambient Intelligent environments.

Acknowledgements. This work is supported by Science Foundation Ireland under grant 07/CE/I1147.

References

1. Delin, K.A., Jackson, S.P.: Sensor web for in situ exploration of gaseous biosignatures. In: 2000 IEEE Aerospace Conference Proceedings, vol. 7, pp. 465–472. IEEE (2000)
2. O'Hare, G.M.P., Muldoon, C., O'Grady, M.J., Collier, R.W., Murdoch, O., Carr, D.: Sensor web interaction. International Journal on Artificial Intelligence Tools 21(02) (2012)
3. de Souza, L.M.S., Spiess, P., Guinard, D., Köhler, M., Karnouskos, S., Savio, D.: SOCRADES: A web service based shop floor integration infrastructure. In: Floerkemeier, C., Langheinrich, M., Fleisch, E., Mattern, F., Sarma, S.E. (eds.) IOT 2008. LNCS, vol. 4952, pp. 50–67. Springer, Heidelberg (2008)
4. Cecílio, J., Furtado, P.: Distributed configuration and processing for industrial sensor networks. In: Proceedings of the 6th International Workshop on Middleware Tools, Services and Run-time Support for Networked Embedded Systems, MidSens 2011, pp. 4:1–4:6. ACM, New York (2011)
5. Aberer, K., Hauswirth, M., Salehi, A.: A middleware for fast and flexible sensor network deployment. In: Proceedings of the 32nd International Conference on Very Large Data Bases, pp. 1199–1202. VLDB Endowment (2006)
6. Botts, M., Percivall, G., Reed, C., Davidson, J.: OGC® sensor web enablement: Overview and high level architecture. In: Nittel, S., Labrinidis, A., Stefanidis, A. (eds.) GSN 2006. LNCS, vol. 4540, pp. 175–190. Springer, Heidelberg (2008)
7. Mandl, D., Cappelaere, P., Frye, S., Sohlberg, R., Ong, L., Chien, S., Tran, D., Davies, A., Sullivan, D., Falke, S., et al.: Sensor web 2.0: Connecting earth's sensors via the internet. In: Proceedings of NASA Earth Science Technology Conference 2008 (2008)
8. Helal, S., Desai, N., Verma, V., Lee, C.: Konark-a service discovery and delivery protocol for ad-hoc networks. In: 2003 IEEE Wireless Communications and Networking, WCNC 2003, vol. 3, pp. 2107–2113. IEEE (2003)
9. Cao, H., Wolfson, O., Xu, B., Yin, H.: Mobi-dic: Mobile discovery of local resources in peer-to-peer wireless network. IEEE Data Eng. Bull. 28(3), 11–18 (2005)
10. Gomes, A.T.A., Ziviani, A., Lima, L.S., Endler, M.: Dichotomy: A resource discovery and scheduling protocol for multihop ad hoc mobile grids. In: Seventh IEEE International Symposium on Cluster Computing and the Grid, CCGRID 2007, pp. 719–724. IEEE (2007)

A Modular and Distributed Bayesian Framework for Activity Recognition in Dynamic Smart Environments

Arun Kishore Ramakrishnan, Davy Preuveneers, and Yolande Berbers

iMinds-DistriNet, KU Leuven, Belgium
firstname.lastname@cs.kuleuven.be

Abstract. Conditional dependencies between the human activities and different contexts (such as location and time) in which they emerge, are well known and have been utilized in the modern Ambient Intelligence (AmI) applications. But the rigid topology of the inference models in most of the existing systems adversely affects their flexibility and ability to handle inherent sensor ambiguities. Hence, we propose a framework for activity recognition suitable for a distributed and evolving smart environment. On the one hand, the framework exhibits flexibility to dynamically add and remove contexts through autonomic learning of individual contexts capitalizing the spatially distributed AmI infrastructures. On the other hand, it shows resilience to missing data by boot-strapping and fusing multiple heterogeneous context information.

Keywords: User contexts and activity recognition, distributed software and frameworks, Smart home/office, Bayesian algorithm.

1 Introduction

Recent advancements in the field of micro-electronics and mobile computing have increased the possibility of acquiring richer contextual information less intrusively at cheaper costs. This prospect for adding more sensors and gathering multiple contexts has made context-aware applications, especially location and activity-aware applications, indisputably the key enablers of AmI environments.

Traditionally, information such as location and time are considered as simple contexts owing to their relatively straightforward acquisition/context management requirements and are extensively used by various smart applications. For instance, an off-the-shelf GPS device can directly measure the geo-location of a user in open outdoor environments with high accuracy. On the other hand, contexts such as activities of daily living (ADL) are considered complex contexts as they necessitate sophisticated (usually computationally expensive machine learning algorithms) inference techniques and are only recently gaining popularity. Together, these simple and complex contexts provide an exhaustive, often a complementary view of user behaviour to effectively detect user activities with fewer false positives and false negatives.

J.C. Augusto et al. (Eds.): AmI 2013, LNCS 8309, pp. 293–298, 2013.

Hence, many AmI applications are shifting focus from utilizing simple contexts such as user profile data and geo-location towards more dynamic and complex contexts such as physical activity of the user as they thrive to provide effective personalized real-time user-centric services. Moreover, given the mobile capabilities of the user and their devices, the operating conditions are continuously changing for the AmI applications giving rise to other non-trivial challenges such as sensor ambiguities (e.g., sensor failures/availability and missing data). In this paper, we propose a modular and distributed Bayesian framework suitable for dynamic and heterogeneous AmI applications to lift these limitations.

2   Related Work

For brevity, here we restrict our discussions to a few prominent activity recognition techniques with inertial sensors and different machine learning concepts that help to combine heterogeneous data sources in those works. Traditionally, activity-aware applications have modelled activities as high-level contexts which are either inferred directly from low-level sensors or indirectly through other context informations such as location.

For instance, [3,1] have studied the possibility of detecting physical activities of a user *directly* using low-level signal from tri-axial accelerometers. The high-level user activities such as standing, walking, running, are modelled as latent state variables of a Hidden Markov Model (HMM) and are trained and inferred *directly* from the probability distribution of observable sensor readings i.e., a body-worn accelerometer. Whereas, in [2,5], the authors have inferred activities *indirectly* through location information about the user which in turn were estimated from low-level sensors. Their paper presented a typical location based activity inference model realized with a Dynamic Bayesian Network (DBN). The low-level sensor data such as WiFi signal strengths are used to infer the geo-location of a user and then the locations are mapped onto the corresponding user activities.

Nevertheless, most of these systems suffer from various technical limitations. They either support direct or indirect sensing of human activities (or other high-level contexts) but not both. This would severely limit the ability of a robust context-aware system to gather information from as many sources as possible. Similarly, adding a new sensor or context is not straight-forward and usually require complete relearning of the model due to their rigid hierarchical structure. Also, learning the structure and parameters of these models are both computationally expensive and require a lot of modelling efforts. In this paper, we propose a novel framework to lift these limitations.

3   Motivating Use Case: A Personal Assistant Application

Smart home (or office) is not a new concept in Ambient Intelligence. For more than a decade, the subject of research of any smart home or office application is to automate the tasks of a user in order to achieve improved comfort, security and energy management [4]. We aim to develop a smart Personal Assistant application to assist a user in smart home and office scenarios without assuming explicit user inputs. As today's ubiquitous smart phones come with an increasing range of sensing, communication, storage and computational resources they play a special role in realizing our Personal Assistant application. For example, the tri-axial accelerometer embedded in the smart phone is used from monitoring the physical activity levels of a user whereas localization sensors such as GPS is used for location based smart notification. Also, we utilize other context sources that are readily available even for a common user such as the CPU load on the work computer, internet connection type, IP address, etc. The significant high-level functional and non-functional requirements identified for the Personal Assistant application are,

- The system should gather as much contextual information as possible from all available context sources.
- The system must implement modular inference techniques for effective inference from heterogeneous and spatially distributed sources.
- The system should be flexible to add (or remove) context sources to cater for the ever evolving list of user devices.
- The system should be resilient to sensor ambiguities (e.g., temporary unavailability of context sources or missing data) to avoid varying quality of service even when certain context sources are temporarily unavailable which is a norm in today's AmI environments owing to the increased user mobility.

4 A Novel Modular and Distributed Bayesian Framework

Technically the proposed framework is a collection of Bayesian networks where each individual Bayesian network models a unique high-level context. For the

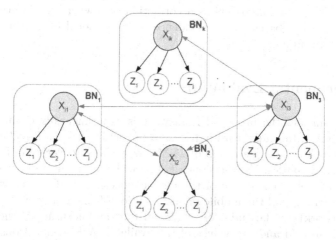

Fig. 1. A conceptual overview of the proposed modular and distributed Bayesian network

ease of implementation each Bayesian network is modelled with naive Bayes assumption. Fig. 1 shows a typical instance of the proposed framework where different contexts are modelled as separate individual Bayesian networks BN_i (enclosed in a box). The parent node in each individual Bayesian network is the high-level context node to be inferred (e.g., physical activities or semantic locations of the user) and their respective children nodes corresponds to the sensors used to infer them (e.g., accelerometer or GPS data). Note that the double headed arrows in Fig. 1 is to illustrate the mutual influence of random variables (contexts) on each other and are implemented as separate Bayesian networks for each of the context nodes.

Learning in the proposed network is simpler compared to a generic Bayesian networks because their naive assumption guarantees fixed network structure. Only the conditional probability density of the nodes representing high-level context have to be learned. First, the prior probability distribution of the high-level contexts are safely assumed to follow a beta distribution with equal prior probability distribution. Then, the likelihoods of the high-level contexts are estimated separately conditioned on (1) the sensor nodes and (2) other dependent high-level context variables and can be easily parallelized as concurrent tasks. Nevertheless, learning the conditional probability densities of the high-level contexts conditioned on other high-level contexts are dependent on the learning in other individual Bayesian networks conditioned on sensor inputs requiring synchronization of those tasks.

Inference in the proposed framework is done in bootstrap mode by recursively executing 2 steps. In the first step, an estimate of each high-level context nodes is generated by combining objective prior probabilities and evidence presented by the other high-level contexts. In the second step, the posterior estimated from the previous step is used as an informed prior to determine the most probable value for each of the high-level contexts. The objective of first step is to utilize the global influence of a context on other co-related context information for improved prediction. The second step acts as a correction step where the informed prior values are adjusted based on the evidence from the local observations of the low-level sensor inputs.

5   Experimental Evaluation

The performance of the proposed framework is experimentally evaluated with the Personal Assistant application discussed in Section 3. Data is collected from 4 users (all male in the age group of 25-35) over a week covering different user locations and activities. Various context sources being monitored are - the call state, the battery level, nature of the data connection (WiFi or network) and GSM signal strength of the mobile phone; location of the user provider (GPS or Cellular network), the latitude, longitude, altitude and accuracy of the position of the user; the ssid and rssi values of the available WiFi connections, if available; the name, address and rssi of the discovered blue-tooth enabled devices; ip address of the computer and CPU load of the work computer; the energy of

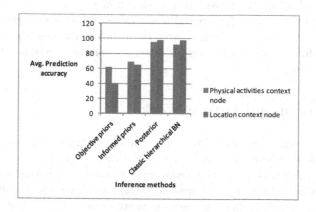

Fig. 2. A comparison of performance of different inference steps and a classic BN

the fft components of the tri-axial accelerometer (to detect physical activities) and binary sensors to detect the user location indoors. The high-level context values of interest are the semantic location of the user (home/work/outdoors-alone/outdoors-public place/car) and the current physical activities of the user (being still/walking/running).

First, we demonstrate the adaptability of the framework by comparing the prediction accuracies of different inference methods (or steps) in the proposed inference algorithm namely, objective prior of the context nodes, the informed prior and the final posterior estimation as shown in Fig. 2. Despite its Naive conditional assumption, the prediction accuracy of the proposed framework is comparable to the output of a classic hierarchical Bayesian network. Especially, for complex context such as physical activity of the user, the increase in performance (accuracy) is achieved at the cost of increased interactions (in the

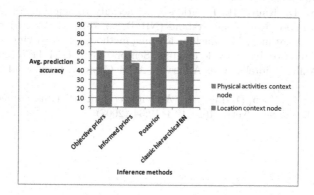

Fig. 3. A comparison of performance of different inference steps and a classic BN model with 30% missing data

global and local inference steps). Also as shown in Fig. 3, the relative decrease in the prediction accuracy (compared to no missing data scenario) of the classic hierarchical Bayesian network is more than that of the posterior estimate of the proposed framework confirming the latter's robustness to sensor ambiguities (i.e., missing data).

6   Conclusion and Future Work

In this paper, we have identified the shortcomings of traditional high-level contexts (such as user activity) recognition algorithms for today's dynamic smart environments. Later, we have proposed a novel framework and analyzed the modularization capabilities of the framework for decentralized and parallel learning of contexts from multiple heterogeneous context sources. Our two-step inference algorithm bootstraps the global and local views of the high-level context nodes for effective recognition of multiple high-level contexts (including activities of daily living) simultaneously. Our experiments on the Personal Assistant application use case demonstrate the flexibility of the framework and its resilience to missing data. In the future, we have planned to incorporate a neural-like inference algorithm where the posterior of the context variable updated iteratively to average out the disagreeing views of individual Bayesian networks and to relax the naive Bayes assumption of the framework.

Acknowledgement. This research is partially funded by the Research Fund KU Leuven, and by the EU FP7 project BUTLER.

References

1. Kwapisz, J.R., Weiss, G.M., Moore, S.A.: Activity recognition using cell phone accelerometers. In: Proceedings of the Fourth International Workshop on Knowledge Discovery from Sensor Data, pp. 10–18 (2010)
2. Liao, L., Fox, D., Kautz, H.: Location-based activity recognition. In: Advances in Neural Information Processing Systems (NIPS), pp. 787–794. MIT Press (2005)
3. Mannini, A., Sabatini, A.M.: Machine learning methods for classifying human physical activity from on-body accelerometers. Sensors 10(2), 1154–1175 (2010)
4. Sadri, F.: Ambient intelligence: A survey. ACM Comput. Surv. 43(4), 36:1–36:66 (2011)
5. Yin, J., Yang, Q., Shen, D., Li, Z.-N.: Activity recognition via user-trace segmentation. ACM Trans. Sen. Netw. 4(4), 19:1–19:34 (2008)

Towards an Integrated Methodology
to Design Sustainable Living Practices

Natalia Romero, Abdullah Al Mahmud, Satish Beella, and David V. Keyson

ID-StudioLab, Faculty of Industrial Design Engineering,
2628 CE Delft, The Netherlands
{n.a.romero,a.almahmud,s.k.beella,d.keyson}@tudelft.nl

Abstract. Sustainable Living Labs (SLL) provide an experimental and interactive infrastructure to enable open innovation processes in the context of real (realistic) home settings. In SLL, home occupants play a role in communicating and discussing their values and lifestyles; they can experience innovations and reflect on the impact of their practices in daily life by means of situated experiments. The Concept House (CH), a SLL built in Rotterdam, the Netherlands, offers such facilities. In this paper, we discuss the development of the Experience Intervention Method (EIM) to obtain a holistic understanding of living practices. We demonstrate the method with a case study on home energy management developed in CH to clarify the role of qualitative and quantitative in-situ methods to get insights, co-design and validate sustainable innovations.

Keywords: Sustainable Living Labs (SLL), in-situ methods, design methods.

1 Introduction

Sustainable Living Labs (SLL) is a research approach that provides an experimental and interactive infrastructure to enable open innovation processes in the context of real homes and realistic home settings [6]. Two elements characterize SLL as a user-centred process: the design is situated in real-life (existing homes) and realistic settings (home labs); and the focus is on behaviours and experiences of daily life practices. In-situ (in-time and situated) design methods facilitate home occupants to reflect on their existing and emergent practices through experimentation, with different levels of design interventions in the context of real homes or of realistic test homes.

Domestic sustainable innovations are designed to co-exist within the dynamic complexity of daily life practices. If home living practices are ignored in the design process, such innovations are doomed to failure [8]. A good example is energy efficient homes that monitor and provide feedback for saving energy. Inhabitants of energy efficient homes often question and neglect advice given on their consumption even when it has been tailored to their specific energy practices [4]. One reason is that energy consumption actions might related to aspects of people's everyday life such as convenience, fashion, or desire for new things, rather than energy conservation. Therefore, a key aspect for the design of domestic sustainable innovations is a comprehensive understanding of people's practices in their daily life settings.

J.C. Augusto et al. (Eds.): AmI 2013, LNCS 8309, pp. 299–304, 2013.

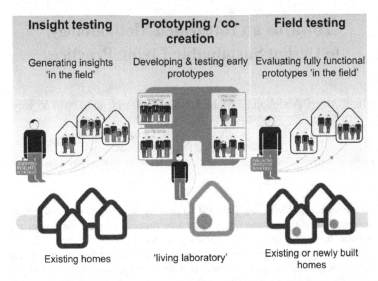

Insight testing

Prototyping / co-creation

Field testing

Generating insights 'in the field'

Developing & testing early prototypes

Evaluating fully functional prototypes 'in the field'

Existing homes

'living laboratory'

Existing or newly built homes

Fig. 1. The three-tier model of Sustainable Living Labs

SLL aims to provide a user integrated research infrastructure [6] for living labs, which is described in a three-tier model that represents three phases of an iterative design process (see Fig. 1). In these phases insights research, prototyping and field-testing, aim to inform, develop and validate sustainable living practices within big and small iteration cycles. The 'Insights' phase is conducted in the realm of existing homes, to a) gain a holistic view of home occupants' behaviours and to b) understand the choices people make regarding daily life practices. In the 'Prototyping' phase, co-design techniques are conducted in realistic home test labs to a) develop scenarios and prototypes within existing daily life practices, and to b) test their impact on different aspects of people's lifestyles. Co-design in living labs facilitates rich design practices, enabling explorations into what is possible rather than being limited to what is factual [1]. Finally, in the 'Field-testing' phase, working prototypes are tested in existing homes to a) validate the adoption of innovations in daily life practices and to b) evaluate their impact on sustainable practices.

The Concept House (CH) has been developed within the framework of the Interreg SusLabNWE project (www.suslabnwe.eu), a European infrastructure of living labs to support activities in the three-tier model. CH consists of the Concept House Proto-type, the house itself, and the Concept House Village, a diversity of communities located in the neighborhood of Heijplaat, Rotterdam. The aim of the Concept House Prototype is to be close to energy neutral or be energy-positive. The exact perfor-mance of the house will be measured in the coming years, with and without occu-pants. The house is fully equipped for people to live there for a period of time. It is also constantly adapted to fulfill requirements of different research studies on energy consumption, such as installation of power sockets to measure single device energy consumption or sensor nodes for measuring climate performance in different rooms.

This paper uses the three-tier model to describe an integrated methodology called the Experience Intervention Method (EIM), to develop innovations in sustainable home technologies within the Concept House infrastructure. A case study on home energy management will be used to illustrate the role of in-situ and integrated methods in each phase, to capture participants' reflections on their daily activities.

2   Towards an Integrated SLL Methodology

The above model requires methods to support design activities that facilitate participants to explain the choices they make on a daily basis. Such design activities refer to interventions that enlighten, guide, involve and even provoke participants to articulate and reflect on their practices and the reasoning behind them.

An integrated approach is needed to provide the desired holistic and ecological understanding of home living practices, that integrates the large sets of quantitative data, collected through the CH infrastructure, with results from qualitative methods. Traditional, qualitative, Human Computer Interaction (HCI) methods such as diaries, surveys, interviews, and questionnaires have been used extensively in SLL studies, and are often complemented by quantitative logging and sensor data [3]. Firstly, the aforementioned methods are not always appropriate to capture the richness and nuances of daily practices nor can they be applied in real homes for extensive periods of time. Secondly, the lack of integration between both data types has made it difficult to provide sound explanations for observable behaviours.

In the following sections, the Experience Intervention Method (EIM) is introduced to explain the proposed vision by integrating behavioural and experiential data in the form of situated design interventions in the three tier model. The method aims to facilitate reporting by participants about their experiences related to existing and emergent behaviours. The situated interventions aim to trigger peoples' reflection on their behaviour and lifestyles by confronting them on their existing practices or by introducing alternative practices. The Ampul project [7] is used to illustrate possible intervention setups for each tier, addressing the envisioned opportunities as well as challenges. Ampul aims to design a home interface that empowers prosumers, people investing in alternative energy home production, to stimulate consumption of energy at the moments when it is produced.

3   The Experience Intervention Method (EIM)

Situated interventions have been applied in the field of ubiquitous computing to evaluate innovations in real settings [2]. Supporting remote and co-located interaction between participants and experimenters, in-situ experiments can evaluate aspects of innovations that consider the whole ecology of user interactions. Momento [2] is one such in-situ evaluation tool based on Experience Sampling Method [5] that uses adaptive prompts, automatic data capturing of context and interactions, and self-reporting.

EIM is based on the same principles behind Momento but goes beyond the purpose of pure evaluation. The method integrates a number of low-fi and high-fi interventions to trigger reflection on daily life practices.

3.1   Phase 1 – Baseline and Low-Fidelity Interventions

In phase 1, EIM aims to create a baseline from the existing practices in the homes of people with minimum intervention. Sensors are used, when possible, to silently capture behavioural data, or minimal interventions in the form of diaries are implemented to help people provide objective information about their practices. This baseline serves as input for EIM to develop low-fi interventions that confront participants with scenarios based on existing and alternative situations. Several interventions can be setup, to explore how different projections of peoples' practices make them feel and how they experience themselves in such projections.

In the Ampul project, research in phase 1 was conducted in six households in the Concept House Village, aiming to gather information on peoples' barriers and drivers to adopt more sustainable practices. The baseline was a map of all electronic devices that a person uses on a daily or weekly basis, defining their average consumption based on technical specifications. Next, an electronic diary was developed to capture an estimation of daily energy consumption per device, in terms of frequency or minutes of use. The tool then calculated the energy consumption per device. Two interventions were designed to study how people experience their energy practices in relation to energy feedback visualizations: one that visualizes home consumption considering energy as a limited resource and one where the appliances with higher consumption are visually compared against the total consumption of a day. In each intervention, information regarding financial and environmental costs were presented, and a questionnaire was administered to report the emotional impact of the feedback (feelings and attitudes) and whether it may lead participants to change something in their current practices.

3.2   Phase 2 – Hi-Fi Interventions and Prototypes

EIM in phase 2, supports co-design by engaging participants to experience prototypes-in-development in realistic settings, allowing the experimenter to use hi-fi interventions to evoke different experiences. EIM collects participants' experiential reports, which can retro-feed the development of the prototypes. Benefiting from a control but realistic home test environment, these hi-fi interventions can be adapted in-situ, depending on observations and contextual factors that describe the current situation. Therefore, possible scenarios can be tried out in different contexts.

In the Ampul project, the intervention was a working prototype implemented in the Concept House; the intervention was designed to prompt people in two ways regarding their energy consumption and production. The goal was to observe people's reaction and understanding of the prompts. An interactive visualization next to the electronic device provided immediate feedback on energy consumption in relation to household energy production. A second interactive visualization was implemented on a tablet to allow participants to see overall changes in consumption and production and to navigate through the consumption of different devices.

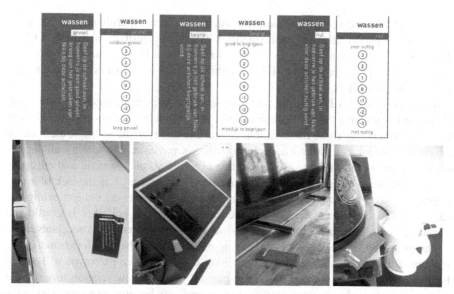

Fig. 2. Situated prompts – the three prompts for laundry: understanding, usefulness, feelings (top); prompts per device (bottom)

Next to each device, a paper based prompt was included to survey people's feeling towards the visualization when using the device. Participants consisted of seven families some of them came from the Concept House village. They stayed at least two nights in the Concept House tasked with performing certain practices: cooking, laundry, preparing tea or coffee, and watching TV.

3.3   Phase 3 – Hi-Fi Working Prototypes

In phase 3, EIM is used in a similar way as in phase 1; to facilitate participants to reflect and report on their experiences around daily life practices. The difference is that in Phase 3, working prototypes are put in the field for longitudinal and large-scale interventions where experiential self-reports and the interactions with the prototype are synchronized. The outcomes are expected to provide evidence on how and why innovations eliciting sustainable lifestyles will prevail over time. EIM offers the possibility to set up situated experiments where prototype functionalities can be remotely intervened on at particular moments, to dynamically test and respond to different conditions observed. As previously said, these interventions can be piloted and fine-tuned in phase 2.

On-going in the Ampul project, is the development of a prototype that can be placed in real homes. The goal is to further explore the impact different prompts may have on the adoption of sustainable practices.

4   Discussion

In-situ experimentation in CH puts people, with their experiences and lifestyles choices, as major actors when designing for sustainable practices. The CH provides unique, real life and realistic home infrastructures where experiments can bring insights that are experiential and contextualized. The main contribution of EIM in CH is that it supports in-situ design experiments where the focus is on capturing experiential reports triggered by low-fi and hi-fi interventions in real-life (own homes) and realistic (living labs) settings.

In phases 1 and 3, EIM enables mid-long term and large scale studies where quantitative and qualitative data collection is deployed to link behaviours with the choices made. By conducting these interventions in real-life and realistic settings, the focus is not on the factual but rather on exploring what is possible, considering all factors within a home situation. In phase 2, adaptive experiments enable vivid and engaging co-design between participants and experimenters. The drawback is the lack of a systematic test to quantitatively compare between cases. However, understanding the subjective and dynamic nature of experiences in daily life practices is considered crucial; therefore, the limitation to only consider qualitative analysis is acceptable.

The presented vision argues that engaging participants in the transformation of existing products into sustainable re-designs in the Concept House Prototype will enable them to both experience and reflect incrementally on their new relation towards the objects. Therefore simple interventions, which gradually become more complex, may help participants become more familiar with the new interactions.

References

1. Binder, T., Brandt, E., Halse, J., Foverskov, M., Olander, S., Yndigegn, S.: Living the (co-design) Lab. Online Proceedings of Nordes 2011 (2011)
2. Carter, S., Mankoff, J., Heer, J.: Momento: support for situated ubicomp experimentation. In: Proceedings of CHI 2007, pp. 125–134. ACM (2007)
3. De Moor, K., Ketyko, I., Joseph, W., Deryckere, T., De Marez, L., Martens, L., Verleye, G.: Proposed Framework for Evaluating Quality of Experience in a Mobile, Testbed-oriented Living Lab Setting. Journal of Mobile Networks and Applications 15(3), 378–391 (2010)
4. Gram-Hanssen, K., Bartiaux, F., Jensen, O.M., Cantaert, M.: Do homeowners use energy labels? A comparison between Denmark and Belgium. Energy Policy 35 (2007)
5. Hektner, J.M., Csikszentmihalyi, M.: The experience sampling method: Measuring the context and content of lives. In: Handbook of Environmental Psychology, pp. 233–243 (2002)
6. Liedtke, C., von Geibler, J., Baedeker, C.: The sustainability living lab as a reflective user-integrating research infrastructure. In: 3rd International Conference on Sustainability Transitions, pp. 206–222 (2012)
7. Rutten, J.: Designing Ampul: exploring future prosumer interactions. Master thesis in Industrial Design Engineering, Delft University of Technology (2013)
8. Spaargaren, G.: Theories of practice: Agency, technology, and culture: Exploring the relevance of practice theories for the governance of sustainable consumption practices in the new world-order. Global Environment Change 21, 813–822 (2011)

Part V

Workshops Descriptions

When Design Meets Intelligence: Incorporating Aesthetic Intelligence in Smart Spaces

Carsten Röcker[1], Kai Kasugai[1], Daniela Plewe[2],
Takashi Kiriyama[3], and Marco Rozendaal[4]

[1] Human-Computer Interaction Center, RWTH Aachen University, Germany
{roecker,kasugai}@comm.rwth-aachen.de
[2] University Scholars Programme, National University of Singapore, Singapore
danielaplewe@nus.edu.sg
[3] Graduate School of Film and New Media, Tokyo University of the Arts, Japan
kiriyama@gsfnm.jp
[4] Human Information and Communication Design, TU Delft, Netherlands
m.c.rozendaal@tudelft.nl

Abstract. This paper illustrates the motivation and objectives of the third international workshop on *Aesthetic Intelligence*. The workshop aims at bringing together researchers as well as industry practitioners from the fields of computer science, engineering, architecture, industrial and interface design to discuss ongoing research activities and emerging trends in the area of smart environments. A special focus of the workshop is on the role of aesthetic design for the acceptance and adoption of services in smart environments.

Keywords: Ambient Intelligence, Ubiquitous Computing, Smart Spaces, Aesthetics, Design, Architecture, Urban Informatics.

1 Motivation

Over the last decades, the nature of computing changed fundamentally. Following the *mainframe era* of the 1960s and 1970s, the two last decades of the 20th century were mainly characterized by *personal computing* as the leading paradigm. Today, we are in the age of ubiquitous computing and are heading towards an era *of smart environments* [1], in which a multitude of computers will be embedded in our physical surrounding and unobtrusively support us in our everyday activities.

However, we did not only see a tremendous increase in computing power, we also experienced a shift in the relationship between computers and users. Especially early mainframe computers required an entire team of engineers and computer scientists to be operated and were jointly used by multiple people, sometimes even entire organizations. The introduction of personal computers in the 1980s was accompanied by a one-to-one relation between computers and users. Today, most people own multiple "computers" in form of notebooks, tablet PCs and smart phones, and continuously interact with these devices throughout their day.

J.C. Augusto et al. (Eds.): AmI 2013, LNCS 8309, pp. 307–308, 2013.

Yet, not only technology changed, also the world around us changed, which has a large impact on the way systems have to be designed. Today's computer users are much more diverse than they used to be in the time of mainframe computers or the era of desktop PCs. Only 20 years ago, computers were mainly used in the office context by users who were relatively computer literate or at least trained for the tasks they did. With the transition away from the office context towards to the home domain, we have to look at completely new user groups, starting with children up to seniors.

In addition, also the context of computer usage changed significantly. Today, computers are used anywhere and anytime. This does not only include different locations (public vs. private spaces), but also varying social contexts (multi vs. single-user situations). All those aspects have a considerable relevance for the design of future systems.

2   Objectives and Research Challenges

Hence, when looking at these developments, it is not really surprising that also the requirements of users changed. In the 1990s, most computer users looked for functional criteria when they bought a computer. Things like CPU speed, capacity of the hard drive etc. were criteria that determined whether a computer was bought or not. Today, other aspects are important as well. Computers become more and more lifestyle devices, which have to meet a broad variety of criteria, ranging from classical usability factors to more hedonic aspects. When designing systems, developers have to take this diversity into account, which means that it is not sufficient anymore to only concentrate on technical problems and performance aspects. Instead, it is vital to make sure that we provide the means – and especially the interfaces – that enable users, who are interested in using the technology we are designing, to actually do so. Therefore, this workshop aims at bringing together researchers from diverse disciplines to discuss best practice examples and research challenges with regard to the inclusion of hedonic and aesthetic dimensions into the design and usage of smart environments. By doing this, the workshop builds on the results and insights gained during the previous workshops held in Amsterdam, the Netherlands [2] in 2011 and Pisa, Italy [3] in 2012.

References

1. Kasugai, K., Ziefle, M., Röcker, C., Russell, P.: Creating Spatio-Temporal Contiguities Between Real and Virtual Rooms in an Assistive Living Environment. In: Innovative Interactions, Elms Court, Loughborough, UK, pp. 62–67 (2010)
2. Kasugai, K., Röcker, C., Bongers, B., Plewe, D., Dimmer, C.: Aesthetic Intelligence: Designing Smart and Beautiful Architectural Spaces. In: Keyson, D.V., et al. (eds.) AmI 2011. LNCS, vol. 7040, pp. 360–361. Springer, Heidelberg (2011)
3. Röcker, C., Kasugai, K., Plewe, D., Kiriyama, T., Lugmayr, A.: Aesthetic Intelligence: The Role of Design in Ambient Intelligence. In: Paternò, F., de Ruyter, B., Markopoulos, P., Santoro, C., van Loenen, E., Luyten, K. (eds.) AmI 2012. LNCS, vol. 7683, pp. 445–446. Springer, Heidelberg (2012)

Introduction to the 2nd International Workshop on Adaptive Robotic Ecologies, ARE'13

Stefano Chessa[1], Mauro Dragone[2], Arantxa Renteria[3], and Alessandro Saffiotti[4]

[1] Dipartimento di Informatica, University of Pisa, largo Pontecorvo 3, 56127 Pisa, Italy
ste@di.unipi.it
[2] School of Computer Science and Informatics, University College Dublin,
Belfield, Dublin 4, Ireland
mauro.dragone@ucd.ie
[3] Tecnalia, Health Technologies Unit, Parque Technológico, Edificio 202,
E-48170 Zamudio (Bizkaia), Spain
arantxa.renteria@tecnalia.com
[4] Center for Applied Autonomous Sensor Systems, Örebro University, SE-70182 Sweden
asaffio@oru.se

Robotic ecologies are an emerging paradigm, which crosses the border between the fields of robotics, sensor networks, and ambient intelligence (AmI). Central to the robotic ecology concept is that complex tasks are not performed by a single, very capable robot (e.g. a humanoid robot butler), instead they are performed through the collaboration and cooperation of many networked devices performing several steps in a coordinated and goal oriented fashion while also exchanging sensor data and other useful information in the process. Such an approach extends the type of application that can be considered, reduces their complexity, and enhances the individual values of the devices involved by enabling new services that cannot be performed by any device by itself.

While these potentials make robotic ecologies increasingly popular, many fundamental research questions remain open. One such question is how to provide sensing and actuating services that are both adaptable and robust. In order to decide the specific behaviours which, in combination, achieve necessary and meaningful tasks, robotic ecologies should not be restricted to only those situations that are envisioned by their designer. Rather than requiring pre-defined models of both the activities of the user they try to assist and the services that should be carried out to assist them, robotic ecologies should be able to pro-actively and smoothly adapt to subtle changes in the environment and in the habits and preferences of their user(s). In addition to adaptability, control mechanisms for robotic ecologies should be capable of synthesizing robust strategies, in the sense that these strategies should take into account both a sufficient amount of exogenous events and the specific capabilities of the devices used to enact the strategies.

ARE'13 is organized under the auspices of the EU FP7 project RUBICON (Robotic UBIquitous COgnitive Network[1]). This edition of the workshop invited contributions to identify and discuss the main research questions that need to be addressed for the development of adaptive robotic ecologies, in order to increase their adaptability, and

---

[1] http://www.fp7rubicon.eu

J.C. Augusto et al. (Eds.): AmI 2013, LNCS 8309, pp. 309–310, 2013.

reduce the amount of preparation and pre-programming required for their deployment in real world applications. The goal of the workshop is to provide a forum to exchange ideas, discuss state-of-the-art results, and set the stage for the generation of a research road-map. In the future we hope to further develop the workshop into an event that increasingly builds and shapes the community of leading practitioners and research experts.

A variety of work has been submitted to the workshop: Michele Girolami, Filippo Palumbo, Francesco Furfari, and Stefano Chessa describe the experience of using ZB4O, an application-level gateway designed to facilitate interoperability between ZigBee sensors and external applications, within the robotic ecology developed as part of the EU project GiraffPlus. Joe Saunders, Michael L. Walters, Maha Salem, and Kerstin Dautenhahn describe the approach pursued within the EU project ACCOMPANY to create an environment where robot behaviours can be taught to a companion robot for elderly people based on events within a sensorized home. Their paper focuses on how to deal with events occurring at different times and in different timeframes and periods. Lia Susana d.C. Silva-Lopez and Mathias Broxvall discuss the need for objective comparisons of algorithms and results of different configuration planning solutions for robotic ecologies. Their paper propose two empiric method for numerically comparing performances of different planning methods. S. M. Mizanoor Rahman, T. Nadia and R. Ikeura present a people-centric adaptive ecology that combines a humanoid robot with a virtual human agent to assist the humans in various real-world complex social tasks in smart spaces. Their paper describe a study performed to assess people's acceptance of the ecology for the performance of collaborative tasks. Finally, Anara Sandygulova and Mauro Dragone illustrate an application testbed built to support interaction studies between human users and robotic ecologies. They describe the design and the implementation of the testbed, and report their experiences in its application to a number of demonstrations and human-robot interaction studies.

We, the organizers, wish to thank the authors for their contributions, the program committee for their reviews, and the conference organizers of the 4th International Joint Conference on Ambient Intelligence (AmI-2013) for making this workshop possible.

3rd International Workshop on Pervasive and Context-Aware Middleware

Hamed Vahdat-Nejad

Pervasive Computing lab, Department of Computer Engineering, University of Birjand,
Birjand, Iran
Vahdat.nejad@gmail.com

1 Introduction

Generally, middleware is a software layer, which by residing between the operating system and application layer in each node, provides new capabilities and facilitates development of applications [1]. Obviously, pervasive computing middleware inherits general tasks of traditional middleware in distributed systems such as coordination, communication, security and tolerance for component failures and disconnections; however, there are some factors separating context-aware middleware from traditional middleware systems [2], as outlined below:

- The infrastructure of pervasive computing is different from that of distributed systems. Besides, heterogeneity is much more here from the standpoint of hardware and devices, software and operating systems, and communication networks. In pervasive computing, a diverse range of hardware devices and software tools has been employed to realize everywhere/ every-time computation vision.
- The notion of context introduces a major distinction between context-aware middleware systems and their predecessors in distributed systems. A context-aware middleware is responsible for context acquisition from context sources, context processing, and context dissemination to the interested applications.

Research on context-aware middleware has been performed under different titles such as architecture, framework, or middleware for context-aware or pervasive systems, infrastructure or platform for context-aware applications, and even context toolkit [3] or engine [4]. Moreover, they originate from different problems and have different capabilities.

Before designing context-aware middleware the characteristics of the environment should be specified. In the ideal situation, a context-aware middleware system, should consider multiple domains [5] such as user personal, mobile, social, urban, and ad hoc environments and also domains that are physically limited to a geographical zone like smart places [e.g. smart room, home, office, university, etc). Each of these domains can support a limited kind of context-aware applications; hence the middleware solution that has been developed for just one specific single domain is very limited in supporting general context-aware applications. On the other hand, these domains are different in nature, so it seems impossible to design generic context-aware middleware for handling all the domains in an identical way.

J.C. Augusto et al. (Eds.): AmI 2013, LNCS 8309, pp. 311–312, 2013.
© Springer International Publishing Switzerland 2013

2   Challenges

In the multiple-domain environments, handling mobility of entities is a challenging issue. Entities such as people, mobile phones, laptops, etc are continuously roaming between different domains such as home, office, university, etc. These entities are usually sources of contextual data, and sometimes hosts for residing context-aware applications (e.g. mobile phone). In either case, they impose new tracing and communication challenges to the system (especially in distributed architecture).

Considering the fact that mobile entities roam between different domains and their context is produced in different domains imposes that these entities should be recognized by a unique name all over the environment. Most of multiple-domain studies ignore this problem by assuming that all the entities already have a unique name, which is known all over the system.

Most of the devices available in the environment are mobile phones and PDAs with limited memory, computational, communication and availability capacities. They cannot play the role of high performance computers and also may sometimes be inaccessible or even off. Therefore, any plan for using them as infrastructure of the middleware should consider these limitations.

Handling a dynamic environment is a traditional problem in the distributed systems. However, a pervasive computing environment is highly dynamic in the meaning that devices join and leave frequently and context changes. Some of the devices such as mobile phones may be regularly switched off and on. Similarly, some of the context types such as a vehicle's location, temperature of a room, activity of a person are changing continuously and rapidly.

References

1. Edwards, W.K., et al.: Stuck in the Middle: Bridging the Gap Between Design, Evaluation, and Middleware. Intel research Berkeley. Intel Corporation, California, IRB-TR-02-013 (2002)
2. Vahdat-Nejad, H., Zamanifar, K., Nematbakhsh, N.: Context-Aware Middleware Architecture for Smart Home Environment. International Journal of Smart Home 7(1) (2013)
3. Dey, A.K., Abowd, G.D., Salber, D.: A conceptual framework and a toolkit for supporting the rapid prototyping of context-aware applications. Human-Computer Interaction 16(2), 97–166 (2001)
4. Carrizo, C., et al.: Design of a context aware computing engine. In: Proceedings of IET 4th International Conference on Intelligent Environments, pp. 1–4. IEEE Computer Society, Seattle (2008)
5. Guo, B., Sun, L., Zhang, D.: The Architecture Design of a Cross-Domain Context Management System. In: 8th IEEE International Conference on Pervasive Computing and Communications Workshop, pp. 499–504. IEEE Computer Society, Mannheim (2010)

Uncertainty in Ambient Intelligence

Juan Ye[1], Graeme Stevenson[1], and Michael O'Grady[2]

[1] School of Computer Science, University of St Andrews, UK
{juan.ye,graeme.stevenson}@st-andrews.ac.uk
[2] School of Computer Science and Informatics, University College Dublin, Ireland
michael.j.ogrady@ucd.ie

Abstract. Uncertainty is a pervasive factor in many sensor-enabled infrastructures, compromising the integrity of the resultant dataset. Incorrect calibration, deteriorating performance over time, or the omnipresent noise within the physical environment, may all reduce the quality and provenance of the data. Imperfect sensor data may result in incorrect inference of real-world phenomena, including human activity recognition for example, thereby reducing the perceived quality of service and experience. Thus a model for handling uncertainty is essential for robust and human-centric ambient intelligence services. The motivation for this workshop is to initiate a research agenda for addressing this critical issue of uncertainty in ambient intelligence, with an emphasis on strategies for detecting, resolving, and programming against uncertainty.

Keywords: Ambient intelligence, uncertainty, sensor networks.

1 Introduction and Motivation

Advances in sensing, communication, and intelligence technologies in recent years have promoted the research theme of "ambient intelligence"; that is, making the real world environment sensitive and responsive to people's needs and goals with the help of invisible sensors and actuators embedded within the environment [1]. Ambient Intelligence (AmI) has thrived in many human beneficial application domains including Ambient Assisted Living (AAL), traffic control, environmental monitoring, and cultural services, to name just a few. However, the possibility for the widespread deployment of AmI applications remains uncertain. One of the most critical reasons behind this is the inherent uncertainty of the perceived sensor data and the resultant consequences of triggering unsatisfactory or even incorrect course of action, some of which could at least theoretically, have life-threatening consequences.

Physical sensors, and sensor networks, may suffer from many types of faults, including hardware failure, disconnection from the network, vulnerability to environmental interference, and poor battery life [2]. Researchers from University of Virginia concluded from their experience of deploying sensors [3]: "Homes are safe environments for humans but can be hazardous for sensors, particularly when hundreds of sensors are deployed over long time durations". During their years of experimentation, there was an average of one sensor failure per day. All these undesirable factors

J.C. Augusto et al. (Eds.): AmI 2013, LNCS 8309, pp. 313–314, 2013.
© Springer International Publishing Switzerland 2013

may result in missing, contradictory, outdated, or even incorrect sensor data. Furthermore, uncertainty may also be introduced at the software level; for example, a crude rule repository or an ill-fitted reasoning model. The net result is that AmI services cannot naively assume data is "clean"; rather an explicit approach to mitigating uncertainty at all layers must be adopted.

2   Workshop Topics

This workshop aims to bring together representative members of the industrial and scientific communities that have experience in and concern over the impact of uncertainty in real-world AmI design. It will consider state-of-the-art uncertainty resolving techniques including fuzzy logics, various statistical correlation models, Bayesian models, and evidence theories, amongst others. A discussion will be initiated on understanding of uncertainties, how to make uncertainty more informative to applications, and how to engineer software that depends on uncertain data. More specifically, the following topics are perceived as archetypical of those that must be addressed so as to enable effective uncertainty management in AmI:

- Detecting and classifying sensor faults;
- Dealing with non-technical uncertainty issues, for example those caused by human interaction with embedded sensors over extended periods of time;
- Aggregating uncertain data from heterogeneous AmI sources;
- Reasoning and classification in the face of uncertainty;
- Characterising uncertainty in knowledge representation;
- Modelling and reasoning about uncertainty in the sensor web technologies;
- Designing and developing uncertainty-resistant applications;
- Programming tools for managing uncertainty.

References

1. Cook, D.J., Augusto, J.C., Jakkula, V.R.: Ambient intelligence: Technologies, applications, and opportunities. Pervasive and Mobile Computing 5(4), 277–298 (2009)
2. Sharma, A.B., Golubchik, L., Govindan, R.: Sensor faults: Detection methods and prevalence in real-world datasets. ACM Transaction on Sensor Network 6(3), Article 23 (June 2010)
3. Hnat, T.W., Srinivasan, V., Lu, J., Sookoor, T.I., Dawson, R., Stankovic, J., Whitehouse, K.: The hitchhiker's guide to successful residential sensing deployments. In: Proceedings of the 9th ACM Conference on Embedded Networked Sensor Systems, SenSys 2011, pp. 232–245. ACM, New York (2011)

Introduction to the 5th International Workshop on Intelligent Environments Supporting Healthcare and Well-Being (WISHWell13)

Klaus-Hendrik Wolf[1], Holger Storf[2], John O'Donoghue[3], and Juan Carlos Augusto[4]

[1] Peter L. Reichertz Institute for Medical Informatics, Braunschweig, Germany
Klaus-Hendrik.Wolf@plri.de
[2] Mainz University Medical Center, Germany
holstorf@uni-mainz.de
[3] University College Cork
john.odonoghue@ucc.ie
[4] Middlesex University, London, UK
j.augusto@mdx.ac.uk

This workshop is designed to bring together researchers from both industry and academia from the various disciplines to discuss how innovation in the use of technologies to support healthier lifestyles can be moved forward. There has been a growing interest around the world and especially in Europe, on investigating the potential consequences of introducing technology to deliver social and health care to citizens (see for example [1]). This implies an important shift on how social and health care are delivered and it has positive as well as negative consequences which must be investigated carefully. On the other hand there is an urgency provided by the changes in demographics which is putting pressure on governments to provide care to specific sectors of the population, especially older adults, a group which is growing thanks to advances in medicine and greater knowledge on the relationships between lifestyles and health.

As a result companies, governments, research centres and consumer groups are developing a growing interest in a number of areas which we explore in this event. A partial list of this is: Ambient assisted living, Mobile health monitoring, Health enabling technologies, Next generation telehealth/telecare, Systems to encourage healthy lifestyles, Wearable sensor systems, Health monitoring from the home and work, Support for independent living, Support for rehabilitation, Environments supporting carers, Decision Support Systems (DSS), Data management architectures, Body area networks, Ambient Intelligence applied to health and social care, etc. We believe these topics will require a careful and long examination because although there seems to be a potential to examine how they can support independency and comfort for some citizens, the technology is not yet mature to reassure users of their efficacy and safety. Progress is steady and encouraging however some of these technologies are associated with safety critical scenarios and require extra validation.

This year the workshop joins forces with the International Workshop PervaSense Situation recognition and medical data analysis in Pervasive Health environments that is its fifth edition as well. This event will build up on the topics discussed during the previous editions of WISHWell (in Barcelona during IE09, Kuala Lumpur during IE10,

J.C. Augusto et al. (Eds.): AmI 2013, LNCS 8309, pp. 315–316, 2013.
© Springer International Publishing Switzerland 2013

Nottingham during IE11, and Guanajuato during IE12), and on the previous editions of PervaSense (during PervasiveHealth in London 2009, Munich 2010, Dublin 2011, and San Diego 2012). Healthcare environments (within the hospital and the home) are extremely complex and challenging to manage from an IT and IS perspective, as they are required to cope with an assortment of patient conditions under various circumstances with a number of resource constraints. Pervasive healthcare technologies seek to respond to a variety of these pressures by integrating them within existing healthcare services. It is essential that intelligent pervasive healthcare solutions are developed and correctly integrated to assist health care professionals in delivering high levels of patient care. It is equally important that these pervasive solutions are used to empower patients and relatives for self-care and management of their health to provide seamless access for health care services. There are multiple synergies between WISHWell and PervaSense which we think are worth exploring and this first joint event will aim at consolidating this confluence for the future.

We would like to take this opportunity to thank everyone involved in the making of this edition, first and foremost the authors and participants as this event is theirs, the program committee which helped to select from those submitted a number of good quality papers to be presented, and the conference organizers who are providing the infrastructure for the meeting to take place.

Reference

1. Augusto, J.C., Huch, M., Kameas, A., Maitland, J., McCullagh, P., Roberts, J., Sixsmith, A., Wichert, R. (eds.): Handbook on Ambient Assisted Living - Technology for Healthcare, Rehabilitation and Well-being. Ambient Intelligence and Smart Environments series, vol. 11. IOS Press (January 2012)

Author Index